D0780154

THE BEST SYSTEM
MONEY CAN BUY

THE BEST SYSTEM MONEY CAN BUY

Corruption in the European Union

Carolyn M. Warner

CORNELL UNIVERSITY PRESS   ITHACA AND LONDON

First published 2007 by Cornell University Press

Printed in the United States of America

Library of Congress Cataloging-in-Publication Data

Warner, Carolyn M., 1961–
 The Best system money can buy : corruption in the European Union / Carolyn M. Warner.
   p.   cm.
 Includes bibliographical references and index.
 ISBN 978-0-8014-4555-2 (cloth : alk. paper)
 1. Political corruption—European Union countries.   2. Corruption—European Union countries.   3. Misconduct in office—European Union countries.   4. Commercial crimes—European Union countries.   I. Title.

JN94.A56C69 2007
364.1'323094—dc22

                                                    2007010664

Cornell University Press strives to use environmentally responsible suppliers and materials to the fullest extent possible in the publishing of its books. Such materials include vegetable-based, low-VOC inks and acid-free papers that are recycled, totally chlorine-free, or partly composed of nonwood fibers. For further information, visit our website at www.cornellpress.cornell.edu.

Cloth printing   10 9 8 7 6 5 4 3 2 1

Dedicated to the memory of Ruth Elaine Norberg Warner (1926–2005)

Contents

Work on this book began with a naive question about what happens when countries with different patterns of corruption become members of an international free trade organization. When Edith Cresson, a French commissioner in the European Union (EU), hired an old friend to be her adviser on a project, was she importing French hiring practices into the EU or merely behaving as any administrator would, given the structure of the EU? When Greece's deputy finance minister Nikos Athanassopoulos was involved in (and convicted of) illegally selling cheap Yugoslavian corn in the EU as subsidized Greek corn, had he merely brought the corrupt practices of his country to the international organization or was he responding creatively to new opportunities?[1] Seeing the point spread of EU countries in Transparency International's now famous Corruption Perceptions Index made me wonder whether countries brought their local patterns of fraud and corruption into international organizations and whether there was convergence of these patterns within such an organization. The EU has gone far beyond being a free trade area, but this question of what happens to patterns of corruption in different countries when these countries join an international organization lies at the base of my inquiry. This inquiry began to reveal that corruption was tied to competition—that is, to efforts to evade and best the competition, whether political or economic. Competition had long been considered one of the remedies for corruption; now it seemed to be one of the causes. I found more cases of corruption than I expected, and they were occurring in countries that were wealthy, Western, democratic, and members and chief movers of an integrated, transnational single market—the European Union.

This book is not an essay merely about corruption within EU institutions nor a study of fraud involving the EU budget. It does not cover corruption in the post-2004 accession countries—much of the former Eastern bloc, Malta, and Cyprus. My interest is in corruption in countries where it isn't expected, and in the role of the EU and the policies that directly and indirectly accompanied integration. Corruption takes many forms; this book, as a first cut at the topic of corruption patterns in the EU, focuses on bribery, kickbacks, and extortion among politicians, bureaucrats, and firms. As I make clear, firms often bribe because they perceive that politicians or parties have demanded the bribe. This book is a modest attempt to raise a flag about relying on competition, privatization, decentralization, and campaign finance regulations as a way to reduce corruption. It is also an effort to assess the limits of the EU in affecting corruption. Readers will find that the EU's impact is less than we might have expected.

The book contains two chapters I did not anticipate writing. In the course of my research I discovered that numerous cases of corruption in Europe were connected to overseas bribery and that the connection seemed not to be accidental. Hence, there is a chapter on "export-led" corruption. Further, most of the cases in Europe were connected to party and campaign finance, which led me to investigate the relationship between spending caps, donation caps, public financing, and corruption. Nor did I expect to find that the subject of the book had manifestations close to home in Arizona. I live approximately four miles from Paradise Valley, where Pierre Falcone, an arms dealer pursued by the French, has a mansion (which he has not used recently due to an international arrest warrant). I also live about twenty miles from Sun City, where Paul Marcinkus (1922–2006) was transferred to appease Italian legal authorities after the Banco Ambrosiano/ Vatican Bank scandal, which left one banker, Roberto Calvi, hanging from under Blackfriars Bridge in London, and another, Marcinkus, conducting mass for retirees in Arizona.

I do not advocate massive repressive efforts to eliminate corruption. One thing the book shows is that regulatory practices of any sort often produce problems similar to those they were trying to solve. Furthermore, I have a strong bias toward civil liberties, which are often casualties of draconian anticorruption laws and enforcement.

I make no claim to having a definitive theory of corruption, nor to having all the evidence necessary to back up such a theory. The cases are limited to those exposed by investigating judges, journalists, nongovernmental organizations, and parliamentary inquiry commissions. The allegations described in the book come from reputable sources. They do not necessarily mean that those accused are guilty, but they highlight possible patterns of corruption. Where feasible, I have followed up on the initial judicial or police proceedings, on which press accounts were usually founded, with court decisions and government reports.

This book would not exist were it not for significant financial support, a year's sabbatical at the European University Institute, a year at the Hoover Institution, and several summers at the Center on Democracy, Development and the Rule of Law at Stanford University. Specifically, the field research was supported by a Harvard University Minda de Gunzburg Center for European Studies research travel grant, by a National Science Foundation Professional Opportunities for Women in Research and Education grant (NSF POWRE no. SES-0074977), a Jean Monnet Fellowship at the European University Institute (EUI), a year at the Hoover

Institution as the Susan Louise Dyer National Peace Fellow, and a grant from the Center on Democracy, Development and the Rule of Law at Stanford University. I have benefited enormously from the intellectual environment and research resources of these host institutions and need to repay that debt partly by stating that the findings, opinions, and arguments expressed in this book are my own responsibility.

At Harvard Jorge Domínguez introduced me to Michel Petite, who gave me an introduction to Alain Scriban of the EU's antifraud unit (UCLAF). Scriban greatly facilitated my exploratory research on fraud against the EU budget by setting up a series of interviews with UCLAF officials in Brussels in 1998. That research provided the seed for subsequent grant applications. I thank the NSF POWRE officers for their confidence in the project, and Yves Mény and Martin Rhodes of the EUI for their strong interest in the research and their willingness to take time to talk about it with me. The Jean Monnet fellowship through the Robert Schuman Centre of the EUI provided crucial support for my field research and a stimulating environment for working through my initial findings. My office mates that year, Lisa Conant and Milada Vachudova, were generous with their moral support, their willingness to brainstorm about the topic, and their inclination to laugh and commiserate. A European Consortium for Political Research seminar on corruption, led by Paul Heywood and Martin Rhodes in 2001, provided a helpful context for assessing my preliminary findings, as did a later seminar at the University of Washington, sponsored by the Center for European Studies and the West European Politics Center, and a conference in 2003 at Stanford, "Corruption: Its Consequences and Cures," sponsored by the Institute for International Studies and its Center on Democracy, Development and the Rule of Law. The Hoover Institution National Fellowship was an unparalleled opportunity for research and intellectual challenges. In particular I thank Larry Diamond and Tom Henriksen for their enthusiasm for my project, and my National Fellow cohorts Juliet Johnson and Jeff Hummel for their collaboration, friendship, and penetrating questions. Bruce Berkowitz, Robert Conquest, David Laitin, Terry Moe, Luis Moreno Ocampo, and Barry Weingast kindly gave of their time to discuss various aspects of my project. Larry Diamond and Coit "Chip" Blacker were instrumental in enabling me to be a research fellow at the Center on Democracy, Development and the Rule of Law at Stanford in the summer of 2003 and again in 2005. I also thank Kathryn Stoner-Weiss and Anu Kulkarni for their insights. Much of what I know of the German cases would not be possible without the assistance of Kurt Wenner, and Lisa Conant has been very helpful with advice on legal research in Europe.

The librarians at the Hoover Institution were instrumental in locating documents. Beth Lewallyn, Ben Thomas, Kevin Githunguri, Risto Karinen, Katie

Jordan, Seth Turken, Staci Kaiser, and Chris Chamberlin provided research assistance.

I thank the EU and member state officials I interviewed for the project, many of whom preferred to speak off the record. I have noted sources in the text only where necessary and with permission. I also thank Karl Laske of *Libération,* Fabrice Lhomme of *Le Monde,* Philippe Nasse of France's Cour des comptes and Conseil de concurrence, André Gauron of the Cour des comptes, Yves Mercat of Transparency International France, David Corner and Laura Blackwell of the UK's National Audit Office, John Colling and Hilary De Vries of the UK's Office of Government Commerce, David Allworthy of the United Kingdom Liberal Democrats, Philip Ayett of the UK's Committee on Standards in Public Life, Laurence Cockcroft of Transparency International UK, Franco Ionta and Giuseppe De Falco of Italy's Procura della Repubblica, Paolo Luigi Rebecchi of the Corte dei Conti, Italy, Joachim Stünker of the SPD/Bundestag, Hans Joachim Elhorst of Transparency International Germany, Volker Neumann of the SPD/Bundestag, John Sullivan of the Center for International Private Enterprise, Eleanor Roberts Lewis, Chief Counsel for International Commerce in the U.S. Department of Commerce, Kathryn Nickerson, Senior Counsel in the Office of the Chief Counsel for International Commerce in the U.S. Department of Commerce, Nancy Boswell of the U.S. branch of Transparency International, and Bill McGlynn, United States Department of State diplomat in residence at Arizona State University. They gave generously of their time and on many occasions provided documentation. Again, I stress that the opinions, findings, and arguments expressed in this book are my responsibility.

Jim Alt, Andrew Barnes, Bruce Berkowitz, Ed Campbell, Lisa Conant, Joe Cutter, Larry Diamond, Jorge Domínguez, Colin Elman, Michael Hechter, Juliet Johnson, David Laitin, Simona Piattoni, Susan Scarrow, and Christina Schatzman provided helpful comments and corrections to various parts of the manuscript. I thank two anonymous reviewers for their detailed comments on the manuscript. I thank copy editor Kathryn Gohl and Cornell University Press senior manuscript editor Candace Akins for their expert assistance. Kurt Wenner and Cornell executive editor Roger Haydon read, critiqued, and edited numerous drafts. I owe special thanks to Larry Diamond, Roger Haydon, and Kurt Wenner for their long-standing interest in and support of this project.

This book reflects my effort to make sense of corruption in the EU, to tease out the connections between EU-driven phenomena such as competition and corruption, to understand how EU-related phenomena such as privatization affect corruption, and to assess the limited capacity the EU has to disrupt corruption in member states. As this book goes to press, forty-two individuals, including Pierre Falcone, the late president François Mitterrand's son Jean-Christophe, and longtime Gaullist politician Charles Pasqua, have been indicted in a case dubbed "Angolagate." Their trial may shed further light on how corruption is a means by which politicians and firms exercise political power and manipulate market forces in the EU and beyond.

I am delighted to thank Joe Cutter, who "met" the project in its last year and was very supportive (and no doubt relieved) as I reached its conclusion. Thanks are due to my sister Evelyn Warner Seuberling and my dad Robert Warner for providing the moral support that only family can give.

The book may really have started with Watergate. As a child I was fascinated by the scandal's revelations of the intricate illicit web of power and corruption that was being used precisely to sustain power and corruption. I was puzzled about how to square what I was required to recite every day at school, a pledge of allegiance including the phrase "with liberty and justice for all," with what was showing up in the papers about how the U.S. government under Richard Nixon actually operated. It was an introduction to the myth of democracy, and the power and rent seeking that underlie it. The slush fund and intricate financing network that defense and aerospace giant Lockheed used to grease the wheels of politics and commerce bears an uncanny resemblance to the slush funds and financing networks Siemens and BAE are, in 2007, accused of maintaining. Thus, although this book is focused on the EU, the United States has never been out of mind, and its particular system of corruption is likely my next subject of study.

With this book I risk seeming to be an American railing against the EU. The reader needs to remember that I started by wondering what happens when a group of countries with different histories of fraud and corruption sets up an international organization that has a budget and rules and regulations that the states and their citizens must follow. My focus became patterns of corruption within the member states, as I tried to see what roles economic and political competition played in them. The EU is the frame not just because of the origins of the project but because of expectations in the scholarly literature and in policy circles that international organizations that push for free trade help to reduce corruption and change norms surrounding it. This book reveals my bias: I don't think corruption is generally a good thing. But this book is also an effort to understand the sources of corruption within countries and within a system in which one might not expect it.

This book is dedicated to my mother, Ruth Elaine Norberg Warner. She never had any patience for duplicitous politicians, whether those politicians were on the local school board or in the White House.

CAROLYN M. WARNER

Phoenix, Arizona

Abbreviations

ACEA	Azienda comunale elettricità ed acque
BEF	Belgian franc
CAP	Common Agricultural Policy
CDU-CSU	Christlich Demokratische Union Deutschlands–Christlich Soziale Union
CIEEMG	Commission interministeriel pour l'étude des exportations de matériels de guerre
CNCCFP	Commission nationale des comptes de campagne et des financements politiques
CNUC	Commission nationale d'urbanisme commercial
COCOBU	Commission du contrôle budgétaire
CSU	Christlich Soziale Union
DC	Democrazia Cristiana
DESO	Defence Export Services Organisation
DGSE	Direction générale de la sécurité extérieure
DLO	Direct Labour Organisation
DM	Deutsche mark
DREE	Direction des relations économiques extérieures
EBRD	European Bank for Reconstruction and Development
ECGA	Export Credits Guarantee Agency
EEC	European Economic Community
ECJ	European Court of Justice
EMU	European Monetary Union
ERAP	Entreprise de recherches et d'activités pétrolières
ESP	Spanish peseta
EU	European Union
EUR	Euro
FDP	Freie Demokratische Partei
FRF	French franc
IR £	Irish pound
ITL	Italian lira
NAO	National Audit Office
OECD	Organization for Economic Cooperation and Development
OLAF	Office européen de la lutte anti-fraude

PCF	Parti Communiste Français
PR	Parti Républicain
PRI	Partito Repubblicano Italiano
PS	Parti Socialiste
PSDI	Partito Socialista Democratico Italiano
RPR	Rassemblement pour la République
SNPE	Société nationale de poudres et explosifs
SOFREMI	Société française d'exportation des matériels, systèmes, et services
SPD	Sozialdemokratische Partei Deutschlands
UCLAF	Unité coordinatif de la lutte anti-fraude
UNESCO	United Nations Educational, Scientific, and Cultural Organization
ZAR	South African Rand

INTRODUCTION

Nothing is easier than buying a politician.

—Léon-François Deferm

In 1991, on the very eve of the launch of the European Single Market, politicians in Italy took bribes of more than $100 million to approve the breakup of a joint venture between a private and a state-owned firm. Also in 1991, the former treasurer of the German Christian Democratic Party used the bribe he collected on one deal to pay his fine for tax evasion on another. In 1988, just two years after Spain had joined the European Union, the French firm Alsthom and the German firm Siemens surreptitiously donated a total of almost $7 million to the Spanish Socialist Party. In 2001, during the phase-in of the euro, Siemens allegedly paid the Italian state-owned power company ENEL a large kickback for a lucrative contract. Italian judges accused the German firm of considering kickbacks a normal business practice. Instead of encouraging free market competition and discouraging corruption, has the European Union fostered the opposite?

Corruption has persisted in the EU because the market and political reforms associated directly and indirectly with it impel and enable some to use corruption to get ahead of their competition. In addition, the EU's structure has been based on institutions that are weak on accountability. The Single Market and the "ever-closer union" of Europeans brought with them efforts to increase trade and competition across states, and they were accompanied by waves of privatization and decentralization in many states, as well as by state promotion of national champions in the overseas (or third-country) export market. These actions have an underside that merits exposure and analysis. This book provides a framework for understanding corruption cases in the western EU countries that have appeared in the news since the 1980s, and for understanding the persistence of corruption in the EU. These cases suggest unexpected connections between liberal market and political reforms, and corruption. And in many cases, politicians' needs for campaign and party financing forge the links.

The EU is connected with corruption in its member states as a result of its heightening of competition in various sectors and its weak institutional structure. It is striking how its ability to discourage corruption is limited. Phenomena not integral to the Single Market project but that accompanied it, such as privatization, decentralization, and campaign finance regulation, come with opportunities and incentives for corruption, and the EU, as a supranational institution, has a low capacity to moderate those opportunities.

Increased competition may goad some firms to bribe politicians or to concede to politicians' extortionist requests. Foreign competitors can be absorbed into the old corrupt system. Privatization gives rise to opportunities for politicians to exercise discretion in new ways. Competition for access to overseas markets and lucrative contracts leads states to overlook international bribery and to set up their own institutions, which, perhaps unintentionally, facilitate corrupt contracting. Although the fifteen western EU countries (EU-15) are wealthy democracies, they are democracies with competing political parties and politicians who need to finance their organizations and campaigns, and when the parties and politicians cannot get what they think is sufficient funding legally, they tend to turn to illegal means. And that is a major driver of corruption in the European Union.

Within the context of the EU, corruption is feasible because of the institution's weak accountability structures at the national and subnational levels. Establishing a free trade area, a common market, or even a political union among sovereign states leads to a proliferation of regulations to implement the arrangement but a paucity of enforcement powers. The international institutions established to govern such arrangements have not been given the necessary enforcement powers and resources by sovereignty-jealous states, and the dynamics of economic and political competition and other forces create their own incentives and opportunities for corruption. The EU and its member states created institutions and processes that should have, according to standard thinking, limited—even seriously diminished—the opportunities for illegal enrichment and corrupt practices on the part of firms, politicians, other public officials, and intermediaries. But those very institutions and processes could be evaded or subverted because of weak standards of accountability and weak supervisory bodies. These failings are inherent in the process of liberalization under the auspices of an international organization and office-seeking politicians: states do not want to give international organizations real power, and national politicians are reluctant to make their own accountability institutions more powerful. In terms of enforcement capacities, the EU still does not rival those of its member states. It is clear that the EU is much more than just an international organization, although I use that shorthand throughout the book.[1]

This is not to say that it is impossible to decrease corrupt practices while undertaking political and economic reforms. Creating institutions that adhere to democratic norms of "openness, publicity, and inclusion" and that are more accountable would further that goal. So too would having independent media and public interest watchdog groups. It is also important for officials to have a strong sense of ethics and public responsibility.[2] Yet in some states such ethics are undermined by efforts to run government like a business; in others, they are often trumped by raison d'état or the exigencies of political competition. In still others they have been noticeably absent from the start.

The unchained liberal market is not self-correcting; neither are political reforms. Competition alone is not a cure for corruption. Even advanced, wealthy, long-standing democratic countries need to pay attention to their institutions and ethics and to have skeptical media and vociferous public interest groups. If states enact political and economic reforms without paying attention to those elements, they are creating conditions for corruption. Thus, these factors likely are even more critical in less advanced, poorer, newer democracies (e.g., the Eastern bloc accession countries). Free trade areas create their own possibilities for corruption, and in this age of the proliferation of regional and international trade organizations, the production of corruption as a side effect should be of concern. Membership in the EU does not inherently drive out corruption, as the EU, in its acceptance of the Eastern bloc countries and Malta and Cyprus, had assumed. Instead, it allows old forms to persist and permits the development of new ones. The EU has a negligible ability to reduce corruption, and it promotes economic forces and political reforms that provide new incentives and opportunities for corruption. Economic and political rationality are at work, but not in the expected ways.

Liberalization is expected to reduce corruption. What we see instead is both old patterns of corruption continuing and new ones emerging. This is surprising. The standard expectation is that corruption decreases once countries, their firms, and their politicians are exposed to competitive pressures and are operating under a common set of market rules and regulations. The British economic commentator Samuel Brittan asserted that for those who decry cronyism, "globalised free trade is their best defence against the corruption of politicised capitalism."[3] Not noticing that corruption was getting worse at the time, the then EU commissioner for expansion claimed in 2002 that the EU integration process for the 2004 accession countries was having salutary effects on the fight against corruption.[4] The U.S. trade representative Robert Zoelleck argued, in support of the Central American Free Trade Agreement, that CAFTA "will strengthen the foundations of democracy by promoting growth and cutting poverty, creating equality of opportunity, and reducing corruption. . . . CAFTA goes beyond cutting tariffs to require broad changes in the way economies and polities operate, challenging those who have grown corrupt and complacent in captive, uncompetitive markets."[5] The unspoken assumption here is that uncompetitive markets facilitate collusive deals; no one has an incentive to cut costs. Public resources can be squandered by firms and politicians who depend on each other, not the economic market or electoral arena, for survival.[6] Uncompetitive markets, with high barriers to trade, "may induce businesspersons to bribe their way to exemptions or special treatment."[7] Nevertheless, corruption is an additional cost of doing business, which makes firms less competitive relative to those not involved in corruption. The ancillary argument is that when there is increased economic competition, firms engaged in corruption will be forced to drop out or to stop their corrupt practices. Thus, when free trade agreements open domestic markets to competition, domestic firms that routinely pay bribes to politicians will be forced out or forced to stop. Politicians, in turn, will be forced to quit demanding bribes, because their electoral futures depend on domestic firms staying in business in order to provide employment for the voters and tax revenues for the state. To quote Sandholtz and Koetzle, "In a closed market, the importer sets the price of imported goods above the international price and the bribe-taking official collects part of the monopoly profits. In a market open to trade, the bribery tax forces returns below the level prevailing in the market, and the producers so taxed will drop out. Thus the competition created by free trade penalizes bribery."[8]

Further, it is suggested that increased trade and competition provide voters (and firms) alternative means of income and doing business. They are less dependent on the government, so they can repudiate the demands for bribes made by the governing parties, politicians, and bureaucrats.[9] Finally, scholars and policy makers have assumed that when free trade and competition are promoted through a rule-generating free trade organization, corruption is both unlikely to occur in the organization and less likely to occur in the participating states—because the organization's rules theoretically limit opportunities for corruption in both. To quote Andrew Moravcsik, "Once we set aside ideal notions of democracy and look to real-world standards, we see that the EU is as transparent, responsive, accountable and honest as its member states. The relative lack of centralised financial or administrative discretion all but eliminates corruption."[10] Given the reality of corruption in the member states, the EU, if it is as "transparent, responsive, accountable and honest as its member states," is prone to corruption.

Privatization is also supposed to root out corruption. Removing the state from economic activity removes the discretion its politicians and bureaucrats have over the direction of economic activity. Gerring and Thacker summarize the logic for their analysis: "the larger a role the government plays in the market—as producer and/or consumer—the greater its capacity to engage in corrupt activity. . . . Whatever functions are not entrusted to government cannot be as easily abused by government."[11] In addition, when the government, not the market, is producing goods and services, the prices are determined politically and, so the reasoning goes, are inherently vulnerable to corruption. Even seemingly technical decisions about state investments will be subject to the pressures of politicians and constituencies. In contrast, privatized firms are subject to market discipline. They cannot afford corruption, so they will be less likely to bribe and more likely to shun officials' requests for illicit payments.

Scholars and EU policy makers assume that the problem of corruption lies elsewhere, perhaps in some of the new member states, and in the less developed countries beyond the EU's borders. Corruption is supposed to be reduced through the effects of membership in the EU. Rather, corruption has adapted to the European Union and persists in a variety of the older member states. Countries formerly considered relatively immune, such as Germany, and countries with a presumed culture of administrative efficiency and impartiality, such as France, have been the sites of both routine and "high" corruption. Another country, Italy, saw a dramatic improvement in general living standards at the same time that corruption there became endemic, and there is some doubt about whether its anticorruption campaign of the early 1990s has had any lasting effect. Ireland has likewise seen extraordinary economic growth and significant corruption. A number of major corruption cases have involved politicians and corporations colluding across borders. It seems as if the European Union created both a common market for trade and a common market for corruption.

Is this simply a case of the old practices of heavy state control of the economy being exposed to the light by the market? The customary interpretation says it is. France was known for its so-called *dirigiste* state, which directed and owned much of French economic activity. Indeed, most European states were known until the 1980s for their extensive intervention in economic activity. The private sector was limited. State officials, including politicians, could use their positions to reward friends and punish enemies, and to extract payments for resources transferred either between state firms or between state and private-sector firms. Transactions were easily hidden; after all, it was the state that controlled the books. The advent of economic competition spurred by the EU and the pressure to qualify for the European Monetary Union (the euro) prompted states to unload state firms and subject their activities in the market to an independent overseer: the European

Commission. Considerable corruption in the old state-controlled system was exposed as Europe adopted the new market economy system and European states integrated their economies into the Single Market. A French case makes the point. In 1992, just before the official launch of the EU's Single Market, the CEO of France's state-owned oil company, Elf, received a letter from the minister of economics telling him to find a way for Elf to save a textile firm from bankruptcy. As the CEO testified to a judge, "we were in the pre-election phase, which for the head of a state-owned firm is a difficult time," that is, it was a time when state firms were expected to rescue insolvent private firms in order to prevent job losses. As the textile firm's owner Maurice Bidermann noted, "these investments were made with the express agreement of two ministers, [Dominique] Strauss-Kahn and [Michel] Sapin [of Industry, and Economics and Finance, respectively]." The only hesitation on the part of the political authorities was whether to use Elf or the state-owned bank, Crédit lyonnais, for the buyout.[12] With the privatization of Elf and Crédit lyonnais, such maneuvers should no longer be possible.

Yet the corruption in Europe that has made headlines since then is not just a temporary disruption during a transition to an Anglo-American-style market system and not just a holdover from the corrupt Kohl-Mitterrand-Andreotti era. In the late 1990s, bribes appear to have been paid by British, German, French, Italian, and Spanish firms to bureaucrats and politicians in a variety of EU and other countries. And although the United Kingdom prides itself on being notably less corrupt than many of its fellow EU members on the Continent, its export credits guarantee agency has subsidized dubious transactions, former prime minister Margaret Thatcher's son was arrested for allegedly helping to finance a coup attempt in oil-rich Equatorial Guinea, Tony Blair's Labour Party has been caught in some unseemly funding deals, and locals in Glasgow have found that a seat on the city council is the road to riches.

As it turns out, corruption in the EU is not uncommon.[13] This book reminds us of the high and sometimes extraordinary levels of corrupt behavior in the core (old) EU. Greater competition and more campaign finance regulations have not done away with corruption. These factors have allowed some new forms to arise, even if perhaps the absolute level of corruption as a percentage of GDP may have gone down. Given that we lack data on historic levels of corruption, these observations are not possible to quantify. The cases, nevertheless, are suggestive of unexpected patterns about which policy makers, citizens, and scholars ought to be aware.

Much of the corruption in the EU is not directly associated with its policies and institutions. Because elections are still member state based, including those for the European Parliament, and because the vast majority of revenue collection and public spending occurs within the individual states, corruption is largely a member state problem, not, despite the extensive publicity in 1999, a problem within the supranational EU institutions such as the European Commission. Newsworthy cases such as that involving Elf in France, the shady financing of Helmut Kohl's CDU in Germany, Enimont in Italy, and the lesser known but more frequent local and regional cases have at their base efforts by political parties and politicians to attain more financing and efforts by firms to best their competition. Decentralization in the name of democratization in many European countries has brought with it the need for more regional and local elections and, inevitably, the need for more parties, politicians, and campaign funding. Those needs have not been given adequate legal funding, nor has the need for more oversight been addressed. Corruption most often occurs through kickback schemes on public works contracts—contracts that account for 10–20 percent of the combined GDP of the EU states. To the extent that these collusive arrangements violate the EU's many regulations regarding public procurement, the corruption in the states affects the EU.

This book surveys various phenomena associated with the European Union's development and their relationship to political corruption. I focus on corruption in the states that were members of the EU before the 2004 accession, when the EU acquired ten new members, eight of which are from the former Eastern bloc. I also analyze how the European Commission's efforts to promote competition in an area prone to corruption—public procurement—has been no match for creative politicians, firms, EU-generated red tape, and the inevitable vulnerabilities of an international organization. Various kinds of corruption exist in any country, and in some places it is endemic. There likely has been hidden or low-level corruption in such countries as the United Kingdom and Germany for a long time, but in this book I do not attempt a historical analysis of particular states. Corruption is neither ubiquitous nor homogenous across the EU, but classifying the differing patterns across states and explaining the historical origins of them must be the subject of another study.[14] The corruption cases herein are, of course, limited to those that have been discovered. Their existence and their range, with many cases reaching the highest level of the state in a wide cross-section of European countries, reveal patterns of political corruption and lend plausibility to the claim that graft can thrive in the very conditions that were supposed to obviate it. The book makes no claim to being definitive or to having definitive evidence; rather, it invites further research.

In many ways, the phenomena and cases examined here are typical of those found in advanced industrial and postindustrial countries such as OECD (Organization for Economic Cooperation and Development) member states. Most if not all OECD states have undertaken privatization, acted to increase free trade and economic competition, decentralized, increased competition in overseas markets, and enacted and revised campaign and party finance laws. At the same time, the phenomena and cases are affected by the states' membership in the EU. These countries have encouraged more competition and undertaken privatization because they are striving to create a single market in which their economies will thrive and expand. Since the 1980s, the view has been widely held that more competition, privatization, and market integration in the EU would facilitate that. The EU member states also have been under more or less the same set of EU rules and regulations pertaining to many aspects of trade, competition, and government contracting. It is in the EU countries, perhaps more noticeably than in other OECD countries, that we have seen the shift from state-directed economies to state-regulated economies, and it is here that most economists, policy makers, and political scientists expected to see the salutary effects of a deregulated, liberal market on corruption. The Maastricht Treaty of 1992–93 is a symbol and tool of the EU states' push toward liberalization. It is not a dividing line between a corrupt past and clean present. The focus on the EU-15 is not meant to exonerate or downplay corruption in other OECD states, especially in the United States and Japan. Instead, it is meant to shed light on the dynamics of corruption in what has become the world's most advanced and integrated free trade area.

Of all international organizations, the EU has gone farthest in integrating the economies of its members, and in being granted some centralized political authority by these states. With the promotion of free trade areas and organizations worldwide and extensive concern about the detrimental effects of corruption on economic growth and political development, it is useful to see what has happened in the EU. In most policy and academic studies of the EU, the organization's effect on corruption within its member states has been neglected; indeed, studies of international organizations in general have largely assumed it away. Various analyses of the correlates of corruption find that membership in international organizations and also higher levels of international trade correspond to lower levels of corruption. Yet the persistence of corruption in the member states of an international organization such as the EU has not been explained.

The intensified effort to create the Single Market in the 1990s had several untoward effects. It created enthusiasm for running government like a business and for promoting economic growth, which led to joint ventures between public agencies and private firms. These joint ventures confuse business and public goals and standards of conduct; they blur lines of authority and lead to conflicts of interest and corruption. To create the Single Market, the EU states have produced a thick web of regulations and directives, but to retain sovereignty they have severely limited the resources for oversight and enforcement of those rules. Expectations that free trade, expanded competition, and economic growth would reduce corruption have been frustrated by the reality that in most countries old habits and practices were applied to and operated within the new arrangements. The old system has historical weight, presence, and influence on norms and behavior patterns in new contexts. In 1992, when politicians on the regional governing council of Abruzzo, Italy, received development subsidies from the EU, they did as they had always done with government subsidies: shared them with kickback-paying political friends and firms. Change, if any, is gradual and subject to deliberate distortion by politicians and businesses wanting an advantage not allowed by the new rules.

Behavioral codes, norms, and expectations have the power to sidetrack new rules such as EU economic regulations. If the unspoken norm in a country, region, or economic sector has sustained corrupt practices, then new rules and institutions will be affected by those old norms. The best information that individuals, firms, politicians, and bureaucrats have about how others will act—information that inevitably affects their own decisions about how to act—is informed by preexisting codes and norms. For instance, if a country, economic sector, or governing body has a reputation for corruption, then new entrants will have an expectation that they need to operate in that system. They will hire locals with the appropriate knowledge and connections. Politicians, firms, and bureaucrats make decisions about how to operate partly on the basis of their expectations of how others will act. If the norm is corruption, they will expect the same, even in the application of a new rule. There may be some uncertainty as a result of the new rule, but the links among individuals (both firms and politicians) in corruption are surprisingly resilient. In such situations, the expectations of enforcement and punishment, or, in a word, risk, are low. It is primarily the EU states that enforce EU rules (and, of course, their own rules), not the European Commission or the European Court of Justice (ECJ). If a state already has a corrupt political economy, then it is not likely to enforce new rules aggressively.

Simultaneously, and to the frustration of those wanting simple explanations, new rules and contexts can create new patterns of corrupt behavior at the same time that old patterns are at work. Under Germany's old corporatist style of governance, the Social Democratic Party tended not to collect kickbacks. With privatization in the 1980s and 1990s, the party started skimming funds off the top of some contracts it awarded in some areas where it held power. Now in Germany, as has long been the case in Sicily and other parts of Italy (not to mention the United States), the garbage collection industry is a locus of illicit transactions between private firms and politicians.

To promote the market and to promote their own industries, whether publicly or privately owned or mixed, states have created agencies that can facilitate corrupt transactions. Export credit guarantee agencies are a case in point. When they are combined with governments' keen desire to sell arms and infrastructure projects to less developed countries, they have allowed public funds to subsidize bribes, kickbacks, and excessive commissions to intermediaries, politicians, and private individuals. A credit guarantee reduces the risk to companies that are investing in corrupt countries, so it encourages governments and companies to ignore corruption. At the same time, states have privatized the delivery of government services, making it possible to demand kickbacks on contract awards and thus opening new opportunities for corruption. States have even privatized the planning of publicly funded, privately constructed projects, enabling them to outsource the entire project to a consultancy that arranges kickbacks and reserves some of the profits for the coffers of the governing parties.

European states have institutionalized the means of corruption in other ways. In a sense, it is a matter of bureaucracy working too well. The export credit agencies' mission is to promote exports, not to police contracts. They focus on the former, not the latter, and thus can, in fulfilling their mission, subsidize corrupt deals. As the UK's Export Credits Guarantee Department said in regard to its providing $200 million in insurance coverage to a Halliburton subsidiary accused of paying bribes to land a contract in Nigeria, "it is not an investigatory body able to look into the matter more deeply."[15] The concept of fundamental national interest is often codified in law, allowing documents to be classified as permanently off-limits if they are judged to affect that "national interest." The earnest, although some might say politicized, officials who staff the boards that make those determinations have the protection of the national interest as their mandate. They employ a generous interpretation of it, which is often invoked when judges try to investigate politically sensitive cases. As the French judge Renaud van Ruymbeke found when trying to track the bribes and murders associated with a $500 million arms sale, well-functioning bureaucracies and democratic institutions shelter corrupt practices. His investigation has been foiled by the invocation of national defense secrecy.

Immunity of office protects other corrupt politicians. Judges can request that the immunity be lifted, but politicians have little interest in voting to lift immunity of their own kind. Even if a politician is not in the governing majority, he or she likely will remain protected. Members of the majority know that after the next election, they may be the ones in the minority. This ethos of mutual protection holds sway in national parliaments as well as in the European Parliament.

Corruption persists partly because the politicians who benefit from it often have the legal means to disrupt law enforcement activity. They can interfere with the supposedly independent judiciary, they can award themselves amnesty, they can refuse to lift the immunity of office conferred on their colleagues, or they can invoke secrecy in the interests of national defense to block investigations. As the

Berlusconi government demonstrated, politicians can pass laws to erase corruption by changing its definition, or by changing the statute of limitations, or by changing penalties. Speaking of corruption in Italy in 2002, prosecuting magistrate Piercamillo Davigo commented, "From 1992 to today the system has done everything to counter the magistrates, but has done nothing to counter corruption and its causes. For ten years the political class has pretended to cure the fever by modifying the scale of the thermometer. Thus it makes believe that there is no fever."[16] If left to their own devices, national judiciaries, tax authorities, stock market commissions, and police agencies in the western European countries function reasonably well. In the course of their work, these authorities find and prosecute corruption cases. For example, the French stock exchange oversight board sent a routine alert to Eva Joly, a financial crimes investigative judge, about an odd transaction involving the Bidermann textile firm, which manufactured clothing for Yves Saint Laurent, Kenzo, Ralph Lauren, Arrow shirts, and Gold Toe socks, among others. The firm had received a bailout loan from the French oil company's Gabon subsidiary. Joly's routine investigation led to the anything-but-routine unraveling of the state-owned oil company and various political and business careers. Official investigators are seldom left to their own devices, however. Sometimes they have been corrupted; sometimes they have been blocked or pulled off cases. Parts of Eva Joly's investigation, and related and more penetrating ones by other French magistrates, were stymied. Even cooperative witnesses have been silenced: when Alfred Sirven offered to reveal the names of French politicians who had received kickbacks from the French oil firm's contracts, he was silenced by the judges hearing the case because his revelations were viewed as too explosive. The judge conducting an investigation that directly implicated the sitting French president, Jacques Chirac, was pulled from the case. Reason of state trumped rule of law, as it often does in the construction and operation of international organizations such as the EU. And, as the following chapters show, the counterintuitive incentives in economic competition, privatization, decentralization, and campaign finance within the EU member states undermine the EU's principle of the rule of law, a principle declared in the Treaties of Rome and reaffirmed in each successive EU treaty.

Corruption continues to serve the interests of some EU member-state politicians, parties, and firms because it allows those involved to beat out their competition or at least gain resources to try to do so; because it allows flexibility that formal rules and regulations do not; because it is a tool in the economic and political struggle for power; and because the various dynamics of privatization, competition, decentralization, export-oriented policies, and campaign and party finance allow for and provide incentives for it. Not to mention that it is motivated by the usual suspect—greed, the desire for more income, revenue, and privileges.

There are informal networks that sustain corruption, and these coexist with and feed off the formal legal networks that sustain political and economic, party and firm structures in the EU and its member states.

As with other OECD states, the EU and its member states are being hypocritical: they preach anticorruption and good governance, but when it comes to the EU, they are lax about it. In 2002, when the EU was criticizing the Eastern bloc candidate countries for their casual efforts and laws against corruption, "only eight of the 15 member states had completed ratification of the 1995 Convention on the Protection of the European Communities' Financial Interests."[17] Germany, Japan, and several smaller EU countries have balked at strengthening the OECD antibribery convention.

The book proceeds with an overview of corruption dynamics in the European Union, then unpacks those dynamics in subsequent chapters. It does not explore the academic debates about what kind of organization the EU is (intergovernmental, multilevel, and so forth) or how to characterize its decision-making processes.[18] Those readers not familiar with the EU are invited to consult appendices 2 and 3. Currency exchange rates were calculated using an online service; they are for the year of occurrence and are not adjusted for inflation. The amounts given in dollars are rounded because the book's argument does not depend on precision to the last decimal place.[19]

Corruption has financial and political costs. Corrupt practices misappropriate public resources at the same time that the public is advised that the state must enact austerity measures. The World Bank estimates that 3 percent of total global GDP is lost to corruption. Corruption also degrades the quality of democracy by breeding cynicism and by limiting those things that should be in the public domain and for the public interest to just those persons involved in the corrupt transactions. It is about a breach of public trust. Corruption affects not just 450 million EU citizens but people elsewhere, because the EU and its member state sustain corruption domestically and abroad.

Specifically, despite claims that corruption is a victimless crime, in Europe it has been anything but. A surprising number of corpses are related to corruption cases, even when classic organized crime networks are not involved. Socialist Party kingmaker and former deputy prime minister of Belgium André Cools was murdered in 1991 when it appeared he was going to reveal a corrupt arms deal. That arms investigation led to the resignation of four government ministers, the suicide of one of them, the suicide of an army general, and the resignation of NATO secretary general Willy Claes. In 2000, Wolfgang Huellen, the chief financial officer of the parliamentary delegation of one of Germany's two most powerful and dominant political parties, the Christian Democratic Party (CDU-CSU), was found dead at the end of a noose. Huellen was involved in what came to be known as Kohlgate.[20] Jürgen Mollemann of Germany's Liberal Democrats (the FDP), charged with tax evasion and fraud, went skydiving and unhooked himself from his parachute. In 1993 Italian business mogul Raul Gardini shot himself shortly before he was due to be interrogated, and Gabriele Cagliari, the CEO of a major Italian public enterprise, suffocated himself to death with a plastic bag in prison. Both men had been key figures in the Enimont affair, which saw political parties rake in several hundred million dollars worth of kickbacks. A weapons sale by France to Taiwan in which hundreds of millions of dollars disappeared into various political and defense pockets also generated several mysterious defenestrations in the 1990s.[21] What all these cases have in common is that the politicians, parties, and firms involved were trying to best their economic and political competition in the European Union and elsewhere. Bribery and graft were instrumental in doing so and were considered feasible alternatives within European political, legal, and market structures. Corruption is more common in Europe than typically thought, and it is sustained by the market and political dynamics thought to root it out.

CORRUPTION DYNAMICS IN THE EUROPEAN UNION

Who ought we to distrust, if not those to whom is committed great authority, with great temptations to abuse it?

—Jeremy Bentham

By 1992, according to some estimates, if the dollar amount of corruption in Italy had represented the gross income of a firm, that company would have been the twelfth largest in the country, just behind Olivetti and ahead of Alitalia. Fraud and corruption take a noticeable portion of the EU's annual budget, and major party-financing scandals within the states have led many to conclude that corruption has become the norm, not the exception, in Europe's democracies.[1] Corrupt deals in Germany in the late 1990s and early 2000s have involved millions of euros, and that figure excludes the cases with which former German chancellor Helmut Kohl was associated in the early 1990s.[2] French firms have routinely paid kickbacks of 2–5 percent on public works contracts to political parties. France's privatized defense and engineering group Thales, formerly Thomson CSF, is, at the time of writing, under investigation for bribing public officials in France, Greece, Argentina, and Cambodia, for collusion with politicians on market distribution in Tahiti, and for fraud against the European Union itself. After the launch of the Single Market, Dutch construction firms set up a racket on public procurement contracts, and evidence indicates that the German industrial group Siemens spent more than EUR 420 million ($553 million) on bribes to win contracts overseas, at home, and in EU neighbors Greece and Italy between 1999 and 2006.[3]

Corruption continues in Europe due to the nature of economic competition, the demands of campaign financing, and the opportunities afforded by privatization. Corruption in the western European Union countries is distinguished from corruption in the former Soviet bloc, and from corruption in other less developed countries, in that with legal, institutional, and economic development,

EU countries see kleptocracy decline; it is then replaced by bribes and kickbacks, primarily on public works projects, to benefit political parties and corporations. Oddly, corruption becomes more "democratic," and the route to personal enrichment via corruption becomes indirect and institutionalized—it tends to pass through political parties, bureaucracies, and firms.

Even if "international flows associated with trade and investment increase the costs of corruption to any given country," those flows do not necessarily also increase costs to the individual politicians, bureaucrats, or individual firms that profit from corruption. Gerring and Thacker note that "greater openness should impose greater discipline on countries to reduce corruption."[4] The problem is that corruption may be costly to countries as a whole, but individual citizens, firms, political parties, and politicians could find it rational to engage in corrupt practices. Costs to the individual politicians, bureaucrats, or individual firms that profit from corruption may not go up. How the phenomena associated with international economic integration fostered by the EU have sustained corruption needs to be understood.

DEFINING CORRUPTION

Corruption is often defined as the abuse of public office for private gain. That description misses a large part of what generally strikes a chord in most Europeans: that corruption also involves violation of the norms, not just procedures, of their democratic processes. When British tabloids headline political sleaze, they are playing on the sense that something in the body politic has been degraded, cheapened, or debased. These cases of sleaze may have been legal yet still be called corrupt. Societal norms may vary across countries and regions, but within Europe the promise of democratic government is that governmental decisions are made according to procedures openly agreed upon, not according to what amounts to a private sale between a privileged few who have the requisite connections and funds. If we allow the standards to be defined by communities, we may have several problems. One is the very real possibility that corruption may corrode community standards, altering a community's sense of the public interest. If we rely on the definition in a community's legal code, we may find that the legal system also contains corrupting laws: "that an act is legal does not always mean that it is not corrupt."[5] Campaign-financing laws, passed by self-interested politicians, may have the effect of giving legal sanction to behaviors, by politicians and political parties, that undermine elected and appointed officials' ability and incentive to uphold some common good, some public interest. Anyone who attempts to define and study corruption also needs to recognize that corruption in the EU is often as much for the purposes of funding political parties and campaigns as it has been for the private gain of those involved. A slightly broader definition is in order. In democracies, political corruption is a violation of the norm of openness and inclusiveness in the decision-making process. Recognizing that it is sometimes difficult to define specifically what is public, I hold that corruption is a violation of the public trust that the public office will be used for public purposes. A French court put it elegantly when convicting a well-known politician: "Alain Juppé, while he was invested with an elected public mandate, deceived the confidence of the sovereign people."[6]

I work with the definitions of corruption as used by the various countries and also with the common understanding as noted earlier. The analysis does not go on to distinguish between instances of "bureaucratic" or "legislative," or "high" or "low," corruption, or among gray, black, and white. In this study of corruption in the EU, I do not cover what could be termed corporate corruption or fraud, or corruption in civil society, or the corruption of or by the media, unless it is corruption in those sectors directly connected to an institution or official in the executive, legislative, or judicial branch of the state.[7]

Many of the cases described in this book were not prosecuted under a country's legal definition of corruption. In France, even when bribes and kickbacks are involved, officials are more often accused of abuse of public funds than of corruption; the former term was adopted after some major scandals in the 1930s.[8] In Germany, there are at least eighteen different legal types of corruption, ranging from forgery to malfeasance in office and contravention of public laws.[9] Statutes proscribing tax evasion or illegal party financing are other common means of prosecuting corruption. Most of the cases in this book are ones in which a number of public and private persons, firms, and political parties benefited from the deliberate distortion of the official decision process, and that distortion had a monetary price put on it. In her early definition of corruption, Susan Rose-Ackerman emphasized "the use of an illegal market as the method of allocation" within a democratic political system. I am interested in the factors that allow or sustain such actions, so my working definition of corruption is suitable.[10]

Scholars have put much effort into determining how corruption affects countries, their economies, and political systems, and it is worth commenting on their general findings. Most research finds that in modern, market-oriented democracies, corruption distorts the democratic process—a process that, in principle, allows citizens to oust one government and choose another. By insulating those who hold power from challenges to their rule, corruption blocks that possibility of change. It can be, therefore, politically inefficient, just as market monopolies often are economically inefficient. Second, corruption diverts general, public wealth to personal wealth without providing accountability, without adherence to rules determined by the democratic process. Third, it distorts market competition because corrupt transfers from public to private wealth occur in the absence of (legal, open) market-driven supply and demand. Fourth, corruption can be economically inefficient. It draws investments toward projects that do not necessarily meet demand (public or private) but that provide kickback schemes, and it dissuades legitimate investors from entering markets. Fifth, it may put countries in violation of their international economic agreements.[11] And surprisingly, it is those international agreements that sometimes facilitate corruption.

FREE TRADE AND COMPETITION

The introduction of free trade and competition between states does not necessarily reduce corruption. The usual expectation is that free trade and competition disrupt collusive arrangements and also make corruption too costly for businesses or governments to engage in. Free trade and competition also should create new economic opportunities, thus reducing the need for individuals to use corrupt practices to stay afloat or get ahead. The standard view expects that free trade and competition inherently reduce corruption because, by definition, free trade and competition mean that transactions perhaps previously blocked as a result of closed markets and regulations are now open. Corruption therefore is not necessary to complete the exchange.[12] However, when free trade creates more competition, it can change conditions sufficiently that some firms have an incentive to resort to corruption. As competition in the private sector increases, landing government contracts can become increasingly important to a firm's bottom line. Paying a bribe to land a contract is often cheaper than bankruptcy (although several of the large firms caught in corruption cases later went bankrupt), and paying can give a firm an edge over the competitor with the better bid. Furthermore, as the EU's experience makes clear, creating the infrastructure for free trade and competition entails setting up a regulatory framework, and inevitably those regulations block some transactions. Particularly in countries with a tradition of heavy regulation and corruption, some politicians will be inclined to take advantage of a firm's interests and accept a kickback for allowing a blocked transaction to go forward.

With the European Union (and the WTO) requiring states to reduce their subsidies to private and public firms, and with state bailouts subject to EU oversight, firms must be more aggressive in the marketplace to stay afloat. Public handouts are less readily available. Competition to gain market share or to land a government contract intensifies. Competition, by increasing the supply of firms in a given market, can also increase the demand for corruption. Also, competition does not necessarily increase the risk of discovery. When competition brought on by economic integration and free trade increases gradually, as it has in the EU, firms, politicians, and bureaucrats can absorb the new competitors into the old system. The new market economy is creatively adapted to old patterns of corruption, not the other way around.

Competition also impels the European states to "export" corruption, as they and their firms vie for markets and contracts in the international economy. As is well known, bribery, kickbacks, and retro-commissions, in which a percentage of the bribe or "commission" paid to a foreign intermediary or official is then paid back to politicians, parties, and firms, are common in the oil, infrastructure, and arms industries. What may be less well known is that European states have institutionalized the means by which such practices can be launched and often turn a blind eye toward them. States have created agencies to aggressively promote sales for their weapons manufacturers. They have created others to support exports to and infrastructure projects in high-risk and highly corrupt countries. They have formalized, bureaucratic procedures for firms to follow in order to declare commissions paid on foreign contracts. Those commissions represent both legitimate payments and bribes; the national customs authority approves them. Even in the EU, states grant exile and sometimes citizenship to those wanted for corruption in other member states.[13] Networks that are useful for legitimate commerce also can be activated for corrupt practices.[14] The European Union has had no dampening effect on the trend, in the advanced industrialized countries of the West, of using corruption to compete in the international economy.

DECENTRALIZATION, DEMOCRATIZATION, AND CAMPAIGN FINANCING

Decentralization and what we might call democratization also have perverse effects on corruption. This observation is contrary to the standard expectation that the loosening of central government control fosters competition among local or regional governments, and that decentralization fosters more local-level oversight. The competition among area governments is supposed to compel local authorities to make the most efficient use of tax revenue, in order to make the locality attractive to businesses and home buyers. Michel Delebarre, president of the Committee of the Regions (an EU organization), puts it this way: "Decentralisation produces government which is closer to the citizen, [has] more transparency, more efficiency, and more likelihood of delivering concrete results on the ground."[15] Corruption siphons away revenue and typically is not an efficient allocator of revenue. Therefore, local authorities will be impelled to eliminate corruption, because it makes their area less attractive to outside investors and potential tax-base-contributing residents.

When decision-making authority is brought down to regional and local levels, however, where formerly it had been tightly held by the central government, the number of instances in which governing authorities make discretionary decisions increases. Effective supervision also decreases, because few citizens watch their local governing authorities with the same care that they do the national government. Voter turnout for local and regional elections is often significantly lower than it is for national elections, even in countries that have been decentralized for decades.[16] Local decision making also reduces oversight because lower-level oversight boards are often weak and lines of authority unclear. Local staff may not have the competence to evaluate complex bids. If the central state decentralizes but still provides the bulk of revenue transfers, localities face few hard budget constraints and thus decentralization has less of a damping effect on corruption.[17] The French state began decentralization in 1982 and is still catching up with the cases of corruption that decentralization spawned. But what really turns decentralization into a production process for corruption is combining it with elections to those new layers of government, and with the privatization of local government services.

Democratization, or more elections, fuels increased demand for campaign financing. Parties and elections need financing yet face a problem: there is little reason to donate to a party unless one gets something directly in return, but such a quid pro quo between a private person or firm and an elected official is usually what we mean by the term *corruption*. Relying on voluntary, legal donations seldom generates enough funding to run a campaign or party. Public financing merely inflates the cost of running campaigns and party organizations, thus increasing the demand of parties and politicians for more funding. Those states that have heavily regulated political financing have exacerbated the problem by restricting the supply of legal donations and spending. What politicians and parties cannot get legally, they may try to get illegally.

Even seemingly well-financed and politically successful parties and politicians often resort to corruption to obtain more funding. Whether working within a two-party or multiparty system, politicians are in an arms race for funding. Efforts to control it are about as successful as controlling weapons proliferation or imposing a prohibition on alcohol. More elections, as a result of decentralization having added further layers of elected officials, mean more campaign and party expenses, and that means more demand for financing to cover costs and get ahead of political rivals. Even the concession to democracy that the EU has created, the European Parliament, has been associated both with campaign finance corruption and with immunity against prosecution for those politicians involved.

PRIVATIZATION

Privatization is supposed to "reduce corruption by removing certain assets from state control and converting discretionary official actions into private, market-driven choices."[18] In the western states of the EU, this process has been corruptible and has led to other corrupt arrangements. The rights to sell off government assets have been appropriated by private individuals in some cases; politicians who already hold office can demand kickbacks from those in the private sector who bid on public works contracts. Contractors are unlikely to complain because the contracts are usually parceled out to include all firms and because often the contracts are padded to cover the cost of the kickback. The risk of getting caught is low. Contractors also prefer not to challenge the governing authority with whom they hope to do more business in the future. Another popular feature of privatization, the creation of parapublic agencies, blurs the lines between public authority and private business practices, thus heightening the potential for conflict of interest and corruption. In countries that are less corrupt, public-private partnerships can erode the esprit de corps that may have promoted "the defence of values such as the 'general good' and 'public service,'" and thus provided an important normative guard against corruption.[19]

Privatization contributes to the corruption potential of decentralization partly because many local and regional government contracts are exempt from EU and national provisions for competitive sealed bids. The exemptions result because the amounts are under the set thresholds, or the amounts can be easily arranged to be under the thresholds; because the number of contracts awarded relative to oversight board capacity is high; and because politicians, firms, and bureaucrats have found it easy to establish an equilibrium in which all benefit. The EU's oversight capacity is sorely stretched; it relies on ad hoc complaints from contractors and private citizens, and on the existence of national laws to which contractors can appeal. Most contractors are reluctant to file suit; they want to avoid the expense, not to mention the worry, that they might be informally blacklisted from future contracts by the agency they are filing against. The EU has recently shifted oversight of procurement contracts under a certain amount back to member states, so supervision now depends on the administrative capacities and ethical norms of each region.

THE ROLE OF THE POLITICIAN

Corruption survives in the European Union for a variety of reasons. Above all, one must remember that despite democratic elections, elected politicians are not always the agents of the voters. The holders of elected office also hold the power to change laws and intervene in judicial proceedings. They use the tools of the state to protect themselves. When it comes to matters affecting their interests, they often write weak laws. Even when facing voters, they are protected by the fact that corruption is only rarely of immediate concern to voters, whose choices are limited, often to a set of parties or candidates, all of whom have participated in one form of corruption or another.[20] In France, several high-level corruption cases have been stymied because cabinet ministers, in the name of national defense, have blocked judicial access to key documents. Thus, for instance, in one of the cases involving the French oil company Elf, information about bribes, which the investigating judge suspects amounted to hundreds of millions of euros per year, remains classified.[21] When the German government of Gerhard Schroeder tried to investigate the various scandals involving former chancellor Helmut Kohl, including the sale of a former East German oil refinery to the French oil company, it found most of the evidence, both on paper and computer disks, had been destroyed by the departing government. When Silvio Berlusconi became prime minister of Italy in 2001, he decriminalized false accounting, conveniently reducing the definition of the act, and shrank the statute of limitations, as well as the penalties, should he or his cronies ever be found guilty of the same. The *Economist* commented that the law would have been an embarrassment even to a banana republic.[22] When French Socialists and Gaullists were embroiled in corruption cases in the 1980s, they agreed to pass laws granting themselves amnesty from prosecution. Voters in the next elections could hardly exercise retribution, because all the major presidential and legislative candidates had tainted, but amnestied, pasts.

INTERNATIONAL ORGANIZATIONS

An inherent contradiction is present in the structure of any international organization that uses rules and treaties to promote free trade and economic integration. Freer trade comes with both more rules and less enforcement of them. To create open borders and a common market, states do not unilaterally eliminate their own barriers to foreign trade; that might be politically foolish, since they have no guarantee that other states will follow suit. Instead, states negotiate with each other to write rules that will tell them what, by how much, and when they each have to alter their regulations on trade and markets. Yet those rules are inherently weak. International organizations lack strong oversight, policing, and enforcement capacity: those are features of sovereignty that states jealously guard. A common set of rules may follow, but more competition may impel some firms to bribe their way into contracts and markets, and if they do, the firms run a small risk of getting caught. They can create a web of transnational transactions that involves multiple jurisdictions, thus frustrating police and investigating magistrates, who only have authority in their own country. Corruption may be simpler than following the EU's complicated directives, whose exact procedures legally can differ in each country. At one level is the myth of a common market with strong oversight and enforcement; at another is actual practice. The EU's anticorruption convention is just that, a convention.[23] It has no teeth. In addition, the sovereignty considerations that impede trans-European judicial cooperation can block investigations in a particular country. In a country such as France, where the concept of national interest is highly developed and the emphasis is on *raison d'état* (national interest), corruption in certain economic sectors becomes one more means to justifiable ends, and hence itself justifiable and sheltered from investigation and prosecution.

The institutional changes wrought by the EU occurred in an environment that was already thick with institutionalized economic, social, political, and cultural relations and patterns. In such conditions, the impact of any one change is likely to be muted.[24] Partly for that reason, the EU as an institution of regulations and agencies has not had a large impact on patterns of corruption in EU countries. The EU has been generated by its member states, in a protracted process in which state interests, traditions, and cultures are all brought to bear on its development. It is not an exogenous "shock" of the sort popular with social scientists trying to test hypotheses by comparing outcomes across different countries exposed to the same stimulus.

What the EU has done is allow corruption through its policies of increasing economic competition within the Single Market, including regulation of competition in the public procurement sector. The institutional and cultural safeguards against corruption have lagged behind the opening up of markets. What the EU has done only indirectly is to host policies that accompanied the Single Market and are part of the standard package of economic and political reforms touted as cures for sluggish and corrupt political economies: privatization, decentralization, and campaign finance laws. These latter forces have their own, often interactive, dynamics that foster corruption.

The EU has also not made high levels of corruption a barrier to membership. Just a month and a half before it joined the EU, Slovakia was criticized by the EU for not having improved its laws against fraud and corruption, but the state was allowed to join anyway.[25] Slovakia had already been criticized a few months earlier for its weak restraints on conflict of interest, party financing, and corruption.[26] The EU guaranteed Romania and Bulgaria membership by 2007, even though anticorruption efforts in those countries have been of limited success. The

EU's reasoning is that once the countries are members, the EU can exercise more leverage. However, it will have lost the major coercive element, since there are no mechanisms for kicking countries out of the EU, and harsh sanctions, even when envisioned, are seldom if ever applied. The assumption seems to be that membership will solve the problem. Yet it does not, because in the EU, dynamics that allow and encourage corruption obtain.

INTERACTION EFFECTS

Each chapter to follow focuses on a phenomenon, such as competition, even though it becomes clear that corruption dynamics are interactive. Discrete policy programs such as privatization interact with others such as decentralization, and campaign-financing regulations and EU public procurement policies, to facilitate corruption in ways probably not imagined by the policy designers. Take, for example, cases in which Charles Pasqua has been implicated. Pasqua was twice French interior minister (1986–91 and 1993–95), sometime presidential hopeful, and cofounder with Jacques Chirac in 1976 of the Gaullist party Rassemblement pour la République (RPR). The cases in which Pasqua's name surfaces illustrate the interconnections of corruption in the European Single Market.[27] One case involves a parapublic agency set up to promote weapons exports; another involves his activities as head of a territorial government that had attained more freedom to maneuver thanks to decentralization; and another pertains to his efforts to obtain financing for his European Parliament campaign. Following the institutional, business, and personal connections between Pasqua and others illustrates how corruption can persist in wealthy, first-world democracies.

Decentralization, Privatization, and Arms Exports

Charles Pasqua was president of the governing council of Hauts-de-Seine, next to Paris, from 1988 to 2004. Thanks to the decentralization policies of the 1980s, these department governing councils had become more powerful institutions. In the process of investigating the myriad cases Pasqua appears to have been involved in, a judge discovered that Pasqua had obtained a loan of about $450,000 (EUR 445,000) to finance his 2002 presidential bid, which he ultimately did not pursue. The loan came from a Cypriot bank, on behalf of a shell society connected to the head of a school in Hauts-de-Seine. The alleged intermediary in that deal, Noulis Pavlopoulos, has been under investigation for money laundering in connection with the loan. The loan's origins and ends have become the subject of a judicial investigation.[28] In 1995, when Pasqua was head of the department, Pasqua created the school and named Pierre Monzani as its director. Monzani has also been investigated by the French judiciary, and when Pasqua was head of the splinter Gaullist party Rassemblement pour la France, Monzani was its general secretary. The school has been financed by major French corporations, and it participates in and receives financing from the EU-sponsored Leonardo da Vinci and Socrates programs. The EU's Leonardo da Vinci program has had problems with mismanagement, which has raised concerns about fraud. False invoicing for some programs has been common.[29] Ironically, Pasqua, the founder of this EU-funded school, is something of a Euroskeptic and has run for European Parliament elections on a "sovereignty of France" platform.

Pasqua's name also appeared on the infamous oil-for-food list from Iraq as the recipient of twelve million barrels. Currently, investigations reveal that Pasqua's political foundation may have received major donations from Elias Youssef Firzli, a Lebanese lawyer who, witnesses say, was the intermediary between Total (the oil company that absorbed Elf) and Saddam Hussein's oil ministry. Firzli allegedly facilitated Total's access to oil by way of and circumventing the UN-sponsored oil-for-food program.[30]

Pasqua's colleague, the Corsican Jean-Charles Marchiani, has demonstrated how to derail the privatization of government services and how to illegally profit from stiff competition in the arms market. Having lost his 2004 reelection bid to the European Parliament and so having lost his immunity, Marchiani was jailed in 2004 and convicted in 2005 for having received FRF 9.7 million ($2 million) as the intermediary in the rigged award of a baggage-handling contract for the Parisian airport authority, Aéroport de Paris, at the Roissy Charles de Gaulle facility to a private contractor. He shared the airport "commission" with Claude Pasqua, a cousin of Charles Pasqua. He also has been convicted of taking DM 2.5 million ($1.2 million) in payment between 1994 and 1999 for having helped the German defense firm Renk sell equipment for French Leclerc tanks. Marchiani claims he was, instead, employed until 1993 by a British subsidiary of the French defense group, Thomson, which has been implicated in a variety of corruption cases, including one which brought down Roland Dumas, former foreign minister and head of France's Constitutional Court.[31] Marchiani is also under investigation for having illegally profited from his efforts to free French hostages in Lebanon and Bosnia, in 1988 and 1995, respectively. Marchiani had become Middle East adviser to Thomson. Finally, he is under investigation for his involvement in what came to be known as Angolagate: a corruption case of illegal weapons sales to Angola, possibly facilitated by France's weapons export promotion agency, SOFREMI (Société française d'exportation des matériels, systèmes, et services).[32]

Pasqua's post as interior minister gave him control over that parapublic agency, SOFREMI, which had been set up to market and sell French policing weapons and training capabilities to other countries. The French state owned 35 percent of the agency, and the rest was held by a group of twenty-six of France's industrialists in the security and arms business. SOFREMI was typical of state efforts to promote select domestic industries: although ownership was divided between the state and the firms it promoted, the agency was run by the French state. Its very existence testified to a conflict of interest between public office and private gain, and, not surprisingly, it was implicated in a major corruption scandal. Decentralization interacted with Pasqua's network in other ways. It was through the administrative director of his Hauts-de-Seine department governing council, a man who also had worked for Pasqua at SOFREMI, that Pasqua was introduced to the international arms dealer Pierre Falcone. Under Pasqua, Falcone became the exclusive agent of SOFREMI, and it was under Pasqua that Falcone allegedly ran a huge illegal arms sale to Angola through SOFREMI, allegedly with Pasqua's approval, and in conjunction with Arkadi Gaydamak, a Russian born billionaire businessman. In December 2001, Gaydamak fled France after an international arrest warrant was issued for him. The warrant is for illegal weapons sales, tax evasion, money laundering, and bribery. He has since been living in Israel.[33]

If the reader is wondering how an agency of the French state (SOFREMI), under the direct supervision of the interior minister, could have approved an illegal arms export, so too is the French judiciary. It is also questioning how an agency whose remit is to promote the sale of French-manufactured weaponry would have sponsored the sale of weapons that were clearly not French. Falcone claims that the deal (between 1993 and 1994) never passed through France, so the arms were not exported from France. Instead, the $633 million dollars worth of weapons were spoils from the Soviet empire and passed through two of the EU's newest members while they were in accession talks, the Czech Republic and Slovakia. He also claims that the Angolan Dos Santos government was not under an arms embargo—only the rival group, UNITA, was—and that the deal was also "morally legitimate." Pasqua asserts his own innocence.[34] The affair, which has reached the highest levels of the French state, has been dubbed Angolagate.

Angolagate

Angolagate began in 1993 when Angolan president Eduardo Dos Santos asked a French contact, Jean-Bernard Curial, how to evade the arms embargo imposed on him, in order to squelch his political rival. Curial, longtime Socialist Party operative and Africa specialist, contacted President François Mitterrand's son, Jean-

Christophe Mitterrand. The younger Mitterrand had made Africa his vocation, working under his father in the Elysée as a consultant. Jean-Christophe Mitterrand had just been transferred out of his job at the Elysée and into a consultancy with Elf, the state-owned oil company, and with a subsidiary of Compagnie générale des eaux, one of France's major multinational water infrastructure firms. Jean-Christophe put Curial in contact with Falcone. Falcone and Mitterrand had been introduced to each other by the director of the Africa sector of Thomson, one of France's major weapons producers. For his troubles, the younger Mitterrand was allegedly paid $1.8 million and invited to Falcone's Paradise Valley, Arizona, mansion (in August, which, given the weather there at that time of year, could mean Falcone didn't think much of Mitterrand). Jean-Christophe Mitterrand was later held in preventive detention in Paris and released after his mother, the widow of President Mitterrand, paid his approximately $1 million bail.[35] Mitterrand has claimed that the $1.8 million were not from the illegal arms sale but were related to a fish factory investment of his in Mauritania. The Mauritanian government is also investigating him for tax evasion.[36]

International Finance, International Connections, and Export-Led Corruption

Corrupt deals make use of legal financial institutions and arrangements, and Angolagate was no exception. When Angola was unable to pay upfront for the weapons, Gaydamak and Falcone turned to Marc Rich, the financier residing in Switzerland, whom Bill Clinton had pardoned in his last days as president of the United States. Rich had been pursued for "tax evasion, tax fraud and running illegal oil deals with Iran during the hostage crisis." Just as the British government had financed a controversial weapons sale to Saudi Arabia that involved sizable bribes, Rich financed their $500 million, SOFREMI-approved but possibly illegal arms sale, through an Angolan oil-for-cash system.[37]

To handle their arms deal, Falcone had opened an account in the name of a Slovakian firm, ZTS-Osos, at Paribas in France. Paribas was the same bank that handled many of the funds from the UN-sponsored Iraq oil-for-food program. Alerted to the arrival of a sizable arms shipment in Angola by one of France's intelligence agencies, the DGSE (Direction générale de la sécurité extérieure), and of probable French financing, the French tax police investigated. Falcone and Gaydamak hired a tax lawyer, Allain Guilloux. Coincidentally, Guilloux was the tax lawyer accused of wrongfully holding a videotaped confession made by Gaullist party government appointee Jean-Claude Méry. Méry, on that videotape, which later was consigned to Socialist deputy and finance minister Dominique

Strauss Kahn, revealed a Gaullist party illegal financing network and directly implicated President Jacques Chirac.[38]

One of the subthemes of this book is the extent to which informal contacts, and networks of personal and professional friends, facilitate corrupt transactions. Corruption relies on the trust and knowledge that develops among friends, colleagues, and ethnic groups. In France, Pasqua, of Corsican descent, is seen as a central figure of a *réseau corse* (Corsican network), which has had strong links to networks in Africa, including France's oil company Elf Aquitaine (now part of Total).[39] Falcone was born in Algiers of a Corsican father; Pasqua's so-called right-hand man, Marchiani, is Corsican. Marchiani is suspected of profiting from Falcone and Gaydamak's illegal arms sale, earning about $300,000 for his role, or about 1 percent of the amount Falcone and Gaydamak are estimated to have made on the sale.[40] Yet another Corsican, Étienne Léandri, has been implicated in several of these cases.[41] Pasqua's son, Pierre, is wanted in connection with Angolagate. He resides in Tunisia, which, conveniently, does not have an extradition treaty with France.

Another of Pasqua's entourage, André Guelfi, of Corsican parentage, is connected to a Franco-Uzbekistan bribery case of a French oil refinery construction firm, Technip. Technip in turn is directly linked to a bribery case involving Halliburton's KBR subsidiary (during Dick Cheney's tenure as head of Halliburton) and the Nigerian government of Sani Abacha. Guelfi was also active in the corrupt aspects of the sale of an East German oil refinery to the French national oil company (see chap. 2). In this Elf-Leuna case, which contributed to the downfall of German chancellor Helmut Kohl, Guelfi provided the bank account through which commissions were paid to several figures who were suspected of sending payments to German politicians and parties. One of those figures, former Bavarian defense minister Holger Pfahls, was thought to have disappeared in Asia but was later found in Paris, living in an upscale apartment near the Eiffel Tower.[42] We see the EU's limited effect on reducing the opportunities for graft when we note that the sale with which those bribes were associated was approved during the normal operations of the European Commission's Competition Directorate.

Falcone and Gaydamak also have been connected to Socialist president François Mitterrand's close adviser Jacques Attali, who used to head the European Bank for Reconstruction and Development. Evidence indicates that Attali, on behalf of the arms dealers, used his high-level ministerial connections to stop the investigations.[43] In addition, Falcone's firm, Brenco, appears to have paid Thierry Imbot $120,000 between 1996 and 1999 for his advice and network access in mainland China and Taiwan. Imbot was one of the alleged defenestration victims of the Thomson frigate sale to Taiwan, with which Roland Dumas, France's foreign minister and later head of its Constitutional Court, was connected.[44]

Falcone has high-level connections to American politicians not only through Marc Rich but also through his own wife's political donations. In 1994, Falcone married a former Miss Bolivia (1988), Sonia Montero de Falcone, who, through her Utah-registered health and beauty products business, Essanté, donated $100,000 to the 2000 Bush/Cheney campaign, and she herself donated the maximum legal amount to George W. Bush and several other Republican Party candidates. The funds more than likely came from Falcone's activities rather than from his wife's unprofitable business. The Republican Party returned the donation after the 2000 election, upon hearing of the arrest of the probable source. Sonia Falcone was arrested at her Paradise Valley, Arizona, home in 2006 on immigration fraud charges. She had become a well-known philanthropist in the Phoenix area, who has said her goal is to "reach out to the abused, homeless, and hungry while helping to fight in the war on the world's most deadly diseases" and to support causes that "will do the most good and help the most people."[45] She is, however, married to someone who is alleged to profit handsomely from civil wars.[46]

Falcone and Gaydamak's arms sale to Angola was discovered through the normal operations of various French administrative services. The foreign intelligence agency DGSE reported in December 1995 that a large quantity of arms from the former Soviet bloc had arrived in Angola through the intervention of a French intermediary. It wasn't until 2000 that Falcone was arrested. And, typical of corruption cases, progress was slow due to the normal operations of various French administrative services. The judiciary had to obtain permission to request and use evidence from other countries, the European Parliament maintained the immunity of two of the major suspects, and as the lines of the case grew increasingly complex, the judiciary had to obtain permission to extend its inquiries.[47] Finally, at the same time that the French judiciary was trying to keep Pierre Falcone in the country, the French foreign ministry, in the course of its normal operations, processed paperwork from Angola requesting that he be granted diplomatic standing at UNESCO.

There is nothing illegal in Angola's use of UNESCO to provide diplomatic cover for Falcone, who had been released from jail in December 2001, after posting a $15 million bail, but jailed again for eleven days in October 2002 when he violated the conditions of his release. It merely shows that with little effort, legitimate institutional structures can be used for dubious ends. Falcone was able to leave France when Dos Santos, president of Angola, one of the most corrupt and poorest countries in the world, and of which it could be said in 2001 that only a quarter of its national revenue was accounted for, appointed Falcone its ambassador to UNESCO in June 2003. Despite Falcone being under investigation by the French judiciary, the French foreign ministry naturally consented to file the requisite papers: its job is diplomacy, not law enforcement. The UNESCO ambassadorship granted Falcone at least limited diplomatic immunity. He abandoned the $15 million bail bond (chump change, as some have observed) and used his diplomatic passport to fly to Angola, where he was to begin setting up institutions of higher learning. He was also free to supervise his extensive oil and diamonds interests (with Gaydamak, among others) in Angola. His wife said Falcone would stay in Luanda until his UNESCO work was done; it is more likely he will stay until he can fly elsewhere without risk of being arrested and extradited to France.[48] The only high point in all this is that a few months later, the much admired and well-known French actress and icon Catherine Deneuve resigned from her post as France's goodwill ambassador to UNESCO in protest of Falcone's appointment.[49]

Some of the factors that enable corruption to persist in Europe are conflicting missions, priorities, and norms at the highest levels of state. To wit, the president of Angola put considerable pressure on France to clear Pierre Falcone, who appears to be crucial to Dos Santos's system of "governance" and economic "development" in Angola. Dos Santos protested directly to President Chirac, and the Angolan state (such as it is) refused to sign off on contracts with France's Total to exploit two recently discovered offshore deepwater oil blocks. It also refused to renew Total's license on another block. Although members of the French judiciary have built a strong case against Falcone and have not, at the time of writing, annulled the international arrest warrant, the French foreign ministry and the presidency worked to appease Dos Santos and find a way to resolve the conflict.[50] The judiciary's mission conflicts with that of the foreign ministry, and anticorruption efforts conflict with business priorities. Reason of state may trump rule of law.

Political corruption has been largely insulated from EU rules and regulations, and not directly diminished by the EU's impact on the European economy. Notable in the cases to follow is that they have taken place not at the fringes of political power but at the very center of it, and all this while the European Single Market has been in full swing. Politicians and firms engaged in corrupt acts appear to have operated easily within the regular institutional arrangements of member states, the EU, and international financial institutions. Regulations to promote free trade, the forces of economic competition, export-led growth in oil, arms, and infrastructure, and privatization, decentralization, and campaign finance laws can provide institutional bases and incentives for corruption to persist within the European Union. There is often a time lag of years between corrupt actions and their discovery. For reasons discussed in this chapter and elaborated in the rest of the book, it appears premature for the *Economist* to have written in 2000 that "corruption in European politics is probably on the wane."[51]

DOES COMPETITION IN THE EUROPEAN UNION CORRUPT?

Colonel Pickering: Have you no morals, man?
Mr. Doolittle: Can't afford them, Governor.

—George Bernard Shaw, *Pygmalion*

On the morning of February 20, 1992, in Orlando, Florida, police were called to a not entirely atypical south Florida scene: a wild, half-naked middle-aged man standing seventeen floors up on a balcony of the Hyatt Regency Grand Cypress hotel, threatening to jump into the lushly planted atrium below. Within little less than an hour, a police officer had talked the man down and back into his hotel room, where a twenty-two-year-old woman from Escorts-in-a-Flash was sprawled on the bed, high on cocaine. The escort, Denise Wojcik, said she and another escort, Sherri, had spent the night with the deranged man, snorting cocaine through rolled up hundred-dollar bills. The man in question was searched and found to have a bit more than thirty-one grams of cocaine in his possession, enough to make him a drug trafficker under Florida law. He was also found to be Ben Dunne, supermarket mogul and scion of one of Ireland's wealthiest families. In a twist worthy of a Carl Hiassen novel, Dunne blamed his behavior on his having been kidnapped by the IRA eleven years previously. Incredibly, the IRA reference turned out to be true.

Although this story may have been dismissed as just another tale of the moral turpitude of the rich, the ensuing legal battle, which triggered a government investigation, revealed that at the debut of the Celtic Tiger's unprecedented economic takeoff, Irish politics was being financed by an elaborate network of illegal financial transactions, undisclosed donations, and tax dodges, and that Charles Haughey, leader of Fianna Fail and former Irish prime minister, was at the center of it.[1]

Some might say that a corruption case such as this is the last gasp of "old Europe" as it confronts the competitive market economy, but indications are that corruption is making the transition to the more competitive economy and into new economic sectors. There are serious allegations that Silvio Berlusconi, Italian prime minister (1994–95 and 2001–6) and founder of the party Forza Italia became Italy's modern media mogul and billionaire the old-fashioned way: by bribing judges and the tax authorities.[2] In Ireland, evidence indicates that in 1995 the bid procedure for awarding the license to run second-generation mobile phones was rigged, and, despite the professed openness to international competition and an EU legal framework that required it, internal memos suggest that the amount of "Irish content" was a factor in determining the winner.[3] In 2001, Dutch television exposed extensive collusion that had been going on for years in public contracting between construction firms and public authorities, despite EU competition rules, and in a market sector with over two thousand firms.[4] In 2005, employees of the French electronics and defense firm Thales (formerly Thomson CSF) were investigated for making payments to win a city rail contract in Nice.[5]

These cases raise the question of whether and how economic competition restructures the opportunities and risks of corruption. Free trade between states is expected to increase competitive pressures on firms, which lowers their ability to tolerate the costs of corruption that they may have been paying. If free trade also includes an agreement to open up a state's public procurement practices to bids from foreign firms, then politicians and bureaucrats should also find it harder to continue corrupt practices. On this virtuous path, even under domestic policing and judicial systems that remain unchanged, everyone should have less incentive to engage in corruption: there is more risk and less profit in it.[6]

This happy scenario assumes that foreign firms cannot be bought off as easily as domestic firms, that an increase in the number of participants in a given market sector will disrupt any preexisting corrupt practices, that the long-term effects of competition will influence short-term business calculations, and that when a country's economy is forced to be more competitive, politicians will not just increase public spending to cover extra outlays for corruption (thus absorbing the costs so that businesses can continue to give kickbacks).[7] It also assumes that the free trade rules and open public procurement rules will be observed and enforced. In other words, international free trade accompanied by an oversight body raises the risks and thus costs of corruption to levels that neither businesses nor governments can sustain.

This assumption is accompanied by the belief that private firms are less corruptible than governments. This book is not out to champion governments, which indeed have predilections toward corrupt behavior, but we should not ignore the temptation for corruption in private firms.[8] If a bribe is less than the potential profit, and has a low likelihood of discovery and penalty, then using one to get entry into a market, to win a contract, is a cost-effective business strategy. The standard view is that firms face incentives that restrict corruption: they have to be profitable, and corruption is like an additional tax; they are hierarchically structured with considerable staff oversight; and their employees are rewarded for performance, which is measurable in terms of firm profits. Yet the emphasis on profits is also what makes corruption a viable business strategy at times. Competition between firms entails risks to each firm. Corrupt transactions with politicians and bureaucrats can reduce that risk. It is a matter of opportunity costs: the foregone transaction (landing a contract, accessing the market, receiving a zoning law exemption, making a purchase or sale) might be more costly than the bribe and its attendant risks and penalties.

As the European Union's experience shows, these risks may exist in theory but not, at least for many years, in practice. Transnational policing and judicial cooperation is slow, cumbersome, and usually requires help from third (non-EU) countries, such as Switzerland; whistle-blowing is rare; and the open borders allow creative forum shopping. EU institutions, heavily dependent on the cooperation and good faith efforts of the member states, can scarcely verify the EU's own budget accounts; sentences in corruption cases are usually suspended, and financial penalties are rarely more than a small percentage of the gain from corruption; and firms that try to expose corrupt actions of their competitors are often excluded from the market they were trying to enter.

The EU's main legal institution, the ECJ, is geared toward resolving treaty disputes, not prosecuting transnational or domestic political corruption. The EU's anti-fraud unit focuses on fraud against the EU budget. Powerful politicians implicated in corruption cases use their positions and connections to foil their own judiciaries. If anything, the EU's regulation–heavy free trade regime has fostered collusion between firms and politicians. The Commission's mantra of competition impels some to take evasive action. Indeed, contractors looking for more business may be willing to pay "commissions," bribes, or kickbacks in order to establish themselves in a new market. Also, some sectors, as a result of their characteristics, do not have a plethora of competitors, so those that enter the market can easily be incorporated into the corrupt distribution network.

Competition in the EU did increase in the run-up to the Single Market and after its launch. Intra-EU exports in manufactured goods rose 14 percent between 1985 and 1995, and exports in services rose by 7.6 percent for the same period. Foreign direct investment "doubled as a share of total EU fixed assets investment." The effect on competition by the EU itself may have been less than the Commission expected, but for various reasons, firms in the EU-15 began facing more competition.[9] The recession of the early 1990s created competitive pressures as well.

This chapter makes two points. First, competition carries with it countervailing pressures that encourage corruption. Second, competition is not able to reach into many of the areas vulnerable to corruption. More competition means that those areas sheltered from it become even more valuable. On the first point, more competition means that expenses, including taxes, matter more. This means, in turn, that firms have an increased incentive to bribe their way out of taxes or other government regulations that add costs or impede transactions. More competition also means that cartels have a higher value to all the firms that are included in them, even if, under the new trade regime, cartels carry a greater risk of discovery and disruption.[10] More competition means firms will lobby to have it restricted, often through regulations that give a particular firm or small set of firms a competitive edge. Favorable or unfavorable zoning laws have a potentially greater effect on a firm's survival and profits.[11] Although much of this struggle for regulatory advantages takes place according to legal rules, evasion of those rules can also offer firms (and predatory, competitive) politicians an advantage. Politicians in the relevant parliaments, regional and local councils, and committees may extract fees to pass helpful laws and exemptions. Former French interior minister Charles Pasqua and former Irish minister Padraig Flynn are two notables who have been under investigation for having done so in at least one instance.[12] Flynn, as EU commissioner for social affairs (1993–99), was a member of the European Commission that resigned in 1999 under allegations of fraud, mismanagement, and nepotism.

On the second point, those sectors most often involved in corruption—defense contracting, water, utilities, and services such as telecommunications—are usually excluded from free trade rules on government procurement for many years. The politicians who have final say over negotiations all have an interest in protecting "sensitive" areas. States may also decide that many of their parapublic agencies (e.g., postal services) are not "public authorities" subject to the rules of the international agreements. It can take years of ad hoc international court cases before a state is compelled to admit that one of its pet parapublic agencies is subject to international agreements on public contracting.[13]

In addition, if competition threatens firms, those areas that can be sheltered from it are more attractive. Since in many sectors the risks of corruption being exposed and the penalties for it have not gone up, corruption becomes a viable short-term business tool. In many countries, it is not hard for a firm to find obliging politicians and bureaucrats with the necessary influence to arrange favorable outcomes. Even under competitive rules, states retain discretion over actions that carry large financial repercussions for firms, among them tax decisions, zoning regulations, authorization of the sale or purchase of arms, and the like.

Some note that the EU, through the treaty articles on competition, limits the amount of state aid and other subsidies that governments may provide firms, thus making it harder for states to protect firms from competition. Indeed, in the European Union, there has been a general downward trend in the level of state aid provided to industry, measured as a percentage of GDP.[14] As time goes by, firms move from having soft budget constraints to hard budget constraints. This shift should make bribery and kickbacks more costly to them, even if the absolute amounts of bribes and kickback percentages remain the same. Intra-EU exports and imports have more or less steadily increased over time in most of the states.[15] Yet a firm's hard budget constraints may also raise its costs of losing a contract; hence, at the margins, corruption may be cost effective in the short run. Also, the European Commission has approved a number of generous state aid packages for troubled firms, further reducing the threat of hard budget constraints.

The EU is also said to impose hard budget constraints on states and firms because those states in the European Monetary Union (states using the euro) need to meet the restrictive criteria of the stability pact. These criteria should make the opportunity costs of corruption higher. Certainly in the 1990s, states worked to reduce inflation and budget deficits in order to qualify for EMU. As an OECD report notes of Italy, "a wide range of reforms has reinforced market principles throughout the Italian economy. Key sectors of the economy have been opened more widely to competition, a sweeping program of privatisation has considerably reduced the interventionist role of the government, and administrative reforms have been introduced to improve the quality and transparency of the regulatory system."[16] By 2003, however, Germany, the country that had been most adamant that there be a stability pact for the euro, was among the first to break it, and soon was joined by France in declaring that the pact was unsustainable and needed to be renegotiated. The president of the European Commission, Romano Prodi (1999–2004), went so far as to call the pact "stupid."[17] Italy, Portugal, and Greece also broke the rules, which calls into question the existence of hard budget constraints due to European Monetary Union.

Finally, old practices, or in the terms of political economy, institutions and norms, become the default mode for individuals', firms', and politicians' expectations about what others will do. Thus, even as external parameters (laws, number, and types of competitors) change, the best guide for any one actor of what others will do is what has been done in the past. If prior institutions and norms facilitated corruption, leading to expectations that each would be behaving corruptly, current practices are more likely to reflect those expectations of the past than those of a new political and economic era of competitive markets. The focal point for coordination will be preexisting norms. It is not so much a change in the rules as a change in the belief that the rules will be enforced and that others will obey them which changes patterns of corruption.[18]

What we see in this chapter are examples of how competition creates incentives for corruption during the move to a freer market and after. The chapter focuses mainly on competition between firms that leads to political bribery or collusion. Willing and motivated politicians and bureaucrats are essential components in the effectuation of bribery and collusion. Competition between political parties is also a force goading corruption, and its effects are examined closely in chapter 6. This chapter does not attempt a painstaking, theory-confirming comparison of cases, statistics, and structures; rather, it brings to light two phenomena often overlooked in the drive to create regional trading blocs and increased economic competition: corruption resulting from competition and corruption impervious to competition.

COMPETITION CREATES INCENTIVES FOR CORRUPTION

Rather than competition making bribery too expensive for firms, firms often claim that competitive pressures force them to resort to corruption or forms of legal "bribery" (e.g., offsets). This reasoning is particularly applicable where demand for obtaining business is high, supply is low, and the consequences of not getting business are substantial. Economists might note that there is a "non-linearity in the incentive structure."[19] Effects are not incremental but sharp. The Spanish high-speed train case is illustrative. In 1989 Siemens was in competition to supply the electric lines along the high-speed rail line between Seville and Madrid. The firm is alleged to have paid into Spanish Socialist Party accounts, by way of fake consulting firms, approximately $3.28 million.[20] The contract, for ESP 100 billion ($8.4 billion), went to Siemens. Perhaps Siemens had concluded, from its failure to win the juiciest part of a dual set of contracts from Spain for construction of high-speed trains in 1988 (it had gone to a rival French firm), that mere lobbying (including use of such heavy hitters as then German chancellor Helmut Kohl) did not produce results.[21]

In that case, Siemens was in competition with the French construction giant Alsthom (which makes the high-speed train, the TGV, Train à grande vitesse) and the Japanese firm Mitsubishi for a contract to build some two dozen high-speed trains and a linked contract to build seventy-five locomotives. Skoda of then Czechoslovakia and Fiat-Ansaldo of Italy had bid for the locomotives but were not considered quality contenders. The contracts were worth approximately $370 million and $160 million, respectively. The Mitsubishi bid was 30 percent lower than those of the other two, and Mitsubishi had been a major provider to Spain of locomotives, but the French firm, due to its TGV, was the early favorite of the state railway monopoly (Renfe). Both Siemens and Alsthom were allowed to resubmit their bids; Alsthom was ultimately selected to build the trains. Siemens was awarded the locomotives contract. Swiss investigations into suspicious funds transfers indicate that Alsthom and Siemens paid an (illegal) fee to the Spanish Socialist Party (PSOE) for the awards.[22]

The competition is fierce for a reason: the rewards are nonlinear. "The stakes are extremely high and centre on who will lead the world in the supply of trains capable of speeds of up to 300 kmh (190 mph). With Britain's attempt in limbo, only France, West Germany and Japan have developed a national high-speed system. But none has been exported yet and the growth, or mere survival, of the technology and the builders depends on opening new markets."[23] The Spanish contracts were viewed as the last in Europe before the century's end, and the bribes, while substantial for the political party involved, were trivial relative to the value of the contracts. Corruption was a means of gaining, not losing, in a highly competitive economic game.

In competitive markets, corruption is not just a tool of the strong but of the weak as well. A case in Belgium is illustrative. In the Agusta affair, the Italian helicopter manufacturer Agusta beat France's Aérospatiale and Germany's Messerschmitt in a 1988 bid to provide forty-six helicopters to the Belgian air force. Analysts in the mid-1980s had already been commenting on how stagnant demand for weapons was causing problems for the Italian arms industry and singled out Agusta as having "major difficulties."[24] The CEO appointed in 1989 said he found Agusta in "a catastrophic situation."[25] The mechanics of a $51 million kickback had Agusta paying an offshore firm, Kasma Overseas, and Kasma writing a false invoice for consulting services.[26] Total value of the contract was approximately $225 million. As the Belgian air force had anticipated, the Italian helicopters were far too heavy for their intended use, requiring major, expensive modifications, which delayed delivery by years.[27] In his testimony on the case, Willy Claes, former minister of economics (and head of NATO), singled out his ministry's authorization committee as being "more attached to the compensations than to the quality of the weapon."[28]

The Dassault case, which merges with the facts of the Agusta case, is another example of how competition, combined with politicians looking for personal and political financing, leads to corruption of the competitive process. In 1988, the Belgian air force opened a competition for the modernization of an electronics system on F-16 fighter planes. After an initial bid, the air force drew up a closed list of two finalists: the electronics division of the French firm Dassault, and Litton, a U.S. firm. The air force favored Litton's offer—arguing it was much further along in the research and development process, that it was more sophisticated, and that Litton's R&D program for the system was economically secure—and transmitted its recommendation to the purchasing department (Service général des achats). Two months later, however, the air force revised its submission, deleting any mention of concerns about Dassault's economic viability and about the less developed status of its system. The air force suggested that the minister of defense make the final decision: "in light of the technical coordination on the one hand, and the financial considerations on the other, the two offers are practically the same and could be presented for decision to the minister."[29]

Why the change in evaluation? Serge Dassault, CEO of the eponymous firm, was looking for a way to develop his firm's electronics division, the Belgian Socialist Party was looking for more financing, and the network was already in place. Through his "tight business connections" with the Syrian arms dealer Mamoun Bashi, Dassault had learned of the Agusta maneuver; he had also learned that in the F-16 modernization competition, the air force preferred the U.S. firm's system. Bashi introduced Dassault to Alfons Puelinckx, go-between in the Agusta affair, and told him that "they already had a network and structure in place to reach the heads of the relevant departments and to secure the path of the funds." The relevant heads were, of course, Willy Claes, vice prime minister and minister of economics, and Guy Coëme, minister of defense. Claes and Coëme, both Socialists, were from rival regions (Walloon and Flemand) and had help from another, Guy Spitael (president of the Walloon Socialist Party). Dassault, on his part, had expressed a willingness to pay off the political party "in charge of the department of defense." The price tag? Approximately $2.5 million. After Dassault reached agreement on financial arrangements, two of Coëme's staffers, Jean-Louis Mazy and André Bastien, informed the air force generals in charge of the recommendation that the report should be rewritten so that the Litton and Dassault bids appeared equal and that they then propose that the minister of defense make the final decision. If not, Mazy and Bastien threatened, the air force risked not getting the modernization system at all. Given that the air force viewed the system upgrade as essential to pilot safety in combat, the generals agreed.[30]

The cases were linked both by the fact that the intermediaries and political parties involved were the same and by the fact that investigation into the Agusta case revealed corruption in the Dassault case. Agusta had been discovered not through what might be thought of as the normal channels of justice, nor through what the EU counts on to facilitate competition: the complaint of a rival firm. Instead, it was discovered when André Cools, head of the Socialist Party, from a stronghold in Liège but a nationally powerful and one-time vice prime minister, was murdered. Cools had expected the Agusta and Dassault kickbacks to go into party coffers, but evidently those were obtained by a rival faction in his party (that of Claes and Coëme) and by private pockets (the interior minister of the Walloon regional government, Guy Mathot). Competition in the weapons sector spurred corruption, but so did the fact that the network, once established for Agusta, was available for Dassault a year later: as the court noted, "the same persons are implicated . . . and that they, at least in part, used the same mechanisms to permit, facilitate or try to carry out these fraudulent schemes."[31]

In essence, Dassault paid the Belgian Socialist Party a percentage of the contract's value in order to have Belgium subsidize Dassault's efforts to break into a new sector of the arms trade. For Dassault, this seemed to be the most effective way of "competing" with other firms. And, in the Belgian Socialist Party, he found ready and willing partners. When interrogated in 1995, Serge Dassault said under his breath, "everyone pays commissions."[32] Indeed, the court said as much in arguing that widespread corruption was not a reason to ignore this case: "it is of no significance that at the time, these practices may have been in general use."[33] The intermediaries helped in that they saw in Dassault another opportunity for commissions. Notably, those involved expected that the process could be corrupted, that they could find others willing to participate in corrupting the process and not defecting.

Again, competition, instead of reducing corruption, is a factor in its increase. Politicians are able to take advantage of this dynamic. It appears that more, not less, competition has been driving some of the lower-level corruption in Germany, most of which involves waste management and construction contracts, sometimes separately and sometimes together.[34] Increased competition, including pressure on Germany to reduce its government spending in the run-up to the euro and after, did not prevent the Social Democratic Party in Cologne and other areas of Germany from asking for and taking kickbacks from garbage collection companies and from the firm to which it awarded the EUR 400 million ($465 million) contract for building an unwanted, unnecessary waste incinerator outside Cologne. These practices were undertaken, according to German documents, in 1994 and continued at least until 1999. The SPD (Sozialdemokratische Partei Deutschlands) politicians involved claim that they only used the funds to finance the party (extralegally, of course), but of an alleged EUR 12 million ($14 million) deposited into Swiss bank accounts, only EUR 420,000 ($490,000) have been accounted for among SPD Cologne funds.[35] Of these, about one-third were from Steinmüller, the firm building the waste incinerator.[36] Although it is unreasonable to expect corruption to be completely eliminated by competition, the Cologne case appears not to have been a fluke. Corruption related to party financing has surfaced in other parties and in other areas of Germany, indicating that conditions have been propitious for a middling level of corruption in Germany since the advent of the Single Market.

The EU, in its efforts to construct a competitive market, sometimes inspires corrupt tendencies rather than deflating them. In the Elf-Ertoil case of 1991, Elf sought to buy (literally) time in order to prepare its case for the EU's Competition Directorate. It did so by paying Nadhmi Auchi, the multimillionaire Iraqi businessman with British citizenship, a sizable commission to buy a Spanish oil refinery, Ertoil, then sell it to Elf after the European Commission approved the Elf purchase proposal.[37] Ertoil was controlled largely by a Kuwaiti firm, and the Kuwaiti government, to get cash during the Gulf War, wanted to sell its stake in Ertoil. Elf had been searching for a position in Spain but faced, in this sale, competition from BP, Total, and Shell. Elf had already been working to buy Cepsa, the Spanish gasoline distributor. The Spanish central bank, the main stockholder of Cepsa, wanted Elf to purchase Ertoil because the bank feared that were Total or Esso to get it, the Cepsa deal would be ruined. Elf's CEO at the time later said that problems developed because the Kuwaitis had put a deadline on Elf's option to buy Ertoil, but Elf, which was also working to buy Cepsa, was unable to get EU approval in time. He noted that "Elf couldn't buy that firm, but also couldn't let it fall into the hands of a competitor." Thus, Elf "had to" find an intermediary who would purchase Ertoil and then be willing to sell it to Elf.[38] The intermediary and original purchaser, Auchi, was paid a large commission (ESP 3.6 billion, or $34 million), and he transferred nearly half of it back it to Elf's general director, Alfred Sirven, who then disbursed chunks of it to various senior Elf executives. Ironically, press reports at the time stated (accurately) that Auchi's firm, GMH, "is believed to view the operation as essentially financial, however, and is ready to resell Ertoil providing it can make a comfortable margin on the transaction."[39] Obviously, it did. Auchi got a loan from the French investment bank, Parisbas, in which he had a 4.5 percent stake, to help pay for the temporary acquisition of Ertoil. The seasoned international businessman told the French court, "I was dealing with a state-owned firm. I didn't think at all that those directors would ask me [to do] something that wasn't right. They asked me to pay, I did, I thought that they had their reasons to do it."[40]

A similar process occurred when Elf bought 20 percent of another Spanish oil concern, Cepsa, through a local agent, Daniel De Busturia, who took $16 million in commission and gave half back to Sirven, "without knowing, according to him, the real recipients."[41] This is another case of competition spurring an oil company to use bribery to beat its competitors, with credible allegations that some of the bribes went to Spanish politicians who "had to" approve the deal. When asked about the sizable "commissions" paid by Elf, Le Floch-Prigent perfectly captured the role of competition in corruption: "I think that the money given to Mr. Auchi represented less of a cost to the firm than if a competitor had purchased Ertoil."[42] The illegal payments enabled Elf to get what it wanted despite delays imposed by the EU's Competition Directorate procedures, which required that the Elf-Ertoil purchase be approved by the European Commission. This is a classic case of firms using corruption to evade government regulation, so it is ironic that the corruption was prompted by rules designed to make the EU's economy more competitive.

There is a sense that new economy "industries" such as media, telecommunications, and information technology are less prone to corruption precisely because they are new. Also, they are run by a younger generation of market-oriented entrepreneurs and managers who shun corruption because it merely adds to business costs and because they prefer the head-to-head combat of the market. Yet when competition between private firms takes place in a context in which corruption is a normal part of the economic and political system, firms are likely to see corruption as just another business tool. Silvio Berlusconi's empire did. In 1988, Berlusconi sought to acquire the controlling interest in publicly held but family-dominated Mondadori, the Italian publishing group that put out *La Repubblica,* one of Italy's two major national newspapers, several of its major national weeklies (*Panorama, L'Espresso*), numerous popular women's magazines, and many profitable local newspapers and owned the major book publishing company Mondadori. Berlusconi's desires were thwarted by Carlo De Benedetti, CEO of Olivetti, who held the majority interest and had no interest in selling it. Instead, De Benedetti and the Mondadori family agreed that De Benedetti would purchase the family's shares no later than 1991, thus giving De Benedetti the majority stake in Mondadori's ordinary shares (50.3 percent) and 79 percent of the reserved.[43] Less than a year after the agreement, however, the Mondadori family (save one, Leonardo) switched sides, enabling Berlusconi to take over the presidency of the firm. Thus began a legal battle to decide whether the agreement of 1988 between De Benedetti and the Mondadoris was still valid. The dispute first went to an arbitration committee, which decided on February 28, 1990, in favor of De Benedetti. The Berlusconi schism (technically, the Formenton group) took their case to the court of appeals in Rome, presided over by Arnaldo Valenti, Vittorio Metta, and Giovanni Paolini. The court held that the original contract violated standards for publicly traded firms and so decided in favor of Berlusconi's interests. A few short legal skirmishes, more arbitration, and a parliamentary law later, Berlusconi's firm Fininvest and De Benedetti's Cir, which was Olivetti's financial arm, divided Mondadori's holdings, with Berlusconi taking the book publishing house, the national weekly *Panorama,* and assorted magazines, and De Benedetti *La Repubblica* and *L'Espresso.*

Investigations into another corruption case brought to light that shortly after the court gave its sentence, nearly half a million dollars wound up in one of Judge Vittorio Metta's bank accounts. It seems the funds originated in an offshore Fininvest account and then passed through holdings of Cesare Previti (defense minister in the first Berlusconi government, long-time Belusco*ni* associate, lawyer for Fininvest [part of Berlusconi's business empire], and at the time of the judicial proceedings, a parliamentarian for Forza Italia, Berlusconi's party) and another Berlusconi associate, Attilio Pacifico. The Roman judge tried to pass it off as an inheritance from a friend (yet another Italian judge whose financial dealings the Swiss judge Carla Del Ponte was investigating), but Milan magistrates were not persuaded.[44]

Berlusconi got off thanks to a creative reading of the statute of limitations as it applies to corruption by a private person, which he was at the time. The statute of limitations as it applied to him had run out at only seven and a half years, whereas the judges in question were held to a fifteen-year period. In June 2001, just a year and a half shy of the tenth anniversary of the EU's Single Market, the appeals court did not merely explain its interpretation of the statute of limitations but added several comments about why Berlusconi in particular should be accorded a generous reading of it. One reason was that he had, "after all," agreed to give back to De Benedetti some parts of the Mondadori holdings. Another reason, and significant when considering the role of competition in reducing corruption, was that he had "been active in an economic and entrepreneurial arena of national importance." In addition, the court cited his particular individual and social life, which "in itself" warranted the consideration of attenuating circumstances. According to the court, because Berlusconi had been operating in national (that is, major) economic circles, and because he had comported himself well since the alleged crime (and at the time of the court's ruling, he had twice been elected prime minister, the second time with a majority in both houses of parliament), he deserved a lenient interpretation of the statute of limitations.[45] In other words, entrepreneurs who compete for high stakes in the national economy (as opposed to small, local markets) warrant special consideration, even more so if they become prime minister. His having to compete in the market was viewed as a mitigating circumstance.

Berlusconi, wanting to be completely exonerated, appealed to the Corte di cassazione, which agreed with the court of appeals and elaborated on its ruling: Berlusconi was due forbearance because of "the conduct of [his] life since the hypothesized crime."[46] For the Corte di cassazione, the gravity of Berlusconi's actions—having possibly arranged the bribing of judges in order to secure a ruling on a business venture—was attenuated by the assumption that he had not, since then, done it again. For observers of Italian politics, this scenario of a conviction for corruption being overturned by higher courts is nothing new; the higher courts had merely applied their traditional reasoning to a more dynamic economic sector—the media.

Another new economic sector, telecommunications, is not immune from illegal activity, despite being an area full of competitive international bidding. The sector is not immune because intervening in the outcome of the bid creates lucrative investment opportunities for entrepreneurs and their political supporters.

In the Irish second-generation mobile phone (GSM) licensing case, an executive from the Norwegian state-owned firm Telenor, one of the members of the consortium that won the GSM license, claims he was told by one of Telenor's partners in the consortium, Denis O'Brien of Esat Digifone, to donate IR £50,000 ($80,000) to the political party of the minister who had overseen the licensing process, Michael Lowry.[47] O'Brien (of Esat Digifone) then reimbursed the Norwegian firm (Telenor). A tribunal has been investigating that claim, in addition to allegations that Lowry had financial connections to the main underwriter of O'Brien's firm—Dermot Desmond of IIU, who was brought in as an investor after the consortium had submitted its bid—as well as financial connections to O'Brien.[48]

Lowry was the focus of an earlier scandal of sorts when he decided to promote competition in telecoms by forcing the state-owned telecommunications firm Telecom Eireann to grant O'Brien's firm, Esat Telecom, use of Telecom Eireann technology for voice telephony. Despite other firms having asked for the same privilege, Lowry did not extend access to any other private firms. Ironically, Lowry's foray into the promotion of competition not only smacked of favoritism but also was, according to the then laws of Ireland, illegal (a point made to Lowry at the time by his staff and by Telecom Eireann).[49]

Avoiding taxes is one well-known way a firm can retain its profit margin. Tax evasion is easily turned into political corruption as those seeking to avoid taxes may try to buy decisions from the politicians or bureaucrats in charge. Penalties are usually far less than the taxes avoided. Take, for instance, the Flick affair. The bribery and corruption charges against Count Otto Lambsdorff (treasurer of the Freie Demokratische Partei [FDP] at the time of the facts and soon afterward economics minister) and Hans Friderichs (economics minister at the time of the facts, who became chairman of Germany's then second largest bank, the Dresdner, and later Airbus chair) were dropped due to the apparent inability of the prosecutors to prove that the favorable tax decisions made by the defendants were related to payments made by the Flick firm.[50] The Bonn court clearly thought bribes had been paid, but it could not convict due to insufficient evidence. Flick allegedly paid Hans Friderichs $138,000 when Friderichs was economics minister, and then Lambsdorff $50,000 when Lambsdorff was economics minister, to get their favorable decision on waiving DM 450 million ($160 million) in tax liability resulting from the sale of part of DM 1.9 billion in Daimler Benz stock ($800 million) to Deutsche Bank. They also paid additional amounts, hoping for additional tax breaks of DM 350 million ($195 million). Friderichs testified that Flick negotiated an agreement in the 1970s to pay the FDP DM 3 million ($1.7 million) over a few years. The Flick firm also paid DM 1.7 million ($950,000) to Rainer Barzel, who allegedly gave up chairmanship of the CDU (Christlich

Demokratische Union Deutschlands) in 1973 in favor of Helmut Kohl, in exchange for that payment. The payments, if only donations to the FDP, were at the time not illegal. What made them illegal was that they had been made to bogus charities so that the contributions would be tax deductible, and they seem to have been made as payment for a favorable tax decision from the German tax authorities. Count Lambsdorff was convicted merely of tax evasion and of aiding tax evasion and fined DM 180,000 ($100,000); Friderichs was also convicted of tax evasion and fined DM 61,500 ($34,000). A year later, Lambsdorff was rewarded with the party chairmanship. The businessman in the case, Eberhard von Brauchitsch, received a two-year suspended sentence and a fine of DM 550,000 ($306,000). Considering that he had evaded paying taxes of almost DM 18 million ($10 million) by his "charitable" donations to the FDP, it was a good deal.[51]

The prosecutions and investigations of the Flick affair, which took place from 1984 through 1987, did not deter even Helmut Kohl, who was himself subject to investigation both for lying under oath to a parliamentary committee and for corruption of a similar sort later, in what became known as the Kohl affair. In fact there were four cases for which he was the central node. Kohl eventually admitted to running a system through which he secretly collected funds for the governing CDU Party from 1993 to 1998.

The Flick affair exposed what was already an open secret, that major firms and banks routinely gave all three major parties donations through front charities. The method ensured that their contributions were tax deductible and, by the time they got to the parties, anonymous. Friedrich Halstenberg, a former SPD treasurer, "has estimated that between them, the major parties have improperly received DM 500 m[illion] since 1948."[52] In his defense, Count Lambsdorff argued that everyone knew about the system and that the tax authorities deliberately looked away. And, as such distinguished politicians as Bettino Craxi and Silvio Berlusconi have argued in their own defense, Lambsdorff also asked why he should be the one singled out.

MANAGING THE COMPETITION THROUGH CORRUPTION

The EU strikingly illustrates the existence of parallel worlds in the universe of markets and politics. On one level are privatizations, ostensibly market-oriented relations between the private and public sectors, and a drive to make the economy more competitive and to reduce the state's involvement in it; on another are corruption, ententes between politicians and firms, and illegal campaign financing derived from corrupt business and government practices. Yet the parallel worlds violate geometry in that they have a point of intersection: the application of market principles—however, not in a free market but in a political cartel. In some cases in France, as in Italy, the political parties succeeded in putting an explicit price on government decisions and then selling them. For example, an "entrepreneurial" figure inside a party decides that there is a business opportunity of sorts to be exploited: that of obtaining systematic "donations" from firms doing a lot of contracting with the state. The entrepreneur then devises a system to extract funds from the firms and reorganizes the procurement market in such a way that even the firms prefer it. Kickbacks, bribes, and preferential arrangements are made under the auspices of the "new public management" thinking, a new relationship between government and the private sector in which parapublic agencies contract out planning and financing to consulting firms that are subsidiaries of political party think tanks. The state has yet to exit the market; it remains, but under a new guise.

During the run-up to the European Single Market of 1992, during an increase in competitive pressures, various countries created ways to manage the competition and make it benefit the coffers of political parties. One of the primary areas in which this occurred was public works. In France, for example, one of the cases allegedly involved Jacques Chirac; he has denied it, although witnesses implicate him. (At the time of the facts, Chirac was prime minister, mayor of Paris, and leader of the Gaullist party; he was president of France from 1995 to 2007.) Beginning in 1986, a date that coincides with the signing of the Single European Act, Chirac's party, the RPR (Rassemblement pour la République), arranged for a front society to collect kickbacks from a set of construction firms that were awarded a prearranged share of government contracts for maintenance and construction of 450 public schools in the Paris area. Risks were minimized by including all political parties and the firms likely to want to bid. One witness testified, and others confirmed, that "there was an agreement between the parties on the Parisian Regional Council to take funds from firms and it was the direct consequence of the enormous public schools construction market."[53] Although competitive pressures from membership in the EU may compel firms in the private sector to be more efficient, these pressures do nothing to compel political parties to be more efficient or to reduce their demands for funding, nor do they reduce the temptation to get funding from public procurement kickbacks. For that to happen, the ethical and judicial environment must change significantly.

The system used by the Gaullists (RPR), and by other parties, had at its core a politico-business entrepreneur, a species in abundant supply in the Single Market era of making governments run more like the private sector. This type of entrepreneur could foresee arrangements that would make all parties to the deal content (save the taxpayer, who was never included anyway), and more content than if they had been left to compete with each other or make bilateral deals. Jean-Claude Méry described his system for financing the Gaullist party from the public housing office of Paris: his account is a description of how to set up a collusive arrangement with high likelihood of cooperation and is worth quoting in full:

> I bring in ten to fifteen firms, we put out a call for tenders, a call for candidates. We select ten firms, then, in order not to have problems [*avoir d'emmerdements*], we divide the contract between the ten firms. They make an offer . . . recalculating and lowering their price. . . . We make the selection, and it's like that, very gently and the most legally [*sic*] in the world, with no one wanting anything or saying anything, we gently manage close to 140 million francs for painting [for one firm], 240 million francs for painting [for another], 400 million francs for painting [for another], 120 million francs per year for windows and frames, 100 million francs for supplies. . . . We manage thus the entire market, tranquilly, which is going to bring a dozen million francs, good year, bad year, I would say, to the [party] machine. It is never more than 1%, 1.5% of the total price, thus we aren't in the midst of falsifying prices. The contractors, *au contraire*, [who are] delighted to have guaranteed contracts for a year, regale us with rubies on the fingernail. Not only are the firms content, they have work, they have a long term contract, the OPAC [city housing agency] has prices which are even well studied, we maximize our string pulling. . . . And we even reach an understanding with the socialists. We share the mana. I'll take the Communist firms, in order to handle, for example, the management of the sewers. . . . We give everyone something to eat. That's how you make everyone get along perfectly and you have work for everyone. And at the same time, the house takes in, either here in France or in Switzerland, larger and larger sums of money.[54]

As Méry puts it, his system is better than the market because everyone who wants work has it, even firms linked to rival parties, and his party gets a cut too. His system was viewed with such admiration within the party that when it came time for the Gaullist-controlled Île-de-France regional council to divide up the public schools' construction market, the party's regional leader consulted Méry.[55] In well-publicized yet characteristic cases, such as Urbatechnic and the public schools of the Île-de-France, the collusive arrangements included only domestic firms (although many of them are also multinationals).[56] Foreign construction and engineering firms may have self-selected out of competing in French public procurement because of practical difficulties. They may also have been aware that there would be strong local preference, something hard to document for a legal challenge.

As Méry described, it was in any case relatively easy to exclude foreign firms by manipulating the tender requirements. The "operation" of which he was most proud was that of putting elevators in the public housing projects. He notes that he followed required procedures: there was a public tender, and the lowest bidder won it. According to Méry, this happened because "it was me who prepared the call for tender. I prepared it with those who were going to be the lowest bidders. . . . I set up the operation in order to be sure that it was my friends who had [won] the operation."[57] Méry took advantage of arrangements meant to make public spending more efficient by relying especially on private enterprise; such arrangements were also meant to make life easier for local governments, which could contract out a massive project and pay for it over an extended period of time. Méry was able to get kickbacks for the RPR and give business to private French firms. He made sure that the financial requirements of the tender were such that only two French firms could qualify. "I eliminated, automatically like that, Kone, Otis, RCS."[58]

The 1992 Single Market program was expected to increase competition in the construction industry, one of the key industries that employed corrupt practices.[59] Various statistical analyses suggest that the European Union's Single Market program did increase competition in the construction industry, although not necessarily in France, if measured by the increase in intra-EU trade.[60] By early 1990, increased competition would only aggravate difficult conditions. The response was cartels, collusion, and corruption. In the Netherlands, which had a long history of (legal) cartels in the industry, the cartels colluded with public authorities to fix prices and rig bids in order to minimize competition, lower risks, and ensure steady revenue. They also paid bribes to public authorities. According to the parliamentary commission that conducted an investigation in 2002, the practices were copied by Belgian and German cartels. Meanwhile, EU law had no effect. Although the Dutch cartels had been expressly forbidden by the EU in 1992 (the cartels were fined by the European Commission), and an anticartel directive was officially transposed in 1986, the practices continued undeterred. Bribes were cheaper than the competitive market required by the EU, and collusion had the advantage of evening out risks, and facilitating innovation and investment in human capital.[61]

The continental countries discussed so far have an economic and political structure characterized by considerable nonmarket coordination, even in dealings that are perfectly legal. They have been labeled coordinated market economies by some.[62] The United Kingdom is the one EU member state in which economic activities in the post-Thatcher years have been structured more by the market and less by formal or informal nonmarket collaborative arrangements.

However, at the same time that the UK has earned the label of liberal market economy, it has initiated programs that undermine that market mechanism—precisely by bringing the market into politics. Government and business are meant to coordinate in launching joint economic ventures. The consequences for corrupt practices in the UK are not auspicious.

As most observers and experts agree, corruption is not a severe problem in the UK. The country has consistently ranked in the top ten or eleven of "cleaner" states in the Transparency International rankings. Sleaze, however, has become a problem, perhaps best defined as gross conflicts of interest or morally questionable activity. Since the Thatcher era, the country has welcomed economic competition, goading it on by privatizations and by making the UK business friendly to foreign firms. Contrary to the expectations that the free market, with attendant competition brought on by free trade, will help stamp out corruption, the UK has seen that the attitudes which accompany economic competition may invade the state. Indeed, that outcome was encouraged by the Thatcher and subsequent governments. The result is an undermining of the ethics of public service, and a marketization of government decisions.[63] In combination, these create a slippery slope to corruption: along with the danger that market logic will encourage public servants to see that their every decision has its price (and therefore can be bought), there is the fact that corruption sometimes invades when public values are in flux.[64]

Another issue is that along with international trade come international businesses with related political demands. These often have to do with tax status, export credits or loan guarantees, and citizenship. Just as, domestically, interest groups and firms hire members of Parliament (MPs) as consultants and pay them for asking questions in Parliament, so too do foreign businesses when they arrive.

With the advent of the Single Market, the United Kingdom saw serious scandals involving MPs taking donations from private citizens and firms in order to ask questions in Parliament. Although in other countries this practice may seem a waste of funds, in the UK parliamentary questions are a means of gaining otherwise inaccessible information and of influencing the outcome of parliamentary debates. Although the sums involved were trivial (on average, about £2,000 [$3,300] per question per MP), a fact that might reflect the low value of the information or the low threshold of tolerance for such sums, several of the cases were of such high profile and so flagrant that they transgressed the public's sense of propriety. Some MPs were suspected of having collected £100,000 ($164,000) in one year by performing such tasks.[65] The ethos of having government run like a business seems to have contributed to the sleazy dealings of British governments, parties, and MPs.

The Labour Party somewhat cynically made a virtue of not accepting donations from foreigners, save from those to whom it had just granted citizenship or those who had dual nationality. For instance, in 2001 Prime Minister Tony Blair

(Labour) sent a letter to the Romanian prime minister supporting the efforts of an Indian businessman, Lakshmi Mittal, to purchase Romania's steelworks, Sidex. Just weeks before, Mr. Mittal had donated £125,000 ($182,000) to the Labour Party. It looked as though Labour had sold a business favor to Mittal. Blair congratulated the Romanians on their privatization program and noted that it had the potential to "set Romania even more firmly on the road to membership of the European Union."[66] Mittal's firm Sidex, competing with a bid from a French firm, won the purchase contract, which was also supported by the UK's Foreign Office, as well as guaranteed loans from the UK government and the European Bank for Reconstruction and Development. Lionel Jospin, French prime minister, was planning to visit Bucharest to lobby for the French firm.[67] Blair claimed there was no connection between the donation and his letter of support. Indeed, he argued that it would be absurd for the government not to support British business. The rub was that the part of Mittal's empire that bought the Romanian plant is registered in the Dutch Antilles and has only a handful of UK employees. UK steelworkers, and their supporters in Blair's own party, were angered that Blair would help a foreign firm build up capacity in Romania to compete against UK steel.[68]

A few months later, the Labour Party was exposed as having accepted a £100,000 ($146,000) donation from British pornography publisher Richard Desmond. At the time, Desmond's firm was trying to purchase another media outlet. The corruption problem was in the timing. Soon after Desmond's donation was made, the Labour secretary of trade and industry, Stephen Byrer, said he would not refer a decision on the takeover to the UK's Competition Commission, thus clearing the way for Desmond's purchase of the Express newspaper group. The Labour Party then took out ads for the 2001 campaign in the group's papers. Perhaps surprisingly, there was nothing illegal in these or the Mittal events, but they struck the public as morally corrupt.[69]

THE LIMITS OF COMPETITION
Absorbing Competition into Preexisting Patterns of Corruption

The level of political corruption can remain fairly untouched by increased competition and free trade. For example, the major cases of illegal party funding in France (Urbatechnic for the Socialists; lycées of Île-de-France and public housing in Paris for the Gaullists) were not brought to light by complaints from foreign firms or the European Commission but by French regional and national courts of audit, by seemingly unrelated French judicial investigations, and by politicians from newer parties (e.g., the Greens). A similar scenario obtained in Germany. Foreign firms shut out from competing in domestic markets as a result of corrupt deals were not the whistle-blowers. Greater economic competition has not reduced the demand for illegal party financing. The state still retains the right to decide to whom to award contracts, and in tight economic times, those contracts become all the more valuable to competitors. Politicians are able to gain party financing that way.

Competition, rather than disrupting corruption, is absorbed into the prevailing system of business and politics. The effort to compete often requires that a firm adapt to home rules. The OECD Convention of 1997 and the EU Convention contain statements that governments agree to prohibit bribing of foreign officials, but the conventions do not carry the force of law, and although most of the EU-15 states (including Italy, France, and Great Britain) have long had laws on the books regarding bribery, enforcement is erratic, manpower is limited, international cooperation with investigations has been slow at best, and the political will has been almost entirely absent.

Firms entering markets where corruption is the prevailing mode of conducting business find that to compete, they must participate, not run to the judiciary. They learn the informal market arrangements. In 1985, as Italy was about to sign the Single European Act, which was meant to inaugurate a competitive open market, Honeywell, a U.S. firm, opted to serve as the conduit of a rigged public works contract for a local firm, Compsyst, and it both paid and accepted funds for its role. Sicily's computer agency of sorts, the CSI (Centro siciliano di informatica), set up a bid whose technical requirements it knew only Honeywell could meet. Although invited to bid, IBM declined, citing lack of competency in the particular area being contracted out. Hewlett Packard, Olivetti, and Buffetti Sistemi followed suit. Honeywell "generously" agreed to subcontract to Compsyst, which was merely a subsidiary of the CSI—a shell through which CSI management could obtain kickbacks and politicians could obtain patronage.[70]

Likewise, in 1991, when the Swiss-Swedish firm ABB and the German firm Siemens wanted to bid on a public works contract for the Roman public water and power company ACEA, their Italian offices sent representatives to meetings between other contractors and the political party representatives who handled the kickbacks and contract awards for that economic sector. Some favoritism for domestic public works suppliers was evident: the four Italian firms (Ansaldo, Redi, Elektra, Riet) each got 25 percent of the overall contract, and ABB and Siemens were granted only the contract (50 percent each) for remaining supplies. The agenda for the meeting states that "for the next 8 contracts [there is to be a] preference for the local firms," meaning those from Rome, of which there were two. They were to get 50 percent of the work.[71] The national firms would have to "compete for the residual 50 [percent]" of the contracts. At the same meeting, the winners of the next contract were decided; work was evenly distributed between the firms.[72] ABB's Italian unit seems to have been involved in bribes for the Milan metro line as well. ABB's general director commented on the overall situation: "We all knew that in Italy, things tended to be done differently than in other countries."[73]

The French multinational computer firm Bull had an Italian unit that also gave kickbacks and regular payments to the leader of the Socialist Party in order to win and retain the party's computer business and in order to win contracts with the justice ministry.[74] Italian party officials had no scruples about asking multinationals for kickbacks or about trying to drum up business with them. The director general of the public administration section of Bull Italia testified that a Social Democratic Party (Partito Socialista Democratico Italiano, PSDI) official, Roberto Buzio, contacted him to see if Bull had any "negotiations in progress" with the Ministry of Culture. Buzio suggested that if Bull did, he could be of service "in facilitating [the removal of] or removing eventual obstacles."[75]

Precisely as the EU was launching its Single Market of 1992, Germany's Bayer and Honeywell illegally financed the Republican Party of Milan, as well as the direct campaign expenses of some of its candidates. The payments functioned somewhat like a retainer, purchasing goodwill and some political axle grease from the Republican Party (Partito Repubblicano Italiano, PRI).[76]

All of these cases share a common characteristic: the employees of the multinational seeking the contract are primarily domestic nationals of the country offering the contract; thus they likely possess the relevant local knowledge and, more important, have the local connections that enable the firm to fit in and profit. In Sicily, the head of the computer agency running the kickback scheme had Italian contacts at Honeywell with whom he was able to arrange the deal, under the protection of an important Sicilian political figure, Salvatore Grillo. The price for Grillo's services was that CSI hire, as superfluous personnel, several individuals chosen by Grillo.[77] Local staff perpetuate the local practices, despite the entry of the foreign firm. Corporate ethics codes take a back seat to profit demands. It takes more than an increase in foreign competitors to shift corrupt practices.

Competition Does Not Uncover Corruption

Which reduces corruption: the lover, the informer, or economic competition? In the EU, it is more likely to be the lover or the informant than economic competition. During the 1980s and 1990s, the Single Market years, countries as disparate as Germany, Spain, and Belgium were the sites of high-profile corruption cases. One might think it was thanks to increased economic competition brought about by the EU that the cases came to light and that they were merely the last gasps of a modus operandi that could not survive in the new competitive environment. Yet a look at the cases indicates that competitive pressures were not the reasons the cases came to light; more often it was routine tax inspections, personal vendettas, a jilted lover, or suspicious deaths.[78] The several cases that implicate French president Jacques Chirac were discovered first by a regional tax inspector. The Flick affair in Germany (involving, as discussed earlier, bribes to avoid a huge tax bill) began when the Flick industrial group's chief accountant was audited.[79] Corruption in the Dutch construction industry was exposed after a manager left a major construction firm as a result of a dispute; in reprisal, he gave the justice ministry documents showing parallel accounts kept by the firm.[80] None was brought to light by what the EU counts on: an excluded firm filing a complaint with the national competition authority. Spanish prime minister Felipe González met his downfall when a lawyer representing a Chilean accountant, Carlos Van Schouwen, called a reporter at the Spanish newspaper *El Mundo* to say that the accountant "could produce receipts for payments made by leading Spanish firms for consultancy work that had never actually been done."[81] The consultancies were false fronts for the tried and often true method of funneling funds (illegally) into political party coffers. But Van Schouwen had more to say: a large chunk of the illegal funds came from Siemens, the German firm, which had interests in winning Spain's high-speed train contract, making the case more than a run-of-the-mill party-financing fiasco. Siemens denied the allegations. Van Schouwen had spilled the beans because he never received his commissions for processing the false paperwork. One of the major cases for which Italian prime minister Silvio Berlusconi was prosecuted began when the girlfriend of one of his close associates went to the judiciary. The case that first showed the wide net of corruption established by the French Socialist Party emerged by accident when a magistrate was doing a routine investigation of worker deaths at a construction site.

The noted German journalist Hans Leyendecker assessed Germany in a 2002 article titled "Excuse Me, Palermo! How Germany Became a Purchasable Commodity and Sicily Became a Bribe-Free Zone."[82] His view was that somehow the market mentality in Germany had promoted corruption while reducing it in its "traditional" homeland. Yet the effect of increased economic competition on corruption is attenuated by the prior context of political and economic relations and by the preexisting level of corruption in the country. Increased economic competition may bring other types of problems, such as an increase in tax evasion. It did not disrupt existing patterns of corruption in France, Italy, the Netherlands, or Germany. Coming as they did in 1992, the official advent date of the Single Market, Italy's anticorruption Tangentopoli (kickback city) trials may seem to undermine that claim, but increased competition and rules promoting competition did not change the incentive and payoff structures of firms and politicians, save to make corruption more important. It took the collapse of communism and the exponentially increasing demands for illegal party financing to change the political climate, which in turn enabled the judiciary to expose corruption.

The impact of rules promoting interstate economic competition is constrained by preexisting institutional and normative arrangements across countries. These arrangements tend to be more powerful, certainly in the short to medium term, than the influence of incoming foreign firms, or the influence of occasional European Court of Justice rulings. As we have seen, firms adapt their behavior to that required in the host country in order to profit.

Political competition is not the cure one might hope it would be. Party systems in many European countries have become "cartelized."[83] New entrants are rare. Furthermore, political competition spurs demands for party financing, and parties are seldom satiated with what is available to them legally. As France, Germany, and Italy show, parties and individual politicians of the left, right, and center have been corrupt and have colluded with each other at times in sustaining corrupt practices. Bringing the traditional opposition into government usually does little more than bring that party into the preexisting system. Some, such as the French Socialists under Mitterrand, get inventive, only to see their techniques copied by the traditional party of government. Fringe parties have been crucial for bringing corruption cases to light (e.g., Greens in France, Plaid Cymru in the UK), but because they are fringe parties, they do not go on to win power. Citizens are left with the usual suspects to run the government, suspects who have little incentive to restructure the system to prevent corrupt behavior. Italy's Tangentopoli could occur because of the complete collapse of the traditional political party system. Yet it was a collapse that also gave Silvio Berlusconi an avenue to political power.

Germans such as Hans Leyendecker may be correct in worrying that they have caught the Italian disease: the pressures of economic competition stemming from the European Union and other free trade organizations have prompted a variety of corrupt schemes by which businesses stay afloat and politicians profit. This chapter is an invitation to further research. It is clear that the EU countries have not converged toward one model of markets and politics; the notable differences in arrangements between the economy and state, including how corporations are governed, have persisted and could not help but affect the patterns of corruption that emerge. Some studies have found that differences in religious heritage affect levels of corruption.[84] This chapter's role has been to point out that corruption persists even under economic competition and that various areas are nearly impervious to competition. Firms resort to corruption when doing so is less costly than losing business, and politicians and bureaucrats enable it by asking for bribes to exercise their discretion in a manner favorable to specific firms. Although at the macroeconomic and societal level, corruption may be an expensive tax, at the microeconomic and political level, it can be a profitable tool. The EU has not altered that dynamic. Corruption is not only a feature of the Single Market; it is a feature of international trade and is sustained by the political, legal, and market structures of the EU and the other OECD countries.

"CORRUPTION IS OUR FRIEND"

Exporting Graft in Infrastructure,
Arms, and Oil

> Thou shouldst rather ask if it were possible any villany should be so
> rich; for when rich villains have need of poor ones, poor ones may
> make what price they will.
>
> —Shakespeare, *Much Ado About Nothing*

When asked to explain how, on his modest government salary, he could have purchased 123 plane tickets costing more than $34,000, a former French bureaucrat, Jean-Charles Marchiani, replied that the funds came from "the savings of his 90-year-old mother-in-law."[1] That excuse failed to convince the French police, who instead suspected Marchiani of being directly involved in the sale of arms to Angolan president Eduardo Dos Santos at a time when the French government had banned such sales, and of surreptitiously using the French oil company Elf to fund Dos Santos's rival in the Angolan civil war.[2] The $34,000 sum was but the tip of the iceberg of profits available from corrupt transactions in the export of arms and import of oil.

In this chapter I review and analyze three major areas of foreign economic activity in which corruption plays a significant if not determining role: infrastructure development, armaments, and oil. The evidence from these sectors directly challenges claims that international organizations such as the European Union and the Organization for Economic Cooperation and Development have damping effects on corruption.[3] For the sake of greater access to export markets and sales, EU member states and their firms disregard their own laws, those set forth in international agreements, and those of other countries.

I call this behavior export-led corruption. Export-led growth has been a means used by some developing countries to rapidly increase their economic growth and become serious entrants in the international economy. Typically, the state leads an all-out effort to enter and succeed in foreign markets; imports and the domestic economy are steered toward facilitating exports.[4] In the case of export-led corruption, corruption is a means of increasing exports, of increasing foreign market share, and it is often state sponsored.

That the global economy involves extensive corruption has been well publicized by NGOs such as Transparency International; after some prompting by TI, international organizations such as the World Bank and OECD followed suit. The extent of the involvement of European states in the creation and perpetuation of corruption in the international political economy is less well known. Not only is corruption an element of transnational business transactions, but it is sustained by European politicians, their parties, and their state-owned firms, including the "national champions."[5] European governments have often condoned or turned a blind eye toward corrupt foreign practices by their multinationals, have encouraged corruption within their state-owned enterprises, and have used it as a tool of revenue generation and foreign policy.

In a reversal of the traditional moral hierarchy, it is more often third-world governments that investigate and try to prosecute the corrupt practices of European (and U.S.) multinationals. European states have by and large ignored corruption in programs they fund through such major international organizations as the World Bank and the IMF (not to mention the UN), as well as toward their own international development and export credit agencies. In Great Britain, where since 1906 it has been illegal for corporations and politicians to bribe foreign officials, not a single individual or corporation has stood trial for breaking that law.[6]

Not only has competition for markets and profits been a factor in cross-border corruption within Europe, but it has been a factor internationally as well, with European countries, including those with reputations as least corrupt, playing host to multinationals that routinely bribe foreign officials and intermediaries in order to land contracts. Furthermore, some of the funds from the contracts revert back to European politicians and businessmen for private or political party use. In some countries this has been standard practice, in others "only" an occasional incident.

Most studies of corruption conclude that increased competition in government contracting and in the private sector will reduce corruption. These studies fail to recognize that calling for policies that increase competition in the market may be irrelevant in some sectors, such as the manufacture of commercial planes, arms, oil, and utility infrastructure. As Tony Blair acknowledged after forcing Britain's Serious Fraud Office to drop its investigation into bribery and corruption surrounding a defense contract with Saudi Arabia, the stakes—mainly profits and rents—are very high; firms and states perceive that winning any particular contract is critical for gaining substantial market share and for maintaining and increasing domestic employment and economic growth.[7] Therefore, as economic competition *increases,* firms are willing to pay bribes, and their domestic governments are willing to overlook or indirectly subsidize the bribes (through export credits) in order to help their firms land contracts.

The hypocrisy is just below the surface. In many cases, the companies involved in or implicated in corruption outside of western Europe are from countries that have signed the Organization for Economic Cooperation and Development (OECD) Convention on Combating Bribery of Foreign Public Officials in International Business Transactions. This convention obliges signatories to adopt national legislation that makes it a crime to bribe foreign public officials. It specifically requires that "investigation and prosecution of the bribery of a foreign public official shall be subject to the applicable rules and principles of each Party. They shall not be influenced by considerations of national economic interest, the potential effect upon relations with another State or the identity of the natural or legal persons involved."[8] Although signatories may have adopted such legislation, they may routinely ignore it as well as the convention's mandate to put aside economic and diplomatic considerations.

Along with economic and political considerations, bureaucratic rationality too is a factor in export-led corruption. Export credit guarantee agencies have the mandate to promote exports; so too do government arms sales agencies. They do not have the mandate to impede corruption.

GENERAL CHARACTERISTICS
Perverse Incentives

It is critical to recognize that those most likely to write and enforce the policies and attendant rules promoting competition often have a vested interest in doing precisely the opposite. First, it costs an enormous amount of time and money to investigate and prosecute such corruption. As several economists have noted, "although a bribe could be considered just a transfer [of resources], punishment involves dead weight losses in proportion to the destruction of resources from which the [prosecuting] group gains nothing."[9] Second, investigating brings to light actions and expenditures that those involved, including the state, would have preferred remained confidential: Elf (now part of Total) did not want rival oil firms to know exactly how much it was paying the Gabonese president for its operations there. Firms and governments prefer that trade secrets, such as amounts of bribes or names of intermediaries, remain secret. In addition, prosecution of major domestic multinationals is bad domestic politics: it can hurt jobs and alienate major supporters. Third, the OECD Convention's mandate to prosecute despite possible economic repercussions loses to the economic argument that even if companies of member states are not involved in bribery, companies of rival states will be drawn in and will therefore win the contracts. The "what's good for the multinational is good for the domestic economy" argument is irresistible to politicians, particularly when the corruption occurs offshore, out of sight of constituents, and practically off limits to domestic investigative agencies. Ditto for the bureaucrats who supposedly regulate the industries in question. A 2005 OECD review of Britain's adherence to the antibribery convention noted that the UK evaluated the economic consequences to the British arms industry of pursuing a case involving corruption between a major defense firm and a Middle Eastern state. The case was dropped.[10] Fourth and finally, the possibilities for personal enrichment compete with officials' sense of propriety.

Commissions

International trade brings firms and governments into frequent contact for economic exchange. Corruption follows. Firms do what is expedient for business, and if bribery lands contracts, gains market access, and moves goods, whereas adhering to legal rules does not, the incentives to use bribery are strong. Western politicians and firms claim that bribery is obligatory in many parts of the world. As one chief executive of a British weapons manufacturer said, "Commissions make the world go round. There's nothing illegal about them. I don't know of a [Saudi] royal who'll get out of bed for less than 5%."[11] Some argue that commissions should not be called bribes, that they are instead like brokerage or realtor fees—a payment to someone who makes a deal happen, who finds terms on which buyer and seller can agree. Yet commissions support corruption. When the commission is 25 percent of the contract, and when it is unclear where all the money from that commission goes, the fee may not be just a commission.[12] A French official in the finance ministry said of commissions that "they go up in certain Asian countries for some types of transactions, because there is very strong competition."[13] An industrialist noted that sometimes the commissions, which are often turned to private ends by the recipient, reach 45 percent of the contract in highly competitive markets because it is necessary to "coax" the client.[14] Commissions are used to purchase the award of contracts, especially in markets in which there is competition between suppliers. When the commission is paid in order to change the outcome of a government decision about the award of a contract, the payment is a bribe.[15] When the client is a government official or political figure, that is corruption. A British exporter noted that Nigerian generals routinely demanded a 70 percent commission, and he candidly (and anonymously) called it what it was: bribery and corruption.[16]

Middlemen are prevalent in export-led corruption. They advertise themselves as having connections to the right people in the right places, and they stress that without their intervention, Western firms will get nowhere. One intermediary who became the subject of several international judicial pursuits stated flatly, "after all, complex relationships in national defence are involved. You can't just call up two or three people and hope you have a deal."[17] Middlemen exploit the intricate and personalistic nature of much of politics and business. And firms, states, and international organizations, with their own lack of familiarity and contacts in the countries in which they wish to land contracts, rely on them. As one firm convicted of bribery noted in its defense, "the use of agents is internationally recognized" by, among others, government agencies, the EU, and the World Bank.[18] When an intermediary is paid a commission, part of it often is transferred to key officials and leaders in the country awarding the contract. Sometimes, part of the commission makes its way back to the home country via the foreign bank accounts of key politicians and industry leaders. For example, one of the French state's oil company intermediaries, André Guelfi, estimated that of the $100 million Elf paid him in commissions for the various contracts he brokered, he spent $70 million paying third parties, including political leaders.[19] Intermediaries also "isolate businessmen [and states] from unpleasant truths."[20] Using an intermediary keeps the corruption at arms length. As a French exporter said, "One is not too curious either about the real power that is behind [the deals], or about the real recipient of the funds."[21] Commissions may reach extraordinary heights in order to buy the compliance of the intermediary, so that the intermediary does not double-cross his or her "employer."

Secrecy

Corruption needs secrecy, and in the competitive infrastructure projects, oil, and arms trade, it has it. Most European countries seldom fully disclose the terms of weapons sales. Information is provided "on an unofficial and selective basis," oversight by elected parliaments is rare, and media coverage is regarded as a nuisance at best.[22] Despite their claims of being democratic, governments keep to themselves information such as "to which countries and in what quantities goods such as artillery shells, land mines and cluster bombs have been licensed for export."[23] Oil companies have protested efforts to require them to "publish what they pay" in bribes (always called commissions) or to reveal their financial circuits, and few countries have signed up for an extractive industries transparency initiative.[24] A Total spokesman said that "whether it's the oil industry or any other industry, obviously you wouldn't want your competitors to know what you pay.

It's not that we're against it, or that there's something to hide; it's just the standard."[25] Infrastructure projects are seldom decided by transparent processes; neither the governments nor the firms involved have an incentive to share their
pricing and payment information with the public or each other.

Even in a country with a robust tradition of public oversight by way of parliamentary committees, the unwillingness to investigate possible corruption in
overseas exports is strong. In its 2005 review of the United Kingdom's implementation of the OECD Convention, the OECD observed: "given the size of the
UK economy and its level of exports and outward [foreign direct investment],
along with its involvement in international business transactions in sectors and
countries that are at high risk for corruption, it is surprising that no company or
individual has been indicted or tried for the offence of bribing a foreign public
official since the ratification of the Convention by the UK [in 2001]."[26] The economic and political costs are deemed too great: in Britain, the state's refusal to release an investigative report on a shady arms deal with Saudi Arabia was justified
on the grounds that "the Saudis would have been upset."[27] One could just as well
have added that the British public would have been upset. This is the same state
that, in other contexts, lectures or "advises" new democracies on the importance
of transparency, openness, and other anticorruption policies in government and
in economic transactions.

It is symptomatic of the problem, but perhaps no surprise, that in France, investigating magistrates have run up against the brick wall labeled "national defense secrets" in trying to investigate bribes and kickbacks possibly associated
with the sale of French military equipment to Taiwan and other similar contracts.[28] Given these domestic secrecy incentives, Western firms doing business in
less developed countries may have little incentive to "publish what you pay" for
access to a market or for landing a contract. When BP did so, it was almost thrown
out of Angola; its competitors, unwilling to do so, were not.[29]

Secrecy is aided by the vast and lightly or unregulated "offshore" economy,
which is supported by sovereign states, including several in the EU (the United
Kingdom and Luxembourg) or heavily tied to it (e.g., Switzerland). Offshore
"spatio-juridical" locations such as the Caymans or Luxembourg establish arrangements enabling shell companies and banks to launder funds for or from corrupt transactions. Between 2004 and 2006, BAE, a large British defense firm, was
under investigation for maintaining a $90 million slush fund used for bribery of
various sorts. The alleged slush fund accounts were held in Switzerland and the
British Virgin Islands.[30] The BAE investigation was dropped, in the name of national security. Secrecy prevailed. Britain's attorney general claimed "it has been
necessary to balance the need to maintain the rule of law against the wider public interest." British banks processed more than $1.3 billion of Nigerian dictator

Sani Abacha's takings from public coffers. British authorities have not prosecuted even one of the twenty-three London banks involved.[31] Indeed, much offshore banking occurs onshore in the EU, the United States, and Japan.[32]

Tied Aid and Other Forms of Financing

Another EU member state strategy for increasing domestic economic and political revenue is increasing the level of aid to a particular country so that it, in turn, can purchase weapons or infrastructure projects from the donor country. Technically this method is not corrupt, but it can foster corruption.[33] The United Kingdom provides an example of how it works. In 1988–89, the UK's aid to Nigeria was £6.3 million. In 1989–90, UK aid to Nigeria increased tenfold, to £67.7 million. Also in 1990, the UK negotiated the sale of eighty "made in the UK" Vickers tanks to Nigeria for at least £50 million. "A Whitehall spokeswoman said £59.4 million of this aid was to finance essential imports. She insisted there was no link between the aid increase and the arms deal."[34] Rather than force Nigeria's corrupt president, Sani Abacha, to pay for the tanks, or for the "essential foreign aid," which the oil-rich country should not have needed, with funds he had sequestered in Swiss banks, by way of British banks, the British government coddled the Nigerian ruler, used public money to facilitate sales for the UK's privatized defense industry, and foisted the costs onto British taxpayers. In essence, the scheme is not unlike that of politicians inflating a contract by an amount more than sufficient for the contractor to pay the required kickback and make a hefty profit at the same time. Significantly, research by the NGO World Development Movement found that between the 1980s and 1990s, foreign aid to "eight of the largest buyers of British arms, including Oman and Indonesia, has risen while aid overall has fallen by 20 per cent. Last year alone, as aid to Africa was cut, ECGD [Export Credits Guarantee Department] increased five times its financial backing for arms sales to 'risky markets.'"[35] This process appears to have accelerated as weapons sales became ever more competitive and, from the perspective of politicians, had the benefit of providing business for their infrastructure contractors too. The system sets up an absurd cycle: for rulers of developing countries, the more subsidies there are for European contractors, the more the countries will have bidders for their contracts, and the more the bidders will be compelled, due to intense competition, to offer bribes.[36]

　　It is well known that Western banks and states have long profited from their role as repositories for illicitly gained funds.[37] What is less well known are the extremes to which Western corporations and states have gone to facilitate this role. France's Elf oil corporation provides an example. Lest the reader protest that this example merely reflects the old industrial Gaullism, where industry is seen as a tool of the state, I note that these practices continued during Elf's privatization and appear to have continued after its merger with TotalFina (later Total).[38] To absorb and selectively disperse some of Gabon's petrodollars, the Gabonese president Omar Bongo set up a bank in Paris (FIBA) in 1975. When Gabon's regime nearly bankrupted the institution in 1978 through deficit spending, Elf stepped in to buy 40 percent of its shares and took over its directorship. FIBA became the personal bank of Bongo and other African elites and their families and friends. The bank helped finance weapons purchases for at least one civil war—fought during June–October 1997, in the Congo, and led by Congo president Lissouba— and made numerous loans to Bongo's friends and even Elf managers. The wife of Congo President Lissouba routinely withdrew over a million francs in cash. When Bongo's domestic bank went bankrupt, Elf stepped in to have FIBA create a branch in Libreville. According to testimony of its general director, Pierre Houdray, FIBA was "at the crossroads of relations between the French oil firm and multiple African states (Gabon, Congo, Angola)." The bank was located on one of Paris's most prestigious streets, and its clients routinely withdrew millions of francs on the strength of a phone call from the Gabonese president. The bank did not keep receipts of the transactions in Bongo's personal accounts. Instead, once a year the director met Bongo and asked him to sign for the withdrawals but did not keep a copy for himself or for the bank. FIBA facilitated the establishment of offshore accounts, such as with Crédit Foncier de Monaco, noted for being both a Corsican stronghold and the bank used by about thirty African elites from Gabon and Congo. Deposits to Bongo's official and personal accounts primarily came by way of Western banks in Liechtenstein, the United States, and Switzerland.[39] In essence, corruption in Gabon, the Congo, and other African countries was not only paid for by Elf (and other Western oil companies) but laundered by Elf.

The following survey shows that in their efforts to increase overseas business for their contractors, to sell arms, and to find oil, the Europeans also increased overseas corruption.[40] Infrastructure projects, arms, and oil have the ingredients for corruption: heavy government involvement and huge potential rents interact with the monopsony position of the developing countries. European states set up institutions that facilitate corruption even as they sign agreements and pass laws condemning overseas bribery. Firms convince government officials that winning contracts and having market access are crucial to their profitability. Because those who bear the direct costs are politically unorganized or disenfranchised—usually taxpayers in European countries or the poor in the less developed countries— and those who profit are politically powerful and well organized, export-led corruption continues.

INFRASTRUCTURE PROJECTS

Competition for business in "emerging markets" generates its own corruption; it is not just the less developed countries that contaminate the "clean" firms and governments of the advanced industrial states. Firms involved in intense competition in overseas contracting are prone to corruption, which has led to such perverse outcomes as firms forming cartels to reduce competition for major projects. The western European market for major development projects has become saturated; economic integration has facilitated mergers and the demise of smaller players, and the big firms have aggressively exported their practices to foreign markets. The projects can be worth hundreds of millions in revenue, are awarded through processes with no independent oversight, and are so large that multiple "competitors" can be included in the award. As a sales manager of a major firm stated, such practices lead "to some strange bedfellows. The big contractors are joint venturing and not trying to do it all anymore." They collaborate to share a hotly contested market, such as Asia: "There are new projects announced every week, which means that everybody is there competing."[41] In forming consortia and other types of alliances, contractors reduce the effective number of competitors in a market and create conditions that facilitate corruption: fewer players, more coordination, less transparency.

The infrastructure projects are so big that numerous firms from multiple countries can be awarded a piece of the action, and the financing also can be distributed. A case in point is the Lesotho Highlands Water Project, conceived in the 1980s to divert water from the Senqu/Orange River in water-rich but otherwise poor Lesotho to water-hungry South Africa. The project, whose first part cost an estimated $2.7 billion, involved numerous different companies from Europe and South Africa, and several international consortia.[42] A Canadian, a German, and an Italian firm have been found guilty in Lesotho of bribing the former Lesotho head of the project, Ephraim Sole. The Lesotho government anticipates conducting additional trials against the other firms and consortia. Bribes ranged from a few thousand dollars to more than one million.[43] The consortia alone had transferred about $300,000 to Sole, with individual firms and consortia making other substantial payments.[44] The Canadian firm, Acres International, after having stated that it "had no knowledge of any payments made by Bam to Sole," and having "denied that the payments which were made to ACPM [Bam's consulting firm] were intended as payments to Sole,"[45] was convicted of a £278,000 ($415,000) bribe and fined £1.6 million ($2.4 million).[46] The UK member of the Spie Batignolles consortium defended itself by noting that "it is the consortia in each case that have been cited, not the individual companies."[47]

Some of the funds for the full five phases of the Lesotho project came from

Crédit lyonnais, a major state-owned French bank that later went bankrupt under negligent, if not fraudulent, management, and Dresdner Bank, whose CEO, Hans Friderich, had been convicted a few years earlier of tax evasion in the Flick bribery affair.[48] Another part of the story is about the unusual, if not illegal, financial maneuvers taken by the World Bank to ensure that the project could be started despite international economic sanctions against South Africa. The World Bank arranged the establishment of a trust fund in London through which payments from international financiers and government export credit agencies could be made: Lesotho was to be the official debtor, even though sanctioned South Africa was to service and pay off the debt.[49]

An investigative report noted that "the companies implicated in this scandal are no strangers to allegations of corruption. For example, Spie Batignolles and Sogreah were involved in Kenya's Turkwell Gorge Dam which, because of bribes reportedly paid to Kenya's president and energy minister, cost more than twice what the European Commission said it should have."[50] Other European firms were also involved in that project (Alsthom, Norconsult, and Knight Piesold).[51] In 2004, the secretary general of the Organization of American States, Miguel Angel Rodríguez, was arrested and accused of having accepted a $1.2 million payment from French corporate giant Alcatel for helping it win a contract from the Costa Rican telecommunications company.[52] As of November 2006, BAE/Saab, a British-Swedish arms consortium, is under investigation for bribing an African political party "in order to secure a public contract to sell fighter jets" to that African state.[53] The French defense giant Thales is under investigation for granting kickbacks to political figures in order to win a contract to renovate destroyers for Greece in 2002 and to win the security market for the Athens Olympics in 2004.[54]

Legal doctrine and practice on the part of Western corporations facilitate such practices.[55] The UK firm involved, Balfour Beatty, argued to a House of Commons committee that the problem lay with the consortium, not with Balfour Beatty: in the business world's "mind," participation in a consortium absolves the individual firm of responsibility for the consortium's actions. Its legal department wrote that "Balfour Beatty PLC is not the subject of any charges in the Lesotho courts. A joint venture [of which it was a part], led by French contractors, is the subject of charges."[56] The firm's chairman, Lord Weir, wrote that "on major contracts, a company may be a member of a consortium, joint venture, or partnership, consisting of other companies, either international or local, but may well not be the managing partner or the partner with prime responsibility for the sales and commercial aspects of the contract." This assertion is not unlike a corporation claiming that because it paid an intermediary, it did not bribe the final recipient of the funds.[57]

Western states fuel overseas corruption through their export credit guarantee agencies. These agencies underwrite export sales and Western built projects in areas considered risky investment environments. On the domestic side, there is also the potential for corruption, if not merely conflict of interest. The agencies enable their multinationals and contractors to conduct business in environments that are so unviable that exporters and contractors would not normally do business there. The official view was well put by Lady Chalker, then United Kingdom's minister of overseas development: the export credit program "finances developmentally sound projects of commercial and industrial significance to Britain. . . . These projects have directly brought us £3.9 billion in export orders. They have created and maintained tens of thousands of jobs for British workers. Hundreds of British companies have benefitted from contracts and subcontracts, which they have won with our help."[58] In 2004, carried away with its mission to support Swedish firms in risky overseas markets, Sweden's export credits agency distributed a handbook to some private firms, saying that "when you are doing business with government authorities or government owned companies, you sometimes have to pay to complete a deal."[59] Italy's export credit agency, SACE, has provided a $1.13 billion guarantee on a commercial loan by German and Italian banks for a highly controversial, massive gas pipeline project from Russia to Turkey, partly by way of the Black Sea. Another Italian guarantee agency, within the state-held energy firm ENI, has backed an $866 million loan for the same project. The deal, which won the European Oil and Gas Deal of the Year award in 2000, has fallen prey to corruption. Ongoing investigations implicate officials and firms in Turkey and Russia;[60] given the size of the contract, and the involvement of Western firms and government agencies, it is unlikely that Italian and German officials and firms would not have been affected. Likewise, Indonesia offers an untold number of cases of corruption in large Western-built and Western-underwritten projects.[61]

Export credit guarantee agencies get involved in their governments' efforts to create markets where they don't exist. An example is the Pergau, Malaysia, dam. It was built with £234 million ($417 million) in British aid, despite Britain's Overseas Development Administration reporting in 1989 and 1990 that such a project was "unnecessary" and "a very bad buy" and that it would be "a burden on Malaysian consumers."[62] Promoting British firms, Prime Minister Margaret Thatcher pledged in 1989 to the Malaysian government that the aid would be forthcoming. The procurement contracts were won by the two UK firms that had proposed the project; Malaysia did not hold a competitive international bid. One of the winning firms, Cementation, employed Thatcher's son, and its parent company, Trafalgar House, was directed by Thatcher's former foreign affairs adviser, Sir Charles Powell. Costs went up 25 percent within two weeks of the British and

Malaysian prime ministers agreeing to the deal.[63] But there is more. "Documentary evidence subsequently revealed that the aid package was linked in writing to a reciprocal arms deal whereby the Malaysian government agreed to buy over £1,000 million [$1.8 billion] worth of British military equipment in return for the UK funding of [the] Pergau [dam]."[64] When the press got wind of this arrangement, the British government backpedaled rapidly to de-link the deals. Efforts to de-link the deals succeeded, but the Malaysian government and the British public were left with the impression that there had been an illegal arms-for-aid quid pro quo, and, in all but the fine print, there was one.[65]

The justification is export trade: France's office of overseas commerce, the Direction des relations économiques extérieures (DREE), states: "For external trade, the designated objective of the Republic is to do contracts, not to set oneself up as the defender of morality."[66] As in other countries, France's export credit agency covers the cost of "commissions," but in France the limit is 8 percent. That ceiling is easy to evade by writing up some of the commissions as consulting fees.[67] Commissions of up to 15 percent of the contract are generally tax deductible.[68] In other words, the state subsidizes corruption as it promotes exports.

ARMS TRADE

Four suspicious deaths, one mistress financed by the state-owned oil company, one foreign affairs minister sporting $2,000 Italian shoes, half a billion dollars in bribes, and six naval destroyers sold for over $3 billion to a country not granted diplomatic recognition by the selling country: such are the ingredients of a Franco-Taiwanese arms sale scandal. Arms sales generate numerous convoluted schemes made possible by corrupt transactions. For weapons-manufacturing states, arms exports are seen as crucial to what they argue is a critical domestic industry, and they go to great lengths to ensure that export sales occur. Since the early 1980s, competition by European firms and states for weapons sales within or outside Europe has been fierce. The end of the Cold War led to a drop in total world military expenditures, and as of 2003, those expenditures had not completely recovered. At the same time, the top producers have been squeezing out their rivals, such that from 1990 to 2003, the market share of the top five arms production firms went from 22 to 44 percent. With the United States and EU countries adhering to "buy local" policies, most of the competition is for exports to the third world.[69] It is because of that competition that the arms sales sector has been prone to corruption. Because the sector is highly competitive, the potential profits are enormous, and in the name of national security and corporate confidentiality, the bid process is cloaked in secrecy. The fact that "the transaction price is rarely well-defined" also makes the sector ripe for corruption.[70] And because bribery has been the norm, firms have little fear that other firms, including new market entrants, will blow the whistle on them: the other firms are also engaged in bribery.

Competitive markets include firms that are less competitive than the market leaders. For the less competitive, a bribe or kickback paid to those in charge of facilitating market access or granting contracts and licenses may represent a lower marginal cost than bankruptcy at the hands of the more efficient competitors in the market. Bribes are used to persuade the buyer (a government official, for instance) to accept lesser-quality goods—a payment for the opportunity cost of having the buyer forego a superior product.

Further, sellers and purchasers seldom face hard budget constraints, because the military industrial complex is usually politically protected from serious budget cuts.[71] If any of the arms manufacturers are nationalized, as they were in France for a time, then "arms and arms export decisions are more than ever shielded from public debate and from societal pressures. . . . Nationalization created more the illusion than the reality of public accountability and elected government control."[72]

The arms trade also sets up a dilemma that is often "resolved" through corruption. As one scholar noted, "governments with major domestic defence industries are required to undertake two contradictory roles: the regulation and control of military exports, on the one hand, and the promotion of foreign sales, on the other." The arms trade is a highly lucrative and yet internationally competitive economic sector, and one for which exports are often critical to the profit margin. Buyers can select from a wide range of suppliers. Yet as an economic sector subject to national security concerns, arms exports face extensive regulatory hurdles. Officials on the weapons export control boards—the oversight committees—tend to be from the industries and agencies that have a direct interest in promoting exports: defense and the military. This conflict of interest can degenerate quickly into corruption. Transparency, often eliminated in the name of national security and relations with other countries, is in short supply. Under the cover of national and commercial interest, parliamentary representatives in Britain and elsewhere have been barred at times from asking the government questions about arms exports.[73] The combination of bureaucratic barriers to sales and lack of transparency creates both the demand for corruption and its supply.

In addition, the EU's structure, with its free movement of goods, can "undermine national [export] controls" by making it possible to export the goods from the EU state "with the weakest legislative or administrative system."[74] Given how loosely some states have interpreted their own guidelines on weapons sales, corruption of their own officials may not be necessary to gain permission to export.

In Belgium, antitank grenade launchers are considered "hunting weapons" and therefore have legally been exported to countries on which there are arms embargoes.[75]

The importance of the arms trade to the major exporters is seen in the government agencies each has established to promote arms sales.[76] By 1961, France had a government agency for promoting the sale and export of French arms.[77] The French also have a special consulting firm (owned 49.9 percent by the French state) that "helps" purchasing countries "define their operational needs, weapon requirements, and specifications."[78] Were it not for the fact that these arrangements are legal, under each state's laws, they would fit the classic definition of "state capture." That definition has been summarized as "actions of individuals, groups, or firms in both the public and private sectors to influence the formation of laws, regulations, decrees, and other government policies (i.e., the basic rules of the game) to their own advantage by means of the illicit and non-transparent provision of private benefits to public officials."[79] Again, the only difference is that the interlocking relationships between weapons manufacturers and government-sponsored defense export promotion agencies are legal.

Even in countries that reputedly keep an arm's length between firms and the government, the arms export business is one of cozy relations. The liberal market economy gives way to the conflict-of-interest economy.[80] In Britain, the committee that approves export license applications, the Export Control Organisation within the Department of Trade and Industry, is staffed by officials seconded from industry to the agency. The "oversight" groups in the UK meant to enforce the rules—a Ministry of Defense working group and an Interdepartmental Committee on Defence Sales to Iran—have been "heavily biased in favour of the exporters. Thus, among the 'non-lethal defence equipment' exported to Iraq during the late 1980s were fighter aircraft spare parts, body armour, gun sound-ranging equipment and machine tools for the manufacture of artillery shells."[81] The UK has a Defence Export Services Organisation (DESO) that "co-ordinates the direct government support for arms exports, providing marketing assistance and advice on negotiation and financing arrangements, as well as organising arms exhibitions and promotional tours."[82] Its staff and leadership are seconded to the Ministry of Defense, of which DESO is a part, from defense industries, and have strong links to 10 Downing Street. The civil service salary of its head is "topped up" by the arms industries.[83]

The arms trade has been a buyer's market for several decades, even when the buyers have insufficient funds or are otherwise poor credit risks. The government of the seller state steps in to provide export credit loans, guarantees, and foreign aid to facilitate the sale. This scenario is also the case for arms sales to oil-rich countries, such as Qatar and Saudi Arabia, not to mention to oil-rich but otherwise poor countries such as Angola and Nigeria.[84] In 1989, when weak oil prices threatened Saudi Arabia's ability to meet its obligations, the UK government scrambled to arrange a loan for Saudi Arabia so it could continue to "purchase" (with oil) the military equipment on order under the "Al Yamamah" defense contract.[85]

The contradiction that results from the intersection of national security interests restricting arms exports and national economic interests promoting those same exports is sometimes likely to be "resolved" by corruption. The case of the sale of German tanks to Saudi Arabia illustrates the point. In 1990, Jürgen Massmann, the head of Thyssen Henschel, the tank unit of the major industrial firm Thyssen, initiated contacts with a middleman involved in other corruption cases, Karlheinz Schreiber, for the purpose of arranging the sale of Thyssen tanks to Saudi Arabia. Thwarting Thyssen's aims were Germany's restrictive export laws prohibiting weapons sales to sensitive, conflict-ridden areas such as the Middle East. Saudi officials, in turn, were eager to buy the Thyssen product, the "famous Fuchs 'sniffer' tanks," a state-of-the-art tank for detecting biological, chemical, and nuclear residues.[86] Schreiber had excellent contacts at Thyssen, in the CDU-CSU/FDP German government, particularly among the Bavarians, such as Walther Leisler Kiep and Max Strauss, and in Saudi Arabia. Thyssen also contacted Mansour Ojjeh, a billionaire Saudi businessman, to ensure that the Saudi royal family would agree to the purchase and to its terms.[87] Despite the Saudi government's official ban on "commissions" for weapons purchases, Thyssen's Massmann, Ojjeh, and Schreiber knew that only commissions would make the deal work. And they knew they needed a contact in Germany's defense ministry. They chose the deputy minister, Holger Pfahls, former head of Germany's counter-espionage service, who had already been contacted by the Saudi ambassador, and who had been considered a protégé of a leading conservative politician, the powerful Bavarian prime minister Franz Josef Strauss (CSU).[88]

Two circumstances made the deal more complex than usual: first, Saddam Hussein invaded Kuwait on August 2, 1990; second, Thyssen had just sold its complete inventory of Fuchs tanks to the United States. The first complication meant that lobbying on the German side would have to be more intense, as Germany was awaiting the American response before making any moves. To deal with the second complication, Massmann, Ojjeh, Schreiber, and a handful of key Saudi and German military officials met and decided to suggest "loaning" the Saudis some tanks from the German army: "Thyssen could refit the equipment for the Saudis' use and immediately begin manufacturing replacement vehicles for the German army."[89] The deal also included some other equipment and maintenance facilities. Total cost was almost DM 500 million or about $300 million, with over $100 million of it going to "consulting fees," the universal euphemism for bribes and commissions. Schreiber has testified that he paid DM 1 million ($600,000) to the CDU and DM 1 million to the CSU.[90] Walther Kiep received about DM 300,000 ($180,000) and used most of it to pay his fines from the Flick affair.[91] Thyssen figured that even with the fees, the company would make a profit of 8–10 percent.[92] By October, Thyssen and the Saudis had reached agreement on the main points, but Thyssen still had to obtain permission to export the tanks. Approval of the Kohl-led German cabinet came in February 1991.[93] Evidence points to the likelihood that corruption enabled Germany's economic considerations to trump its national security considerations. The conflict between having a defense industry that inherently demands a steady stream of sales and a foreign policy that restricts or bans exports to certain countries, thereby blocking sales, got resolved by corruption.

Likewise for the sale of six French destroyers to Taiwan in 1992. France did not have diplomatic relations with Taiwan and was wary of further disturbing already unsettled relations with mainland China, with which it did have diplomatic relations, so when the then state-owned defense firm Thomson-CSF applied to sell its destroyers to Taiwan, the foreign affairs minister, Roland Dumas, opposed the sale (which the weapons export board had approved).[94] The case was all the more urgent in that Thomson risked losing out to its German and American rivals.[95] To the rescue came Alfred Sirven, number-two man at the state oil company, Elf, and Christine Deviers-Joncour, who later chronicled her experiences in her book *La putain de la république* (Whore of the republic).[96] Sirven exploited Deviers-Joncour's personal relations (mistress) with Dumas, setting her up as Elf's off-the-books lobbyist who was to convince Dumas to allow France's defense firm, Thomson, to sell destroyers to Taiwan.[97] Although Elf had nothing formally to do with Thomson, high-level managers at Thomson believed that Elf (via Alfred Sirven) had a network of connections to Beijing (which were needed to pacify Beijing's opposition to the sale) and to the French Ministry of Foreign Affairs (which were needed to obtain approval for the sale to Taiwan).[98] Indeed, Thomson and Elf may have had closer connections than is generally known: it was Thomson's director of operations in Africa, where Elf had extensive dealings characterized by corruption and political manipulation, who brought Deviers-Joncour into Thomson. It appears that Sirven and Christine Deviers-Joncour saw the Thomson deal as one from which they could profit handsomely to the tune of FRF 160 million ($32 million), not counting the $10,000 a month Elf paid to Deviers-Joncour nor her Elf credit card for her expenses.[99] Charged with making things happen, Deviers-Joncour and Sirven did. Ironically, when, via a Swiss shell firm, they tried to collect on the promised "commission" for their services, Thomson's CEO refused to pay. Apparently not willing to see a corrupt deal violated, then president François Mitterrand had his office lean on Thomson's CEO to pay the bill.[100]

The bill that Thomson seems to have paid was for far more: half a billion dollars, to a Chinese intermediary, Andrew Wang. Wang reputedly used some of the funds to purchase the acquiescence of mainland Chinese leaders to the sale of the destroyers to Taiwan, and, as alleged by Roland Dumas, French foreign minister at the time, to purchase the acquiescence of various political or other figures in France.[101] The commissions continued to be paid even as investigations became public knowledge.

The destroyer sale appears to have involved massive and coordinated corruption at the highest levels of government and industry in France and Taiwan. Close connections between the defense industry (much of which was state owned) and politicians, with the addition of national security shielding deals from public scrutiny, facilitated corruption. So too did extensive competition for sales in defense: immediately after the French firm Dassault (of Belgian bribery fame) lost a sale of French fighters to Finland, the French minister of defense, Pierre Joxe (and currently a member of the Constitutional Court), advocated selling a hundred of the fighters to Taiwan. The failure to sell the Dassault planes to Finland was expected to lead to severe financial difficulties: Dassault hadn't had a weapons-for-export order in over four years.[102] The solution: sell them to a country with which France had no formal relations (Taiwan) and whose receipt of the planes would irritate a major ally (China). What with Andrew Wang as the point man for such deals in Taiwan, he again served as intermediary, and enabled other French firms to piggyback sales onto the fighter sales.[103]

Exposure of such high-level corruption has deadly costs. In 2000, the commercial attaché to Taiwan at the time of the Thomson destroyer and Dassault Mirage jet sales in France's external secret service (DGSE) told his father, also of the DGSE, that "there were men in Taiwan and in France, at the highest level of Thomson, who had made colossal fortunes from these contracts." Not long after, the attaché, Thierry Imbot, was found dead, allegedly having fallen from his apartment window one dark and stormy night.[104] He may have known too much.[105] A Thomson employee, Jacques Morisson, met a strikingly similar end five months later. He too had told a confidant that he feared he would be assassinated because of his knowledge of the underside of the destroyer sale. The Taiwan chief of naval procurement, Captain Yin Ching-feng, was assassinated in 1993 after pressing too hard in his investigation of the inflated price paid for the destroyers, knowing full well that the inflated price covered the bribes.[106]

Similarly dubious deals have taken place across the Channel (not to mention across the Atlantic, but that is the subject of another book), even in a so-called liberal market economy and even under the auspices of that presumed advocate of the free market, Margaret Thatcher. A spectacular case in which not just the transaction price but the price of the entire deal was anything but clear is the

British Al Yamamah arms sales to Saudi Arabia.[107] The sale had two phases. Phase 1 was signed in 1986, but even while it was being negotiated, a British newspaper lodged serious allegations that the deal involved bribes of more than $750 million (£600 million).[108] Perhaps just as extraordinary were the terms of the deal: the 72 (Tornado) fighter jets and 24 Hawk trainers would be "paid for almost entirely in oil."[109] The privatized British oil firm BP, and also Shell, was to pump the bartered oil, sell it on the open market, and deposit the funds in the account of the UK defense ministry, which would then reimburse the (recently privatized) arms manufacturers, such as BAE. The details were not public, and it is not even clear the Thatcher government could put a real figure on the sale, which was reputed to be worth about £5.5 billion ($9.8 billion). But this was trivial relative to what was to come: a deal—phase 2 of Al Yamamah—worth at least £10 billion ($18 billion). As the *Financial Times* put it, for the United Kingdom it was the "biggest sale ever, of anything, to anyone."[110] The Saudis' choice of the United Kingdom yet again may have been partly due to the UK government's refusal to make public the details of the first agreement.[111] It did not make public the details of the second either. Although the arms trade rewards secrecy, that secrecy also sets up conditions for corruption.

The British had perhaps learned from Lockheed's misfortunes in the 1970s that to remain competitive in the arms trade, silence is best: even when allegations of corruption were to have been investigated by the UK's National Audit Office, the subsequent report was not published, in contrast to the publication of thousands of other investigative reports the NAO has produced.[112] In Al Yamamah deals, partisan competition was negligible: at the time, the head of the parliamentary committee with authority to release NAO reports was a Labour MP (Robert Sheldon, now Sir Robert). Despite allegations of bribes paid to Saudis and kickbacks on those bribes paid to the British Conservative Party and to Margaret Thatcher's son, Sheldon kept a lid on the report, as has Blair's Labour government. Blair instead has maintained the same strategy, stating that "winning exports is vital to the long-term success of Britain's defence industry." In the Al Yamamah arms deal with Saudi Arabia, numerous allegations of bribes surfaced, one of which was actually admitted to by the chairman of Thorn EMI, subcontracting with BAE, the main contractor for the Al Yamamah deals. The chairman, Sir Colin Southgate, said that his firm had paid a 25 percent commission on a £40 million ($71 million) shipment. When the managing director of the same firm was told that Saudi law prohibited "commissions" on arms deals, he replied, "Then they got a big problem with Al Yamamah."[113] Evidence indicates that the British Ministry of Defense approved of that arrangement and itself took £2 million from it. As to the complicity of politicians, Prime Minister Thatcher's office asserted that no commissions had been or were being paid on the deal.[114] Other evidence contradicts this. In addition, in 1994, allegations and some evidence surfaced that Thatcher's son Mark had been given a £12 million ($21 million) payment by the Saudis as a "gift" related to the deal. British authorities with competence to do so refused to investigate.[115] Mark Thatcher was later arrested in South Africa for helping to finance a coup attempt against the president of oil-rich Equatorial Guinea.[116] When the Saudis halted negotiations on an additional order of seventy-two BAE Eurofighter Typhoon jets potentially "worth as much as £40 billion ($78 billion)," in 2006, in an effort to force Britain's Serious Fraud Office to drop an investigation into corruption associated with earlier Al Yamamah deals, Britain complied.[117]

Increasing the effect of secrecy on corruption in a competitive economic sector is the fact that British political parties were not required to disclose donors or amounts until 2001. For example, if some funds stemming from the Al Yamamah deals had come in to Conservative Party coffers, they could have done so in complete secrecy. The party did not even have to resort to shady financial dealings to hide the donations: no one was allowed to audit party accounts.

Competition in the arms industry is another factor that fuels, rather than reduces, corruption. Indeed, competition was a major factor in the Thatcher government's extensive efforts to land the Saudi contract. For Britain's major military aircraft firm, BAE, "the long-awaited Saudi contract has underpinned the future of BAE's profitable military aircraft business." In the opinion of BAE's CEO, Dick Evans, "If we had not received the Saudi order we would have had to shut down completely the Tornado line in a couple of months' time."[118] The Saudi order was for forty-eight more Tornado fighter jets at £5 billion ($8.9 billion), under the umbrella of the Al Yamamah deal. During the 2006 negotiation of the deal to purchase seventy-two BAE Eurofighters, the British were well aware that their French rivals were lobbying hard for the Saudis to switch to the French-built Rafale jets.

Both the Franco-Taiwanese destroyers case and the Al Yamamah deal demonstrate the high political and business levels at which arms sales corruption transpires. Arms corruption is not merely a matter of lower-level bureaucrats taking advantage of their position to skim a few thousand off a contract; it is high-ranking government and business elites, and middlemen, reaping enormous rewards from their participation in the corruption of their own export control systems, from the corruption of UN and national arms embargoes, and from the corruption of foreign officials. They exploit the fact that judicial and press investigations are blocked by the claim of national defense secrets and by the fact that the arms trade is global but judicial authority is national.[119] They exploit their personal and business connections to profit from, and thereby reinforce the institutionalization of, the bribery connected to arms sales.

Compounding the corruption in weapons sales is the fact that the weapons are often paid for with petrodollars from oil owned by the purchaser country but ex-tracted and distributed by an oil firm from the seller country, which earlier had undoubtedly paid enormous "commissions" if not also outright bribes for drill-ing rights.[120]

OIL

In order to import oil, a number of European oil companies export corruption. As in the arms industry, in the oil industry it has long been routine to give com-missions to the agents who broker deals, and to the official state and its public of-ficials with whom a contract is established. One oil industry businessman said it was like giving advances on royalties.[121] Ceteris paribus, commissions will be higher the more valuable the firms judge the resources to be. As BP said of oil con-tracts in Angola in the late 1990s, "noting the significant discoveries made in the last two years in the adjacent deep-water blocks, it was widely believed that the ultra-deep water blocks would possess significant volumes of oil. Hence, compe-tition for access to these licenses was keen and the signature bonus was high re-flecting the anticipated prospectivity."[122] As for investments in poor countries where political authority and the legal system are unstable, one can make a ra-tional argument for commissions: they are payments intended to keep state offi-cials from expropriating the oil company's fixed assets. They are a means of surmounting a commitment problem: local rulers can credibly threaten to ex-propriate assets, so Western firms pay local rulers a bonus to dissuade them from cheating on contracts. The bonus payments, though, set up what an economist might call a situation of moral hazard: they create incentives for local rulers to continue to be bad bets, to "need" payment so as not to cheat on the next con-tract. For this reason, multinationals (and Western states) are vulnerable to the claim that they coddle corrupt, derelict regimes.

Concerning commissions, the chief auditor at BP told a House of Commons committee that in the extractive part of the business,

> there is usually some form of bidding for the right to explore or the right to develop in that country. . . . We are very sensitive, of course, given the sums of money involved to ensure that the payment flows which are in-volved end up in official bank accounts, so that, as far as we have con-trol over events, these activities are clean and above board. Now, of course, in some of these countries it is alleged that when those payments pass into what we will call government bank accounts, there may be things that go beyond that—but of course that is not within our con-trol. We are aware of it but we cannot control it.[123]

One of Elf's former CEOs, Philippe Jaffré (1993–99), admitted that there may be kickbacks on the commissions themselves. He said these may go to the "collaborators of the [oil] firm" in a deal, and, washing his hands of the problem, he added that "it is up to the judiciary to settle the matter." Another witness before a parliamentary committee said that it was routine practice for Elf to take "5–10% to fund French parties or politicians."[124] Elf was also used to collect funds from African leaders for the electoral campaigns of French politicians.[125]

Intermediaries are prevalent in the oil industry. For corrupt activities, there is of course no legal authority to enforce contracts, so an intermediary may be employed to vouch for both sides and act as a third-party enforcer of sorts.[126] Once this agent is in business, he looks for more business, and he may suggest new corrupt deals. An agent functions similarly for deals that may be legitimate but nevertheless require secrecy, say, in the interests of proprietary commercial information or state national security. Agreements between groups from different countries face the additional problem of trust between the contracting parties. Thus the value of agents who make contacts is high—and even higher for those whose make corrupt arrangements, where trust is at a premium.

For instance, Elf's activities in Africa, then in Latin America, Asia, and the former Soviet Union, were sustained for decades by a *réseau corse*, a Corsican network headed by André Tarallo and seconded by André Guelfi.[127] Tarallo and the connections and financing he provided to African leaders were widely regarded as essential to Elf's continued presence in Africa. When Tarallo was arrested in France, one of his assistants in Corsica voiced what was generally believed: "given the quality of his relations with numerous presidents, and especially [Omar] Bongo [of Gabon], rebuilding his African network would take years. Tarallo gone, imagine thus that Bongo wants to nationalize Elf-Gabon. With the entry efforts of the Americans, who already are pushing in Zaire, it would be a terrible blow for France."[128]

Transparency

Corruption also thrives in oil transactions because oil is a sector in which transparency is in short supply. As a French parliamentary committee investigating the then two major French oil firms, one state-owned (Elf) and one private (Total-Fina), found, governments prefer not to shed light on the oil industry. According to a 1992 law, the French government was required to "present a report intended to bring to light the real costs of production, transport and refining of oil products." As the committee stated, "that report had never been submitted."[129] Firms are sensitive about corporate information. Each firm might prefer that there not be corruption and that the required commissions paid be lower, but it cannot afford to share information with other companies for fear that they will not reciprocate. In the arms trade, the rationale is voiced that if we don't sell weapons to a client, someone else will. Similarly, in the oil trade, in the absence of collective institutions to enforce an agreement not to pay bribes, each firm proceeds on the assumption that payments are necessary and that if they don't pay them, someone else will—and that that someone else will take the market.[130] BP was blunt: "The major controversy surrounding signature bonuses centres upon the lack of transparency in the process, and this is an area of great concern to many, including ourselves, and . . . which we are striving to address. What is certain is that any British company which refused to participate would merely leave the field open to foreign rivals."[131] Where the corporate culture has been one of subterfuge and obfuscation, this lack of transparency can become endemic. In commenting about Elf's role in a controversial pipeline from Chad to Cameroon, a French parliamentary committee stated that they "can't help but underline once more the lack of transparency in the decision process, and [can't help but be] surprised at the taste for secrecy that seems to pervade the decision makers when it comes to Elf and Africa."[132] Although some secrecy is inevitable (corporations have reason not to reveal all their financial data to rivals), secrecy has become unnecessarily exaggerated, thereby fostering the payment of larger commissions and larger retro-commissions.

Because the bonuses or commissions are often paid into foreign-held bank accounts, domestic authorities and even private auditors cannot easily track the amounts or their ultimate destination. Legitimate commissions may go into a state account and illegitimate ones into the private accounts of state officials. In addition, the latter may tap into the former, as Gabon president Omar Bongo routinely did. Although illegitimate commissions may be against a company's code of conduct (e.g., BP), competitive pressures combined with low risk of discovery create incentives and opportunities to pay them. Elf executives and agents testified that the *bonus occulte* (hidden bonus) was expected by African rulers and therefore was a necessary business tool. According to Elf operatives, these commissions were all approved by Elf's CEO (whether Le Floch-Prigent, Jaffré, or earlier CEOs) and were signaled to the general secretary of the French president. Hidden commissions were also paid when one African ruler provided introductions for Elf to another.[133] Significantly, even though Elf had a new CEO in 1994 and was privatized in 1995, the firm, with the CEO's approval (whether Le Floch-Prigent or Jaffré), continued to pay hidden commissions.[134] According to witnesses who testified before the French judiciary in the Elf affair, this practice continued at least until 1998, even as Elf's practices were being investigated by the French and Swiss judiciaries.[135] Billions of dollars paid by European (and

U.S.) oil firms to Angola's oil ministry and national oil company, Sonagol, never were registered in government accounts and instead seem to have filtered into the private offshore bank accounts of Angola's president and other major public officials.[136]

Opaque Organization

The identification of a state's strategic interests with the material interests of its oil firms also facilitates the export of corruption. Elf is a revealing example. France has long had a state-directed, coordinated market economy in which most major economic transactions and developments took place through close, nonmarket negotiations among politicians, bureaucrats, and firms. That was particularly the case with the state-owned oil company. As one analyst said in discussing Elf, "there is an osmosis between the political class, the firm's world, the press and civil society and the African governments, which accounts for why certain controversies are avoided. . . . The network of [former French Interior Minister] Charles Pasqua remains very active and strongly appeals to African governments, among others, because they work through decentralized cooperation."[137] The firm started as a state-owned enterprise, and its first CEO viewed Elf as France's blood supply. As another analyst stated, "Elf was France: to attack one was to attack the other."[138] Although there were occasional run-ins between cabinet ministers and Elf, Elf's policies often prevailed. An evaluation by France's main audit body, the Cour des comptes, stated that "it seems that the State did not want to nor could make explicit the precise goals of Elf, beyond the sole search, obviously, for profitability and development."[139]

Sirven was, officially, director of general affairs at Elf. In practice, he handled everything from negotiating the terms of the divorce of its CEO, Loïk Le Floch-Prigent, to hiring and funding Roland Dumas's mistress to convince him to authorize destroyer sales to Taiwan, to overseeing French intervention in several African civil wars, to coordinating the network that allegedly paid kickbacks on the Elf-Leuna deal, to working out a deal guaranteeing Elf no disruptions in production should the rival party (UNITA) win the election, to funding the election campaign of the Angola opposition (UNITA).[140]

Italy was not left out of corruption related to oil. The state oil firm, ENI, became a fief of the Socialist Party, and in 1979 its CEO, Giorgio Mazzanti, "had to resign over kickbacks on crude oil deliveries from Saudi Arabia's Petromin."[141]

For some observers, including many NGOs, the mere fact that oil revenues are used for weapons purchases by regimes with notoriously bad human rights records, ranging from Saudi Arabia to Burma/Myanmar to Congo to Angola to Indonesia, is an example of corruption. Further, it is evidence of corrupt collusion between the West and the developing world, and the corruption of the arms and oil industries. Certainly the case histories are appalling. In addition to that moral corruption, however, arms for oil and oil for arms promote political corruption.

One of the extraordinary offshoots of oil-based corruption is the extent to which Western oil firms, sometimes with the support of their home governments, become involved in the violent conflicts in host countries. Thanks to the investigation and prosecution of Elf officials, we have substantial detail on the activities of the French firm. Given the overall structure of the situation, it is unlikely that Elf was the lone firm engaged in such activities. Elf used revenue from its exploitation of oil fields in Angola, which it realized through its contracts with the Angolan government run by Dos Santos's Mouvement populaire de libération de l'Angola (MPLA), to also support that government's challenger, UNITA, led by Jonas Savimbi. Savimbi, wanting funds for his own private army, was "furious that Elf paid Dos Santos [so he could buy] the helicopters that machine-gunned them. Mr. Savimbi threatened to blow up Elf's oil wells in revenge." An intermediary, Yves Verwaerde, who was a member of a conservative French party (Parti républicain), lobbied Elf to give funds to UNITA. Elf's CEO, Loïk Le Floch-Prigent, had made it clear to several of his officials that "the support of the opposition could be worthwhile in case there was a change of regime." At a later meeting, however, Le Floch-Prigent told Verwaerde, then a deputy in the European Parliament, that he "was very doubtful about things falling into place between Elf and UNITA." Elf "supported the government in places which controlled the oil wells." Elf's Alfred Sirven, confidentially instructed Verwaerde to make arrangements with Unita, letting them know that "the new team was more receptive and that [Elf's] support for the government in place [MPLA] was due to the former [Elf] team, that of Mr. [André] Tarallo [head of Elf's Gabon subsidiary]." Nevertheless, Sirven told Verwaerde to make sure "not to disturb Elf's official policy" toward the Angolan government. In addition, the oil company funded UNITA's election campaign in 1992.[142] This situation, involving illegal weapons exports to Angola, via French and Russian intermediaries suspected of having paid off high-level French politicians, has led some observers to characterize it as "a conspiracy to rob the country of its oil money through over-priced military procurement, kickbacks and the mortgaging of future oil reserves for ready cash in the form of oil-backed loans."[143]

STATE-ENFORCED CORRUPTION

In addition to the usual foreign policy justifications, the competitive pressures of the market render instrumental Western states' interest in the rule of law: often, when less developed countries try to investigate and prosecute corruption concerning contracts and projects undertaken by European corporations in their countries, Western states try to block the investigation. At the same time, Western states complain of the corruption in less developed countries. The less developed countries, some of which are among the world's poorest, such as Lesotho, sometimes run out of funds to continue investigations. Despite the OECD agreement to do so, Western states seldom investigate allegations that their own firms have violated their own laws against bribing foreign officials. In the Lesotho Highlands Water Project, the United Kingdom made a deliberate decision to leave the investigation to the Lesotho government.[144] But facing the loss of this potential revenue for their multinationals and smaller contractors, states have little incentive to enforce the international anticorruption measures they have agreed to.

Three cases illustrate the pattern. First, in 1998, Pakistan, under the new but short-lived government of Nawaz Sharif, accused the Western-dominated electricity consortium Hubco of having bribed Pakistan's previous prime minister, Benazir Bhutto, and of recovering those costs by overcharging on electricity rates. Under the agreement with Bhutto's government, Hubco had built, owned, and operated a 1,200-megawatt power plant on the Hab River. In addition to the allegations of kickbacks to Bhutto and her cohorts, Pakistan's Accountability Bureau, established by Sharif to investigate corruption under Bhutto, "had claimed that Hubco's project costs were marked up by $400 million." The World Bank, ten U.S. senators, and the British government, to name a few, intervened to block Pakistan's efforts at investigation. Spurred on by a U.S. energy firm with interests in the project, and motivated by a similar situation in India involving the now bankrupt Enron, the U.S. senators wrote to the World Bank, which had provided a controversial and scarcely used underwriting provision to cover approximately one-third of the $1.5 billion project (for reasons of "political risk"). In their letter, the senators complained that Pakistan's actions were part of "an alarming trend in several developing countries where federal and state governments use unproven allegations of corruption, collusion and even nepotism to rewrite existing commercial contracts." The World Bank concurred.[145] Once Sharif was deposed by military dictator Pervez Musharraf, Pakistan settled its dispute over the electricity rates and withdrew its case against the Hubco consortium and officials.[146] The post-Suharto government of Indonesia faced a similar situation when it tried to renegotiate contracts that had all the hallmarks of Suharto's corruption.[147]

A second case involves Taiwan and France. Despite efforts of Taiwanese and French judges to cooperate in their investigation of bribes paid as part of the sale of French destroyers and fighters to Taiwan, and of the deaths of a number of men involved in the negotiations, the French ministries of Justice and Foreign Affairs ended all collaboration with the Taiwanese investigators in 2002, claiming that

Taiwan was not recognized as a state.[148] Taiwan has retaliated by suing Thales for breach of its contract, whose provisions stated that no commissions were to be paid. This move has left French authorities scrambling for access to the frozen assets of Andrew Wang, in order to repay Taiwan the bribes the French state officially claims were never paid.[149]

In the third case, involving possible bribery during arms sales by a Swedish firm, Bofors, to India, the Swedish government refused to cooperate with the Indian investigators, saying, "It can not be seen as common international practice for a country's government to approach another country's government with a request to get documents that concern this country's dealings with a former government."[150] The previous Swedish government had been accused by Bofors executives of tacitly condoning bribery, as well as illegal arms sales to banned countries, in order to support the Swedish weapons industry and to avoid public knowledge of where Swedish weapons were being used.[151] Bofors was on trial in Sweden for a short time, for allegedly having paid $50 million in bribes for a $1.3 billion weapons sale to India. The bribe was necessary "to counter stiff international competition."[152] Once again, competition spurs, rather than reduces, corruption, and once again, Western states block investigations. As the Indian Supreme Court said in 1992 of India's Central Bureau of Investigation, it had been hindered at "every stage," and it had been "forced to spend most of its energy in court proceedings rather than in investigating the payoffs."[153]

Western states, it seems, despite their verbiage about the rule of law, have no problem colluding to pressure less developed countries to honor contracts signed under dubious conditions. For example, "in July 1999, the ECAs [Export Credit Agencies] of Japan, Germany, Switzerland and the United States took another approach and put considerable pressure on the new post-Suharto government in Indonesia to honour contracts awarded to Western companies to supply power to Indonesia during Suharto's regime. The total cost of these contracts had been inflated by as much as 37% on average, the contracts had not been won through competitive tender, and there were strong suspicions that they were infused with corruption."[154] Labour's foreign minister in 1997, Robin Cook, had previously campaigned for ethics in arms sales. But in 1997, when the export licenses for a suspect weapons deal with Indonesia, agreed to by the Conservative government, came across his desk, he signed the papers. His defense was that "he received legal advice that he would place British firms in breach of contract if he refused to sign the licences."[155] Politicians and firms have found the Holy Grail: the state itself enforces contracts reached as a result of corruption.

Fierce competition by firms and their home states for export markets, particularly in the realm of infrastructure projects, arms, and oil, suggests that corruption is not in opposition to the export market but is a feature of it. Export-led corruption thrives on competition where the rewards of winning are significant: it might be cheaper to bribe and collude than to compete. This chapter has covered a number of cases in which corruption was used to avoid competition in the awarding of a contract or access to a market. The more profitable the market, the more demand there is to participate in it and to gain a large share of it. As demand grows—for instance, when the number of competitors in the international construction industry increases or when traditional markets are saturated—the price of getting into the market goes up. This includes legally permitted "offsets" and also illegal bribes. In essence, export-led corruption exhibits market logic.

Export-led corruption also thrives on a collective action problem: firms and governments might prefer not to pay bribes, so as to reap higher profits, but they cannot trust others not to bribe. The OECD Convention is a case in point: thirty-five countries had signed and ratified the convention by 2004, a number too large for easy monitoring. Within each state there are thousands of exporting firms, again too many for effective monitoring of each group member's adherence to the agreement. As Transparency International notes, "there are more than 60,000 multinational corporations operating around the world with more than 600,000 foreign affiliates."[156] The group's statistics on bribe paying in 2002 show the convention's limited effect. Italy has ratified the convention, but on a scale of 10 to 0, in which 10 is *least likely to bribe,* Italy's firms are ranked 4.1, France's 5.5, and Germany 6.3. (The United States, the Foreign Corrupt Practices Act notwithstanding, ranks 5.3.) Of the countries most frequently discussed in this book, Belgium is highest ranked at 7.8, that is, its firms are least likely to bribe.[157] Construction and public works contracts were the sector in which bribery was most likely to take place, followed closely by the arms and oil and gas sectors; these same sectors were judged, in that same order, to be those in which the biggest bribes were made. The western EU countries have ratified the OECD Convention, and all have agreed to an EU statement, with no force of law, about their opposition to corruption. International organizations are inherently bad at policing their members; enforcement is largely left to the individual, highly self-interested state authorities, who often find bribery for export market access an acceptable evil.

There has been a trend for states, in the name of the free market, prosperity, and national defense, to promote their industries' exports. This trend has two effects related to corruption. First, supply starts to push demand. Markets have to be created, demand cannot be allowed to develop "naturally," so states are tempted to bribe or condone bribes for the sake of their firms' international market share. The corrupt practices of Elf, the French oil firm; the alleged corruption in the Saudi/Al Yamamah arms deals with the UK and the British government's quashing of all efforts to investigate and make public findings about those arms sales; and the huge infrastructure projects in less developed countries that are promoted by Western states and their construction industries: all illustrate this phenomenon of supply pushing demand and an accompanying willingness to overlook corruption for the sake of market share. Second, the trend establishes institutions that facilitate networks between potential buyers and sellers. These networks form part of the structure necessary for corrupt exchanges to occur. The networks do not create the corruption but are a tool that can be used, and reused, in that way.

The efforts to promote exports in competitive sectors lead to a search for individuals with access to those in less developed countries who have power of decision. Those individuals, in turn, have an interest in increasing the amount of business they do, so they too start pushing demand. Intermediaries thrive on making themselves useful, so they show up in multiple cases. The same two men who have been investigated for their alleged roles as middlemen and collectors of large commissions in various Elf affairs are under scrutiny for playing a similar role in illegal weapons sales to Angola. Once the intermediary structures are in place, that infrastructure lowers the costs of corrupt transactions.

Arms embargoes to lucrative markets such as oil do nothing but force the arms market underground, making corruption inevitable. Virtually all major arms-exporting countries violated the UN arms embargo against Iraq; Iran benefited from an extraordinarily complicated evasion of a ban on weapons sales, courtesy of not only the United States and Britain, but France, Germany, Saudi Arabia, and Israel. Illegal arms sales to Iran between 1982 and 1986, if not 1987, helped save the fortunes of nearly bankrupt French weapons manufacturers Luchaire and SNPE (Société nationale de poudres et explosifs). There were also credible allegations that the weapons sales resulted in retro-commissions that helped finance election campaigns of the French Socialist Party in 1986. Luchaire, taking advantage of the Common Market, used its Italian subsidiaries to move the weapons; when the weapons left Europe, they were declared to be going to Latin American destinations, but in reality they landed in Iran. The case was signaled to the Ministry of Defense, reports were filed, and magistrates were blocked from investigating.[158] French politicians appear to have financed electoral campaigns from kickbacks on illegal weapons sales to African countries, but further investigations into those matters have been stymied.[159]

There is room for action: if public outcry is strong, and if penalties are real, there may be a slight change for the better. Studies by the OECD are finding that when laws and procedures require business managers and program heads to be liable for the legitimacy of foreign business transactions, firms at least voice an inclination to become more circumspect about bribing to secure contracts. The drawback is that these OECD-inspired programs only apply to the bribing of "foreign public officials." The intermediaries, who are key in corrupt international transactions, are seldom "public officials."[160] Public standards also matter, as illustrated in the Lockheed case, which had repercussions in the Netherlands and in Italy. Its legacy also includes the U.S. Foreign Corrupt Practices Act of 1977, which outlaws bribery of foreign officials by U.S. firms. Lockheed was the typical case of a foreign firm bribing government officials—in this case, in Italy, the Netherlands, Japan, Turkey, Mexico, Columbia, and possibly Germany—in order to beat out the competition for a major weapons sale.[161]

The European responses to the Lockheed case are telling and offer some lessons on how to reduce corruption. A French official in the Ministry of Defense merely wondered at the naiveté of the Americans, first for investigating the case, second for publishing the committee's findings, and third for being outraged at the fact that a major corporation paid bribes to win contracts. His conclusion: "They are really crazy."[162] The Lockheed scandal changed nothing in France; indeed, Lockheed had complained that when it refused to pay a bribe in Indonesia, the French won the contract, presumably because the French were willing to pay.[163] Most thought that "Lockheed had spilled too many beans and embarrassed too many old friends when it got caught." Ironically, for having done so, Lockheed was no longer seen as an honorable corporation in the eyes of foreign multinationals—it had violated the unspoken code.[164]

In Italy, there was a public outcry, the government fell sooner than the average (lasting only 79 days instead of the usual 270), and elections actually were called, but the Christian Democrats, whose top politicians were among the main beneficiaries of the Lockheed bribes, were not unseated and instead retained control of the new governing coalition. They were able to do so because at the time, the Communist Party, their major rival, was seen by the majority of Italians as an unacceptable party in government. The Cold War sheltered the Christian Democrats from voter retribution. As one victorious Christian Democrat said, "we won this one on fear."[165] Other parties were likewise spared. The Social Democrats renominated their former leader to head their party, despite his having resigned earlier for accepting a Lockheed bribe while he was defense minister.[166] Perhaps as significant, Italy passed a law banning all corporate donations to political parties. Because Italy had no public financing of parties but did have enormous election and party expenses, this legislation merely drove the search for funding underground.

The Dutch reaction was public outrage, a parliamentary inquiry, and full disclosure of its report, including parts unfavorable to the Dutch prince. Since he was married to the head of state, this was no small disclosure. The report was even available for purchase in bookstores. The Dutch prince Bernhard escaped prosecution as a result of concern that a trial might unhinge the current Dutch government, but he was forced to resign all business and military posts. Nor was he was allowed to be reinstated to them, in contrast to outcomes in many corruption cases.[167]

State-sponsored secrecy facilitates and protects what seems to be state-sponsored corruption of exports. Most European states have blocked investigations into illegal arms sales and their accompanying bribes on the grounds of national security. In contrast, the effect of transparency is telling. The Swedish government, after the Bofors bribery scandal on the sale of $1.3 billion in weapons to India, began regularly providing its parliament with information on weapons sales and also including members of the opposition parties in the "information flow."[168] Sweden is one of the countries whose firms are judged to be least likely to bribe to secure arms contracts.[169]

Compounding state-sponsored secrecy is the existence of state-sanctioned offshore banks, financial institutions, and shell societies, some of which are "on shore" in the EU. Firms and politicians are able to channel funds through these structures in order to render invisible the source of the funds. They also play a major role in complicating and delaying investigations, because investigating authorities must gain cooperation and formal legal permission to obtain information across international boundaries.

One might be tempted to dismiss the sordid affairs recounted about export-led corruption in Germany, France, and the United Kingdom as relics of the Kohl, Mitterrand, and Thatcher era, destined to fade away as a new generation takes over. The "new generation" has signed international antibribery conventions, has upped penalties for some violations, and then blocked investigations. Yet there is little cause for optimism. The forces of supply and demand remain the same; if anything, competition for export markets and for access to oil and other energy reserves has increased. Politicians still have the same motives to turn the tables on those who elected them, using their power of office to evade transparency, and to write new rules making corruption harder to expose, or legalizing it. National defense secrecy is still a reason to block investigations into weapons export corruption; diplomacy a reason to block publication of damaging reports on oil, arms, or infrastructure projects. Arms and oil are still regarded as strategic goods in which reason of state trumps rule of law.[170] If the choice of whether to investigate and prosecute is a political decision, or if politicians can intervene in the decision, then, as Germany shows, corruption can continue for decades.

EU membership and ratification of the OECD convention against international bribery have little effect on the propensity of firms to bribe and their home governments to facilitate such actions or to turn a blind eye. First, these international organizations do not have significant oversight or enforcement powers, and some major member states block efforts to extend anticorruption rules.[171]

Second, they seldom exercise what leverage they do have: Slovakia was allowed to join the EU even though the EU chastised it for failing to meet the EU's requirements about arms exports and even though the country is a major conduit for arms sales to embargoed countries.[172] Germany has violated arms embargoes, and evidence suggests it has bribed its way into defense sales.[173] France and Britain have long had laws against paying bribes for weapons or other export sales, and they have long turned a blind eye toward their violation. Italy is routinely in the top five (along with Russia, South Korea, Taiwan, and mainland China) of countries most likely to pay bribes in order to land major contracts, while France, the United States, and Spain are not far behind.[174]

Western states tend to blame the countries with which they do business. In justifying bribes and commissions, Western firms often adopt the view of former Elf CEO Jaffré: "not all countries make the same distinction between public money and private money, between service to the State and serving oneself. . . . I clearly don't share those values but I can't judge them."[175] It is the Western countries that continue to feed the demand, despite various anticorruption conventions and occasional prosecutions. And it is the Western countries that are desperate to win markets and contracts for their multinationals, creating a competitive situation in which corruption becomes an important business tool. It is the Western countries that have tried to block the less developed countries from investigating or revisiting contracts apparently reached through corruption. In other words, in the pursuit of exports, it is the Western states that have used their own legal machinery to enforce corrupt contracts.

THE MYTH OF THE MARKET

Privatization

Il n'y a pas de corruption, il n'y a que des occasions.

—Talleyrand

In the spring of 1991, when Loïk Le Floch-Prigent, CEO of the state-owned oil company Elf Aquitaine, wanted to divorce his wife, Fatima Belaïd, he spoke of it to the president of France, then François Mitterrand. Noting that Belaïd was head of Elf's charitable foundation and that she had accompanied him on numerous business trips, Le Floch-Prigent told Mitterrand that she posed a rumor risk to Elf. Mitterrand replied, "Sort it out yourself. Take care of it." Le Floch-Prigent interpreted this to mean that Mitterrand was authorizing him to use the state-owned company's secret funds to pay off his wife and buy her silence. Use them he did, by way of his number-two man, Alfred Sirven, who told Belaïd that she was "nothing but a nuisance," and by way of several close friends (who had been involved in other questionable Elf dealings), who handled the illegal fund transfers and eventually even the terms of the divorce.[1] Advocates of the free market would be quick to argue that the Elf-funded (and therefore publicly funded) divorce of its CEO is a prima facie case for privatization. Stockholders, including major institutional investors, would not tolerate such practices, if they could find out about them.[2] As Vivendi Universal (France), Parmalat (Italy), Skandia (Sweden), Ahold (The Netherlands), Mannesmann and Siemens (Germany), and Fininvest (Italy) (not to mention cases in the United States, such as Enron, World-Com, and Tyco) have shown, private firms are not immune from fraud and corruption, nor does privatization guarantee corporate transparency.

Privatization of government-held firms is one piece of the standard political and economic reform package proposed to reduce corruption. Among its other advantages, privatization hinders corruption because it makes transparency possible. States are no longer able to hide corrupt, internal activities, some of which rival those of private firms in their complexity. Instead, illegal rent-seeking on the part of the state is exposed to the public when the state contracts out public works rather than controlling them internally. Second, the supply of ill-gotten gains shrinks when the pool of state-owned enterprises does. Third, privatization, to the extent that it increases a free market's competitiveness, reduces the demand for corruption, since corruption often arises from efforts to engage in economic activity blocked by government regulation and ownership.

Although such may be the theory behind privatization, the practice is a bit different. It is difficult to say that there has been an increase in corruption within Europe as a result of privatization, but it is possible to say that privatization has brought with it its own forms of corruption. This chapter examines the creative efforts of politicians, bureaucrats, and firms to engage in corrupt practices even as they are taking their anticorruption medication: privatization.

The ills of public ownership are said to include inflated costs, patronage posts, ghost jobs, and untraceable revenue that disappears into politicians' and bureaucrats' pockets. Although these phenomena may be present more often in a public firm, they certainly emerge with disturbing frequency in private firms delivering government services, obtaining government contracts, or taking over state-owned firms. Corruption can exist in the market just as it can in a state-controlled economy. The techniques may be different, due to shifts in the structure of the state and market, but because it is a tool of transactions, a tool of profit, of political funding, the market alone does not drive it out of existence. Markets mean rules, and someone always tries to cheat on the rules, or change the rules so that what was cheating becomes a rule, even while playing the "market" game.

Privatization takes place within the context of preexisting state-economy-society structures and practices, so it should not be surprising that politicians and firms tend to resort to the techniques and contacts they used under the old arrangements. Even when parameters such as state-market arrangements are changing, preexisting behavioral norms and routines will strongly influence the interactions of politicians, firms, and bureaucrats. In contexts in which the state sector is highly politicized—for instance, when the sector is divided into fiefdoms controlled by the various political parties—its privatization will also be highly politicized.

Privatization in countries that already have something resembling a market economy is not a requirement of membership in the EU, nor of qualifying for the euro. Since the 1980s, however, privatization has become an element of economic policy for virtually all EU member states. The greatest wave of privatization started in 1993, with countries aiming to meet the so-called Maastricht criteria for the single currency. Privatization enabled countries to obtain one-off profits and to reduce continuing budget expenditures, which was critical for meeting the standards they had agreed to for the common currency but that have been conveniently loosened. For instance, in 1993 France obtained $12.16 billion from privatization sales; Italy obtained a similar figure in 1994. Between 1990 and 2001, the EU-15 generated $431.69 billion from privatization. As is well known, the Thatcher government (1979–90) launched a privatization drive that was unrelated to EU common currency concerns but rather was an effort to get the government out of running businesses.[3] The British government now runs numerous "public private partnerships" instead and has state agencies compete with private firms for state contracts. All of this privatization activity has changed the institutional structures in which corrupt transactions could take place. Where corruption was already part and parcel of dealings with the state (e.g., in Italy), privatization did not prompt people to be less corrupt; rather, it prompted them to find different ways to reach the same end: personal profit at the expense of the taxpaying public. In other countries, the shift in emphasis and format of government economic activity led to somewhat confused ethics as well as new problems that were not outright illegal but that appeared corrupt: conflicts of interest. In essence, privatization in the EU has created, rather than eliminated, various opportunities for graft and bribery.

One technique is for politicians to provide political assistance for a deal between private firms or between a private firm and a government agency, in which politicians, bureaucrats, and firms all reap profits greater than those immediately available without corruption. This political assistance is sometimes "required" because the state still has the right of decision and regulation over certain transactions. Politicians and bureaucrats, often in consultation with private corporations, are those who write the rules.

A second is to privatize but take kickbacks for the award of contracts to the private firms that deliver the services formerly provided by government agencies. The financing still comes from public funds. This arrangement need not lead inexorably to corruption, but it creates opportunities for it. So long as the government retains the right to decide which private firm will deliver what services at what price, there is an opportunity for officials and politicians to collect a bribe. When government contracts constitute a significant part of an economic sector or firm's revenue, or are the key factor on the margin, the firm will have an incentive to pay a bribe, if one is demanded by the bureaucrat or politician. Alternatively, a firm may take the initiative and offer a bribe in order to capture market share. The cost of the bribe can be recovered in fees charged to consumers who have no alternative source of service, perhaps by inflating invoices or by skimping on maintenance and safety procedures.

A third is to infuse the public sector with private "initiatives" and market techniques, often by creating jointly financed projects. Although privatization and the infusion of private financing and business practices into government agencies may seem to bring with them the benefits of economic competition, they can also bring opportunities for bribes. Indeed, when the idea of running government like a business is held as the new operating standard, but the "business" is still that of wielding public authority, agents of the government may see nothing wrong with asking for a commission in order to arrange a particular deal. After all, isn't that what real estate agents do in the private sector? The public official is merely acting on behalf of the seller (the state) and so takes a commission (from the state, in the form of a kickback from the state-funded public works project) to supplement his or her salary. Precisely because it is meant to bring market practices into government and meant to get the government out of the "business" of delivering basic services, privatization also chips away at the ethos of public service.

All of these modes are plagued by a lack of transparency. As has been observed of the United Kingdom's aggressive private finance initiative for government projects, "for such a huge programme, one that has committed the government to more than Pounds 130 bn of forward payments on hundreds of PFI [private finance initiative] projects, with at least the same amount to come from projects in the pipeline, it is remarkable how little genuinely robust data there is on its performance and value."[4] Privatization, rather than increasing transparency as its supporters contend, thus enabling citizens to see what their taxes are paying for, actually decreases it.

These patterns are analyzed in the next three sections. The conclusion discusses the ramifications of these modes on the modalities of corruption and their relationship to patterns of governance.

POLITICIAN-ASSISTED PRIVATIZATION

The former Soviet Union and its successor states are not the only ones in which the privatization process was corrupted. The EU provides its own stellar examples. European politicians have used privatization to reward their political friends, to placate enemies, to obtain party financing, and to otherwise structure the process so that it suits their political interests, not necessarily to craft a market-based, efficient, competitive outcome. The case of the Elf-Leuna deal is exemplary, if not also extraordinary. In 1991, Germany's privatization agency, the Treuhandanstalt, established to sell off the holdings of the former East Germany, was looking for a buyer for the Leuna refinery and Minol network of service stations. As a reunification and campaign promise, Chancellor Kohl had promised a "blooming landscape" in the east, and specifically that his administration would turn the chemical industry complex at Leuna into Europe's most modern refinery. The former "Walter Ulbricht" Chemical Works, as it was known, would be modernized to process ten million tons of crude oil into methanol, liquefied gas, gasoline, diesel fuel, and home heating oil in an environmentally sound fashion; this development would provide 2,250 jobs, and in time the associated industries that would result would provide an additional 10,000 jobs.[5] Given that Europe was already saturated with refineries, that Leuna's inland and eastern location meant that it could only be supplied by Russian oil, that it had 20,000 employees, and that it was a polluting, antiquated complex, the glories of Leuna were a hard sell. The Minol service station network was the real draw: it would enable the buyer to significantly increase market share in Germany. Three consortia at first competed to buy Leuna and Minol: one was led by Elf and Thyssen, the German industrial conglomerate of bribes-for-tanks-sale fame; another was led by BP, and one by Kuwait Petroleum. Elf's was the highest, and winning, bid.[6] It probably didn't hurt that a member of the board of directors of a firm held by one of Elf's partners, DSBK, was on the Treuhandanstalt board of directors.[7] Some analysts also highlight the personal friendship between Kohl and Mitterrand, arguing that Mitterrand was helping Kohl's reelection prospects. Evidence suggests that Kohl and Mitterrand shared a DM 1.2 million payment ($600,000) to their political parties without feeling obliged to know or disclose the donors.[8]

The Treuhandanstalt refused to make details of the sale public, not even the sale price. The only information divulged was that the Treuhandanstalt would make a substantial investment to offset some of Elf's expenses.[9] Later accounts suggest that Elf's consortium offered DM 4.8 billion, in the expectation of DM 2 billion in German subsidies, but even the parliamentary committee investigating the case couldn't figure it out.[10]

A number of years later, when the French judge Eva Joly began untangling the knot of Elf's activities, her investigations began to uncover indications that Elf had used bribes to clinch the deal, particularly in order to receive a commitment of investment subsidies from the Treuhandanstalt. Elf's CEO, Le Floch-Prigent, wanted to obtain DM 2 billion (about $1 billion) in subsidies from the German government for Elf's purchase of the Leuna refinery. According to court documents and his testimony, Le Floch-Prigent therefore "decided to engage in a vast lobbying exercise." He and Alfred Sirven, Elf's director of general affairs, agreed to Sirven's proposal of a $51 million lobbying campaign, which allegedly had among its final recipients two well-placed German officials. Court documents named recently retired parliamentary secretary of state Agnes Hürland-Büning (CDU), who took a post at Thyssen, and former minister of the economy Hans Friderichs (FDP), who was on both Leuna's and Minol's board of directors. The party coffers of then chancellor Helmut Kohl's CDU were also an alleged recipient. Sirven also said he paid a consulting firm headed by Edith Cresson, former prime minister of France, about $600,000 (FRF 3 million), to do a study of economic conditions in eastern Germany.[11] Sirven, under the auspices of Elf, turned to an intermediary, Pierre Lethier, a former French secret service agent with good contacts in Germany. Lethier in turn contacted and allegedly paid about $10 million to Holger Pfahls, then deputy minister of defense (who later went into hiding, in Paris of all places),[12] and about $32 million to Dieter Holzer, who was also involved in the kickbacks and bribes on the sale of German tanks to Saudi Arabia. Thereafter these funds were transferred and transferred and transferred again through a complex array of accounts of different companies, foundations, and persons. The Thyssen connection was used to pay several key Elf figures: it paid a "commission" of $7.8 million (DM 13 million) on June 14, 1993, into an account in Geneva, which was then distributed among various Elf operators. Intermediary André Guelfi received $2.7 million, or about DM 4.5 million; Elf's Sirven received about $2.1 million or DM 3.5 million; Elf's refineries director Alain Guillon received about $1 million or FRF 5.5 million; and Elf's Hubert Le Blanc Bellevaux received about $600,000 or FRF 3.5 million.[13] In the meantime, the EU approved the merger of Elf Aquitaine-Thyssen-Minol, which was how Elf acquired the Leuna refinery and the Minol network (or most of it).[14] The deal was handled at the "highest organisational level" of Elf and involved exchanges of letters between French president Mitterrand and German chancellor Kohl, and also between Elf's CEO Le Floch-Prigent and Chancellor Kohl.[15]

But that's not all. Prosecutors in Augsburg, Bavaria, began investigating Max Strauss, son of Bavaria's dominant political party leader and state prime minister Franz Josef Strauss (of the CSU and also a former defense minister), for having helped Dieter Holzer hide $31 million (DM 50 million) from Elf for CDU and personal accounts, and launder $252,000 (DM 400,000) for himself. Walter Leisler Kiep is also suspected of having received funds illegally.[16] In 1995, Kiep was also linked to a payment for the Thyssen tank deal.[17] Furthermore, Thyssen's "consultant," Agnes Hürland-Büning, was paid extraordinary amounts for trivial "work," and it has been suspected that she acted as a conduit for additional illegal financing and bribes. For example, she assisted Thyssen in obtaining a piece of property at the former border crossing of Dreilinden (between West Berlin and the DDR), which was to be part of a Thyssen industrial project called Europarc Dreilinden. Her job, she testified, was to "clarify" title and ownership aspects of the property. For this, she received an honorarium of about $3.1 million (DM 5 million).

Privatization can spur competition, which actually spurs corruption. The new Leuna refinery would create sharply increased competition for other German oil and chemical firms. To get around the Elf-Leuna deal, a number of consortia proposed various alternative pipelines for the oil, which would have had the effect of rendering Elf's and Thyssen's Leuna investments unprofitable. Evidence suggests that certain individuals were bribed on behalf of Elf-Leuna in order to stop some of the alternative pipeline projects; others were ruled out on environmental grounds by the state governments concerned. Agnes Hürland-Büning testified that for her work in preventing the construction of one alternative pipeline, dubbed Wilhelmshaven, she received about $500,000 (DM 1 million), half paid by Thyssen and half by Elf.[18] Thyssen and Elf, also fearful of competition, used bribery to halt efforts by other consortia to circumvent the competition created by the new Elf-Thyssen Leuna refinery. One might have expected the other consortia to resort to bribery, but it appears they were less well connected politically: the Leuna deal had the full backing of French president Mitterrand and German chancellor Kohl.

The financial trail has been obfuscated, and the German state and federal judiciaries have refused to investigate beyond work that had been done earlier by other prosecutors. As used to happen regularly in Italy, potential cases were sent to the burying ground of a cooperative judiciary, in this case, to Bavaria. The death of one prosecutor, Jörg Hillinger, in a car accident on the very day he was to file papers, may have had something to do with others' reluctance, so too the destruction or "disappearance" of relevant documents and files from both the chancellor's and the Munich prosecutor's office. Kohl's party did all it could to block a parliamentary investigation into kickbacks paid by Elf and Thyssen for the Leuna-Minol purchase.[19] As the investigating parliamentary committee said, "Shortly after the federal election of 1998, and the change in governing party associated therewith, there took place a wide-ranging destruction of documents and erasing of electronic data in the offices of the Bundeskanzler." A study of the situation found that in the period between the election on September 27, 1998, and the transfer of power on October 26, 1998, to Gerhard Schröder of the rival Social Democratic Party (SPD), two-thirds of all electronic data stored in the offices, approximately three gigabytes, were completely erased. The report documents a detailed effort at destruction of evidence, and its author did not believe that this destruction was coincidental, as was alleged by a couple of the CDU witnesses to the committee. Among the documents destroyed were those having to do with the sale of the Thyssen tanks to Saudi Arabia, the Leuna-Minol deal, and the sale of Bundesbahn housing projects. The report concluded that without those documents and others (a secretary of Kohl admitted to destroying 1.4 million pages) it could neither confirm nor deny the suspicions of corruption, nor even the motive behind the destruction of the documents. "If the motivation for this erasing of data lies in the effort to destroy evidence of corruption, we cannot be certain."[20]

Corruption was possible, indeed, highly likely, given that both the French and German governments were using privatization as a political tool for Franco-German relations, for party funding, and for corporate welfare, and given that the process was not subject to public scrutiny. Furthermore, the sale of German state assets to a French state-owned firm was occurring in politico-economic systems in which the market seldom determined merger and acquisition outcomes. In "coordinated market economies" such as those of France and Germany, firms and the state tend to rely more on inside contacts, interlinked groups of overseers, and the private exchange of information.[21] A case in point is former minister of economics, Dresdner Bank and Airbus CEO, Dr. Hans Friderich, who had been convicted of tax evasion in relation to the Flick affair (see chap. 2). A year later (1988) he was appointed chairman of the supervisory board of Airbus, then in 1991 also became a consultant to the investment bank Goldman Sachs, which drew up the contract for the sale of Leuna and Minol, and then in 1992 became an "adviser" to Elf. In the next three years, he was paid more than DM 1.6 million for "restructuring" the Minol corporation, ending the contracts that Minol had signed with other companies in the past, and advising Elf in its relations with the Treuhandanstalt, various German federal ministries, various German state governments, the federal antitrust office, and the European Commission, with respect to the investments to be made in Leuna. That is not all. In 1992, Friderich was also elected head of the board of directors of Minol and the Leuna-Werke AG and was involved in negotiations with the Treuhandanstalt over Leuna's sale.[22] Although that level of conflict of interest may seem extreme, it was the norm in Germany's coordinated market economy. Arranging a deal such as Elf-Leuna, with its attendant commissions, bribes, and kickbacks, was within the prevailing politico-business culture of the two countries. The enormous German taxpayer–financed subsidy to the Leuna refinery and the enormous French taxpayer–financed investment commitment by Elf illustrate "a political and business culture that encouraged and endorsed the payment of millions of dollars in *Schmiergelder* (bribes) to ensure contracts for government-supported industry" and to ensure financing for the dominant political parties.[23]

In addition, the Elf-Leuna sale occurred in a context in which the necessary networks for corrupt transactions already existed. The men who had been involved in several of Germany's major corruption cases were still around; so too were their counterparts in France. Karlheinz Schreiber, Dieter Holzer, Holger Pfahls, Walther Leisler Kiep, and Max Strauss all resurfaced in the investigations as entrepreneurial brokers in the illicit deals. On the German side, the same shell company, Delta International Establishment, that was used for bribery in the Thyssen tank case and in the Airbus sales to Canada, was used in the Elf-Leuna case. And through the intermediaries with whom Elf and the Germans were ac-customed to dealing, other accounts could easily be accessed.[24]

Privatization in Italy, not surprisingly, also went awry. Italy produced the spec-tacular case of Enimont, in which, first, bribes were paid to all political parties to bring about the merger of the chemicals division of ENI (the state-owned utility company) and Montedison, a private firm. Then, a few years later, when the politicians behind the Enimont deal decided the marriage hadn't worked, they backed Montedison's CEO Raul Gardini into a corner, with the help of a corrupt judge in Milan.[25] Gardini was compelled to pay approximately ITL 150 billion (about $100 million) to the governing political parties so that they would approve the divestiture. (The technical details required the state to give a "favorable regu-latory decision permitting the sale of the shares held by the banks.")[26] The parties made it financially feasible for Gardini to sell his Enimont shares, by having ENI buy them for $500 million more than financial analysts observed they were worth. Nevertheless, Gardini committed suicide the morning he was to be interrogated; no politician has served time for demanding and accepting the bribes.

Privatization was taking place in a context in which the political parties were accustomed to using public funds, public enterprises, and public decisions as means of generating funding for the parties. Thus, as court documents note, it was clear that decisions by ENI's board of directors were "following instructions coming from the political world."[27] These were not just general cues about policy direction but specific instructions about discrete actions, including precise pay-ments to political parties via their offshore and Swiss bank accounts.[28] Illegal party financing was so common that the Socialists had a *sistema Troielli* (named after its manager, Gianfranco Troielli) of foreign firms and bank accounts rang-ing from Hong Kong to Liechtenstein by way of the Cayman and Channel Islands for collecting, transferring, and laundering kickbacks.[29] It was a ready-made tool, easy to redeploy for the illegal proceeds of privatization. Privatization Italian style fit the contours of preexisting practices. After the board of ENI forced CEO Gar-dini of the privately held Montedison to either sell all his shares in Enimont or buy all of ENI's, something Montedison could not afford, Gardini reached the conclusion that, in the words of his adviser Carlo Sama, "he was about to lose the game; he realized in particular that the real power of the political system was much stronger than the entrepreneurial logic of which he was an expression. . . . Gardini realized he had to accept walking in step with the political party system."[30]

On a smaller scale, as soon as word got out in Italy that garbage collection would be privatized, a major private firm contacted the Naples politicians whom it knew would determine the contract award. "Everyone knew that the planning and the possible execution of big projects in Naples passed exclusively through the 'imprimatur' of these men."[31] Market decisions would not be left to the market, precisely because politicians were deciding whether there would be a market, and who could enter it. Despite privatization, despite the drive toward the Single Market of the European Union, decisions were still being made the traditional way.

Ireland's effort to begin opening television and radio to private enterprise was immediately corrupted. In 1989, Ireland's minister of communications, Raymond Burke, solicited and received a political "donation" from a private radio firm after he issued a directive limiting the fees that the national radio service could charge private companies for use of its transmission lines; the amounts were considerably lower than what the state-owned firm had hoped to charge.[32] The state-owned firm had a statutory mandate to maximize its revenues. Whereas the minister of communications had earlier agreed with the state radio firm that an annual access fee of IR £252,000 ($388,000) was reasonable and would help maximize potential revenue, Burke's new directive reduced this annual amount to a mere IR£ 35,000 ($54,000). He was paid IR £35,000 for using his power of office to benefit one private firm, Century Communications Limited. Other fees were also reduced, such as maintenance, one-off installation, and the like. In addition, Burke ordered the state broadcasting company itself to purchase the equipment that the private firm needed "to broadcast its signal." A year after having accepted a "donation" from the private firm that won the first private broadcasting contract, Burke also promoted legislation to reduce the amount of advertising revenue the state firm could earn, expecting this strategy to redound to the benefit of private firms. Burke, as communications minister, said this was part of the trend toward "relaxing the state monopolies which existed in the broadcasting sector, and allowing greater competition."[33] He had merely imported standard business practices, such as performing quid pro quos for friends, into the government.

Many of the corruption cases in France involve the privatization of services. To take but one example, in the region around Paris (the Île-de-France) a firm that was the "major beneficiary of the policy, begun in 1988 by the Regional Council, of privatising the heating systems of schools," gave kickbacks to Jacques Chirac's Gaullist party (the RPR). The linkage was facilitated by the fact that the firm was the heating subsidiary of the major public works firm Lyonnaise des eaux, which was directed by the former general secretary of the Gaullist party, Jérôme Monod. In a related case, a private financial institution specializing in the financing of local government initiatives (possibly thanks to decentralization) gave kickbacks to the local Gaullist party.[34] As the next section shows, when the transfer of ownership is complete, the subcontracting process can still be corrupted.

SUBCONTRACTING OF GOVERNMENT SERVICES AS PART OF PRIVATIZATION

A lucrative and controversial example of the subcontracting of government service delivery and the corruption thereof is in the area of water privatization. An official at the European Bank for Reconstruction and Development stated that "water and its infrastructure are the final frontier for private investors to invade."[35] And invade they have, and at the behest of politicians benefiting from kickbacks on the privatization of water delivery, distribution, and treatment, and swept away by the idea that privatization cures economic and political ills. The EU itself is pushing water privatization globally and promoting competition in water privatization everywhere but France (which, no surprise, has no foreign firms with water concessions operating within its borders, despite the fact that 80 percent of its water services market is being run by private firms). One example of the EU's enthusiasm for water privatization: through its eastern European expansion program, PHARE, the EU paid PricewaterhouseCoopers over $700,000 to assess the bids for water system privatization in Sofia.[36] The firms most likely to win the bids are also the firms that have been involved in graft and bribery in western Europe and other parts of the world.

Clearly economic statecraft is involved: the world's three largest water companies are European: Veiola Environnement (formerly Vivendi Environnement, which was formerly Compagnie générale des eaux), Suez (a merger of Compagnie de Suez and Lyonnaise des eaux), and RWE. The former two are French, the latter German.[37] In view of the EU's competitive advantage and market strength, it makes economic sense that it should push water privatization. But in view of the subcontracting process's vulnerability to corrupt transactions, the EU's policy does not bode well for good governance.

Privatization is supposed to rid the world of inefficient, poorly managed, and corrupt municipal water services. To quote a World Bank official, John Briscoe, contracting out the service to a private firm is beneficial in that "issues that have long been submerged will be brought into the glare of public scrutiny: what is the service level to be provided? How will it be monitored? What will be paid for the service by whom?"[38] Yet, were advocates to look at privatization in France, they might be forced to change their optimistic assessment. It is not necessary to invoke third-world horror stories in order to raise doubts about water privatization.[39] In the reputed bastion of democracy, public officials and politicians have limited the public debate on privatization of water services, not allowed public comment on the setting of rates or types of services, evaded the oversight commissions or staffed them with interested supporters, and taken kickbacks on the contracts (not to mention had their houses remodeled). As to public oversight, once the water system is privatized, the public has no right to see the financial reports of the firms that have the water monopoly in their area. As Britain has found with its "private finance initiatives," efforts to study the efficiency and value for money of such projects "rapidly crash into issues of commercial confidentiality."[40]

To entice private firms to purchase state firms, the government may cover the costs of making state assets economically sound before sell-off. In cases of privatizing the delivery of services, the state may guarantee a minimum revenue or even profit level to a firm. In addition, many privatized sectors are those for essential services and resources, such as water, roads, and utilities. If a private firm goes bankrupt or otherwise fails, the government is virtually compelled to step in. In many cases, the private firm faces no real budget constraint—it can leave the state holding the bag. When the privatized water system in Adelaide, Australia, run by a consortium of the French firm Vivendi and the then British firm Thames, supplied the city with foul water and foul smells, the government stepped back in and bailed out the consortium. There are seldom hard budget constraints for major privatization projects, even though such constraints are touted as a major reason for privatizing government-provided services.

Grenoble, France, has experienced taxpayer bailouts of privatization schemes.[41] Following on the heels of decentralization, the Gaullist mayor of Grenoble, Alain Carignon, privatized the water system by contracting with Lyonnaise des eaux, the firm whose CEO had been general secretary of the same party as that of the Gaullist mayor, the RPR. The mayor collected kickbacks for his party and all others on the municipal council and left residents with a sharp rise in water bills. The Greens refused the kickback and eventually were able to get the case investigated. Water experts note that overbilling "is a generalized practice" and includes the cost of the kickbacks to politicians. The water company was later found by the courts to have overcharged consumers through the use of fraudulent accounting techniques.[42]

Consistent with government bailout of privatized firms, in 1996 the new Grenoble city council "remunicipalized" the water system by creating a firm that was 51 percent owned by the city and 49 percent owned by Lyonnaise des eaux (now Suez-Lyonnaise). This firm immediately subcontracted with a firm wholly owned by Suez-Lyonnaise, while the city council had to cover more than FRF 30 million in debt from the original contact that Carignon's council had set up. The city council also conceded to the Suez-Lyonnaise subsidiary most of its dividends from the joint-venture firm, to cover supposed losses incurred by Suez-Lyonnaise in the original contract. The losses included the kickbacks. When courts eventually declared all the contracts null and void, Grenoble created a wholly owned government agency to operate its water system.[43] Suez-Lyonnaise barely suffered: "Two (replaceable) executives spent time in prison, the illegal entry fees were repaid to the company, no real losses were made during the period."[44] The firm also was not barred from work elsewhere.

With the Single Market officially in place and plans for the euro well under way, a subsidiary of the French water firm Vivendi nevertheless paid the mayor of Milan a $2 million bribe in 1998 on a $100 million contract to construct a water treatment plant, as part of Milan's privatization plans. Vivendi thus beat out twelve other competitors. The mayor was a member of Silvio Berlusconi's party, Forza Italia. The French manager responsible for the bid had said he had "excellent contacts" with the parties in Milan's governing coalition and was predisposed to pay up to ITL 4 billion ($2 million) to obtain the contract.[45] The mayor has been sentenced to three years in prison for taking the bribe.[46] This corruption cannot be blamed on Mitterrand or Democrazia Cristiana era politics; it is the regrouping of forces for corruption that is finding new venues, and they are in privatization.

Waste management is another lucrative and corrupt area of privatization. In Germany, there have been cases of corruption that involved privatizing government services. In Cologne, Norbert Rüther, local head of the Social Democratic Party (SPD) took bribes in exchange for the award of a construction contract worth more than EUR 400 million ($465 million). A waste management construction firm, Steinmüller, co-owned at the time by businessman Helmut Trienekens and the German utility conglomerate RWE, paid Rüther and several other SPD politicians who were in charge of the award decision in order to win the contract for building a massive waste incinerator plant. Investigations indicate that Steinmüller deposited about EUR 12 million ($14 million) in Swiss bank accounts as bribe payments between 1994 and 1998. Only about EUR 420,000 ($490,000) were recovered.[47] These funds were divided into small-enough amounts to avoid having to publish donor names and then given to a set of party activists, who in turn gave them to the SPD. Those contributions were tax deductible. Although the national SPD leadership has sought to argue that the Cologne scandal is an isolated incident, not at all like the vast network of illegal financing that the CDU/CSU operated under Helmut Kohl, its claim is not convincing.[48] At least forty party activists were involved, and the former regional SPD leader from 1998 to 2001 and close adviser of Chancellor Schröder, Franz Müntefering, was implicated. Müntefering was SPD general secretary from December 1999 to September 2002, and in 2004 became chairman of the SPD. Given that Cologne is the center of the SPD's power in the state of North Rhine-Westphalia, it is possible that the SPD leadership knew of the bribes.[49] It is also plausible that some of the SPD officials implicated in the scandal saw the contracting out of a public service to be a fairly easy target for kickbacks. And it may be indicative of a political culture that sees the use of state resources as a "legitimate" means of

obtaining party financing and of minimizing the disruptive effects of competition between firms.[50]

POLITICAL PATRONAGE THROUGH PRIVATE FIRMS

It has been argued that privatization prevents politicians from stuffing state firms
with employees who work for the politician instead of working for the state
agency. But does it? In Europe, private firms sometimes take on fictitious employees as partial payment for the award of a contract. Usually these employees
are political party activists, even politicians, who do nothing at the firm and are
thus able to work full time for a political party. The Paris housing office, under
the leadership of RPR activist Jean-Claude Méry, hired, in his words, "an impressive number of elected officials, diverse and varied, on the right or left, seconded,
at the demand of [Chirac's right-hand man] Michel Roussin [who had previously
been a consultant to the president of Compagnie générale des eaux, Jérôme
Monod, who was a close friend of Chirac's], in all sorts of firms, large or small,
guaranteeing them a salary and thus ensuring that these men or their spouses
could work for the RPR without other cares." He gave several examples, referring
to a firm that specialized in repairing exterior walls: "it was the contracts that we
gave them . . . which allowed [us] to have [our men] employed by them."[51] A firm
connected to Charles Pasqua (RPR, sometime minister of the interior) paid the
salary of Méry's secretary. That same firm subcontracted with Compagnie générale des eaux.[52] The privatization of government services did not put an end to
party patronage; at best, it merely made it illegal.

QUANGOS AND PUBLIC-PRIVATE PARTNERSHIPS

Parapublic agencies and public-private partnerships, also called quangos (for
quasi nongovernmental organizations), have become the means of financing and
service delivery for many government services. The catch with this "new public
management" concept is that it leads to the "hollowing out of the state" through
subcontracting and the formation of multiple private-public partnerships. It
balkanizes the state, rendering control, including audits, much more difficult. It
creates a situation in which the state is not sure what it "owns" anymore, and
where property rights are unclear, corruption thrives. As Italian prime minister
Amintore Fanfani said of the proliferation of parapublic agencies in Italy at the
end of the 1950s, "the public administration is really a clandestine organization,

no one knows anything about it." Another observer suggested it was the "only true Italian forest."[53]

Quangos can cover everything from hospital cafeteria services to campgrounds to marketing firms for weapons. They tend to lead to conflict-of-interest problems, to kickbacks and retro-commissions on sales, to nepotism, and other ills. They more easily escape official audits, because they may fall under the audit thresholds, and even if they are audited, the applicable standards are uncertain. Many quangos in Britain involving private finance initiatives (PFIs) escape audit merely by dint of the proliferation of quangos and limited staffing at audit agencies. Of 583 such initiatives to finance school construction, only 8 underwent any independent audits by the National Audit Office. A union audit report in 2003 found that British PFI schools were characterized by higher operating costs as a result of poor insulation and other construction features, higher financing costs than if the local government agencies had borrowed the funds, shoddy construction, unbudgeted-for classroom furniture, and the occasional bankruptcy of the private "partner," which would leave towns without schools and the government holding the bag.[54]

France's SOFREMI (recall chap. 1) illustrates how quangos can be easily diverted from their legitimate purposes. Established in 1985 under the Ministry of the Interior to promote the sales of police weaponry and related internal security equipment to foreign countries, SOFREMI was owned in part by the French state (35 percent) and in part by weapons companies such as Thomson SA, Alcatel, and Aérospatiale. According to some observers, when Charles Pasqua became interior minister in 1986, "a clique of gunrunners soon assumed control of the organization" and retained it at least until 1997.[55] One of those "gunrunners" was Pasqua's contact Pierre Falcone, who became "the sole broker for Sofremi" in contract negotiations.[56] SOFREMI usually gave commissions in the range of 5–10 percent of sales to its brokers; Falcone is alleged to have received sums much higher, some of which seem to have gone to Falcone's "friends." The CEO who took over in 1997 said, "I have the impression that Falcone paid everyone over the years." Given the amounts involved in sales, even the 5–10 percent commissions were substantial. At 10 percent, a sale of arms to Colombia for $28 million (concluded in 1993) would have generated $2.8 million for the broker.[57] According to judicial and other investigative records, Falcone was able to use the parapublic agency as a cover for his own personal arms deals and other operations, and, evidently, with the cooperation of those responsible for SOFREMI (the CEO and the minister of the interior). Falcone's weapons deals were sometimes anything but merely domestic security weapons for policing agencies; they included missiles, tanks, and landmines, and, contrary to the mission of SOFREMI, they were not even French made. As covered in chapter 1, one of those personal deals involved illegally selling arms to Angola.[58]

Conflicts of interest also surfaced when President Mitterrand's adviser Jacques Attali earned over FRF 1 million ($200,000) as adviser to Falcone at SOFREMI. Another, Bernard Poussier, the vice president of SOFREMI, in 1997 at the end of his term allegedly accepted over $100,000 from Falcone.[59] Still another intermediary and friend of sometime interior minister Charles Pasqua, Étienne Léandri, "earned" FRF 21 million ($4 million) and gave half of that amount to an organization founded by a friend of Charles Pasqua.[60] The public aspect of the agency was turned to private uses, an all-too-common occurrence.

Contracting out the Contracting-out Process

European governments have been establishing programs and legal bodies not only to contract out the building of infrastructure or the providing of a particular service (say, hospital meals), but also the planning, financing, building, and operating of "public" services. In France, these are known as *marchés d'entreprise des travaux publics* (public works markets), and they have proved popular with those interested in collecting kickbacks or engaging in other corrupt activities. For instance, in 1990 the Île-de-France region around Paris decided to renovate two hundred of its schools and to build seventy new ones, at a cost of about FRF 20 billion ($4 billion). According to one official under investigation for corruption of the renovation project,

> rather than consign the management of the work to its school facilities and planning office, the region "externalized" it and consigned it to Patrimoine Ingénierie.
>
> Such a system owes nothing to chance. It allows firms, individuals and agencies to escape the eventual control of the administrative services of the region. The technical steering was consigned to Patrimoine-Ingénierie under the supervision of political "pilots" who watched over the awarding of public contracts. The result was that two-thirds of the contracts went to the major construction firms and the last third to regional firms. Curiously, no firm external to the region participated in the tendering process. That partition/division [of contracts] was known in the regional assembly.

When a reporter asked the official if he felt any pressure to say nothing, he said, "not real pressure, but surveillance. In fact, the politicians were convinced that there would not be any follow up, because, to the extent that the system had always functioned that way, there was no reason that it stop. They had a sentiment of impunity."[61]

In southeastern France, another regional council created a parapublic consulting and finance firm (Société d'économie mixte, or SEM) for its school renovation plan. It too became a locus of illegal party and personal financing through kickbacks.[62] Meanwhile, in Paris, parapublic agencies allowed Jean-Claude Méry, the entrepreneur of Paris's public housing office, to rig the bidding for public contracts. He hired a private consulting firm to review and adjust the offers various firms made so that the outcome was the one he desired. The firms did not complain, because he was careful to ensure that everyone got work in their turn.[63]

As part of privatization and decentralization, regional councils in France have been granted the power to delegate the analysis of procurement tenders to a *bureau d'études* (consulting firm), such as Patrimoine Ingénierie. In the Île-de-France region, the firm acted as an intermediary between construction firms and the elected regional politicians. There is also a *commission des marchés* (procurement market commission) for the region, which assesses the files that have been evaluated by the consulting firm. In a number of cases, the director of the consulting firm, Patrimoine Ingénierie, participated in the work of the regional evaluation commission, even though such directors were not allowed to be involved at that stage. Predictably, "the commission, whose politically pluralist composition is charged with discouraging all manipulation, decided on the basis of its [that is, the Patrimoine Ingénierie's] analyses."[64] From 1990 to the end of 1994, Patrimoine Ingénierie had a "quasi-monopoly" on the planning and contracting process. According to witnesses, the consulting firm was "in flagrant violation of the procurement rules." Among the obvious violations were frequent use of the negotiated procedure (40 percent of cases) and frequent use or abuse of the restricted procedure.[65] Both procedures evade open, competitive bidding. In the negotiated procedure, the contracting authority invites contractors of its choosing to discuss the project and then awards the contract to its preferred contractor. The restricted procedure allows the agency to bring in a firm, during the contract review phase, that hadn't been in the initial group. Also, France allows an agency to favor certain firms in order to shore up competition. Thus, a member of the president's cabinet of the regional council could legally suggest to a firm that it submit its candidacy for a project on the very day of the commission's meeting, which was a month past the official closing of the call for tenders. Sometimes contracts were actually awarded before they were passed to the legal control service, which must vet and approve of the contract award, and sometimes before the meeting of the commission des marchés.

The United Kingdom's version of this contracting out of the contracting process has been to create a public-private firm (51 percent private, 49 percent public) called Partnerships UK, which is said to help the public-private partnerships (PPPs) expand investment opportunities and exploit assets more efficiently.

It is meant to help "public bodies on specific PPP transactions, aiming to improve the process of planning, negotiating and completing PPPs."[66] In essence, the state, to get more "value for money" out of public-private partnerships, created yet another one, which acts as a management consulting firm to, and investor in, PPPs (which themselves are funded through investments from consortia of public agencies and private firms). Launched in late 1999 as a wholly owned firm of the UK Treasury, Partnerships UK went parapublic in 2001 and has expanded its remit to include overseas consulting work involving other countries' PPPs. As yet, corruption strictly defined has not surfaced, but a host of other problems have: the lines between investors, firms, and public agencies have been blurred; public money is used to generate profits for specific private firms (the select investors); and it is unclear who has auditing authority over Partnerships UK or its projects. Public access to the records of Partnerships UK is not clear. Such conditions create a fertile environment for corruption.[67]

Partnerships UK is also a study in conflict of interest. Of the nine firms that constitute the private shareholders, five have directors who had served or still serve in the British government or in the Bank of England, Britain's central bank.[68] Typical is shareholder Abbey National Treasury Services PLC. Its chairman, Lord Terrence Burns, had been chief economic adviser to the Treasury and head of the Government Economic Service from 1980 until 1991, when he became permanent secretary to the Treasury Ministry, a post he held until 1998. More recently, Lord Burns has been a nonexecutive director of Legal and General Group PLC (1999–2001) and chairman of the National Lottery Commission (2000–2001). He is also a member of the House of Lords Economic Affairs Select Committee, appointed a life peer when he stepped down from the Treasury in 1998. But the clever aspect of Partnerships UK is that its mission winds up justifying conflict of interest: one of the primary goals of PPPs (and private finance initiatives) is to enable individuals to invest in and profit from government-sponsored projects and services. For the government to profit as well, it makes sense to have on board investors who know how government operates and thus have the expertise to become advisers on the public-private partnership boards as well as on the consulting and investment firm for PPPs, which is also a PPP: Partnerships UK.

Privatization of Public Ethics

In a country that has relied more on a sense of public ethics to minimize corruption than on rules and prosecutions, the merging of a public agency and a private business risks replacing public service ethics with the standards of private business practice. This prospect has become evident in the UK: "the new agencies are monopolies, with autonomy, and might spend more money on themselves."[69] Two large quangos were targeted by the House of Commons Public Accounts Committee for inappropriate expenditures and dubious management; the report decried the general decline in standards of ethics in public and parapublic agencies.[70] For example, the parapublic Welsh Development Agency allowed its executives free use of its cars for private purposes. Granting executives access to a company car is standard practice in the private sector; it is not in the public. Another scandal was the large payments, up to $300,000, given to laid-off or fired employees. Again, this practice probably would not raise too many eyebrows in the private sector, but it has not been a generally accepted one in the public sphere.[71] Aggravating these tendencies has been the fact that "Britain lacks a formal system of law for public authorities and the 'opportunistic pragmatism' in setting up many governmental bodies on various and unpredictable bases . . . has been the result. Even these bodies' basic authority varies considerably, let alone the rules or customs of their work."[72]

In Britain, government's immersion in business development plans with the private sector has led to a confusion of ethics, in addition to instances of corruption. Private finance initiatives, in which private contractors put up most of the financing for public projects, have seen extensive profiteering in some sectors (schools, prisons) and more costly, poorly built projects as a result.[73] In the city of Doncaster, for instance, a city government initiative for development, called Doncaster 2000, led to investigations of city officials and the developer for improper conduct. As the press commented, "Gifts and hospitality can be seen from two quite different viewpoints: out of order under strict public interest codes or part of the way that business operates perfectly legally in its own world."[74] Another commentator stated that "the phrase 'conflict of interest' doesn't do the job, either. Rather, there is a community of interest between politicians and executives so lost in free-market ideology that the distinction between the regulated and the regulator has become all but meaningless. They are comrades—'partners,' to use the cant of new Labour and the old Conservatives—in the struggle to centralise power, privatise services and conduct public business in private."[75] Although that structure in itself may not be corrupt, it provides the opportunity for corruption.

A civil servant or government bureaucrat can become infused with an entrepreneurial spirit that turns to corruption. This prospect certainly occurred in the case of Jean-Claude Méry. In charge of the public housing office of Paris, and also an activist in Chirac's party, the RPR, he saw market and revenue possibilities where others had not. Moreover, he thought that, because the kickbacks he collected from the contracts his agency awarded amounted to "only" 1.5–2 percent, he "wasn't in the middle of falsifying prices."[76]

The entourage of Charles Pasqua (French Interior Minister 1986–88, 1993–95) also got into the entrepreneurial spirit of public-private partnerships. When Pasqua was president of his departmental government—the wealthy Hauts-de-Seine, adjacent to Paris—he created a parapublic agency called Coopération 92 (the number of the *département*), with the participation of what seems a "who's who" of corrupt deal makers in France and overseas: Elf-Aquitaine, Bouygues, Lyonnaise des eaux, and Compagnie générale des eaux. Coopération 92's purpose, to create public works programs in Africa, was financed by the local taxpayers at about $14 million a year.[77] In 1991, Elf sold a parcel of land in Hauts-de-Seine to a firm, Thinet, which then sold it six days later to Coopération 92 for almost 50 percent more. Thinet was headed by Bruno Guez, the director of Coopération 92. Allegations are that the extraordinary difference in price, totaling FRF 95 million or about $19 million, went into political and corporate pockets. At least $12 million landed back in the personal accounts of Elf directors. The 50 percent higher sale price was based on a decision by the city council, taken the evening before the sale, to rezone the land for office buildings. The city council was headed by an André Santini, who is the brother of one of Thinet's directors, Dominique Santini. André Santini was also on the board of directors of Coopération 92. Thinet was granted 30 percent of the rights to develop the property, and a subsidiary of Compagnie générale des eaux was granted 40 percent. And thanks to the zoning change, the buildable surface tripled. In court, Thinet's Bruno Guez admitted that if they hadn't paid commissions to Elf officials, they would not have been granted the sale. And just like real estate agents in legal transactions, the Elf officials commented that they could earn good (albeit illegal) commissions from the deal.[78] The entrepreneurial spirit of the French elite was not lacking; it was just misdirected.

PRIVATIZING CORRUPTION

In 1999, Philippe Jaffré, CEO of the by then privatized Elf, declared to a parliamentary committee investigating corruption in the oil industry that "for its part, Elf does not use corruption and Elf condemns it."[79] Yet in 2002, that same CEO was being grilled by the French judiciary about Elf's payments of more than $140 million to Nigerian leaders for their permission to construct a refinery. Jaffré later took his business practices to privatized Alstom, as CFO. In 2004, Alstom was on the verge of bankruptcy, and the French government was negotiating with the European Commission over bailout and restructuring plans.[80]

In the UK, the proliferation of pubic-private partnerships, with private finance initiatives, and the arrival of outright privatization have vastly increased the number of private-sector and parapublic positions that former cabinet and high-ranking civil servants have available to them upon leaving government service.[81] The relationship between government regulators and officials, and the firms they are charged with regulating, appears to have grown closer, more difficult to control, and less transparent. The British state has entered an Alice in Wonderland world of state-market relations. In the name of "value for money" and better use of taxpayers' monies, the government has compelled its agencies to compete with private firms for government contracts and has created a public-private firm whose mandate is to generate profits for investors and to help government agencies exploit opportunities for public-private partnerships. The state competes in the very market it also ostensibly regulates. And public agencies are goaded to develop profitable projects, with the likelihood that one of the main justifications for having a state in the first place, provision of public goods, is dropped in the process. The potential for erosion of ethics, leading to corruption, is enormous.[82]

In Italy, Silvio Berlusconi, prime minister for nine months in 1994, and then from 2001 to 2006, is the poster child of legalized corruption. The obvious conflicts of interest between his business holdings and his position in government have been well documented.[83] His governments made a practice of changing laws to cover his tracks, and he has evaded several convictions for corruption thanks to the statute of limitations. Oddly illustrative of the extent to which Berlusconi has used his public powers for personal ends, in 2003 his government bowed to Berlusconi's deep-seated fear of arachnids by banning the importation of scorpions and poisonous spiders into Italy.[84] In Germany, the major political parties have both been so enmeshed in a series of privatization scandals involving bribery, diversion of public funds, illegal party financing, and kickbacks, as well as personal graft, that they have tacitly colluded to bury potential investigations. Ironically, this is precisely the kind of corruption for which less developed countries such as Thailand and Indonesia are being condemned. Describing corruption in Thailand, political scientist Thittinan Pongsudhirak said, "The biggest business groups are in power, in the cabinet legislating their way to fill up their pockets." As in Italy, the Thai government has made extremely favorable decisions regarding the media holdings of the prime minister. Transparency International has commented that the Thais do not seem to understand the term *conflict of interest;* it could say the same about most Western governments.[85]

Privatization is supposed to reduce corruption by exposing transactions between government and business to public scrutiny, or at least to the scrutiny of competitors. However, the institutional arrangements of privatization can be exploited by opportunistic individuals. It takes only the cooperation of a small number of individuals, well placed, to agree to profit illegally from government–market transactions. Taxpayer scrutiny is notably absent. The demand comes from two directions: politicians wanting campaign and party financing, and firms wanting revenue-generating contracts and market access. The supply also comes from two directions: politicians with discretionary control over administrative levers, including but not limited to the judiciary and to procurement oversight boards; and firms with funds to pay the politicians for their efforts. In a striking number of cases, privatization has merely transferred the locus of corruption so it is more likely to be called corporate fraud. Why? Few firms have a short-term interest in competing in a genuinely competitive market, and many are able, through convoluted accounting schemes and complex stock market, subsidiary, and offshore transactions, to hide their activities from oversight—if not forever, then for long enough to enrich upper management. Italy used to be known for having a price on every government action: government decisions were, illegally, routinely sold to private bidders. Put another way, the market mentality had been brought into all areas of the government, albeit illegally. Now, throughout the European Union (and elsewhere), using market practices to determine government actions and policies has by and large been legalized. Europe has validated Talleyrand's statement: "there is no such thing as corruption; there are only opportunities."

DECENTRALIZATION, DEMOCRACY, AND GRAFT

If I'm not paid, I won't sign papers for anyone.

—Former deputy mayor of Marbella, Spain, Isabel García Marcos

Did the mayor of Lyon and minister of foreign commerce steal his daughter's diary? Would the information therein implicate his son-in-law in a bribery and kickback scheme hatched not long after decentralization in France? Are illegal kickbacks from local public works projects actually income subject to alimony considerations? Do living in a home given to one's mistress by a property developer and then altering the local zoning plan for that developer constitute corruption? Such are the questions European judges have had to address in investigating and prosecuting corruption in local and regional politics.[1]

Decentralization has become an accepted remedy for the perceived and real ills of centralized government. Its advocates, from the European Commission to the OECD to the World Bank, suggest that putting governance in the hands of local authorities creates competition between authorities of adjacent communities, with the expectation that government or administrative competition will lead to better services and economic growth.[2] Local government is also expected to respond better, that is, more efficiently and effectively, to specific local needs. Decentralization is also hailed as a way of bringing transparency to government activities, since local citizens are supposedly best placed to act as watchdogs over their local authorities, as opposed to their trying to keep track of distant central government authorities.

There are countervailing pressures, however. Precisely because local governments can be held directly accountable by citizens for the state of their communities, local governments have a strong incentive to favor local businesses in awarding contracts, thereby foregoing the benefits of forcing price competition among contractors for government services. Hence, any gains from accountability are lost in local preference. Although in the long run these inefficiencies may force the government to increase taxes to pay for increased expenses, elections occur in the short run, and there are few hard budget constraints—central governments tend to bail out local debt.

In turn, the elections, including the much-touted reforms in Italy and France that provide for the direct election of mayors, substantially increase demands for campaign and party financing. If that financing is not forthcoming through legal means, then kickbacks from local public works contracts become a desirable means of supply. These new decentralized arrangements, even when they are inserted into uncorrupt areas, coincide in democracies with new, local elections, which bring with them the demands for financing.

Combining devolution of authority with privatization of service delivery, but not with privatization of the authority to decide who delivers what services, creates opportunities for corruption. Auctioning or awarding public works and service contracts to private firms or licensing private firms as qualified to deliver certain services actually creates incentives for corruption on two sides—by those who supply or contract for the work, and by public authorities or members of a commission who award the contract.

These incentives dovetail with the incentive to favor local businesses over out-of-area firms in awarding contracts. Giving local governments the authority to manage the social and economic development of a territory gives them discretion over whether to deliver services themselves, to privatize (contract out) the delivery, or to not deliver services at all. The third option is electorally untenable, and the first two leave considerable scope for favoritism and corruption. If there are oversight and monitoring commissions, these can be co-opted by the local agencies they monitor. Decentralization's goal of reducing the size and scope of government bureaucracy may facilitate corruption because trust and cooperation, essential elements in any transaction, corrupt or honest, are easier to create in smaller groups. In addition, "the organisation of institutionalised corruption also requires networks,"[3] and networks are more likely to exist at the local level.

An additional countervailing force is that the processes of devolution tend to obfuscate the delineation of public authority, as in which agencies and institutions have "property rights" over the exercise of what aspects of public authority. In the business community, wining and dining potential clients is an accepted way of doing business; providing material incentives to potential clients is as well. What are automobile cash rebates but kickbacks from the manufacturer to the purchaser for having "awarded" the contract to the manufacturer (that is, buying the car from the company)? When taking out a mortgage from a bank, home buyers pay points to obtain lower interest rates. Yet these transactions, considered legal and normal in the private sector, are of dubious legality and morality in the public sector. The proliferation of public-private initiatives and the extensive contracting out of "public" service delivery have inexorably led to questionable and sometimes decidedly corrupt actions on the part of public officials and private-sector firms.

Complexity creates other incentives or opportunities for corruption. Although central government authorities may have the competence and critical mass to evaluate and process public works tender competitions, for which technical details and rules have become extremely complex, smaller regional and local authorities may not. EU directives merely add another dense layer to the applicable regulations.[4] The European solution has been to allow even this function—that of organizing the competitive bid and often that of conceptualizing and designing the project—to be contracted out to consultancies. These *bureaux d'études, società di servizi,* or consultancies can serve as much-needed organizations that perform state-mandated functions in a private-sector context, thus enabling the state to provide "value for money" in its use of public funds. Or they can serve as much-needed focal points for coordinating the illegal rent-seeking activities of firms, politicians, and government officials. What happens may depend on other factors, such as sources for campaign financing, political party competition, the risks attached to corruption, the local economy, and local norms.

The downsizing of the state while supersizing the regulatory requirements leads to pitfalls that the perceptive former mayor of Reggio Calabria describes. As Agatino Licandro states, public agencies use *società di servizi,* which are hybrid public agencies, to organize and process everything, because the local, provincial, and regional governments are incapable of dealing with all the regulations and all the technical requirements of government-approved projects.

> To oversimplify: the State (under the form of state participation) profiting from the fact that the State (under the form of the public administration) is not capable of handling the procedures stipulated by the State (under the form of the government and Parliament) creates [a] "società di servizi" (in reality an emanation of the State). This is what happens, officially and according to legal norms. In reality, it is much worse. . . . In reality there are middlemen linked to the consultancies who arrive in town and explain, "We have the means to enable you to have the financing. Let's be clear: without us you will not succeed in seeing it even with binoculars. The minister who must give the money is ours. We will see him about this. You must simply write up the contract with the conditions that we stipulate and afterwards you can't do any-

thing. We will even specify the conditions protecting your interests. Our lawyers will do that. We pay them well, they are the best. You just must sign here."

If the municipality or provincial government protests, "no harm done: the consultancy, together with the certainty of the financing, moves on to graze in greener pastures."[5]

Italy has never been noted for having a strong, well-functioning administrative apparatus, but the devolution and privatization of government functions have also been problematic in countries with a strong administrative tradition, such as France.

Decentralization in France, Italy, and parts of the United Kingdom was accompanied by much fanfare. In 1982, the Socialist-led French government passed enabling laws to shift much of governance and administration to regional, provincial (called *départements*), and local authorities. In 1970, the Christian Democratic–led Italian government finally enacted legislation provided for in the 1948 Constitution, to establish regional governments in sixteen ordinary regions of Italy (five already had special status). In 1999 the Labour government of the United Kingdom devolved authority to the regions of Wales and Scotland, and reestablished the mayor's office in London. In the 1980s, all three states undertook substantial privatization measures in an effort to reduce state control and involvement in the economy, with the proclaimed intention of increasing economic growth and reducing government spending. Although I discuss privatization in a separate chapter, it is essential to consider its interaction with decentralization. Both phenomena led to the unintended consequence of facilitating corruption at the local and regional levels of government.

Decentralization and the local corruption it can facilitate often have links to national politicians and parties. What appeared to be a case of local party corruption in Milan, involving the director of a state-financed retirement home, turned out to be directly connected to illegal financing of sometime prime minister Bettino Craxi and his Socialist Party.[6] Likewise in France, when local tax inspectors uncovered false invoicing, the payments for which wound up in the regional Socialist Party's coffers, they also discovered that this system was directly connected to the party's financing of François Mitterrand's 1988 presidential campaign. An elaborate scheme of kickbacks from public school construction and maintenance projects around Paris was traced to funding of Jacques Chirac's mayoral and presidential campaigns. Perhaps the biggest surprise in all this was that one of these three prominent politicians—Craxi—was actually prosecuted, found guilty, and sentenced to jail; he fled to Tunisia and died in exile. The investigation of Mitterrand's indiscretions was shut down by his party, in collusion with the parties of the opposition, and to ensure that no one would pay a price, the government promulgated and the parliament passed an amnesty law. Chirac escaped investigation by virtue of a court decision declaring that he could not be prosecuted while president.[7]

This chapter analyses decentralization in France, Italy, and the United Kingdom and then concludes with a discussion of the failure of theory to match practice.

DECENTRALIZATION AND CORRUPTION IN FRANCE

The cases that have come to light in France show that local governance, local administration, and local oversight commissions had the effect of democratizing and decentralizing corruption. No longer was corruption limited to the Paris elite; it was now available in all regions of the country, to all elected officials no matter how humble. French decentralization, with its massive transfers of budgetary authority and expenditures to the local and departmental level, substantially raised the value of holding local office. It also created another layer of elected governance, but one with limited budgetary powers—regional councils. In addition, and ostensibly under the pretense that the representatives of the people would make better watchdogs than technocrats, local and departmental oversight commissions for public works contracts were staffed by elected officials. Yet those same local elected officials needed funds to finance their campaigns and parties, as well as related operating expenses.

Decentralization handed off to ill-equipped local officials far more spending power than they had ever had before. If the Socialist Party, which sponsored the legislation, had wanted to democratize the possibilities for fraud and corruption, they could not have devised a better means than decentralization. The national Court of Auditors (similar to the U.S. Government Accounting Office, or GAO) already had been remarking, in its annual reports, that local government offices were unable or unwilling to manage expenditures responsibly or to follow public works contracting procedures.[8] The court questioned the proliferation of "associations" used by local governments to deliver some public services but that often were the means of evading the detailed rules governing local agencies.

In contrast, from the 1950s until about 1970, virtually all public construction was overseen by a national government agency, the Société centrale immobilière de la Caisse des dépôts et consignations, created in 1954. For school construction, for instance, the particular construction firm was selected by the local government, but the price, the structure, and all the details save aspects of the external appearance were determined by the national ministry. Most of the contracts went to the *grands groupes,* or large construction firms favored by French industrial policy. Because the price of the contract was set at the national level, and because the project was overseen, from initial call to tender up to the final payment to the contractor, by the central state's administrative authority (the departmental prefect), there was little discretion at the local level. This arrangement substantially circumscribed the institutional opportunity for demanding kickbacks. Similarly, because the value of the contract was centrally controlled, firms could not afford and did not need to give large bribes at the local or regional level. Further, before decentralization, there was little local demand for campaign and party finance. At most, local mayors asked the selected firms to make a donation to the soccer club or rest home, or to do some remodeling on the mayor's personal residence.[9]

In 1982, France devolved much of its governance to 26 regions, 100 departments, and 36,763 municipalities. The new arrangements changed the power of the prefect, the state's representative in the departments and regions. Before decentralization, all activities of departments and communes were subject to a priori control and supervision of the prefect. After decentralization, the prefect only exercised ex posteriori control over regions, departments, and communes. Departments and regions received "their own decision-making powers, and their own powers of execution." Local authorities receive tax revenue for which "the tax base is set and the taxes are collected by the state." They may borrow "without having to obtain authorization from any higher authority," although the departmental prefect may rule on the legality of the loan procedure.[10] Loans may not be used to cover previous loans.

Decentralization à la française created vast potential for pork barrel politics, if not also for corrupt practices. Two of its aspects warrant some examination. First, in terms of fiscal decentralization, the new arrangements altered the framework for the collection and distribution of tax revenues, but not in a way that imposed fiscal and performance responsibility on the subnational governments. Whereas in the past such revenues had been collected and spent by the central government through its agencies throughout the country, now local governments and administrations received block grants as well as the direct transfer of some centrally imposed taxes. As a result, local, departmental, and regional governments came to depend "for a significant portion of their revenues on grants based on automatic formulas having nothing to do with the health of the local economy or the soundness of local administration."[11]

Second, and illustrative of the new opportunities for creative local spending, is the way in which the construction and maintenance of public schools, and the financing thereof, were to be done. No level of subnational government was without its potential kickback supply. The *lycées,* or high schools, became the regions'

responsibility; the *collèges,* or junior high schools, became that of the departments; and the cities and towns (the *communes*) had responsibility for the elementary schools. The communes were given the authority to set up their own
zoning plan and to issue building permits; the departments were given control of
the building and upkeep on "public thoroughfares." Local governments were allowed to subsidize local businesses in difficulty, with the result that "communes
were increasingly falling into debt as a result of the defaults of businesses" on approximately 10 percent of the local guaranteed loans. In 1988, the state transferred this authority to departments and regions.[12] The state retained control
over major national highway systems and over the construction and running of
hospitals.

The potential supply was met by a potential demand: given the new governing powers, local, departmental elections had more significance, and an entirely
new layer of government and elections was added: that of the regions, whose representatives were elected every six years.

Symptomatic of the potential for corruption in newly decentralized France is
the system that developed in Grenoble, a major city in the French Alps; it combined all the elements of decentralization, privatization, and democratization.
Known as *le système Carignon,* it was named after the man who became mayor of
Grenoble in 1983 and soon thereafter head of the departmental council. Granted
the power to privatize the delivery of public services by the 1982 legislation, Alain
Carignon created a complex and lucrative system of kickbacks from all municipal public works contracts, whether multi- or single year. The kickbacks were funneled to Carignon himself, to his party (that of the Gaullists—the RPR), and to
all of the other major parties. One of Carignon's assistants, Guy Névache, testified that Carignon told him to "do only like everyone else and ask the firms that
participate in many of the public tenders" for kickbacks.[13] With Névache acting
as coordinator for the mayor, eight construction firms, most of them subsidiaries
of the large national construction firms, agreed on how to divide up the public
works "market" of Grenoble. In return for avoiding the uncertainty and expense
of the competitive bid process, the firms willingly paid for pleasure trips of elected
officials, donated cash to them, and gave kickbacks of 2–5 percent on public
works contracts.

In turn, the political parties on the municipal and departmental councils divided the proceeds among themselves. All political parties but the Greens were
involved. As Carignon noted, because the system benefited all, it permitted him
to "neutralize" his political adversaries. The proceeds sometimes were extraordinary: for a waste water plant, $12 million went to the local RPR-UDF (Gaullist-
liberals) and $5 million each to the opposition Socialist and Communist parties.[14]
For a refuse treatment system and for a new tram line, the contractors paid a 5

percent kickback to the main parties, who divided it among themselves, with 60 percent going to the mayor and his RPR-UDF supporters, 25 percent to the Communist Party, and 15 percent to the Socialist Party.[15] As an elected official stated during interrogation, "There was, effectively, a system of taxes on the firms participating in public works contracting. From 1987 to 1988, the firms, and in the first place the large construction firms, understood that the local governments constituted a huge potential market. . . . I think that this system exists in many other departments, [it is] simply that in Grenoble and [the department of] Isère, the level of political life was too high and it allowed for some slippage."[16] In other words, the main difference between the governance and corrupt practices of Grenoble and other cities in the 1980s and early 1990s was that the Grenoble mayor got caught because of his high-profile politics.

Because these projects had exorbitant costs, one might wonder why, since voters themselves would be paying the bills, elected officials would opt for something that could trigger voter backlash at the next election. The answer is that, first, the contract was structured so that voters would not see the costs until after the election, and, second, the contracts provided substantial payments to all participating political parties, so there was no motive to turn corruption into a campaign issue.

The much-touted capacity of the European Union to force competition on recalcitrant government agencies and hence reduce corruption has been exaggerated. Most local and many regional government contracts come in under the EU thresholds; some are deliberately divided into separate lots so as to evade the thresholds. When they are above threshold, however, they involve sectors that until 1990 were excluded from EU directives.[17] As of 1994, local elected councils managed three-quarters of France's public investments, but only about half of that was subject to competitive bidding. Until a 1993 law, *loi Sapin*, transposed the relevant EU directives, the rules on competitive bidding did not apply to water, garbage, or urban transport.

Even where the EU rules should apply, they are not regularly applied. For instance, in 1986 the elected government for the region Provence-Alpes-Côte d'Azur created a public-private development agency named Semader. One of its projects was to upgrade public schools, and to do so it awarded contracts by special invitation, not by competitive bidding. A firm specializing in prefabricated classrooms won more than FRF 8.5 million ($1.5 million) in contracts that way. Between 1991 and 1998, the same firm won about FRF 33 million ($6 million) in offers for tender, none of which followed an EU requirement of specifying the maximum allowable expenditure.[18] In another case, for the construction of the second phase of the regional office building (approved in 1987), the regional public tendering commission, the Commission des marchés du conseil régional, declared the open tender process a failure. The commission went to the negotiated procedure and awarded the contract to the firm Mistral, which had placed the most expensive bid in the open tender. This case was noted by the regional audit board, which complained that the legal controls were defective. The prefect's office had not examined the case—which was not trivial, costing about $42 million. Though the contract was over the EU threshold for public procurement it did not trigger the application and enforcement of EU rules.

Parties and Decentralization in France

Until 1988, French law prohibited political parties from accepting donations and did not provide for public funding. The only legal source of funding was membership dues. This stipulation drove the search for funding underground, particularly as traditional sources of campaign support, labor unions and the church, weakened. After 1988, a set of laws allowed for limited donations—initially about $4,000 per person and about $40,000 per corporation—and some public funding of candidates and parties.[19] What with important subnational elections taking place, as well as the European Parliament elections, and limited public financing, legal supply could not keep up with demand.

Quick to take advantage of the opportunities for corruption that decentralization provided was the French Socialist Party. Until 1981, the Socialists had been in the opposition at the national level since the Fifth Republic had been established in 1958. Once they became the majority party, they quickly discovered how to use government resources at all levels to sustain their hold on the central government: by exploiting decentralization. The deaths of two construction workers in Le Mans, the inflated invoices of a consulting firm in Marseilles, and the 1988 presidential campaign of Socialist Party candidate and incumbent French president François Mitterrand came together, illustrating the nefarious connection among decentralization, privatization, and campaign finance demands. When Thierry Jean-Pierre, a judge in Le Mans, began investigating the fatal work accidents, he received a phone call suggesting he contact the former secretary of the regional Socialist Party, who would have "revelations" to contribute. The politician in question said it was routine for certain firms to give "commissions" to various consulting firms "in order to obtain public works contracts."[20] There were allegations that in order to make up for the kickbacks, the firms cut expenditures on construction site safety. These consultancies were connected to a firm in Marseilles, which in turn was connected to the Socialist Party. In 1989 in Marseilles an officer with the financial "police," Antoine Gaudino, came across evidence that a local construction firm (and subsidiary of a major national firm) had been paying inflated invoices for the research and consulting services of a firm, Urbatechnic, chosen by the local Socialist-led government. In turn, Urbatechnic sent the funds to the regional Socialist Party, which then, allegedly, funneled them to the national party for François Mitterrand's presidential reelection campaign of 1988, among other expenses. The goal was cryptically stated in a confiscated document: "2 March 1984. Goal of Urba-Gracco: bring money to the Socialist Party, the [membership] dues are no longer sufficient, no direct support from business."[21]

In the Urba case, it was Socialist-led city and regional councils that approved the public works contracts and that picked the firms they were awarded to. It was, indeed, common practice for the governing majority of a city to "force the companies applying for [government] contracts to hire these research organizations [consultancies], which then levies a 'research fee' of 2 to 2.5 percent of the value of the contract."[22] The consultancies were set up to launder the kickbacks the firms were asked to give to the parties awarding government contracts.

Thanks to collusion between the Socialist and Conservative parties, knowledge of the extent of corruption in decentralized France is limited. Where the Socialists had Urba threatening to expose their true colors, the Conservatives had their own "Urba" (Cogedim). The fact that an Urba employee had kept meticulous notes in his appointment book of all his contacts with national-level Socialist Party officials concerning funding meant that a large number of Socialist Party and government ministers could have wound up in an investigating magistrate's office. Nevertheless, the facts of the case are unknown because the investigation was deliberately shut down, the police officer was fired by the interior minister, and the government, with full support of all major parties in the parliament, passed a series of amnesty laws covering party finance crimes committed by politicians. The amnesty laws left vulnerable those politicians who used corruption for personal enrichment. The Conservatives were only too happy to support such laws when it came to light that they too had been actively involved in illegal party-financing schemes.

Nicknamed *arrosage municipal,* the process of financing party expenses through municipal budgets is well entrenched in France. Some of it is legal but dubious: party activists set up an association, and then the party-led municipal council gives it municipal subsidies. Other aspects are illegal but too common to prosecute. "In France, all roads lead to . . . commissions: construction of housing, roads, schools or hospitals, factories or supermarkets. The entrepreneur, in one way or another, passes by the 'caisse.' These practices enable [the party to] establish a veritable war chest." In France, decentralization, and the local and regional elections it entailed, led to the local tenet of, as an elected official commented, "do whatever you can" (*le régime de la débrouillardise*). As the same official remarked, "a businessman friend runs my mailings through his stamp machine, a paper merchant who supports the RPR gives me paper for printing."[23]

In the 1960s and 1970s, national business federations, such as the Metal and Mining Industries and the National Construction Federation, made large donations to the parties. The national businessmen's organization (CNPF) had a central office (Service des études législatives) that gathered funds from its members and donated them to the parties of the right. Decentralization disrupted that system, as regional party federations and local branches sought to fund their own operations first.[24]

After decentralization, those contracts that were put out to "competitive" bids often were rigged in order to finance the local and regional parties' expenses. In the French department of Yvelines, near Paris, three supervisors of various departmental building services advised the regional council of which firms to award contracts to.[25] Most of the businesses involved later went bankrupt or otherwise out of business. One, which did all of its work with the department, admitted that it had to give 10 percent of revenue to the local civil servants. The payments were made in cash in envelopes stashed alongside the road, in a café, and even in the public administration offices. On average, every fifteen days, from 1991 to 1993, it was one envelope of cash containing FRF 3,000–5,000 ($550–900). "If I didn't bring an envelope, I didn't have work," said one businessman. One official protested that the regional council approved more than five hundred contracts each year and processed 145,000 invoices. "How can you check everything?" he asked. By 2001, seventy-four people were under investigation. They evaded the oversight of the regional Competition Commission by making sure that the contracts each totaled not more than $50,000 (which also evaded European Community control).[26] In another case, the accused politicians' lawyers blamed their clients' crimes on decentralization, arguing that the development transferred enormous sums to local councils that hadn't the means to follow the correct procedures.

A newly elected Socialist on the municipal council of a town of about 50,000 said that

> it was surprising, all those oddball customers lining up to come to the mayor's office. We didn't know it would happen like that. One day, some guy came to us saying, "we will give you a car, it's the custom." We refused. When one just got elected on a platform of transparency and morality in political life, one doesn't make concessions. But it is clear that if we had talked to the [party] federation, they would have told us, "shut your mouth and take the car."[27]

Another comments that "it's not a rip-off. It's them [businessmen] who come to us, because they find it in their interest." An architect commented that "firms operate in complete immunity because they 'water' everyone. Moralizing, in the subject of party financing, happens by way of a reform of the public tendering code. Above 180,000 FRF [$36,000] you have to have a public tender. I exposed this to higher ups in the PS [Socialist Party]. They told me to shut up." Contemporary observers noted that "the 'normal' politician is the one who agrees, on the proposal of the regional council, that the maintenance contract for 41 schools in the department be awarded to one single firm. The firm rubs its hands, the regional council also: it collects large sums." A mayor stated that "to be an elected official is to know how to count. It is also to know how to manage one's calendar. The first year, you study the projects; the second, you launch them; the third to the fifth, you inaugurate them. The last year, you don't do anything . . . for fear of being beaten and thus to see your adversary pocket the dividends of the projects."[28]

Those implicated in corruption cases in decentralized France have run the gamut from obscure local and regional politicians and firms to major national party figures, government ministers, and large national firms. Whether the politicians were obscure or household names, the technique used was by and large the same: a bribe, euphemistically called a "gift," given to close a deal with the government. The currency varied: overseas vacations, home remodeling, campaign donations. One businessman gave about FRF 235,000 ($47,000) to the electoral campaign of the vice president of the regional council in exchange for the awarding, in a competitive bid process, of a school roof renovation project. Another business was awarded the building of an elementary school; in exchange, it gave about $120,000 to various persons via the consulting firm owned by the wife of an intermediary. Between 1989 and 1994, that firm processed FRF 8 million ($1.6 million) in bribes.[29] The president of the regional council was also involved.

Another illustration of the complex motives, financial arrangements, and consequences for campaign finance in France is provided by the case of a parliamentary deputy, Michel Noir, who was seeking to become mayor of Lyon. In 1989 he received a "donation" of FRF 1 million ($200,000) for his campaign from one of France's largest construction firms, Bouygues. The donation was delivered about four months after Noir assured Bouygues and its minority partner, another construction colossus, Dumez, that they would be awarded a major construction contract, without competitive bidding, to build a circumferential highway around Lyon. Although Noir claimed he awarded the contract on the basis of the firms' international reputation, the two firms were the only ones invited to bid and oversight boards were ignored, or they conducted their business in secret meetings. A later investigation, by judicial authorities, revealed the total lack of competitive bidding, despite EU directives requiring it. The judge involved in the investigation later remarked on the "uncanny timing" of the electoral campaign, the large donation, and the award of the contract.[30]

In a related incident, Noir's son-in-law (who was the intermediary in the construction contract) was convicted of abuse of public funds for payments he received from firms for services not rendered, including a firm involved in corruption in Grenoble. It was found, although Noir denied it, that much of the funds went, via Panamanian shell societies and a Swiss bank, into Noir's account for his electoral campaigns.[31] These incidents are only a few among many that illustrate how an individual's rise to political power can be traced to the manipulation of private construction firms seeking public contracts.

Privatization facilitated, and may even have encouraged, these corrupt transactions. For instance, the transactions of Grenoble mayor Carignon were handled by the parapublic agencies that he and his local and departmental governments set up. At arm's length from normal civil servant control, these agencies were used to plan, coordinate, and contract out big- and small-ticket development projects and, of course, to collect the "commissions" demanded from contractors. The contractors, accustomed to the French tradition, long institutionalized in France's industrial and governing structures, of state protection and management, did not protest. Coordination, with kickbacks, was more familiar and less costly than competition.

CORRUPTION IN DECENTRALIZED ITALY

In Robert Putnam's famous study of civic culture in Italy, the governing institutions of Lombardy rank high in terms of performance. The cause, according to Putnam, is a healthy civic culture. In contrast, the institutions of the southern regions rank abysmally low.[32] Yet it was in Lombardy's capital city, Milan, considered Italy's financial, publishing, and design, if not also industrial, capital, that the thick web of Italian corruption first was exposed. As a southern newspaper gloated, "Milan: the south without the sun." It was local corruption and its connections to national parties that brought down the First Republic of Italy. And it began with a seemingly ordinary case of corruption: in February 1992, Mario Chiesa, director of Milan's largest public retirement home, was caught taking a bribe of ITL 7 million ($7,000)—partial "payment" from the firm awarded the contract to provide custodial services to the home. The total bribe was double that, or about 10 percent of the contract's value.[33] The contractor, evidently irritated at the high price of the bribe and dismissive of the consequences, had complained to the judiciary that he was being asked to pay for what should have been a competitive bid. Magistrates, led by Antonio Di Pietro and Gherardo Colombo, had been building a case against Chiesa for over a year. Using the contractor as the lure, they snared him. Chiesa's case was not helped by the fact that he had recently tried to reduce the amount of child support he owed his estranged wife, while simultaneously taking on a mistress. His wife challenged his effort to reduce child support by arguing that his wealth was far greater than his official $70,000 a year salary. To prove it, she turned over to the civil authorities copies of records showing his illicit financial holdings and business transactions, which Chiesa had kept at home.

Chiesa, however, was not acting entirely on his own: he had attained the directorship of the retirement home courtesy of his rank in the Socialist Party, which he had attained, in turn, by demonstrating his vote-getting and money-raising abilities. By the time he won the directorship of the local public facility, he was a favored client of the Socialist Party leader and sometime prime minister Bettino Craxi.[34] The flexibility afforded to political entrepreneurs like Chiesa by decentralization provided numerous opportunities for creative political party financing and career building, not to mention personal enrichment. Before decentralization, corruption was not unknown in local government, but the bulk of the evidence indicates that what was most frequent was not outright corruption but patronage: the exchange of material favors for votes.[35]

In terms of its political institutions, by the 1970s Italy would seem to have been a model democracy, with frequent nationwide elections and party conventions, and with the major parties having active branches in each village, town, and city in the country. Italy has devolved power to regional, provincial, and local governments; it holds frequent elections for public offices at a range of levels; and it has an active multiparty system.

The results were not what one expects of a model democratic structure, however. Paradoxically, where inter- and intraparty competition was most intense, so was corruption. Competition among parties and politicians, rather than leading to cleaner politics, led to its further corrosion.[36] The devolution process started in 1970 with elections of representatives to fifteen new regional councils. Political rivalry and reluctance to release vast patronage resources to the regions delayed further decentralization until the late 1970s:

> Henceforth the regions, or the municipalities under regional supervision, could found and staff their own specialist agencies for welfare, run their own subsidy schemes for farmers and artisans, and organize their own co-operatives and nursery schools. They could draw up regional development and land use plans; they could take over the Chambers of Commerce. . . . The Southern [regions], for example, acquired a role in industrial planning for the South in 1975; all of them were expected to

run the youth employment scheme in 1978. By 1980 the regions were spending 18 per cent of the national budget, and had become the main bodies responsible for health and social services.

They also gained "real powers of patronage and policing" by virtue of their new control over the licensing of public establishments and services, such as restaurants, taxi drivers, and the like.[37]

With every administrative post and every elected office infiltrated by patronage-seeking and corrupt politicians, decentralization merely provided more spaces into which the parties and their rent-seeking behavior could flow. Decentralization increased corruption because it increased the number of people who had to be brought into the system through bribes. As one regional official said to the head of a parapublic consulting firm, while negotiating for a higher kickback amount, "But you know, sir, that I also have to pay the Coreco [regional audit committee]?" Indeed, bribing the Court of Auditors cut into the funds that politicians could give to their political party in order to maintain their standing. When Agatino Licandro became the newly elected mayor of Reggio Calabria, capital city of Italy's poorest province, he was told that his "job as mayor was to distribute the money [from kickbacks] to the municipal councilors." Licandro had been inserted into a very complex system of kickbacks, one feature of which was to prevent "the municipal councilors from becoming discontent. . . . Money in politics became a means of establishing and consolidating oneself. I understood that I had to do this. It was connected with the job of the first citizen [mayor]."[38]

Every holiday brought with it the obligation of the directors of public agencies to give resources to politicians, who "wanted money for the additional expenses of representation." For those who directed the agencies, holidays were "a calvary, a crucifixion worse than that of Jesus Christ." As the number of politicians increased exponentially with decentralization, so too did the demand for resources. Local politics in Italy had long had the tenor of an arms race, with candidates outbidding each other in offering patronage and other favors to voters and to the local notables who controlled blocks of voters.[39] Decentralization merely increased the number of participants in the race.

Campaign Costs

Funds for campaigns were also critical to survival. Local politicians who had no largesse to distribute risked losing their supporters and hence reelection. Kickbacks were the currency of power in the parties—the means to advancement, the means to strengthening a faction over its rivals.

Italy was a recipe for corruption: decentralization coincided with campaign finance laws that severely limited corporate contributions to political parties and prohibited contributions from public and parapublic agencies. With decentralization of the management of government services came new layers of elected governments, thus increasing the need for campaign financing at the local and regional levels. In most localities, the parties looked to kickbacks on public works, and the system was such that no one party stood to gain more from being a turncoat than it did from participating. New public works projects were judged on their kickback potential, not on their public value. The new Milan metro system was a case in point. So, for example, "the traditional Milanese parties (DC, PSI, PCI, PRI, PSDI) had the opportunity of guaranteeing themselves a different channel of financing with regard to that which was foreseen by the [campaign finance] laws."[40] As Bettino Craxi admitted, "the Milan metro was an opportunity for all the parties to collect funds."[41] Furthermore, decentralization was grafted onto a system already rife with patronage, and with parties and their internal factions vying for control of parapublic agencies, ministries, and subministries.[42] Politicians and party activists had already institutionalized norms of heavy political intervention in the economy and society, norms of using state agencies for explicit political gain such as building reliable blocs of voters and their handlers. As Valerio Bitteto, a Socialist, noted, public agencies were meant to produce votes. When he was appointed to the board of directors of the national energy corporation (Enel), the party leader, Bettino Craxi, told him, "don't just sit there warming the seat"; he was expected to use the position to "get votes for the PSI [Socialist Party]; get money for the party."[43]

As Mario Chiesa, the accused politician whose confessions gave way to Mani Pulite, stated in the late 1970s, "the costs of politics began to be stratospheric."[44] The vice secretary for civic affairs of the Democrazia Cristiana (DC) in Milan, Maurizio Prada, cited a list of elections and other expensive organizational events: "in 1979 the legislative [elections], in 1980 the administrative [local], in 1981 a referendum, in 1982 the national congress, in 1983 legislative [elections], in 1984 the European [elections], in 1985 the administrative, in 1986 the national congress, in 1987 the legislative, in 1988 some referenda and the national congress, in 1989 the European, in 1990 the administrative in 1991 a referendum, in 1992 the legislative."[45] Italian democracy was expensive, and corruption was a way to finance it.

In terms of accessibility to the local public, the party was admirably decentralized. The DC of Milan had both a regional branch headquarters and a separate one for the local and provincial branches. In Milan alone the DC had forty local sections. This expensive political machine would seem to be in part the happy result of a healthy, competitive democracy: the goal was to match, section for section, the Communist Party's local presence. As Prada said, it was the result of an era in which the Communist Party had one cell "for every Church bell tower," and the Christian Democrats countered each cell with a section of their own.[46] The local sections had "no means of autonomous financing." Their fate rested on the Milan DC, meaning that with such a high number of party sections and also such a high number of elections, "we had a very expensive political machine." Prada, who handled party finances, said that although the national DC gave the Milan party around ITL 70–80 million ($70–80,000) per year, the party's expenses amounted to well over ITL 1 billion ($1 million) per year.[47] The irony of such a competitive party system, with such frequent electoral and organizational activity, was that it led to corruption, which is hardly a phenomenon we think of as conducive to or desirable in a democracy.

In the 1970s party activists who were willing to work for free disappeared. Within the Socialist Party (PSI) but, as Chiesa added, "not only in the Socialist Party, the activists left and the clients arrived, those who . . . saw in the party a shortcut for reaching personal goals."[48] Supporters had to be paid for their backing of individual politicians, else they would turn to a rival within the same party: "Often the activists would ask for money not for the party but for themselves. Behind the request for a contribution to pay the rent for the party section headquarters hid a banal demand for small change for futile expenditures. But, here is the point: it would be dangerous not to meet those demands. There is always your closest competitor ready to close not one but two eyes in order to pacify the most outlandish requests."[49] It was not that interparty competition had become fierce, as it indeed had, but that intraparty competition had as well.[50] As one party official stated, "Each [section] leader was out for himself and saw in his neighbor the enemy. The collection and management of resources are tightly linked to the strengthening of one's own political weight. This created in the PSI a grid of centers of parallel political power and an eternal battle among themselves."[51]

It is often assumed that an active opposition will help reduce corruption. Italy, however, has put its own spin on this expectation. The Communist Party, having been excluded from all real positions of governing power until the 1970s, entered local and regional governments not as the anticorruption party but as one all too willing to be bought off. In 1975, when the Communists entered local government, the Christian Democrats began collaborating with them for, among other things, illegal finances. According to the DC's "cashier," the parties lost their ideologically based competitiveness and replaced it with a system of sharing kickbacks collected on public works contracts.[52]

Decentralization expanded the practice of allowing cities to designate subcontractors for public works that were planned and financed by the central state. There was no fiscal incentive for cities to choose the lowest bidder. Local preference could operate, and no one had a political or financial incentive to enforce the rules of competitive bidding. This system encouraged and allowed firms to create cartels, dividing up the public works market. As Mario Chiesa, the accused politician whose confessions gave way to Mani Pulite, noted of the situation in Milan, firms established "'a nonbelligerence pact' such that in the various hospital and health facilities one knew from the start which firms were going to win the contracts."[53] Permissive norms and the financial exigencies of inter- and intraparty competition meant that cities looked to the contractors most likely to be politically useful, that is, the ones that offered kickbacks. The political parties within city councils and those controlling various local public agencies selected the firms known to them to be reliable bribers, not reliable contractors.[54]

Contributing to corruption in local and regional government was the fact that with decentralization, the main national party organizations reduced their funding of their local and regional branches. The Christian Democratic Party, the dominant party of the national government since the end of World War II, for instance, reduced to trivial the funding it allotted to its branch in Milan. The local party, complaining of being hemmed in by party-financing laws that prevented parties from accepting corporate or public agency donations, turned quite naturally to kickbacks from public works projects and operations. The treasurer of the national DC organization knew that the local federation's money "had been given by firms operating in the Milanese public agencies such as the metro, the train, the airport, the bus service, the Ira, the city planning department, etc."[55] If the local party federation proved adept at attracting illegal financing, the national party demanded a cut. The DC national treasurer, knowing "that our sources of alternative financing brought substantial sums, took it upon himself to ask us to contribute to the national needs."[56] In Milan, Craxi insisted that the kickbacks from local agencies be divided between the local and national Socialist Party.[57]

Kickbacks from projects that received state financing but that involved local planning were coordinated by multiple meetings between the interested politicians and firms. As part of the planning for the new Milanese airport, Malpensa, construction firms, the DC national secretariat, its economic planning commission, and local party representatives met to prearrange the division of the spoils. These meetings also brought in the other political parties, including the Communist Party; each was allotted a portion, first by verbal, then by tacit agreement of national and local party officials. There were occasional complaints and disputes between the parties, as when the Republicans lamented that despite their being a "stable participant in the distribution system, it was not remunerated in a satisfactory manner."[58]

Parapublic agencies set up to build and operate public services were easily turned to illegal uses. The Milan metro system was 90 percent publicly funded, with an oversight commission, seven of whose members were nominated directly by politicians (the members of the city council) and three of whom were approved by the city council but nominated by other parapublic agencies. As explained by a Communist Party treasurer in his testimony, those nominated had been "pre-chosen by the various party secretaries and were those who in the final analysis were the designated recipients of the kickbacks" coming from the firms working on the metro.[59]

As the report of an investigation of local government contracting in Italy noted, "Many illegal acts occur right during the phase of awarding a building contract, when the discretion of the local administration is, instead, supposed to be extremely limited."[60] Awarding greater authority to local governments for both planning and putting projects out for tender merely increased the penetration of corrupt practices. The rules were meaningless and, if anything, increased the payoff for corruption, because applying complex, tight rules to cases would result in more work and perhaps trigger retaliation by contractors not awarded contracts—those surprised by a change in the unofficial rules.

Brokers used, and the awardee often paid, 25 percent of the net amount due in payoffs before the work was even approved by the legal entities in charge of such approvals. As in France, frequently the mediator of corrupt deals was a consulting firm. "The task of the broker was to make contact with public administrators and negotiate the 'affair' with them."[61]

Formal Structure of Subnational Governments

At the same time that Italy began to decentralize many government functions, it almost completely centralized its tax-raising powers. As a result, neither the new regions nor the provincial and local governments were self-financing. Instead, between 1972 and 1977, the state suppressed all local taxes (save trivial ones such as dog-licensing fees) and replaced them with budget transfers from the state.[62] The resulting fiscal structure removed local and regional responsibility for spending projects, with predictable results: planning went toward pork barrel projects, and spending went out of control. As in France, local administrations borrowed heavily to cover operational expenses and investment projects. Many localities went further into debt to finance the interest payments, but in the end at little cost to themselves: in 1977, the state bailed them out by taking over the amortization of the debts incurred between 1972 and 1977.[63]

The Italian regions do not lack for oversight institutions. Each region has its own Court of Auditors. As of 1999, regional authorities are also supervised by a government commissioner, who must sign regional laws unless the government objects. There is a state-run supervisory commission for each region, which oversees the legality of regional administrative acts. Chaired by the state commissioner for the region, the body includes "judges, civil servants, and experts." Its control is ex post facto in that regional acts become "effective if not overruled by the commission within thirty days." Municipalities are "supervised" by a board of auditors, which the municipal council itself selects from "among chartered accountants." In other words, there is little external control.[64] The regional council is elected every five years on a party list system; each province within a region is an electoral district. The municipal councils are elected every five years and can have between fifteen and eighty members. The local city council elects a junta to run things when it is not in session. The structures have the potential to operate effectively.

The Real Structures of Subnational Governments

Decentralization Italian style means that, allegedly to discourage corruption, ever more controls were added to local, provincial, and regional government spending. These rules merely gave the controllers more veto points and, if the controllers were so inclined, more leverage with which to extort bribes from the local governments. As one mayor described it, the regional audit board, Coreco, told him,

> We can bring you to your knees. We can paralyze you. Imagine that we reject your budget: this blocks the release of funds and you can't pay salaries, heat or gas bills. The buses don't move a meter. You then have to resort to emergency procedures. It's true that you can spend the money without having it approved by the Coreco. But later we have to verify the procedures. . . . If we reject them, and you have already spent the money, you bear personal responsibility. You'll end up at the Court of Auditors and pay with your own money. . . .
>
> Who says that our bureaucrats are incompetent? If they wanted they could, without any effort, find the trivial points by which to block [a project] when they could pass it, or pass it when they ought to block it.

It was from these discretionary aspects of their work that the bureaucrats on the control committees derived "their great power."[65]

The bureaucrats who "were supposed to exercise administrative control over the acts of the political bosses" had been nominated by other political bosses. And because the political bosses were using local, provincial, and regional governance to improve their own positions in their parties, they would signal to "their" bureaucrat on the regional audit board how to deal with various projects. As Licandro stated, "It was necessary to take out the funds for the parties, the bosses, the underlings, the election bosses, and others of their ilk out of the public funds: can the controllers jam a rod in the wheels? Simple: just give something to eat to the controllers, who are more insatiable than the others." What was intended to be an auditing mechanism became "a structure of extortion."[66] The city's political boss relied on his supervision of Coreco to control the city. "The acts, before going to the appropriate bureaucrats at Coreco, were examined by the political secretariat of Palamara in order to decide which ones should be 'returned.' In addition, he [the political secretary] used Coreco as an instrument of pressure. . . . The instrument for guaranteeing transparency and propriety was made perfectly functional for its opposite." The regional audit body was a useful tool for the political bosses of the region to learn about every public works project under consideration and, in that way, "turn everything into a politico-business affair" from which they demanded kickbacks.[67] In a context in which corruption already was the norm, Coreco provided a transparency that gave politicians precisely the information they needed to conduct more corrupt transactions. Indeed, as a central feature of Italian decentralization, it gave politicians more opportunities for corruption.

Decentralization Italian style reversed the expectation that cities compete with each other to be more competitive for business, thereby attracting jobs and a bigger tax base. With local public works funded from the center, decentralization merely put the regions, provinces, and cities into competition with each other for public works funding. Corruption gave it an Alice in Wonderland character. Central state politicians and bureaucrats played on this configuration, awarding projects not to the city presenting the "best" project according to some relatively objective standards but to the one promising the most kickbacks. In something of a historical stretch, former mayor Licandro stated, "Paris was worth a mass, a public works project is worth a bit of a kickback even if it feeds this [corrupt] system. . . . Either this or no public works." This became an excuse for corruption: "To obtain financing, even with these [corrupt] methods, signifies that we are carrying out a useful function for the citizenry and for the welfare of the city."[68]

All these extra palms to grease amounted to considerable expense, yet it was borne by the Italian taxpayer at large, not by the particular locality or region in which the corruption took place. Hence local residents had little incentive to overcome the standard barriers to collective action and protest the corruption in their own local governments and administrative bodies.

In sum, the program of decentralization and regionalization, which was intended to make Italy a model of democratization and local governance, failed. It corrupted the political parties as a result of their frenzied desire to obtain operating capital for their many campaigns, it undermined the system of public administration, it eroded any real efforts at oversight of the expenditure of public funds, and in the end the costs of providing public services escalated dramatically as a result of the many mouths that demanded to be fed. Decentralization was not able to break the propensity toward corruption in government; instead, it aggravated corruption, becoming a self-reinforcing system.[69]

THE CONTRAST OF THE UNITED KINGDOM

Without decentralized governance as found in France and Italy, save recently in Scotland and Wales, the United Kingdom has not seen the development of local corruption in the way that Italy and France have. There are other factors as well, but with local governments tightly controlled by the central government, and with the national party organizations bearing the costs of campaigns, fewer local opportunities and incentives for corruption are present. By French or Italian standards, cases of local government corruption in the UK are as rare as they are comical.

Local expense account fraud has been more common than corruption involving bribery or kickbacks. Corruption in public procurement contracting is rare, because the projects and contracts are decided at higher levels. Perhaps indicative of this trend is the fact that relatively small-scale fraud and bribery in one locality became the major local political scandal of the 1990s. In what came to be known as Donnygate, a city councilor was jailed for twenty-eight days for having padded his expense account by a couple hundred pounds. The accused, Jack Riley, said at his trial, "It was standard practice. It was not right but I went along with what I was told." Another city council member, having falsified four expense accounts by about £300 (about $450), was sentenced to eight months in jail. The judge in the case stated that "a certain amount of fiddling expense claims has been almost traditional in England. But what you have been doing went far beyond."[70] With thirty-one convictions for various sorts of malfeasance or corruption, the Donnygate scandal was the largest since the Poulson affair of 1974. In both cases, political party financing was not a motive; personal enrichment of elected public officials was.[71]

Arrangements that had greater financial repercussions were those between council members and developers. What is striking is how cheap the bribes were, given what the developers stood to gain in exchange. Developers gave travel vouchers and other goods in return for revised town plans that greatly increased the value of their land and development projects. For instance, within months of a move, by a city council's planning chairman, into a "£175,000 [$310,000] grade II listed farmhouse" owned by real estate developer Alan Hughes, the "planning committee had approved a series of controversial land deals which promised to make Hughes millions of pounds. But he [Peter Birk, the planning chairman] failed to declare the conflict of interest."[72] Investigation of the case found that Hughes's application to build on a site was initially rejected by the city council. Hughes then transferred ownership of the farmhouse to Birk's mistress, and Councilor Birk moved in with her. Shortly thereafter, at Birk's urging, the city council approved the housing project. Hughes also appears to have won approval of three other developments estimated to make him £5 million ($8.8 million) merely through the support of a friend on the planning committee. It was for personal, not partisan, profit, and the bribe amounts were small.

In an odd mix of public and private malpractice, Doncaster 2000, the joint venture between the Doncaster city council and a private developer, Keepmoat, gave a councilor travel vouchers worth £1,000 ($1,600) when he retired in 1995. The private developer is said to have "made millions" from its links to the city council.[73] To the extent that a retirement gift and free housing can be considered bribes, their low value may indicate the high risk of being caught. Which is to say, if there is a high risk of being caught and penalized, the firm involved will have to see a very high profit margin in the corruption, sufficient to create profits in excess of what would have obtained without corruption. The odds of getting the ultimate payoff affect the amount an "investor" is willing to pay for it. One of the costs to be covered is the risk-and-penalty fee. In Britain, the greater the risks to corrupt actions, the cheaper it is to buy favorable government decisions.

Another incident that shows the low value of bribes relative to the value of government services illegally purchased is that of "Donnygate." Conservative Party councilor John Dainty was convicted of having accepted (or, as the briber argued, demanded) a £5,000 ($7,800) bribe in exchange for dropping his opposition to a seven-acre housing development project. In 1994, Dainty sent the developer an invoice for that amount after a zoning change was granted. The developer, Alan Hughes, sold the lot for half a million pounds ($780,000). It appears that Hughes had to pay off one other city council member, a Labour Party leader, in the amount of £30,000 ($46,900) over several years. Other city officials implicated in Donnygate were arrested and convicted of falsifying expense accounts, not of accepting bribes. Penalties were stiff, in comparison to those meted out for more serious cases in France and Italy: Birk was jailed for four years; and Hughes for five years. Dainty, for his acceptance of a £5,000 ($7,800) bribe, was jailed for fifteen months.[74]

In contrast to cases in Italy and France, political party financing in the UK was not a motive for local government corruption; personal enrichment of elected public officials was. Candidates in British parliamentary elections have little incentive to use local resources for campaign financing. The structure of local and national governance is such that they are not able to. In addition, given that British parties, not their candidates, carry most of the costs of parliamentary elections, there is less demand for corruption at the local level as a way to finance parties.[75] Further reducing incentives for corruption at the local level is the fact that elections in Britain, at all levels, are referenda on the national parties much more than they are on particular, constituency-based candidates. Individuals matter, but mainly at the level of prime minister, who is, in the British system, also party leader.

More common in the UK is patronage, here defined narrowly as the exchange of jobs or contracts for votes. Its legal status is less clear. A scholar investigating what was said to be corruption in one district noted that it was mostly in the form of nepotism. In the municipal councils dominated by Labour, "corruption has traditionally centered on jobs for manual workers and on the allocation of scarce council housing."[76] One investigation concluded that "Labour operates with local authorities, certain law firms and public relations companies on a 'scratch my back and I'll scratch yours' basis."[77] In another case of patronage, the board of Scottish Enterprise Glasgow, which is an agency of the Department of Enterprise, invited tenders for its advertising and public relations contract. The contract was awarded to a firm set up by the former press secretary to a major figure in Scottish Labour, Donald Dewar. In Scotland, "the local machines 'delivered,' they 'did the business,' keeping Labour in virtually unchallenged municipal power and giving it a bloc of MPs impervious to Thatcherite challenges."[78]

Several features of local patronage politics in the UK are similar to features in corruption networks in France and Italy. One commonality is that "local authorities create groups such as tenants' associations or community councils," in other words, the local government creates a parapublic agency to deliver services. Then, "recruits usually close to the council are chosen to run them and apply for grants from the local authority which created them. . . . Not surprisingly, they are successful." The grants fund activities with material benefits; also, the parapublic agency created by the grant publishes "a newsletter promoting their activities, in which the virtues of the local Labour councilor are extolled. The circle of mutual backslapping goes on and on."[79] The strategy has political payoffs: in the 1999 local elections in Glasgow, Labour won seventy-four seats, a combined opposition won four. The difference between the countries seems to be that the UK local councils do not extract kickbacks from the community grants.

Local politicians used patronage to build up electoral strongholds. Partly the result of the structure of local central governance, kickbacks on public works were not readily available at the local level. In the Doncaster case, a group of Labour councilors "with strong links to the National Union of Mineworkers seized power in the [city council] authority in 1981. . . . By 1996, 58 of Doncaster's 63 councillors were Labour" Party representatives.[80] The main sources of patronage, particularly in Labour-controlled districts, were the direct labor organizations (DLOs), which were the in-house agencies delivering local government services. When compulsory competitive tendering, allowing private firms to bid on public service contracts, was introduced by the Thatcher government, many DLOs and Labour councils were suspected of having rigged contracts to discourage private-sector tenders.[81]

The DLOs were the means by which many public works were constructed and delivered. The corruption has been at the level of "fiddled accounts, cash handouts and trips to the World Cup."[82] In one case, eighty Glasgow city council employees were investigated for having defrauded the city of a total of £500,000 ($800,000) in benefits.[83] Investigators found evidence of lax monitoring and use of public funds for dubious purposes, such as twinning trips to other European cities (for example, Paris and Saint-Denis). These local government problems in Scotland most frequently occurred in Labour Party strongholds.[84]

With the exception of Scotland and Wales, the structure of local government in the UK has changed somewhat since the 1950s, but seldom in the direction of greater discretion. With the Thatcher years, the central government "acquired new types of powers over local authorities," including being able to reduce grants to local governments as a penalty for local overspending.[85] Local authorities have no discretion over major public works (schools, roads, hospitals, and such). They get "84% of [their] money from central government, which also has the power to limit its spending through 'capping.'"[86] The central state took over urban development and the building of public housing, and it reduced the real level of financing given to local governments while not allowing them to raise their own revenue through local taxes. By the 1990s, local councils only handled such things as maintaining roadside shoulders, public walkways, and other minor public facilities. District and county councils had more responsibilities. Rendering local governments anemic also rendered them less susceptible to corruption. Even excluding oversight, risk, and cultural norms, the frequency of local corruption in the UK likely is lower because the institutional opportunities for it at the local level are lower.

Although party financing is not a motivating factor in local corruption, personal enrichment could be:

> Certainly no councillor would seek election in order to get rich. Although the allowances paid to the leaders of large authorities may in a few cases appear generous . . . , they are in no sense commensurate with the size of the council's budget or the responsibilities attached to the post. Allowances for "backbench" councillors or members of smaller authorities may be modest in the extreme.[87]

Yet the frequency of local corruption is surprisingly low.

> The Audit Commission (established in 1982) appoints auditors to 460 English and Welsh local authorities. The 469 authorities have over 20,000 councillors and 2,000,000 employees. They spend over GBP 50 bn [$82 billion] per year. In 1995–96 there were 1,475 proven cases of fraud and 21 cases of corruption affecting these authorities. 99% of total local government fraud (in terms of number of cases) is committed by outside persons against local authorities.[88]

The structure of local government oversight in the UK may counteract the incentives of local officials to illegally supplement their salaries. The Audit Commission, responsible for auditing the accounts of local governments, is formally distant from the governments it audits. It is part of the central state; its norms and operational procedures are, for better or worse, a reflection of national norms and practices. It is more likely to be a disinterested observer of local governmental practices. This survey of practices in France, Italy, and the United Kingdom suggests that decentralization creates structures and incentives that foster rent seeking. The latter need not be illegal, but in many instances it is, particularly when decentralization coincides with privatization and the contracting out of government services.

In theory, decentralization, and the "democratization" that accompanies it, is supposed to reduce corruption and promote transparency. This chapter has argued that, in practice, as France and Italy clearly demonstrate, those forces can facilitate corruption and hinder economic competition. Both forces create greater demand for campaign financing because decentralizing democratization typically comes with the establishment of new layers of locally and regionally elected governments. If that financing is not forthcoming through legal means, then kickbacks from local public works contracts become a desirable supply. This incentive dovetails with the incentive to favor local businesses over foreign or other out-of-area firms in awarding contracts; familiarity and trust are key elements of the collusive arrangements undergirding corruption.

Decentralization and local democracy bring with them demands for campaign and party financing; so too do elections at the international level—for the European Parliament. The remedy is not necessarily re-centralization. The flaws in subnational structures can be mended, well-staffed regional level oversight boards can be created, the moral hazard of no hard budget constraints can be reduced, and better provisions for legal campaign financing can be introduced. Yet as France has seen, for countries with an institutionalized tradition of social solidarity, equity, and centralized planning, allowing decentralization to occur as the political economists prescribe, with largely self-financed regions competing with each other for revenue and citizens, is politically difficult, if not impossible.

The phenomenon of kickbacks has been relatively rare in the UK. This may have something to do with public officials' ethics, but it may have even more to do with the fact that what is illegal on the Continent is legal in the UK. Corporate and private donations to political parties are not limited, and the national party-financing market is basically unregulated. UK political parties need not look to illegal kickbacks for campaign and organizational financing, because they can get it in an "open market."[89] This development suggests that we need to look at how campaign finance laws may drive underground the parties' and politicians' search for funds.[90]

In defense of the potential for decentralization and devolution to reduce corruption, one could point out that France and Italy did not follow the "correct" recipe. The central states retained extensive control over local, departmental, and regional governments. Nor did they require these governments to be self-financing and so did not force them to compete with one another for business or civic support. Italy only seems to have introduced competition among municipalities and regions for central state financing, which merely creates incentives for local authorities to bribe central state politicians and all others who might have a say in the financing decision. And that competition is greater after decentralization than before, since with decentralization, local authorities are under more pressure to deliver their own pork barrel projects to their local constituencies in order to win reelection. National efforts to ensure "solidarity," meaning equality of financing and benefits, indicate that the central states have not left the regions and localities to fend for themselves.[91] Under these conditions, local government corruption does not have immediate repercussions for local politicians, firms, and citizens. Instead, it becomes a tool in the system of local governance.

In addition, and especially in Italy, national politicians maintained strong links to regional and local party sections, politicians, activists, and "clients." Even in corruption of local contracts, national politicians kept track of the distribution of finances, and the party system rewarded those local politicians who sent large contributions to the national party, and specifically to their faction leader on the national level.

Other ingredients for successful (that is, uncorrupt) decentralization are imaginable in theory but not likely to obtain in practice. For decentralization to not be accompanied by an increase in corruption, citizens must become local government watchdogs. Yet local government rarely elicits citizen interest and involvement. To create pressures on local governments to be fiscally responsible,

citizens need to be able to move from the city they live in when they are dissatis-
fied with its management (to "exit") easily. As the European Union is discovering
at the international level, citizens, even when legally able to, are slow to uproot
and move elsewhere. And, as Italy demonstrates, mobility may mean nothing: Milan was as corrupt as Reggio Calabria. The potential for illegal gains in local government undermines the democratic promise of decentralization and degrades
the quality of democracy.

THE CORRUPTION OF CAMPAIGN AND PARTY FINANCING

Show me a limit and I'll show you how to get around it.

—Retired British party official

The French like neither political parties nor taxes, and we are going to ask them to pay more taxes to finance political parties?

—French deputy Jean-Claude Gaudin

An Italian CEO dying mysteriously in Mexico; a dead Taiwanese navy captain found floating in a Taiwan harbor; the commander of the Belgian air force killing himself with an overdose of whisky and tranquilizers; a German party treasurer shot to death in his bed; a German judge dying in a car "accident" the day he was to file papers in a corruption case; a Spanish court clerk jumping off a rooftop and plunging to his death to avoid revealing who was paying him to remove case files: illegal party financing in Europe has high stakes.[1] It is also an area in which the EU and the Single Market have had limited impact. Corruption across the EU is partly driven by the desire for financing on the part of politicians and their political parties. Judging by the amounts spent by parties on elections in recent years, diminished state sovereignty within the EU has not reduced politicians' desire for obtaining and holding onto national office. Nor has it reduced their demand for funds to finance their campaigns and the operating expenses of their parties. The Single Market also has not provided an alternate means of campaign and party finance; instead, some of the structures created to govern market integration have become a locus of occasional campaign finance corruption.[2] It becomes clear that market and political reforms that are expected to reduce corruption are not able to stop the corruption derived from campaign and party financing. One reform, the creation of subnational and supranational elected institutions, has itself fueled further demand for financing.

Efforts to regulate campaign and party spending have been about as successful as wage and price controls. Party and campaign financing usually relies on self-interested donors: an individual or firm will not contribute unless assured of getting something specific in return. Although ideologically motivated or "altruistic" donors do exist, there are not enough of them to meet the financial demands of the parties and their election campaigns. For instance, in the absence of a specific return, a firm may hesitate to give a portion of its revenue to a party. It knows that other firms, which may similarly benefit from the policies of that party, can reap the benefits for nothing. This situation creates incentives for quid pro quos, legal or illegal.

Financing electoral competition is similar to an arms race: every competitive innovation and increase in expenditure must be matched by the other parties; attempts to regulate only generate new forms of subversion of the original goal of reducing corruption and "bought" politics; politicians will circumvent and violate their own rules in order to get desired funding; and the watchdog agencies seldom if ever have the resources or authority to monitor effectively what they are charged with monitoring. As with sovereign states, it is almost never in the interests of the politicians who write and vote to pass the campaign finance laws to impede, in any significant way, their own freedom to maneuver later on. In addition, governing parties frequently use their power to block or circumvent investigations into party and campaign finance corruption. It is only in exceptional circumstances that politicians and parties come under scrutiny, and the charges usually wind up being dismissed or reduced to near triviality.

Party and campaign finance regulations that do not take into account donor self-interest and arms race dynamics are doomed to fail. Although one might protest, as did the treasurer of the British Liberal Democrats, that "argument should influence policy, not money," parties need money, and potential donors have little incentive to give it unless they get "policy" back.[3] A variety of methods have been tried, in Europe and elsewhere, to deal with this conundrum. The main ones are caps on spending, caps on donations, and state (that is, public) financing. The first two approaches often engender corruption or other illegal practices; the third approach, public financing, has not prevented parties or politicians from searching out illicit financing to supplement the public funds, which they often deem insufficient. The competitive pressures of democratic politics, the inability of politicians to guarantee policy delivery through the legislative process to donors, and the fact that it is ultimately politicians who write the laws meant to regulate themselves undermine efforts to ensure fair play and to limit corruption.

Most of the cases discussed in earlier chapters of this book involve parties and politicians seeking funding by taking advantage of political and economic dynamics in the EU. Focusing as it does on financing mechanisms, fairness, and the impact of spending on election results, most of the literature on campaign and party finance ignores corruption.[4] It is worth understanding why parties and politicians resort to corruption to finance their activities and how this effort might be connected to the very laws meant to keep them in check. This chapter analyzes the three major mechanisms that have been proposed to deal with the problems associated with financing parties and politicians in some major European states (and, indirectly, other democratic countries). Also, it shows how each regulatory mechanism is undermined by donors' self-interest and the "arms race" problems of electoral competition and representation in democracies. The literature on campaign and party finance generally gives two reasons for campaign and party finance laws, in light of the evident problems. The first is that politicians and parties need funding, and the second is that various publics have demanded that political party and election financing be regulated. This chapter is not concerned with the origins of the regulations but rather with their connection to corruption. In it I set up the donor self-interest problem and then move on to explain the features of the arms race. In three subsections I show that the major forms of regulation often lead to as many problems as they solve. The conclusion points to some alternative mechanisms for dealing with the problem. Nevertheless, corruption, which in this chapter is synonymous with illegal campaign-financing activities, is virtually inherent in democratic politics.

THE COLLECTIVE ACTION PROBLEM OF FINANCING

Political donors fund parties and politicians in order to influence policy. On average, they are more likely to fund when there is some likelihood of a favorable policy return. Thus, to get donations, parties and politicians have an incentive to provide quid pro quos, that is, favorable decisions. But even generally favorable, sympathetic decisions fall prey to donor self-interest: policies are usually too ambiguous to elicit a lot of funding, since each potential donor knows that others could benefit from the policy that the donor helped finance. There would not be enough donors to generate the continuous and large donations that the parties claim they need. Even if donations are not capped by financing regulations, the arms race toward more expenditure and the problem of eliciting donations without the promise of discrete benefits create incentives to resort to corruption: exchanging specific benefits for donations, as has been common in the United States and Britain, and demanding kickbacks in exchange for the award of government contracts, as has been common on the European continent.[5] Finally, politicians seldom if ever have the power to guarantee that they will deliver the requested policy. They cannot commit to giving a return on the investment, unless there exists an illegal market for the sale and distribution of public policies. And that is corruption.

In the absence of a quid pro quo, potential donors have little reason to finance parties. To give them a reason, parties resort to extortion, although they never call it that: arranging to take kickbacks from contractors on public works projects, making a decision in favor of a firm contingent on a specific donation, or, like the Mafia, preventing problems (that they themselves have the means to cause) in exchange for regular payments. Italy was infamous for its system of regular corporate and small business payments to parties in exchange for political insurance against "trouble." Less well known was the occurrence of the same practice in France. Asked why he made illegal payments to the Gaullist party, one businessman said, "I am going to tell you frankly, my concern wasn't to support the RPR, my concern was to avoid problems."[6] Donor interest in getting something in return for the contribution is compounded by the arms race dynamic of party and campaign financing.

ARMS RACE EFFECTS

The arms race dynamic has three characteristics: (1) parties and politicians must match each competitive move made by the others, thus increasing the demand for funds; (2) participants have low incentives to establish adequate enforcement mechanisms; and (3) participants have high incentives to evade restrictions imposed by caps on spending, donations, and public financing.

Matching Each Move

Nowhere else in Europe has the arms race been more intense nor the corruption more egregious than in Italy. The spending of one party has had to be countered by a similar level of spending by all the others. Efforts to regulate the race are subject to the same pitfalls of traditional strategic arms treaties: no state/party has an incentive to create effective oversight and enforcement mechanisms, and each state/party has an incentive to search for alternatives not proscribed by the treaty/ regulation. A careful estimate in the mid-1980s suggested that if the amount of kickbacks to political parties equaled the gross income of a firm, that company's annual revenue would have made it the twelfth largest in Italy, just behind Olivetti and in front of Alitalia. By the early 1990s, the best guess was that the parties had taken in a sum well above the country's total national debt.[7] Media and technology costs increased dramatically at the same time that traditional sources of societal support, such as unions and religious organizations, dwindled, and, more than ever, politics became a full-time career. Italy added some pressures to the demand side that were less prevalent in other European countries: factionalism within parties, decentralization, and extensive interparty competition at all levels of governance and in almost all localities. Politicians ensured that they had a more than adequate supply of financing by colonizing the public sector at, again, all levels of government, by granting parliamentarians immunity from prosecution and by blocking the judiciary's efforts to disrupt the system in any way. As the prosecution's notice to the Italian parliament in 1993 stated, the phenomenon of politicians taking kickbacks from public works contracts and agencies and distributing them to the parties according to a resource-sharing formula "involved the entire national territory." In one of its cases against former Socialist Party leader and sometime prime minister Bettino Craxi, the reporting judge noted that "the illegality brought to light by the investigations has impressive dimensions, not only for its deep-seatedness across time and for the broad diffusion of the phenomenon, but also for the number and distinctiveness of the persons involved, if not also for the amounts handled."[8]

What is of importance here is that this activity began at a time when private (corporate and individual) contributions to parties were *not* capped. Clearly, the parties had long ago decided that they could not get enough funding through legal and unlimited donations, so they resorted to a variant of extortion, thus "solving" the collective action problem of party finance: firms, to do business with the state, had to give kickbacks on the contracts they were awarded.

Even in parties seemingly flush with public funding and legal, private donations, politicians scramble for more in order to retain or expand their position in office and to exert control over party operations. The head of the parliamentary investigative committee for the Kohl affair observed that Helmut Kohl's dubious if not corrupt practices enabled him to amass funds that he then deployed to "take care of" problems in particular CDU federations. Having significant funds at his disposal allowed Kohl to retain strong control of his party in every part of the country.[9] In other words, party leaders, whether elected politicians or organizational leaders, have incentives to amass special resources to control their parties.

One often-suggested remedy for a corrupt political system—more elections and more parties—has the effect of requiring more financing. More elections and thus more party and candidate competition mean greater demand for party and campaign financing. Local, regional, national, and European elections raise parties' and politicians' overall operating costs; their search for funds intensifies. Noting the phenomenon, the chair of a UK House of Commons committee investigating options on party funding observed in 2006, "We are almost into continuous elections, are we not? We have general, local, European, regional, devolved assembly, mayoral elections and maybe even House of Lords elections."[10]

Since 1979 and the European Parliament elections, Germany has averaged six elections per year. Reported spending for national legislative elections per registered voter rose nearly 50 percent over fourteen years.[11] From 1983 to 1997, general election expenditures in the UK rose (in constant prices) almost 22 percent for the Conservative Party, and an incredible 550 percent for the Labour Party. In 1998, Labour's treasurer stated that "to fulfil its role in the democratic process, the Labour Party needs to raise between £20 million and £25 million per year [$33–42 million]."[12] The Belgian Socialist Party had some disagreement about whether extracting a kickback from those involved in the Dassault weapons purchase would be a good idea; the winning argument was the insistence of some that, in light of upcoming campaign expenses, it was necessary.[13]

Weak Enforcement

Creating a regulatory and electoral structure to facilitate party financing and reduce corruption is impeded by another aspect of the arms race. If there ever were a case of the fox guarding the chicken coop, it is that of politicians writing the laws that regulate political financing. One might wonder why they regulate themselves at all. There seem to be two main reasons: they need funding, and they need to avoid distressing too many voters. This is an area in which it is inherently impossible for politicians to create a self-regulating system. Once elected, politicians and their parties are not the "agents" or "representatives" of their electorate but rather their rulers. They can create rules they have little intention of obeying or enforcing.[14] In regulating themselves, they have an incentive to create weak rules so that if they lose power for a time, the opposition cannot use those rules to block their ability to return to power. Campaign- and party-financing laws have the effect of restricting politicians' access to funding and of establishing penalties for infractions. Because politicians do not benefit from this form of "institutionalization of political accountability," they do not set up strong campaign and party finance enforcement agencies and penalties.[15] These aspects of politics are amply demonstrated by campaign and party finance regulations in Europe and elsewhere.

In Italy, even after a major scandal in 1974 involving oil derivatives producers (Unione Petrolifera), the Italian national electricity company (ENEL), and all the major political parties, the governing parties did not have the incentive to prosecute themselves or to create laws with teeth. The Cold War and the extensive use of patronage insulated them from the threat that voters would tip the balance in favor of the Communist Party. As one politician later stated, "this process [of illegal systematic financing] took on a strong expansion first in the 1960s, with the enlargement of the governing formula, that is with the center left and with the consociational [power-sharing] political culture, because that political feature significantly reduced the role of the opposition and thus the function of control."[16] So the dominant parties wrote a law that "did nothing to constrain competition between the parties in their struggle to exploit public resources for their own political ends." Parties whose expenditure *exceeded* by 20 percent the state's contribution to their financing could be *exempted* from the requirement (as of 1974) to publish their annual budgets.[17] Italian politicians left their immunity from prosecution intact, they established a feeble publication-of-accounts requirement, and they eliminated previously legal forms of financing, the latter with the tacit understanding that the judiciary would not successfully prosecute cases of illegal financing.

In Portugal, when the electoral system winnowed the number of parties down to a "quadrangular cartel," it "helped to create a climate of connivance amongst major political parties in relation to the abuse of public office and money." When scandals forced the parties to create a regulatory agency, the parties created a predictably toothless institution whose "actions consisted of non-interference in party affairs." There was decided absence of motivation to create reporting and oversight mechanisms that functioned effectively.[18]

The power of office can convey a sense of immunity. The CDU-CSU's illegal financing system in Germany continued to operate even during media and government investigations. The CDU leader, Helmut Kohl, was described at his appearances before the parliamentary investigative committee as having "showed no regret or guilt. Rather, Kohl in a high-handed and overbearing manner, claimed his 'word of honor' was superior to the law, ridiculed the committee, and refused to answer any of the relevant questions [posed by the committee]."[19] Italian prime minister Berlusconi used his governing majority to try to grant himself immunity from prosecution while in office, and he reduced the length of the statute of limitations for crimes and infractions he is accused of having committed. French politicians have given themselves amnesty from prosecution for illegal funding no less than three times in seven years. In 1995, the government passed an amnesty bill for crimes that had resulted in suspended sentences of nine months or less. Given that a nine-month suspended sentence was a common sentence for those convicted of illegal party financing, the amnesty swept party corruption under the rug.

When politicians do pass laws that establish oversight commissions and require publication of accounts, they routinely leave out effective enforcement mechanisms and usually restrict the amount of information they are required to post as well as the location of the posted data. This inevitably leaves room for corruption to occur and remain undetected or unpunished. The oversight mechanisms are deliberately weak. In Spain, the electoral commission can only report irregularities in party accounts to the public prosecutor, who usually has other things to do. Further, and as in Portugal and Italy, party and campaign auditors can only examine the accounts the parties themselves provide. In Spain, it is only the parliament that can impose fines. Hence, "it is perhaps not surprising that, despite the many irregularities in the party accounts and sometimes apparent infringements of the law, effective sanctions have been hardly imposed in practice."[20] In France, the oversight commission has noted that it is not adequately staffed to examine even the skeletal accounts the parties and candidates give them, nor do they have the authority to pry into the nebulous relations between the parties and their foundations and think tanks. When the auditors do find an infraction by a candidate, they can report it to a special electoral judge, who can decide to impose the limited sanctions provided for in the law. For infractions by parties, auditors are limited to referring the case to the public prosecutor, who has discretion to pursue the case or not. Furthermore, as one would expect of self-interested politicians and their parties, the sanctions they wrote into the law are trivial.

Politicians also tamper with parliamentary investigative committees. The long arm of German chancellor Helmut Kohl reached all the way into the parliamentary commission that was investigating whether any of Kohl's political decisions were purchased. Kohl met on a regular basis with the CDU-CSU members of the investigating committee. Various witnesses and CDU-CSU members of the committee apparently agreed in advance on what testimony the witnesses would give.[21] Prosecutions of German politicians in the Elf-Leuna case, and in other illegal party-financing cases involving Helmut Kohl, have been blocked, dropped, or sent to jurisdictions where Kohl has friends on the court.[22] In the UK, the government blocked the release of parliamentary committee reports that would have exposed dubious if not illegal financing from illegal arms sales.

Politicians claim to be victims of politically motivated witch hunts when the judiciary investigates party and campaign financing. Yet such investigations cannot help but be political if only because they are of politicians and parties. The European Parliament, allegedly the watchdog of the EU against fraud, is anything but when it comes to its own parliamentarians. It almost never lifts parliamentary immunity from prosecution, on the grounds that investigations of politicians are prima facie proof that the investigation is politically motivated.[23]

The extent to which politicians can engage in corrupt practices yet evade prosecution and penalties is evident in the fact that those who take the fall are usually the businessmen and women who made the requested illegal payments. In France, for example, forty-seven businesspersons were tried for bribing public officials in the Paris public housing office, with the bribes then going to a slush fund for a political party, yet not a single politician stood trial. In Germany, in the case of corruption surrounding the construction of a waste incinerator plant, the SPD politician who accepted a large bribe was nevertheless acquitted, while the two businessmen directly fingered were found guilty.[24]

Incentives to Evade Oversight Mechanisms

Spending Caps

Spending caps are designed or thought to help avoid the perception, if not the reality, that the more money a candidate spends on a campaign, the greater the likelihood he or she will be elected. Caps are also thought to help level the playing field, that is, to create greater equality among the parties competing in any given election. In addition, they are thought to stop the seemingly inevitable dramatic growth in resources spent on campaigning (which, by implication, would be more wisely spent elsewhere).[25]

The evidence for the effectiveness of this technique is limited, at best. For one, how can reasonable spending limits be determined? The political market is highly imperfect, prices are not obvious, nor is "need." It is hard to know, save by a proliferation of corruption cases later on, that the limit is too low, or, save by an explosion of expenditure, that it is too high. And what do we mean by "too high"?[26] That parties campaigned "too much"? Going by the expenditure data offered by parties leads to less than accurate predictions: parties tend to underreport expenditures if spending has been capped, and overreport if they have a sense that it might be capped in the future. Further, different parties may have vastly different sources of income, different campaign practices, and different expenditure needs.

A late 1990s survey of twelve European countries showed that all five of the countries with caps on campaign expenditures—Ireland, France, Italy, Portugal, and Spain—have had problems with corruption.[27] Setting spending caps only breeds creative efforts to evade them. For instance, in Britain, in response to public outrage at the way local votes appeared to have been bought during the 1880 parliamentary election, spending caps at the district (constituency) level were introduced in 1883.[28] Parties shifted expenditures to the national level and, in the process, gained more power over individual representatives. They also appear to have exploited efficiencies of scale: rather than hundreds of candidates individually raising money to support their individual campaigns, a handful of large parties raised money for them. Yet once caps were put on national parties' expenditures in 2000, spending went up locally.[29]

Spending caps generate incentives to cheat; although each party would be better off if none cheated, all have strong reason to suspect that another will do so. And because no party can trust the others not to cheat, each is "better off" cheating—a version of the prisoners' dilemma. For example, in Britain, constituency candidates find their spending caps for the general elections adequate; in 1987, individual Conservative and Labour candidates spent an average of 78 percent of the legal limit.[30] By-elections, however, are often extremely contentious, and the parties find the legal limits for their candidates too low. Thus, they tacitly agree to break the law. As a BBC reporter stated, "Each party knows the others do it; each makes it clear to the others—more by what it does not say than by what it does—that, provided the other parties' overspending is not too outrageous, no complaint will be made or action taken." He noted that for a 1997 by-election, the two main parties "had probably spent more than £100,000 [$164,000] on their campaigns, when the official, legal limit was about £31,000 [$51,000]. I now suspect that Labour may have spent as much as £250,000 [$410,000] on winning the seat." Given that by-elections occur with some frequency between general elections, which themselves occur at least once every five years, the British parties find it easy to cooperate to cheat on the rules that they themselves voted on at an earlier point. They know they will be facing each other in future elections and that squealing in the present competition will not eliminate the rival party from the future. The BBC reporter commented that "ironically, despite the intensity with which by-election campaigns are fought, the over-spending is protected by an extraordinary amount of collusion between parties. No party dares to challenge their opponents, since they all know that, if not in this by-election then in many others, they have all been guilty at some time."[31]

Whether it is true that money buys elections or voter turnout, the parties think it does, so they often do what they can to evade spending caps, which they judge to be set too low. For campaign and other organizational supplies, they suggest that their suppliers give them discounts; likewise for advertising; for staff, they suggest to firms that they sponsor employees; and they exploit the lack of specificity in the finance laws in order to creatively classify or not report expenditures.

Another complication: it is difficult to specify what constitutes "expenditure" and to make sure that parties follow the same rules. Politicians prefer not to restrain themselves, so they tend to leave the specifications anything but detailed. Then there is the additional question of expenditure by whom? Most European countries now allow party foundations and think tanks to fund parties but are more restrictive of private individual and corporate donors.[32] By establishing think tanks and related foundations, whose regulation they conveniently had left out of the party-financing laws, politicians immediately exploited the very loopholes they had built into the laws.

Contribution Caps

Does limiting the amount of money any one individual or corporate entity can donate to a party or campaign reduce the corruption of the democratic process? Hardly ever. Parties and politicians in democracies have a determined will to live that overcomes even the most concerted efforts to starve them out of existence or restrict their access to resources. It is common knowledge that parties in post–World War II Italy penetrated the entire state administration, using it for political financing and control, but it is less well known that parties in other European countries infiltrated supposedly autonomous state agencies to use them to their ends. The French Fifth Republic is a case in point. Despite President Charles de Gaulle's contempt for political parties, and despite their being subject to the same draconian regulations that interest groups faced,[33] they survived and multiplied. Deprived of virtually all means of financing (membership dues, donations from individuals or corporations, state subsidies), French parties collected funds by whatever illegal means they could. The party that held the presidency funneled official "secret funds" to itself, the Communists obtained funds from the Soviet Union, the Socialists perfected the technique of having its municipal governments allocate grants to Socialist-connected organizations, and the more business-oriented Gaullists had corporations pay the salaries of party staffers who were listed on city payrolls but worked full time for the party—and everyone took kickbacks from public works projects.

Until 1988, French political parties were governed by the 1901 law pertaining to associations. Parties were prohibited from collecting more than FRF 100 per person (about $17) in membership dues, although the law did not stipulate whether that was monthly or yearly. Parties "were also prohibited from accepting donations and gifts."[34] Reflecting the general distrust of political parties, state funding was minuscule. The only noticeable funding allowed after 1958, the year of the founding of the Fifth Republic, was to presidential candidates, not parties, who had won at least 5 percent of the vote in the first round.[35]

In 1988, after a variety of corruption cases pertaining to campaign and party finance erupted, including illegal arms sales to Iran, the French government proposed, and the legislature, with the cynical abstention of the Socialist Party, passed a series of party and campaign finance laws providing public subsidies to candidates for presidential and legislative elections. Donations were legalized and made tax deductible.[36]

The arrival of legal but capped donations and limited public funding, however, did not alter patterns of illegal party financing. French politicians used their legislative powers to protect themselves from prosecution for previous illegal activities by granting themselves amnesty. They also left intact the systems they had used for illegal financing. Before *and* after the 1988 lifting of the total ban on donations to parties and candidates, the state-owned oil company, Elf Acquitaine, gave funds to the major parties. Elf's number-two man Alfred Sirven stated, "I made the payments in cash. I will not say anything more."[37] In another arena, one of the key movers in the so-called Urba case of Socialist Party corruption that led to the 1988 party-financing law, Henri Emmanuelli, soon was one of the lead suspects in a new case of illegal Socialist Party financing, which also involved widespread corruption by local politicians. Evidently, the legal donations had been considered insufficient. Supermarket chains and other large distribution "warehouse"-style firms such as Auchan, Carrefour, Leclerc, Casino, and Rallye were routinely asked to make contributions in exchange for permission to purchase land or to build in specific locales. The exchange was precise: a "donation" to the party of FRF 3,500 ($600) for every square meter authorized by the planning commission.[38]

Some background detail might be useful. In 1973, in response to fears of local merchants that they would be put out of business by "big box" stores, the French government and parliament passed a law—the *loi Royer*, after its author—requiring that large stores (*grandes surfaces*) be approved for construction by the Commission nationale d'urbanisme commercial (CNUC). The law also set up equivalent departmental (that is, regional) commissions (CDUC). The national commission was staffed by a mix of politicians and merchants. The president of one of the warehouse-style firms testified that the "national representatives of the political parties in place at the time [early 1990s] at the CNUC were charged with collecting funds rather than with giving an opinion on the application files."[39] He complained that the law, "in appointing a too large number of elected officials to the CNUC and the CDUCs has created a system of political party financing at a level which has taken on a considerable scope and which, in the end, has become inescapable for the large firms." Indeed it had. According to testimony of another key figure in Socialist Party financing and the subject of judicial investigations, Jean-Pierre Destrade (the PS deputy from Pyrenées-Atlantiques), the Socialists had designated an official to oversee the "establishment of large warehouse stores." For a time, it had been him. Destrade described a system in which he carefully followed the application files to and through the national approval commission, and then let the cabinet of the minister of commerce and artisanry know the amounts and transactions the Socialist Party wanted from each applicant.[40]

The firms next turned to consulting firms that were linked to specific parties, in order to "process" their applications. The head of one such consultancy estimated that he and one large distribution chain had given at least FRF 3 million in a five- to six-year period. Investigations turned up indications that from at least

1991 to 1995, the approval and illegal-funding circuit extended to the cabinet level of government.[41]

The parties of the center and moderate left were not the only ones to find the amount of legal private financing they were able to receive inadequate to supplement public funding. The Gaullists, Communists, and independent conservatives also pursued additional means of (illegal) financing, usually by using the tried and true method of extracting payments from firms in exchange for granting contracts.[42]

The political solution was to ban all legal corporate donations, even though the corruption had been the result of inadequate legal funding. Individuals could still give up to FRF 50,000 ($8,400) per year.[43] Although some public financing was provided to compensate, the parties and politicians were basically back where they were before 1988—and it is unlikely that their response to funding starvation will be any different.

Another means of evading contribution caps, known as "fictitious employment," takes several forms. One involves having firms pay salaries of full-time government employees who are in actuality working full time for the party; another is to have the government pay the salaries of employees who instead work, illegally, full time for a political party. French president Jacques Chirac's Gaullist party appears to have perfected this technique (save that it was caught). Businessmen testifying at the trial of several of Chirac's key political allies, including former prime minister and Gaullist party president Alain Juppé, noted that they consented to the arrangement after being frequently pestered by a party activist and pointedly asked to come to the party's office (at the time, known as the RPR). There they were told it was "necessary to aid the RPR, either by donation or by employing someone." As one businessman stated, "I understood well that if they asked something of me, it was not the case that I could leave without accepting." The party was able to coerce "compliance" because it controlled Paris's municipal services, including the procurement market. The governing party also took advantage of the fact that, despite the European Union's launch of the Single Market, France was in something of a recession. In response to the question of what would happen if the firm had refused to comply with the RPR's request, one businessman replied, "It was assumed that one would have problems. And we were sitting in the dark years of our profession. Retaining the public procurement contracts was an absolute imperative."[44] Others noted that their firm's business dealings with the RPR-controlled region of Paris amounted to more than 15 percent of their revenue. One businessman testified that he agreed to fund the fictitious employment of two RPR staffers (listed on city payrolls), including the secretary of the then president of the RPR, Jacques Chirac, because he "wanted to neutralize the nuisance capacity of the party." In addition, he was assured by the RPR that "this practice is commonplace."[45] Chirac's party turned its governing majority and the recession into leverage for extorting subsidies from private firms, thereby evading the caps on contributions from private firms while supplementing their public subsidies. It also used its control over the mayor's office to have several public employees work full time for the party.[46]

The subtleties of the Gaullist system of avoiding donation caps pale in comparison to the flagrancy of the Italian parties. The illegal funds collected by Italian parties in the three decades after the passage of the restrictive 1974 party finance bill were astronomical and made a mockery of contribution caps and donor qualifications. Granted that the Italian case is extreme, it underscores the pitfalls of trying to limit the ways parties raise funds and the amount they may raise. The kickback system that had been run in Milan by the major parties for at least a decade before its exposure by the judiciary enabled politicians to finance their personal expenses and their parties or factions within their parties.[47] As one party activist stated, "in this way, the traditional parties of Milan (the DC, PSI, PCI, PRI, PSDI) had the opportunity to secure for themselves an alternative means of funding with respect to that envisioned by the law [on party financing]."[48]

When the Italian party system collapsed in 1994, disgusted Italian voters, spurred on by an opposition party, used the power of referenda to eliminate all state funding for parties and to reduce campaign funding to anemic amounts for candidates only. A subsequent law set a strict candidate spending cap, required public disclosure of campaign donations over about $10,000, allowed no donations over $20,000, and stipulated equal access to the media, which are privately and publicly owned and apparently not free. With the traditional parties in disarray and many of them bankrupt, billionaire media mogul and often-indicted Silvio Berlusconi was able to form his own party and become prime minister in 1994, then return to that office in 2001, with an absolute majority in parliament.[49] Rather than having to bribe parties to enact laws favorable to his business interests, as he had been accused of doing in the past, Berlusconi, in his position as prime minister with a governing majority, was able to enact such laws democratically.[50]

Efforts to limit corporations' ability to buy political influence through campaign and party donations can lead to other conundrums. In the United Kingdom, unfavorable public reaction to some donations from foreign individuals and firms prompted the government and parliament to consider banning foreign donations. Yet the question of how to define a foreign firm became complicated. As one expert testified to a parliamentary committee,

> Already we see the problems likely to emerge with respect to European companies; there is no reason it seems to me in principle for consider-

ing that [a European firm is] a foreign company in the context of an election which, in part and parcel, is about the Government that will rule this country as a part of Europe. It would be wrong in principle to try to exclude those sorts of interests once we admit that they are also involved in our economy, social and political life.[51]

Particularly since the advent of the Single Market, many European firms have merged with non-European firms; some have major non-European shareholders. Efforts to create enforceable limits on foreign contributions, to reduce the likelihood that political decisions are bought or influenced by those with only a narrow economic link to the country, are vitiated by creating a free trade area.

As Germany's experience shows, party and campaign finance regulations primarily generate creative means of circumventing the caps. In 1967, the Bundestag passed a new Law Governing Political Parties and Their Funding: state funding of political parties would be limited to providing funds for running campaigns.[52] The parties were required to provide a public record of their income: contributions of DM 20,000 ($5,000) per calendar year by "natural persons" had to be listed with the name and address of the contributor; contributions by "juridical persons," that is, corporations and businesses, had to be listed if the total donated was more than DM 200,000 ($50,000) in a calendar year. With this law, the current system of party finance, along with a tradition of *Umwegfinanzierung* or evading the rules, was essentially begun.

Immediately, the parties invented a variety of ways to skirt the law. They claimed that they received much larger amounts from anonymous contributors, and therefore they could not give the source of the contributions. These contributions often came through charitable, religious, scientific, or social organizations before being passed on to the parties, and so they could be deducted from applicable federal taxes by the donors.[53] These organizations commonly moved the contributions into accounts controlled by the parties, and the public reports listed the charitable organization as the donor.[54] The CDU went so far as to make the incredible claim that the funds it received illegally in the 1990s came from the estates of Jews who appreciated what the CDU had done for them and did not want their names and addresses made public. The former federal minister of the interior, Manfred Kanther, admitted that the CDU of Hessen had, under his direction, transferred DM 17 million into foreign accounts: "speculating that no one in Germany would dare question the estates of Jewish emigrants and their distribution, [and] in order to hide the origin of these funds, Kanther and his colleagues declared that they were the legacies and bequests of Jewish emigrants."[55]

Another way that parties, candidates, and their contributors evade finance laws is to exploit the absence of fine print in the laws. If there are caps on corporate donations, parties can "ask" that a firm have each of its subsidiaries donate, including those overseas. In 1993, one of France's major construction firms, Grands travaux de Marseille (GTM), got around the ceiling of FRF 500,000 (about $100,000) per party by using that method. Chirac's party, the RPR, thus received FRF 500,000 ($100,000) from GTM-BTP, FRF 450,000 ($90,000) from GTM-Entreprise, FRF 450,000 ($90,000) from GTM-Entrepose-Electricité, and FRF 120,000 ($24,000) from GTM-International. Thanks to its subsidiaries, GTM was able to donate, legally, over three times the lawful amount to the Gaullist party. The Socialist Party similarly benefited from the subsidiaries of another major construction firm, Lyonnaise des Eaux-Dumez, receiving FRF 500,000 ($100,000) from that company and FRF 150,000 ($30,000) from its subsidiary Dumez-SNC, FRF 150,000 ($30,000) from Dumez-EPS, and FRF 50,000 ($10,000) from Dumez.[56]

Public Financing of Election Campaigns

Public financing is an often-tried technique for remedying the problems that accompany private financing or its complete ban. As Thomas Jefferson noted long ago, however, "To compel a man to furnish contributions of money for the propagation of opinions which he disbelieves and abhors is sinful and tyrannical."[57] The approach has its drawbacks. Another problem with public financing, in addition to the issue that Jefferson raised, is that parties never find that the amount they receive from public financing is enough, so they evade the limits and regulations that are a part of this method. Furthermore, the parties in power may want the financing, but they are loath to see their opponents benefit, and the general public may be similarly loath to see their tax money funding the very politicians they claim they detest.[58] Public funding seems to have the same effect on parties and campaigns as it does in the economy—it subsidizes inefficiencies, allows organizations to become bloated, and in the long run, keeps prices—in this case the cost of running a campaign or party—artificially high.[59]

In Italy, Spain, and Portugal, as in Germany, public funding has been generous and easily available. And political corruption for the purpose of party and campaign finance is just as common. Through a set of laws passed in 1985 and 1987, Spain has severely restricted private donations, both corporate or individual, and substantially increased public subsidies to parties.[60] Although the assumption is that public financing levels the playing field and fosters clean politics, that is not always the effect. As one expert says of the situation in Spain, "the reality of Spanish party financing presents a very different picture."[61] Despite what seems to be generous public funding, the major Spanish parties routinely have requested kickbacks of 2–4 percent on public works contracts, particularly in construction. In addition, both before and after the switch to substantial public funding, parties illegally financed their election campaigns. The Flick group of Germany allegedly funneled money to the Spanish Socialist Party in 1977, and in 1989 three firms (Filesa, Time Export, and Malesa) apparently used false invoicing to finance that party's electoral expenses.[62] In the 1990s, a variety of party-related scandals emerged, including the Socialist Party's treasurer collecting bribes from Volkswagen for its purchase of SEAT, and Siemens for its contract with the AVE high-speed train. In 2003, corrupt linkages between parties and construction firms were exposed.[63] Leveling the playing field through public financing is important for fairness and access but goads some to try to augment their resources through other means in order to best their competition.

Despite receiving public funding, parties have resorted to extorting kickbacks in order to extract "donations." The CDS (Democratic Center) Party's director admitted that "outside of membership dues, our finances essentially depended on the allocation from the public Treasury . . . and from revenue drawn from advertising in our magazine, *Commune moderne* [*Modern Town*]. . . . In 1989, we did not receive any donations of the type from individual or corporate donors."[64] The combination of legal state and private funding did not meet the party's demand for funds, so it resorted to taking kickbacks from government projects for which their politicians could influence the award. In 1986, before state financing, the CDS set up a system enabling it to finance itself by way of a Swiss bank account into which firms put their "donations" or proceeds from inflated invoices.[65] When state financing became available in 1988, the party continued to obtain suspect contributions from large and small firms. Investigations determined that the party's leadership were directly involved in running the system.[66]

In 1995, public funding for French parties was increased and corporate donations were banned. In France, the RPR, PS, PCF, and PR all continued their system of getting (illegal) kickbacks on public works projects in the Paris region, despite the 1995 financing law providing for fairly generous public financing of campaign and operating expenses.[67] Yet according to the president of the national regulatory commission for parties and elections, Jacques Bonnet, the system is more or less adequate for now. In part thanks to extensive prosecution by the judiciary, businesses are reluctant to yield to parties' demand for illegal funding, and the politicians themselves may be more cautious now. Bonnet noted that they now have a tendency to "rat" on each other, which they didn't do earlier.[68] Yet there is already evidence that the parties are trying to worm out of these restrictions. The Gaullist party created, in 2003, a foundation that solicits contributions from corporations and individuals, allegedly to support the party's think tank. The lines of separation between the party, the foundation, and the think tank are any-thing but clear.

Most of the time, politicians do not believe that public financing provides enough for their needs. Charles Pasqua illustrates the conundrum of campaign financing: unable to raise legally what he thought were enough funds, he perhaps chose to raise them illegally. He is accused of using his discretionary powers of office, as French interior minister, to illicitly extract funds of up to $1 million in 1994 from a major firm, GEC-Alsthom, in exchange for his permission to move their corporate headquarters.[69] He is also under investigation for receiving ap-proximately $1.5 million to finance his European Parliament campaign in 1999 in exchange for granting permission to one of his Corsican contacts, Robert Fe-liciaggi, to develop gambling at a casino in the Alps. As interior minister at the time of the payment, he had the authority to make that decision. As of Decem-ber 2006, Pasqua is under investigation by the Cour de justice de la République (CJR) in this affair.[70] Evidence also suggests that Pasqua, through his son—who is evading an international arrest warrant by residing in Tunisia, a country with which France has no extradition treaty—received about $1.9 million from the in-ternational arms dealer Pierre Falcone. Various witnesses have alleged that the il-legal payments were intended "to finance the political activities of Charles Pasqua."[71] Falcone's payments wound up, via bank transfer from Zurich to Geneva to Madera to Buenos Aires to New York and back to Geneva, in a bank account controlled by Pasqua's son; evidently they were used to finance Pasqua's political campaigns and publications. Conveniently Pasqua had been elected to the European Parliament before these facts came to light, so he was covered by the immunity offered its associates, which the European Parliament steadfastly refused to lift. In this case the EU, rather than discovering and exposing corrup-tion, sheltered it. After Pasqua's 2004 reelection bid to the European Parliament failed, he cashed in some political debts he had accumulated over the years (for instance, he reminded Chirac that if he, Pasqua, had run for president in 2002, he would have won enough votes to prevent Chirac from winning) and got himself elected to the French Senate.[72] The Senate seat has granted him immunity from the "coercive" aspects of a French judicial investigation, such as preventive de-tention, and blocks his prosecution unless the Senate votes to lift his immunity. What we seem to have is the paradoxical scenario of a politician turning to bribery to finance a political campaign and then apparently campaigning for reelection in order to avoid prosecution for the initial case of bribery.

All of this brings us to the French solution for corruption: bestow amnesty on the politicians, prosecute the businessmen, and then provide fairly generous public funding for parties and candidates, cap spending, block corporate contri-butions to parties but allow them to be tax deductible if given to party "foundations,"[73] set up a modestly staffed oversight board that has no power to enforce the law or to levy of penalties, and see what happens.

The Libertarian Solution?

The sense that rules will solve or at least minimize the problem is confounded by Sweden. It is one of the least corrupt countries in the world, but it has no rules about party or campaign donations, spending, or reporting, nor does it have rules about media access.[74] Political parties in the UK may have reduced the demand for illegal funding simply by allowing their demand to be unregulated and therefore met legally. Until 2001, the UK had no spending limits, contribution caps, or donor restrictions. By the early 1990s, party financing had taken on an unseemly appearance in that it looked as though large party donations bought favorable outcomes. A suspicious number of party donors were granted "honours" by the party in power, whether Labour or Conservative, or placed on the boards of quangos.[75] Both parties came to rely more heavily on large donations from wealthy individuals, many associated with large firms.[76] Such donations do not necessarily pay a party's costs, and opposition parties can find their funding dwindling, given that campaigning is an almost a continual activity and that parties have high overhead and substantial running expenses.[77] As a Labour Party general secretary testified, "if we are to raise that kind of finance, we have to be able to seek donations and to do so at a fairly high level."[78]

Legal donations may not meet the level the party needs or perceives it needs. The supply of such funding may be limited by public financing (lower than a party wants), and by the lack of incentives for donors to give to a party when there are no guarantees that the party can repay the donation with specific policy or material benefits. Corruption provides the guarantee. To wit, the multinational French construction firm Bouygues donated major funds to the French Center Party after it won the contract for a major bridge construction project. The party's leader, Pierre Méhaignerie, was infrastructure minister at the time and well positioned to arrange the deal.[79] The level of demand for legal funding also appears dependent on the organizational structure of party systems and the parties in those systems. Most of the legal funding for the CDU-CSU, for instance, goes to the *Land* branches of the party, leaving the federal CDU-CSU heavily reliant on donations. To increase those, Kohl turned to secret financing methods. In Germany, quid pro quos still occur, but the participants evade prosecution because the payments often come after the favorable decision.[80]

Until the late 1960s, Germany did not have party finance regulations, yet party financing had an aura of impropriety. The role of political parties in the new

German state after World War II was summarized in only one sentence in the Grundgesetz (Basic Law), and only one sentence governed their financing: "The parties must provide a public accounting of the source of their funds." Between 1949 and 1954, there was no direct or indirect financing of the parties by the state. The SPD was able to fund its activities through the contributions of its members, but the CDU-CSU got its funds through the contributions of major corporations and businesses. The CDU-CSU–led government soon arranged the tax laws to suit its funding interests. In 1954, contributions to charitable, religious, scientific, and social organizations that undertake socially "useful" activities became tax deductible.[81] As a result, in 1956, CDU leader and chancellor Konrad Adenauer and several German industrialists in Cologne created the Staatsbuergerliche Vereinigung e.V. (SV) as a juridical "person" to accept contributions to the center-right parties (CDU, CSU, FDP), and with its creation came a massive influx of funds. Thereupon, the SPD in Hessen asked the German Constitutional Court to provide an opinion as to whether this was a constitutional activity. The court said it was unconstitutional, because it benefited one set of parties more than others.[82]

The SV then changed the wording of its charter and said it would no longer accept funds to be transferred directly to political parties. In essence, however, the SV lied.[83] It was later discovered that the center-right party foundation used a variety of detours to hide its activities, including the transfer of funds into accounts in Switzerland and Liechtenstein. In 1972, the CDU, through this shell foundation, established an account at the Swiss Bank Corporation; from there the money was transferred to another account in Switzerland, thence to Luxembourg, then Frankfurt am Main, and finally from there to a bank in Cologne, from which the CDU withdrew funds.

This system of financing went on for twenty-five years completely unknown to the general public.[84] The first investigations of the system took place in 1975, when the head of the Tax Evasion Bureau of St. Augustin discovered documents concerning a "European Office of Management Consulting" in Liechtenstein, which he learned accepted money for fictional shares in fictional firms on behalf of the CDU.[85] Even in countries where the laws concerning party financing are nearly nonexistent, with legality being established primarily through high-court interpretations of the constitution, parties and politicians resort to corruption when they cannot get the funds they want legally.

Indeed, parties may legally obtain loans in the UK, but Tony Blair and several high-ranking officials in his Labour Party are seriously implicated in an arrangement in which the party may have obtained loans in exchange for promoting the awarding of life peerages to their creditors.[86] The Conservative and Liberal Democrat parties also have accepted loans, but at the time of the facts they were not in a position to nominate or award peerages.

As this book makes clear, a country's status as a model wealthy democracy and staunch EU member is no guarantee against corruption: Germany, with its federal multiparty system, free press, high per capita income, and major role in European integration, also hosts a political system whose party financing suffers from fairly widespread corruption.[87] The Single Market, the increased economic competition following from it, as well as privatization do nothing to address the conundrum of campaign and party financing. Those who give sizable donations expect a return; they will hesitate to donate if others who do not donate can nevertheless benefit from a political favor. So politicians strive to ensure that benefits are tailored, bestowing goods such as access, official honors, government contracts, and patronage. If funding demands still are not met, politicians will coerce donations, extracting "bribes" from the recipients of the contracts they award. No funding scheme is ever going to solve the collective action problem of party and campaign finance, and its close connection to corruption.

Corruption can occur because political parties usually have some influence over the operations of the judiciary (despite formal independence of the latter), so they can impede investigations. It can also occur because political parties and their politicians are the ones who must write and pass reform bills, so they can write laws with loopholes and create anemic oversight agencies.

The remedies to these dilemmas are themselves confounded by the dynamics of electoral competition and representation. Transparency is often suggested as a partial solution. The catch is that to have transparency, those least interested in it, politicians, must enact enabling legislation to create regulatory agencies that keep track of party income and outgo. They must also grant those agencies genuine enforcement and penalty powers. Making party income public somewhat limits efforts and schemes by political parties to demand and use inappropriate funds for electoral or programmatic purposes—that is, to collect from those sources that give funds in the expectation that they will receive favorable legislation, policy outputs, and the like. It has the drawback of increasing the disinclination of private donors (including firms) to donate funds. As the head of a major coal mining firm in the UK stated, "It is a private decision made with tax-paid money and I ought to have the right to distribute that money without any public disclosure."[88] It also has the unintended consequence of making the public more suspicious that government decisions are being bought by the wealthy. In commenting on the Labour Party's voluntary disclosure of the names of large donors, former minister Peter Mandelson (EU Trade Commissioner, 2004–present) said, "I think we probably didn't foresee that, in opening the books in this way, the [Labour] government would create possible perceptions of conflicts of interest."[89] Nonetheless, the public perception is an improvement over a secret occurrence.[90]

The effectiveness of disclosure seems to depend in part on the context. In Italy, ever the negative example, disclosure requirements were useless in inhibiting party finance corruption, and laws did not provide for budget disclosures by regional or provincial parties.[91] Since many of the parties' activities took place in the subnational regions and provinces, the discrepancy between real and revealed expenditures most likely was enormous. And that's not counting the effect of factionalism within the parties, which gave each bloc an incentive to keep its rivals from knowing the amounts in its war chest.[92] As Martin Rhodes notes, "in the late 1970s it was estimated that the inclusion of income and expenditure on the part of local branches would have doubled the sums presented in official accounts— and much of this revenue would have come from illicit sources."[93] Besides, disclosure to whom? If merely to a parliamentary president or similar official, or to regional government agencies, it is unlikely that any but a dogged journalist or academic would review the accounts.

Although written tongue in cheek, the American humorist Dave Barry's suggestion may be the most direct way to solve the disclosure problem. Noting that at televised auto races, "the drivers wear uniforms plastered with the logos of the companies that sponsor them," he goes on to explain that "what I'm actually proposing is that we require candidates to wear signs clearly identifying who is paying them to hold their current set of opinions. This would clear up a lot of confusion. . . . Imagine how much easier it would be to understand George W. Bush's environmental policies if he had an oil company sign tattooed on his forehead."[94] This suggestion might elicit the same complaint directed at professional sports—that it's too commercialized—but electoral politics has already become commercialized, and pretending that it is not merely helps to hide the corruption. Some truth in advertising would be refreshing and would expose the quid pro quos to public scrutiny.

Another solution would be to empower public interest groups to intervene effectively to limit campaign finance corruption. The idea is to make it easy for watchdog groups to sue to enforce campaign finance regulations. Politicians may object that they will become the victims of politically motivated lawsuits, yet the threat of legal action may impel some adherence to their own weak laws.

Evening out existing regulations may help, since lopsided regulations, which focus on only one or two aspects of party and campaign finance, can create problems. Two European countries with serious corruption in party finance have a history of no expenditure caps: Germany has not had them for many decades, and Italy imposed them only in 1993. But Germany has an overall cap on how much funding each party can have, and Italy has contribution caps, giving their parties an incentive to keep some financing sources and activities off the books.[95]

Spending caps seem tailor-made for billionaire media magnates, such as sometime prime minister Silvio Berlusconi: the restrictions on advertising expenditures place a premium on those who own media outlets, so that they can advertise free of charge or at artificially low rates. They can also have themselves favorably covered as "news" by the media they own and strictly limit unfavorable news coverage. Berlusconi's Pubitalia was found to have given heavy discounts to Berlusconi's party during the 1994 legislative election,[96] and when Berlusconi, as president of the EU and prime minister of Italy, suggested that a European Parliament deputy would make a good Nazi, his TV channels, and the state-run channels, did not cover the international news-making incident. Although this sort of episode may not be corruption strictly defined, it clearly is conflict of interest.

It is not enough to assume that the competitive economic pressures of the EU will eventually make it difficult for politicians to extract illegal funding from firms and government agencies. As other chapters have shown, competitive pressures create their own incentives for corruption. Nor will the EU, merely by virtue of its being an international organization, reduce corruption: its politicians, including those elected to the European Parliament, need campaign and party financing. If anything, the EU, through the European Parliament, has proved something of an impediment to national efforts to prosecute illegal campaign financing or other sorts of corruption. The diplomatic immunity it confers on its elected officials and its extreme reluctance to lift it stymie the efforts of national judges to investigate and prosecute. Between 1981 and 1999, the European Parliament granted requests to lift immunity in only 16 of 88 cases. It reasons that because the person in question is a politician, the request to lift the immunity is inevitably politically motivated. If a judge requests a member of the European Parliament's voting records in an effort to check whether a quid pro quo may have occurred, the European Parliament views the request as evidence of a biased, tainted investigation.[97]

The public and the media are factors in anticorruption drives. If the public is outraged that major donors expect something in return from parties and candidates, then the public needs to support alternative financing, and at a very generous level. The Clean Elections project in the state of Arizona appears to be an option that allows a high level of public financing coupled with small but numerous individual donations to candidates (currently capped at $5). There is an independent and active oversight board. The public needs to demand that its politicians establish effective oversight and enforcement mechanisms and needs to withhold votes from those who engage in illegal or dubious actions; it cannot just say that such behavior is inevitable. The media need to be investigative, despite accusations that they are being political when exposing the misdeeds and corruption of politicians. The risk, of course, is that advertisers will disagree and that the public will come to see various media as partisan. Granted, the political system as well as the structure of media and capital are stacked against investigative media and public retribution for corruption. Voters often do not have a choice of clean candidates or parties, or decide that other issues are more important. In addition, voters with an anti-corruption agenda find that collective action obstacles make it difficult to organize popular reform movements.

Context matters. For instance, the British media have been alert to improprieties, and the public sensitive to it. When, in 1997, the media discovered that Labour had been given £1 million by Bernie Ecclestone, the Formula 1 racing owner, shortly before the Labour government was going to consider granting Formula 1 an exemption from the ban on tobacco advertising at sporting events, an embarrassed Labour Party was publicly goaded into returning the donation to Ecclestone. Even though parties may be tempted to extort kickbacks on public works projects, the weight of governing norms is such that the risk of doing so is quite high. The British voting public has not become inured to its politicians being corrupt. The first party found to have collected under-the-table donations in exchange for awarding a contract likely risks serious electoral reprisals. Negative publicity in a number of cases seems to have reduced the flow of business-related contributions.[98]

Regulations do not, per se, create corruption, nor does the absence of them eliminate corruption. When party finance was still completely unregulated in Italy, there were several impressive cases of party finance–related corruption.[99] Applying some measure of regulation to party finance in the UK has not (yet?) bred corruption.[100] As with other instances of institutional design, the effects vary according to the context in which the institutions (whether rules, agencies, regulations, or laws) are situated. Nevertheless, regulations that deprive parties and candidates of all legal means of funding lead to illegal, corrupt party financing. Closing down the legal market for a good that is much in demand—in this case, party and campaign financing—merely produces a black market for it. It is also clear that when parties decide they need more funding than legally allowable, they will subvert the law by resorting to illegal means or by creating new techniques that subvert the law's spirit. Finally, it is not the rules that make ethical choices but the politicians. And, to quote Croce, "only idiots expect their politicians to be honest." It is, however, the "idiots" who have less corruption.[101]

THE PATHOLOGIES OF AN INTERNATIONAL ORGANIZATION

When the World Bank thinks it is financing an electric power station, it is really financing a brothel.

—Paul Rosenstein-Rodin, Deputy Economics Director, World Bank, 1947

As previous chapters have shown, the institutions of the EU have a limited role in reducing corruption in member states. Compounding the EU's feeble influence within the states are the new opportunities for creative funding and outright graft that the EU provides. This is because, when divorced from its laudatory agenda of uniting the peoples of Europe and promoting peace and prosperity, the EU is a thick tangle of negotiated rules and regulations, most of which govern economic transactions. In an elaborate process, states and others promulgate these European Union rules and regulations, which they then leave to the states and their national and subnational government agencies to implement and enforce. State interests may lie in deliberately tolerating fraud in certain economic sectors, and behaviors that were thought to be culture or state specific may be universalized through the new institutional context.

To understand this process, and the generally weak policing and judicial structure, we must take into account the peculiar structure of international organizations, including the possible differences in attitudes toward corruption that may affect member countries' institutional responses to corruption. In an international organization such as the EU, the member states have delegated *to themselves* the collection and distribution of an enormous percentage of the EU's budget and have also delegated *to themselves* the operation of most of its regulatory structure. A 2006 House of Lords report noted that "as over 80% of European funds are disbursed within the Member States, the Commission alone cannot be held responsible for the regularity of these transactions."[1] If combating corruption involves policing the agents, then it is the member states that must be controlled.

States, however, do not easily give up sovereignty, and the states of the EU are no exception. The real investigative and enforcement capacities of the EU are limited. Most of the detection and pursuit of fraud and corruption, as well as their prosecution, are reserved to the policing and legal systems of the member states. As an official in the EU's antifraud unit stated, there is a "complete lack at Community [EU] level of any judicial powers relating to investigations by the police and public prosecutors."[2] The European Commission's 2001 proposal to create the job of European Prosecutor has, not surprisingly, not been adopted. The deliberate decisions to keep the international supervisory institutions, such as the Commission, relatively weak tends to insulate the officials of those institutions from accountability. Those officials can ignore calls to reform the system. As a former chief accountant of the Commission wrote in 2006, "the hierarchy of the EC [European Commission] has adopted an attitude of permanent state of denial of the depth and nature of the [financial management] problems and from this point no real resolution can be pursued. All we have is window-dressing and promises for the future."[3] Given weak international controls, a new pot of money for government subsidies, and an exceedingly complex set of frequently revised rules (which can be applied EU-wide, as one size fits all *regulations,* or as *directives,* which each country adapts to its own legislative structure), it is not surprising that the EU's budget and programs are themselves subject to fraud and corruption, and also integrated into national patterns of fraud and corruption.

Regional or international economic integration has been said to reduce corruption by improving norms of business and government practice and, through economic competition, making corruption's drag on the economy more noticeable.[4] These macrolevel trends may exist in theory, but at the microlevel they often fail to obtain. International economic integration tends to remove barriers to trade and increase economic competition but fails to install effective regulatory and enforcement agencies. Some have pointed to the EU's Convention against Corruption as evidence that the EU promotes norms of clean government. But the convention does not have the force of law, and it merely masks a more significant but informal convention, the one that agrees to tolerate corruption because to expose it would be to further undermine the tenuous popularity of Brussels. If anything, the EU (to say nothing of the UN) should lead us to question whether international organizations promote norms of clean government. Other chapters in this volume show that the positive effects of the EU on reducing corruption are hard to find, and an examination of the EU's treatment of its own whistle-blowers raises doubts about how seriously the EU takes norms of good governance.

The EU has not been characterized by its member states' unilateral dropping of their barriers to trade. Instead, in multilateral negotiations, the states create a complex set of rules that each is supposed to follow in order to promote free trade and competition. It gets even more convoluted because in most cases the rules can be implemented in different ways by different states, provided the overall outcome is the same. So, firms wanting to do business in other countries face not just one intricate set of EU rules but often different sets of rules that vary by country. That in itself is a recipe for corruption. A closer look at the EU's regulation of government contracting, in the name of promoting more competition and free trade, and its responses to whistle-blowers, is instructive.

The EU has a limited ability to monitor transactions in member states that tend to be vulnerable to corruption, and it has a limited ability and inherent incentive *not* to aggressively monitor its own programs. Malfeasance and corruption are probably not rampant within the institutions of the EU, but the permissive culture is itself an incentive to dubious behavior on the part of officials, firms, and private individuals.[5] And this permissive culture is one of the pathologies inhering in international organizations.

BYZANTIUM RESURRECTED: PUBLIC PROCUREMENT IN THE EUROPEAN UNION

Government contracting is a major area in which corruption takes place, and many scholars, policy specialists, and legal experts think that the openness and transparency of the procurement process are keys to reducing corruption. To attain openness and transparency, states may create rules and join international organizations that create rules binding them to a common set of regulations. The EU's public procurement regime is an outstanding example of such an arrangement. Within the EU member states, corruption most often occurs through kickback schemes on public works contracts issued by member-state authorities. Those contracts account for 10–20 percent of the combined GDP of the EU states; an estimate for 2002 puts the figure at 16 percent or EUR 1.5 trillion.[6] To the extent that these collusive arrangements violate the EU's many regulations on public procurement, it is here that corruption most often intersects with the EU's rules and regulations.

Pitched as a cure for noncompetitiveness, and even as a possible means of limiting corruption, the European Union's rules on public procurement are anything but. They have limited reach in local and regional government and, if anything, due to their complexity and onerous technical requirements, provide an incentive for corruption. Oversight by the EU is virtually nonexistent, and legal remedies are difficult to activate. In 2000, the European Commission's Internal Market division, which handled public procurement, had a staff of 50; that same year, an estimated 595,986 contracts were put out to tender by EU states, with only an estimated 14.9 percent of the contracts advertised as required by the EU.[7] The staff of the antifraud unit, OLAF, was increased by only 29 (up from 329) after the 2004 accession, which added ten states, none of which is known for clean government.

Decentralization and devolution have also dampened the impact of the EU rules. Generally, subnational governments' awareness of EU rules is low. The French state, when one of its regions was accused of violating EU procurement rules, admitted that "the infringements committed are essentially the result of the inexperience of the contracting authorities in question in applying the Community rules on the award of public contracts."[8] In addition, the "structure of sub-central government in Member States is likely to exacerbate non-publication [of calls to tender] particularly where procurement is devolved to (small) independent units, whose procurement is not aggregated."[9] Furthermore, much subnational procurement spending is under the thresholds at which the EU rules kick in, and local governments can ensure that they fall under the threshold by parsing out pieces of the same project as if they were separate contracts.

Decentralization has other effects. In Italy, mayors were given the apparently logical powers to respond to local emergencies by issuing orders "relating to public health, building construction and the local police."[10] In the Italian context, where market competition was outside the norm, this mechanism became a convenient way of avoiding the competitive bidding procedures of EU public procurement law. Indeed, in 1988 the waste management agency of the northern coastal city La Spezia was "taken to court" by the European Commission for invoking an emergency procedure when an emergency did not exist. The European Court of Justice ruled against the Italian entity, but that did not stop repetition of the practice.[11]

In addition, political factors intervene. Just as "domestic business and labour can make life uncomfortable for both bureaucrats and vote-sensitive politicians if domestic bids are rejected in favour of foreign ones, particularly in recessions," local business and labor can be significant factors in local elections, and hence give local politicians and bureaucrats an incentive to favor local firms over out-of-area firms in public contracting.[12] A mid-1990s survey of large and small businesses by the European Commission found that "a very large number of respondents, however, allege that local preference and the reluctance to take on board new suppliers . . . are still standard purchasing practices. Almost 50 percent of larger companies reporting obstacles to accessing procurement markets believe that purchasers are awarding contracts on the basis of criteria other than price and quality. Similarly, some 40 percent of small firms indicate that their access to procurement markets is hindered by the lack of publication of calls for tenders."[13]

The EU rules, rather than changing behavior, merely are absorbed into the local patterns.

A 1996 EU survey of the 110,000 procurement notices in the EU found that about 30 percent of the "notices of invitation to tenders do not specify the award criteria" and that only about half of the calls to tender then later post the contract award notices, which the Commission sees as critical for informing competitors about the structure of the industry. Also, procurement agencies often fail to publish advance information about upcoming calls, and in the award notices they often fail to give relevant data such as the price or value of the contract.[14] In other words, after nearly twenty-five years under EU procurement directives, the process still lacks transparency. In addition, foreign import penetration of the domestic public procurement markets in the EU states appears to be increasing, but slowly, and it is far below the rate of import penetration in private enterprise procurement. Along with indicating national biases, the data suggest that it would be possible for foreign competitors to be incorporated into corrupt tendering systems—since the increase in foreign bidders is very slow.

As of 1994, there was "no evidence of price convergence between Member States for products bought by the public sector. . . . Since no clear price convergence has been identified, it can be assumed that the competition effect predicted by the Cecchini Report [of 1988] in relation to the opening of public procurement has not yet materialized." For all EU countries, national import penetration is much higher in the private sector than in the public sector.[15]

A 1988 study for the European Commission on the potential impact of the Single Market program on the construction industry estimated that the opening up of public procurement would have "relatively limited consequences."[16] A case in point is the United Kingdom, which has been an aggressive promoter of compulsory competitive tendering. In 1995, however, "the Audit Commission, the local government watchdog, said . . . that there was still 'little effective competition' for many local contracts, and that 70 percent of authorities did not actively encourage private-sector bids. Contractors said the worst offenders included the big-city Labour authorities such as those in Manchester and Glasgow."[17]

The same ruses used for corruption in national and subnational contracting are used on EU-sponsored programs. Overinvoicing is common: the contractor sets up shell companies in different countries and uses them as subcontractors; they don't actually do the work but enable the contractor to present the necessary invoices while keeping his or her own firm's books clean.

In Italy, EU programs were absorbed into the local traditions. The night of September 30, 1992, nine of eleven Abruzzo regional councilors were arrested on charges of corruption. In July of that year, they had approved the awarding of grants to firms for projects cofinanced by the regional funds of the EEC. They awarded about ITL 7.3 billion ($6 million) to 350 firms and community entities, without providing the required list of awardees and a statement of how they met the project criteria. Their cover was blown only when Francesco Mannella, a disgruntled applicant and contractor who wanted financing for a hotel he was trying to complete, called the regional council office; he was told he had not been awarded a grant and was not allowed to see the list. He then called the local police to complain. Investigations revealed that the criterion for the decision was political favoritism. Although the case provoked the ire of the EU's commissioner for the regions, it did not result in significant changes to operating procedures, and some of the politicians involved have come to be seen as elder statesmen in certain Italian political circles. There was an odd disconnect between the exposure of the case and the EU's (in)action on it: the annual antifraud report covering 1992 made no mention of the Abruzzo events.[18] The EU did not pursue the case, which would have entailed trying to force Italy to pursue it in the courts.

Monitoring Byzantium

Even though the EU has widened and deepened the scope of its public procurement rules, many public contracts now escape the high standards because (1) they are below the financial thresholds, or (2) they are held to a lesser standard because they are considered public concessions, not public works contracts. The latter is particularly significant in the era of privatization, of governments contracting out not just the building of infrastructure or supply of goods but the running and delivery of services—known formally as public concessions. A government's effort to capitalize on the alleged advantages of private enterprise running government services means that the contracting process will be less transparent. Examples abound. A recent one is the Thessaloniki metro contract in Greece. Because the winning consortium would not just build the metro but would run it and, in the European Commission's words, would "bear risk" in that "its income from the project remains uncertain," Greece could legitimately define the contract "as a concession contract, rather than a public works contract, which would be subject to tougher procurement rules."[19] Many major public works contracts in Europe now are run as concessions: airports, toll roads, water and waste treatment systems, subways, trains, stadiums, public housing, and the like. The capacity of EU public procurement rules to force competition and impose oversight that might discourage corruption is significantly limited.

The EU is severely understaffed to monitor the states' adherence to the very procurement directives they promulgated and agreed to. As noted previously, the

Internal Market Directorate in Brussels has a small staff of professionals to handle implementation and oversight, and to follow up on complaints about procurement. The Commission optimistically relies on the states to police themselves, and especially on contractors to bring suit, because allegedly effective remedies are in place; the remedies too are an EU-level set of rules that states are supposed to apply. As the 2003 Annual Monitoring Report states, "Complaints are the chief source for detecting infringements."[20] The Commission asserts that monitoring can be done by firms themselves: "With the Remedies Directives in place, economic operators in every Member State have the possibility of lodging before a national court or tribunal (or body whose decisions are subject to judicial review) a complaint for violation by purchasing entities of the rules laid down in the Directives. . . . The extent of the remedies available to suppliers should make them the most effective means of protecting the rights of firms bidding for contracts."[21] But as has been documented in other areas of the EU, real access to remedies is difficult to obtain and, even where successful, is typically limited to the specific case for which the complaint was lodged.[22]

Firms can be justifiably concerned that if they litigate they will be discriminated against in future public tender awards.[23] As the UK House of Lords Select Committee on the European Communities reported in 1988,

> A tenderer contemplating taking legal proceedings in a national court against a public authority claiming breach of the Community's procurement rules faces fundamental problems. It is likely that the tenderer still hopes subsequently to do business with the procuring authority; and, as witnesses were keen to emphasise, he will not want to bite the hand that feeds him. . . . It is, therefore, unrealistic to expect that tenderers will collectively police the Community rules. Most tenderers will prefer to cut their immediate losses in the hope of establishing a longer term relationship of trust and confidence.[24]

Also, cases brought by contractors are often thrown out of court on a technicality. The "poster case" for the effectiveness of EU rules on public procurement fizzled when France's highest administrative court, the Cour de cassation, ruled that France's Competition Commission (which investigated the case) had violated the "human rights" of the firms charged with collusion, price-fixing, and exclusion of a foreign competitor. In this case, the subsidiary of a large Italian public works firm, Condotte acqua, had tried to bid on large contracts for the construction of a high-speed train line and an associated bridge project in France. Thirty-one French contractors, apparently in collusion not just with themselves but with French rail authorities, had already divided up the projects and knew what the outcome of the bid process would be. The Italian firm complained to the French

Competition Commission that the French firms were pressuring it to withdraw. The French commission looked into the complaint, found it valid, and levied large fines on the firms in question. The latter appealed. Their fines, ranging in amounts from about $1,000 to $25 million, were thrown out when it was determined that the firms' "human rights" had been violated on a procedural issue.[25]

Absurdly, the EU's leadership has not always helped the oversight and enforcement process: the Single Market commissioner in the early 1990s, the Italian Raniero Vanni d'Archirafi, "called for a truce in the prosecution of Member States for violations or non-implementation of single market legislation." He reasoned that "public procurement is a sensitive area and all sensitive areas deserve special treatment."[26] Romano Prodi, EU commissioner in 1999–2004, did not exactly underscore the importance of adherence to the rules when he called the EU's stability pact for monetary union "stupid."

Although the investigations and trials of the 1990s might seem to have disrupted efforts to maintain or create corrupt public procurement systems, the French state and EU directives are providing means to re-create them. The EU public works directive implemented in France in November 2001 allows a threshold of EUR 6.2 million before EU public procurement regulations must be applied, and the 2003 French law moves the domestic threshold from EUR 90,000 to the EU level of EUR 6.2 million. This means that over 94 percent of the central state's and over 98 percent of local governments' public works contracts will not have to be put out for bid. In addition, a public accountant and a representative from France's competition oversight board no longer must be present at the meetings where contracts are awarded, and dividing contracts into smaller lots to avoid the threshold no longer is penalized. The only nod to transparency or openness is a clause requiring public agencies to publish a list of the previous calendar year's contracts and awardees. Even the large construction firms objected, perhaps because they feared they would become easy targets of politicians and bureaucrats demanding bribes for the award of markets, or because they would be on the wrong end of occasional favoritism.

Agency Capture

Further contributing to the potential for fraud is the fact that in many member states, the implementation and oversight of EU programs are heavily influenced by the very groups meant to be regulated. Take agriculture, for instance. Until the early 1990s its multitude of subsidy programs consumed almost 80 percent of the EU's annual budget. Administration of the subsidy programs was in the hands of the states; the programs, in turn, were tightly linked with agricultural interests. In

France, for example, the national farmers' unions have official voice on the many national, regional, and local farm administrative bodies that write the rules and manage the programs. In many countries, for the purposes of various subsidies and crop "interventions" (in which a product never goes to market but is put in storage or destroyed), the local farmers' cooperative has the authority to "verify" the size and quality of the crop and to issue the subsidy check to the farmer. If there is an inspection by a government agent, which rarely occurs, the farmer and cooperative are typically given extra time, beyond the maximum allowable two days' notice, to get their fields and accounts in order. For instance, the Court of Auditors found that Italy gives farmers ten days' advance notice of upcoming inspections of declared field plantings (instead of the required two), and that French authorities also routinely give farmers more than the EU-stipulated forty-eight-hour warning. Required field measurements sometimes are not carried out.[27] The penalty? Nothing. As an Italian judge and legal scholar said of the situation in Italy, the monitoring system is "absurd."[28]

EU funds are sometimes regarded by member-state governments and citizens alike as free money. A Dutch agriculture official commented that "it is doubtful if the industry considers committing fraud with EC money to be a serious crime. Sometimes one gets the impression that in professional circles such fraud is considered a skillful practice."[29]

The states' priorities have not included control systems. In a 1994 report, the Italian Court of Auditors lamented the "weakness of inspection services" in the Ministry of Agriculture and noted that the ministry itself had signaled its structural inadequacies in the area of control, which meant that Italy was barely, if at all, meeting the minimum number and standards of inspections required by the EU. The report concluded that the central fraud inspection office was unable to carry out its duties.[30] The extent of the problem is evident in that the EU has no commonly applied definition of fraud,[31] so that what constitutes fraud in Germany may not constitute fraud in Belgium. There is considerable variation among the states as to how the EU's interests may be represented in a legal procedure concerning EU funds. When it comes to obtaining legal standing, from the EU's perspective it is best if the fraud occurred in Belgium, France, Luxembourg, or Spain. There is also considerable variation in applicable penalties, with member states obligated only to ensure that penalties have a deterrent effect—an unenforceable obligation. European legal scholars have raised doubts about the effectiveness of the states' existing penalties, including their deterrent effects.[32] States' priorities are clear in that it was thirty-seven years after the European Economic Community (now EU) was established that they passed the first framework legislation meant to allow the harmonizing of penalties for fraud against EU funds. Yet as of 2006, they had not followed through with actual harmonization. This, along with the open borders of the internal market, encourages forum shopping by those looking for easy ways to profit from the EU.

So too does variation in the effectiveness of member states' legal systems. As a legal expert elaborates, reaching a noteworthy conclusion,

> the financial interests of the Community receive very varied protection under the various criminal law systems. The differences concern the nature or level of the penalty, the definition of punishable acts and the applicability of certain general institutions. . . . With regard to criminal law in the economic field, marked differences between various countries with respect to sanctions for criminal acts of identical negative value could constitute a phenomenon likely to distort competition. In particular, where provision is made for fines for infringements, the risk of criminal sanctions may become a commercial risk in many cases. Thus the amount of the fine becomes a cost that can be reflected in the price of the finished product. Consequently, if between two Community countries there is a difference in the level of penalties, firms established in the country with the lighter penalties have a clear competitive advantage.[33]

Although there has been an increase in the powers of the European Court of Justice (ECJ) and the European Parliament, it is noteworthy that the European Commission's only means of enforcement has been to bring member states before the ECJ for infringements of the EU treaties or regulations. Yet even when corruption has been documented, such as the time a Greek minister tried to cover up a case of fraud against EEC funds in 1986, the ECJ has not had the power to impose penalties. It was only after the Maastricht Treaty that member states agreed to give the Commission the power to impose fines for state and firm violations of market competition rules and to withhold future subsidies in agriculture and regional development. As late as 1989, the EU did not have regulations for minimum standards for the carrying out of customs inspections of goods leaving or entering the EU member states. The states set up their own implementing provisions. Likewise for the administration of agricultural programs, in which, on the basis of unverified statements by the states of their need, the Commission automatically grants funds to the states. Only later, during the annual accounting procedure, are the states required to account for expenditures and report irregularities. And at that point, they have no strong incentive to do so: if they report irregularities, they either have to recover funds from the individual or business in question, or reimburse the EU for those funds from their public accounts. As the House of Lords noted in 1988, "Member States have been unwilling to notify the Commission of established fraud unless they are certain to collect the amounts due [from the fraudster], or unless they will not be re-quired to pay up the sums to the Community. The result is that [to quote a Eu-ropean Parliament report] the Commission 'has little idea of what is actually going on.'"[34]

The situation continues. Former EU chief accountant Marta Andreasen wrote in 2006 that, "amazingly," 85 percent of the EU's budget is given as an advance to the member states for which "no documentation is presented to support the eligibility, legality, regularity of the said payment." There is, therefore, "no mech-anism of determining which funds should be recovered."[35] While the EU's statis-tical agency, Eurostat, was embroiled in a financial scandal, it came to light that Greece had been cooking the books, as it were, for four years in order to qualify for the euro and to (artificially) stay below the 3 percent budget deficit require-ment. Most of the time, Greece's deficit had been over 4 percent. Eurostat, which collects data from the member states that are used to determine, among other things, whether the euro's criteria are being met, had not noticed. Nor had it no-ticed that Italy had engaged in shifty accounting. However, Eurostat's new direc-tor (who was replacing the one caught up in the fraud scandal) pointed out that the organization's data were only as good as those given to them by member states: Eurostat and other EU agencies have no authority to audit member-state budgets. If member states wanted to cheat, they could.[36] They have even struc-tured the system so that if they break the rules, there is virtually no penalty. In the case of Greece repeatedly breaking the rules for euro eligibility, the Commission has found that there is, nevertheless, no legal basis for throwing Greece out of the monetary system.[37]

Aggravating the situation is the fact that although most agricultural and other trade is transnational, both among EEC members and between them and third countries, administrative and judicial systems are national. As one member of the European Court of Auditors stated, "the national control systems did not appear capable of providing a consistent response to the problem of fraud, which is no respecter of frontiers."[38] Between 1994 and 2004, the structural funds were plagued with "numerous errors of legality and regularity," whereas the Common Agricultural Policy (or CAP) still had no effective control systems.[39] Although there have been ad hoc efforts, and some work by the Commission, to improve coordination, the member-state governments have done little to overcome the significant gap between the scope of the community's internal market (and in-ternational trade) and their nation-state-based legal and administrative systems. The gathering of evidence requires cooperation among numerous national and local jurisdictions; evidence admissible in one state is not in another; suspects may have to be extradited, which generally does not happen in revenue crimes; and bank accounts may be offshore, including onshore in Switzerland, Liechtenstein and Luxembourg.[40] A legal expert commented about member states' ambivalence toward prosecuting EU fraud that "you may find their falling over each other to prosecute [fraud] but you're more likely to find that each of them hopes that the other one will do it."[41] Prosecution is costly and complicated, and if funds are recovered, they revert to the EU, not to the prosecuting state.[42]

Some scholars apply principal-agent dynamics to account for these feeble monitoring and enforcement mechanisms. The states could not agree on or find a method for ensuring that, if they delegated real administrative, monitoring, and enforcement powers to supranational institutions, the agents' actions would not diverge from those preferred by the principals.[43] Yet this implies that the concern of the member states is that the agents would be *too* effective in monitoring the behavior of the principals. If the concern of the member states were that other states would be defecting from the treaties' obligations, then a supranational institution would have been better situated than each of them individually to monitor the behavior of the other states. It appears as though the states have made various agreements they don't really want to keep, and the best way to not keep them is for the states to retain the bulk of administrative, monitoring, and enforcement powers.

As one might expect under such conditions, the states were not quick to establish auditing and monitoring agencies for the EU. In 1977, almost twenty years after the EEC's founding, and mainly in response to adverse publicity about fraud, the member states created a Court of Auditors to provide audits of the EEC's budget. In 1992 they accorded the court status as an independent institution obliged to provide a statement of assurance about the regularity and legality of expenditures in the EU's budget.[44] In 1988, again in response to adverse publicity, this time from press reports on findings of the Court of Auditors, the EEC created a separate antifraud unit to facilitate the Commission's efforts to coordinate the detection and verification of fraud among the member states. This agency, UCLAF (Unité coordinatif de la lutte anti-fraude), was modified and renamed OLAF (Office européen de lutte anti-fraude) after questions about the management of the Commission itself surfaced, leading to the Commission members' resignations in 1999. Eurostat, the statistical agency upon which the EU relies for the data needed for its analyses and projections, including eligibility for the euro, has a staff of sixteen. Its employees cross-check the data that all (now) twenty-seven member states submit, but it has no authority to perform real audits of the figures. The edifice of the EU rests on the appearance of reliable data, strong legal authority, and enforcement capability. It is no wonder that, as much as possible, scandals are buried: to do otherwise would be to point out that the emperor has no clothes.

SILENCING THE WHISTLE-BLOWERS

International organizations start life with tenuous authority. To avoid giving their opponents reasons to reduce their authority, organizations have the perverse incentive to reduce the exposure of fraud, mismanagement, and corruption within their institutions. This motivation means that an organization creates a culture of tolerance of the very phenomena that, if exposed, would seriously weaken the legitimacy of the organization. The European Union exemplifies this dynamic. It explains why the European Commission and Court of Auditors have by and large smothered their whistle-blowers and closed investigations into malfeasance. Several examples are illustrative.

In 2002, the European Commission's chief accountant, Marta Andreasen, told the president of the Commission and several members of the European Parliament that the financial and administrative controls on the EU's $123 billion annual budget were weak, making the budget an easy target for fraud, graft, and waste. For instance, there was no good monitoring system for the more than 200,000 external contracts that the European Commission had financed. Andreasen was hired in 2002 to "oversee reforms to the Commission's accounting system."[45] Unfortunately, her boss had created the computer system that she announced needed to be drastically overhauled. Immediately after her declaration, she was suspended by the EU, which charged that by going directly to the Commission president and ten European parliamentarians, she had broken her oath of confidence and loyalty to her employer. She appears to have made the mistake of telling the commissioner for the budget, Michaele Schreyer, and the Commission vice president, Neil Kinnock (responsible for reforms) that the EU's accounting and oversight systems were "insufficient to guarantee the accuracy of the accounts."[46] Her charges received support from the EU's previous chief accountant but not from her immediate supervisor. His blockade prompted Andreasen to go around him. On the technicality that Andreasen had not used the proper channels and was merely telling the Commission what it already knew, the Commission refused to accord her the status of whistle-blower and instead fired her.

An accountant for the European Court of Auditors was fired after he went public with allegations that the Court was covering up systematic fraud and corruption and that some of it involved senior Court and Commission figures. The accountant, Dougal Watt, has argued that he went public only after his comments to the court were ignored. (The Court has one head auditor from each member state as well as a large staff of accountants, economists, and lawyers.) One of his duties had been to investigate the apparent tobacco fraud case of Antonio Quatraro.[47] An extraordinary detail of Watt's case is that the staff of the Court of Auditors held a secret vote on whether to voice support for him and his claims; more than 40 percent not only favored support but also called for the resignation of the then fifteen heads of the Court. Partially vindicating Watt, the EU's antifraud unit investigated and recommended to Luxembourg (where the Court is based) that the auditor from Greece, Kalliopi Nikolaou, be prosecuted.[48] Paul van Buitenen, the whistle-blower whose allegations of fraud, nepotism, and mismanagement brought down the Jacques Santer Commission in 1999 (they resigned en masse under threat of being deposed by the Parliament), was also removed from his job: they cut his pay in half and then shifted him to a job in the Netherlands that had him "monitoring outlays for objects such as lightbulbs." Why? He had taken his claims to the European Parliament after being ignored by his immediate superiors in the Commission. The complaints were verified by the Committee of Independent Experts assigned to investigate. Van Buitenen has since obtained a small measure of retribution: he was elected to the European Parliament in 2004 and has a seat on its budget control committee.[49] However, as he noted, little has changed.

Van Buitenen's complaints were also validated by the eruption of the Eurostat case. In 2003, news reports revealed that Eurostat had set up peculiar "black" accounts with some of its contractors, enabling it to engage in false invoicing and to collect the proceeds in reserve accounts. Incredibly, the European Commission, which is in charge of Eurostat, defended itself by claiming ignorance.[50] In this case as well there was an ostracized whistle-blower whose crime was to notify the EU's antifraud office after her superiors ignored her warnings about one of Eurostat's contractors. It appears that Eurostat's director, Yves Franchet, was at the heart of the off-the-books accounting schemes and also that there were conflicts of interest between Eurostat officials and its contractors. The EU's antifraud unit, not known for exaggeration, described the Eurostat system as "a vast enterprise of looting of [European] community funds."[51]

DOES THE EMPEROR HAVE ANY CLOTHES?

On March 30, 1993, Antonio Quatraro, a European Commission official who worked in the EU's agriculture directorate, committed suicide by throwing himself out of his sixth-floor office window. His death came just a few weeks before the start of an internal inquiry into tobacco fraud in which he'd been implicated two years earlier. As head of the EU's tobacco subsidy division, he had allegedly received a bribe of ITL 2 billion ($1.3 million) from Italian tobacco producers in order to vote for a set of rules for EEC tobacco aid that enormously favored Italian tobacco producers. Quatraro appears to have run, from inside the Commission, a tobacco cartel that benefited himself, several firms, and some Italian politicians. His suicide also came the day after he had met with his godfather, Vito Lattanzio, member of the then dominant and corrupt Christian Democratic Party and foreign trade minister in a recent Andreotti government. There were suspicions that the connection was more than familial, and some reports have indicated that Quatraro killed himself (or was defenestrated) after he revealed to investigators that he had not acted alone. Once he killed himself, the Commission dropped the inquiry.[52] Just as the Commission's actions against EU whistleblowers have shown, the EU has little desire to air its own misdeeds. Where possible, it sweeps questionable activities under the rug.

To promote free trade and remove barriers to competition, international trade organizations such as the WTO, the EU, and NAFTA promulgate extensive rules and regulations. As one commentator editorialized, Brussels bureaucrats have a "hypnotic attraction to regulating anything that moves."[53] Yet where regulations are not suited to local economic and administrative conditions (or are more expensive than the costs paid to avoid them), firms, politicians, and bureaucrats may find it in their interests to coordinate on bribery in order to allow the desired economic exchange to take place. Lowering the threshold at which EU procurement rules apply may only impel collusive arrangements. These may be less difficult to set up and maintain than to follow complex, rigid EU rules. The basic idea is that if it costs more to put in a competitive bid, or to pay the full tax assessed, than it does to pay a bribe, the bribe will be market clearing and thus meet the interests of those in the transaction.

Further contributing to the problem is the EU's tendency to add more rules but not add better and simpler control systems. Regulations and their accompanying penalties, and new oversight boards, are meant to impose higher risks for engaging in corrupt behavior or, even if not corrupt, in malfeasance. But in the European Union and its member states, these risks so far have been minimal: additional oversight is trivial, penalties are negligible, and competitors seldom wind up with an incentive to protest malfeasance. Opportunities have the same sources: an inadequate international legal system; enforcement largely left to the very governments that may be directly involved in corruption; and low risk of discovery and penalty, partly because the states seldom if ever intervene in each other's affairs. In addition, firms sometimes find it cheaper to pay a bribe as part of a collusive arrangement than to confront the costs of a competitive market.

The fact that cases such as the one involving Eurostat do eventually come to light may reassure some that the EU is not inherently vulnerable to fraud, mismanagement, and even corruption. Yet what the cases reveal is less reassuring: the EU is not structured to instill good governance, and it has a culture of obfuscation, not transparency. Further, as is typical of an international organization, its member states do not allow it to be properly staffed or empowered to be an effective barrier against fraud, nepotism, and graft. In defending the Commission's shoddy supervision of Eurostat, Commissioner Kinnock came close to the truth when he stated that "we are dealing with something which has its roots in the 1950s."[54] Of course: that's when this international organization was launched. But rather than build a superstate, it might be useful to consider the consequences of creating complicated and extensive rules that cannot be adequately enforced. Ever-increasing dissatisfaction with the EU and ever-decreasing turnout at European elections may be among the results.

THE EUROPEAN UNION,
THE INTERNATIONAL POLITICAL
ECONOMY, AND CORRUPTION

Ideally, we should see a virtuous circle of benefits. . . . Real life, however, is rarely so simple.

—European Commission

When gli Azzurri, Italy's national soccer team, took to the field for the 2006 World Cup, more than half the players and the team manager were from Italian teams that had rigged matches. To those observers who gave it any thought, it may have seemed like situation normal: someone always tries to cheat in professional sports (and, *che sorpresa*, it happened in Italy). Those who gave it further thought may have noticed that someone always tries to cheat in *any* competitive situation. And thus, as the EU strives to create a more competitive Single Market, and while its leaders embrace globalization and condemn the "populism" that fears it, its leaders and citizens should not be surprised to see corruption in the market and in the intersection between market and politics.

The euphoria of the Single Market waned in the late 1990s, overshadowed by continuing high unemployment, weak economic growth, and a number of corruption cases involving those who had been at the heart of the Single Market project. When the furor over the scandals involving German chancellor Helmut Kohl and French president François Mitterrand had faded, many concluded that the cases were vestiges of an earlier era of the EU. This book has argued otherwise: those cases were a logical offshoot of the effort to construct the Single Market and make European economies and governments more competitive and streamlined. These cases were propelled by politicians' and firms' efforts to beat the competition. The politicians sought increased party financing, and the firms sought market access and profits. Their efforts received institutional support, both through formal bureaucratic mechanisms and through their absence. Although it has become apparent that liberalization in the emerging markets, including the eastern

EU 2004 accession states, led to corruption, it has not been acknowledged that liberalization in the western EU did so also.

Evident in the EU in the few decades pre- and post-Maastricht is not a disappearance of corruption, nor a quantum leap in it, but a recalibration of it. Since the 1970s and the increased expansion and development of the Common Market, the opportunities for corruption in the various EU member states have changed somewhat, but they have not gone away. Fewer state-owned companies means fewer opportunities for politicians to embezzle, but more contracting out of public services to private firms also means more opportunities to demand kickbacks on contracts. More EU-wide competition can translate into more, instead of less, EU-wide corruption because the cross-national enforcement capacities have not caught up with the cross-national opportunities for collusion. Firms now face increased pressures from competitors for survival; government contracts, gained if necessary through bribery, are all the more important. Competition makes bribery and collusion attractive business strategies, and evasion of prosecution becomes just another cost of doing business. Economic growth does not necessarily reduce corruption, as the example of Italy shows. As European markets in arms and infrastructure have become saturated and the United States creates stiff competition in those sectors, European firms and states have used corruption to penetrate new markets elsewhere. Bribery becomes, under conditions of tight competition, an attractive short-term business strategy. Starting in the late 1970s, a new level of elections to an EU-wide institution, the European Parliament, plus elections to new subnational levels of government in Europe, have required more party funding. However, the legal supply of party funding has not kept up with the demand for it. Although elected politicians add more regulations in response to financing scandals, these regulations further restrict the legal supply of funds. The "solution" for parties and politicians has been corruption.

The incentives, opportunities, and demand for corruption are the result of some features of economic competition, privatization, international exports, decentralization, and campaign and party financing. At the heart of each of these concerns is competition, which carries with it countervailing pressures. More competition means that expenses, including taxes, matter more. So, for example, firms have an increased incentive to bribe their way out of taxes. More competition also means that cartels have a higher value to all the firms that are included in them, even if, under the new trade regime, cartels carry a greater risk of discovery and disruption. Free trade and ensuing competition may not reach into all areas vulnerable to corruption. Even under competitive rules, states retain discretion over actions—such as tax decisions, zoning regulations, or authorizations of the sale or purchase of arms—that have large financial repercussions for firms.

Politicians with the relevant powers may extract fees for their "services." Their reason for doing so is often connected to the financing of their electoral campaigns and their political party organizations. Corruption can persist in wealthy European (and other) democracies because political competition has become something of an arms race: every move and innovation by one party must be countered by the others. At the same time, politicians and parties, if often in competition with each other, may tacitly or, as in the case of Italy, openly collude to illegally finance their parties. They agree to engage in corruption and agree to be generous with each other should a scandal erupt, which is one reason mainstream parties seldom defend or praise the work of police and judges who expose political corruption.

Campaign financing is a conundrum in democracies. It is clear that regulatory frameworks are connected with corruption; it is not clear how to solve the problem. Spending caps, contribution caps, or generous public financing do not do away with corruption; indeed, the former two merely spur it on. An open market system in which contributors and the amounts donated are not merely revealed to a parliamentary committee or oversight agency but made easily accessible to the media and general public may help. Still, it does not end the problem that donors may expect and get something in return, which is part of what makes U.S. politics so unseemly, and what has gotten Blair's Labour Party into trouble.

This cynical behavior by politicians highlights the extent to which democracy and markets rest on a lie: there is the myth of inclusiveness, of fairness, of the rule of law, and there is the practice of exclusion, favoritism, and illegality. The latter practices are required by the competitiveness of the system, the high stakes of winning, and the fact that democracy does not eliminate self-interested behavior and markets privilege it. The myth is an illustration of what W. Michael Reisman called the operational code: "a *private* public law in systems in which public law is supposed to be public; those authorized to play control functions and those who deal directly with them come to accept procedures that deviate from the myth system as licit."[1] A French appeals court's commentary on a case is instructive. In upholding a lower court's verdict that Alain Juppé was guilty of illegally financing the Gaullist party through fictitious jobs at the mayor's office from 1988 to 1995, the appeals court stated that "it is particularly regrettable that at the moment when the legislature became aware of the necessity to put an end to the criminal practices that surrounded party financing, Mr. Juppé did not apply to his own party, of which he was the secretary-general with uncontested authority, the rules that he had voted for in parliament."[2] The laws are a facade, behind which the politicians apply alternative rules and practices.

Some sober assessments of the economic impact of the EU suggest that European integration mainly made firms more competitive in the international economy at large.[3] However, it is also clear that member states liberalized their economies to a significant degree and that there was increased free trade, economic competition, and privatization, even if their occurrence cannot be pinned exclusively on the EU and its regulations. No matter what its source, increased competition has goaded corruption, and privatization has created new means of graft. Additional dynamics not directly part of the institutions of the European integration project but that paralleled it, such as decentralization and campaign finance law revisions, have had unexpected and untoward effects on corruption. Decentralization created opportunities for more politically exercised discretion in a context in which politicians need campaign funds for elections to new regional and local governing bodies, and to sustain subnational party organizations. Campaign finance revisions often blocked politicians' legal access to desired amounts of funding; this combination has bred corruption.

Decentralization and devolution within the EU member states have brought with them more elections. The much-touted reforms in Italy and France that provide for the direct election of mayors and for new local, departmental, and regional governments substantially increased demands for campaign and party financing. Cases in Italy, France, and elsewhere in Europe have shown that if that financing is not forthcoming through legal means, then kickbacks from local public works contracts become a desirable source. Decentralization, in turn, provides the possibilities for extracting those kickbacks.

This book has focused on how corruption is associated with various phenomena of liberalization and also with campaign finance regulations across a number of EU countries. It has not sought to isolate types of corruption associated with national forms of state-market structures or with national histories.[4] When these national forms and histories allow for privatization, for instance, it is crucial to understand how and why that privatization fosters corruption. Whereas in the 1970s and 1980s, the United Kingdom evinced more of an arm's-length distance and short-term outlook between the private sector and the state, the 1990s saw a shift to extensive state involvement in the private sector. Public-private partnerships have mushroomed, creating questionable conflicts of interest and conditions ripe for corruption. Although many EU states have unloaded most of their state-owned firms, these same states have reentered the business of business through what are in essence joint ventures with private firms and through extensive promotional activities. This has also blurred the lines between so-called liberal market economies (e.g., that of the United Kingdom) and coordinated market economies (e.g., that of Germany). The states have converged toward what Shleifer and Vishney termed the "helping hand" model, in which the state actively intervenes in the market and in business operations to promote business.[5] Furthermore, when it comes to overseas oil, infrastructure, and weapons markets, the EU countries and their firms, despite differing histories and state-market structures, engage in similar corrupt activities.

These dynamics are not exclusive to the EU-15, but they flourished there as a result of the Single Market project's lack of effective oversight coupled with its emphasis on removing barriers to trade through extensive regulation, which was largely left in the hands of the states to enforce.

THE MYTH OF THE MARKET AND THE DEMISE OF OVERSIGHT

Political and economic reforms intended to give further scope to the market come with risks of corruption. Institutions of accountability are important and have been the ignored element of many of the changes that have come along with the EU. The belief that markets are self-correcting and the fact that states want neither increased supranational supervision of their activities nor increased subnational supervision of subnational activities have led states, national politicians, and policy makers to soft-pedal institutions of accountability. In addition, politicians have little incentive to establish effective oversight institutions and penalties for corruption related to campaign and party finance, or to support stronger enforcement. As legislators and ministers, they have some means to avoid doing so. If such institutions are weak, then politicians and firms will manipulate the reforms to their advantage, thus undermining the reforms. That manipulation can take various forms of corruption.

One might have thought that the EU, with the oversight of the European Commission, the European Court of Justice, and the antifraud office, would have been able to reduce the possibilities for corruption. However, free trade areas and more extensive international organizations have a structural peculiarity: the member states tend to delegate *to themselves* the operation of most of the organization's regulatory structure. Thus, much of the time, the supervisor is one of the things that needs to be supervised. Andrew Moravcsik's prominent work on the subject of European integration contains no mention of corruption or fraud, and he writes as if the European Union's legal system is adequate to the task. Moravcsik goes on to explain that states have no problem delegating sovereignty for "adjudication, implementation, and enforcement" because those "are narrower functions." Governments "can afford looser control and greater efficiency."[6] But it is difficult to see how allowing the policing and enforcement of EU rules to be carried out primarily by the member states' interior and judicial ministries could be seen as a delegation of sovereignty.

One possible institutional remedy is to create a supranational police and customs agency, perhaps with overlapping controls between the Commission and parliament. That is the expectation of international regime theorists. Yet hanging over any institutional solution is the fact that the member states are reluctant to cede further sovereignty to the EU. It is paradoxical that the institutions created by the member states to promote economic growth are in turn fostering what has been shown to hamper it—corruption. With Europe-bashing having spread even to Germany's government, with France and Germany joining the United Kingdom in clamoring for more "subsidiarity" and decentralization of EU functions, and with France and the Netherlands rejecting the EU Constitution, it is unlikely the EU will acquire the means any time soon to combat one of the factors that leads so many Europeans to regard the EU as, at best, a necessary evil.

Another problem is, of course, that the potential for corruption may just "move up" to the supranational institutions. Certainly firms and NGOs in the EU have discovered that it is necessary to have a presence in Brussels. Several scenarios seem possible. One is that the locus of corruption will follow the power. Another is that corruption will be deterred if actors cannot predict whether others will tolerate and participate in corrupt transactions, because they are coming from different states and regions, where norms, practices, and ethics vary considerably. Yet another is that the networks of corruption that have been resilient in the member states will be resilient under the new conditions. As Avner Greif has theorized and demonstrated, institutional patterns and the cultural expectations that support them can be self-reinforcing, even when parameters shift.[7] But again, rather than build more institutions and more regulations, it might be useful to put energy into enforcing those laws that exist and reviewing those that seem to encourage rather than discourage corruption.

It may also have been expected that the national oversight institutions would block many of the cases that emerged, particularly in the states with long histories of rational administration, such as Germany and France. However, national politicians had strong incentives to enact economic reforms, the pain of which they could blame on Brussels, but not strong incentives to create effective oversight institutions. Politicians prefer not to limit their own freedom of maneuver, so when privatization and decentralization provided new sources of kickbacks and new demands for campaign and party financing, they were not likely to legislate in favor of institutions (and staffing levels) that could monitor the exchanges. They may also not want to be perceived as placing burdensome regulations on business. This is not to say that the EU and its member states are, everywhere and always, woefully lacking in oversight agencies and enforcement capacities but to point out that those agencies and capacities are less than their promise—as a result of the interests of the politicians who create them.[8]

A TURNING POINT?

It is tempting to think that corruption in the international political economy is at a turning point. Despite the many factors encouraging corruption, thirty OECD states and five others have signed on to the OECD antibribery convention; OECD firms are becoming aware of possible penalties; a few OECD states' judiciaries are investigating and prosecuting egregious cases of bribery; some major firms, spearheaded by BP, have signed on to the Extractive Industries Transparency Initiative; the World Bank and the IMF have made corruption reduction a recognized policy area; and NGOs such as Transparency International and Global Witness have made corruption an international issue. Could it be that the tide is turning and corruption in the EU will recede?

The evidence is mixed. The United States has been using post-9/11 extradition treaties, antiterrorism laws, Sarbanes-Oxley, and the U.S. Foreign Corrupt Practices Act to snag European as well as other businessmen and firms. Recently ABB, the Swiss-Swedish construction and engineering giant, was snared by the U.S. Department of Justice and the Securities and Exchange Commission. Its subsidiaries in the United States and the United Kingdom bribed Nigerian officials in 1998 to land contracts; the United States claimed jurisdiction over the UK subsidiary because the U.S. subsidiary had several employees acting as agents in the United States for the UK subsidiary.[9] Although the unusual reach of U.S. law enforcement may discourage some corruption, its potential impact is muted by the selective scope of the reach: the Department of Justice has not investigated corruption allegations in the Coalition Provisional Authority of Iraq and has done little to investigate corruption in Halliburton's contracting practices in Iraq from 2003 to the present. The senior army procurement officer who questioned the dubious practices of Halliburton and the contract award process has faced retribution, while Congress has stymied efforts to investigate. By 2005, Halliburton had been awarded more than $10 billion in U.S. government contracts for reconstruction in Iraq, with at least 10 percent of that amount being of questionable use or entirely unaccounted for.[10] Corruption continues because firms and politicians correctly perceive that the level of coordination and enforcement needed from the major states and firms will not materialize.

States use corruption to engage in economic statecraft, and the EU states are no exception. Despite the fact that the largest firms based in any EU country are usually multinationals and have their tax liabilities spread across numerous jurisdictions, domestic governments still regard them as their national champions. In addition to state subsidies, which fly in the face of EU norms on competition, corruption is a means of protecting national champions from competition, and it is a practice that ranges across the EU-15.

In the international political economy, EU states and their firms are competing not only with each other but with other major players. Failing to play by the illicit but standard rules would be economically and politically costly, because international rivals would gain market and critical resource access, and political influence. When the French judiciary refused to drop its charges against alleged illegal arms dealer Pierre Falcone, an ally of the Angolan government, Angola refused to renew the French oil company Total's concession on a major Angolan oil block. China, which tends to ask few questions about good governance and transparency, has been increasing its influence in Africa and Latin America.[11] Saudi Arabia successfully pressured the United Kingdom to stop investigations into a BAE slush fund because a Saudi prince was one of the alleged recipients. The Saudis had threatened to take their business for a huge defense weapons purchase to France.[12]

Several major countries, including Germany and Japan, have opposed efforts of the OECD antibribery unit to require applicant companies to disclose to their export credit guarantee agency the names of overseas agents, the amounts paid in commissions, and the purpose of those commissions.[13] A rare United Kingdom investigation into a case of overseas bribery conveniently involves not a British firm but a Halliburton subsidiary in the UK, and the alleged corruption (in Nigeria) took place at a time when Dick Cheney was Halliburton's CEO.[14] A cynic might note that the UK's investigation into the matter started after the United States began extradition proceedings against three UK bankers allegedly involved in Enron's collapse. It should surprise no one that only a handful of the more than 2,000 companies and individuals that paid bribes in the Iraq oil-for-food scandal are being investigated. Given that the bribes provided firms access to a market, and Western politicians with remuneration, and that the harm was borne by distant Iraqi civilians, investigations and prosecutions have had low priority.[15]

Adding it up, there are dynamics that should disrupt corruption in the EU, including the EU having a fairly free flow of capital, labor, and goods, with supranational oversight institutions, and a number of states that not only seem to have norms against corruption but also score very high in international anticorruption indices. Yet the EU also has contractors looking for more business who may be willing to pay commissions, bribes, or kickbacks in order to establish themselves in a new market. As a result of their characteristics, some sectors do not have a plethora of available competitors, so those firms that enter the market can easily be incorporated into the corrupt distribution network. And the politicians and parties needing campaign financing are an inherent part of every democracy.

Economic integration is supposed to reduce corruption by spreading the (assumed) good governance norms of the dominant states in the organization and by making corruption's drag on a national economy more noticeable because of the increased exposure to foreign competitors. These macrolevel trends may exist in theory, but at the microlevel they often fail to obtain. International economic integration tends to remove barriers to trade and increase economic competition but fails to install effective regulatory and enforcement agencies. The EU claims that a state must reduce corruption before being accepted as a member, but it has never allowed high levels of corruption to block a country's accession. Bulgaria appears to have noticed: its anticorruption efforts flagged in the year before its accession to the EU.[16] The experiences of EU member states underscore the extent to which political and economic competition can drive corruption.

International commerce is a difficult area in which to reduce corruption. There will always be countries that find a comparative advantage in money laundering, bribery, and harboring those in the sights of international arrest warrants. European governments have an incentive to ignore bribery, because if their firms don't pay, the firms of another country will. For corruption in the international political economy to be significantly reduced, states and firms have to recognize that bribery and corruption are not in their particular interest, and major coordination and enforcement problems have to be solved. The hidden nature of corruption makes the judging of compliance with anticorruption conventions extremely difficult, as the OECD has discovered in its review processes.

Another reason there may not be a dramatic shift toward an anticorruption norm in the international political economy is that bribes are integrated into the dynamics of the export market economy. As cases in chapter 3 showed, bribes respond to market incentives, though not as economists traditionally expect. That is, instead of the market driving bribes out, it incorporates them into the supply-demand function. When there are more competitors for government-sponsored contracts overseas, the increase in demand enables government officials to raise the price of the bribe they require for award of the contract. In some sectors, such as commercial aerospace, arms, oil, and utility infrastructure, the stakes in profits are very high, and firms and states perceive that winning any particular contract is critical for gaining substantial market share and for maintaining and increasing domestic employment and economic growth. As a result, as economic competition *increases,* firms are willing to pay bribes up to the point where the cost, including nearly negligible risks of prosecution, matches the profits. Their domestic governments are willing to overlook or indirectly subsidize the bribes, through export credits, in order to help their firms land contracts.

On the other hand, continual changes in laws, the market, and political conditions would help disrupt the "legal certainty" that corruption will hardly ever be punished. Were changes in these areas unsettling enough, they would destabilize some transactions. Corruption relies on the expectation of those involved that the action is not likely to be discovered. Many of the cases covered in this book were governed by the additional expectation of the actors that the corrupt transaction was the norm. When laws change and are enforced, there may be a disruption of these expectations, which should eventually discourage some from using corruption to best their competition. It may take time for the news to get out and for learning to occur. One question for research is how much impact selective enforcement of anticorruption laws has on what might formally be called corruption equilibria: the systems of corruption and the norms and beliefs integral to them. Another might pick up on the analysis begun here, to see under what conditions corruption networks are destabilized or how much change in market or political conditions is needed for that to occur.

FURTHER RESEARCH ON CAUSES AND SOLUTIONS
Data

I make no claim to having quantitative or cumulative qualitative evidence of aggregate or sector-specific corruption levels in EU states since the 1970s, nor specific amounts and numbers of corruption cases associated with campaign and party financing. This book, as a work on a subject for which data are scarce and difficult to quantify, uses the evidence available to put forth and explore a new argument.[17] One interpretation of this evidence is that it is random background noise. Another is the one I put forward in this book: the evidence is associated with the economic and political dynamics of constructing the EU and of financing political parties in democracies. The argument developed here has a predictive logic that is borne out by the cases. The evidence invites further testing with other cases. In this book I also rely implicitly on counterfactual reasoning: in the absence of condition X, outcome Y would not have happened. Certainly this is controversial and not something on which one should blindly base public policy.[18] But the corruption cases associated with privatization, competition, decentralization, export promotion, and party financing are frequent enough to suggest that there is a nonrandom dynamic and that the standard cures—competition, privatization, and regulation—may not be sufficient to root out corruption. Competition may impel efforts to game the system, privatization may create new opportunities for kickbacks, and regulation without real enforcement leads to evasive action.

Further research needs more data. The databases, such as Transparency International's Corruption Perceptions Index, that rely on surveys have been limited

to starting points in the mid-1990s. The World Bank Institute has worked to develop comprehensive indices of good governance. These include measures of corruption, though because of their partial reliance on corruption perception
surveys, results go back only to the mid-1990s. In an effort to improve on survey
data, move beyond perceptual measures of corruption across countries, and to
make quantitative, cross-national historical research possible, Miriam Golden
and Lucio Picci suggest a measurement based on the amount the government has
paid for physical infrastructure and the cost of the physical quantities of infrastructure. As they note, the "intuition underlying this measure is that, all else
equal, governments that do not get what they pay for are those whose bureaucrats
and politicians are siphoning off more public monies in corrupt transactions."
Although their database for Italy comes with numerous caveats, it allows for measurement of variations in corruption levels over time, for many decades.[19]

Interaction Effects

Competition, privatization (which is meant to increase competition, among
other things), decentralization, and, in general, free trade need to be examined
more closely to see under which conditions they *do* discourage corruption and
under which they do not. This book has suggested a number of ways they encourage or allow corruption yet recognizes that further research with carefully
controlled comparative cases, as well as developing quantitative measures of the
sort that Golden and Picci have compiled for Italy, is important to advancing
knowledge of corruption dynamics. Furthermore, the research needs to test for
interaction effects. As this book has shown, the liberal consensus reforms are
thought of as separate, independent policies, but they interact in ways that are
perverse.

Role of Bureaucracy

Bureaucracies are usually condemned by anticorruption activists and free mar-
keters alike for their excessive red tape. The problem in the western European bureaucracies is sometimes red tape (as, for example, the EU public procurement
regulations), but sometimes it is the fact that public bureaucracies can underwrite
corruption even when their officials are doing their jobs properly. Because bureaucracies in modern democratic states are differentiated, specialized, and efficient, they focus on their specific, narrowly defined tasks: for example, promoting
exports through subsidizing and insuring firms' deals, and retaining as classified

all documents pertaining to national security interests. If there is corruption in export-subsidized contracts, it is the role of auditing agencies and the judiciary to find and sort it out. Bureaucracies, merely by fulfilling their mission, can provide institutional support for corruption. The fact that they can offer this support sheds some light on the nature of corruption in modern capitalist democracies: it is sustained by the formal institutional structure of the state.[20]

Certainly there are differences in levels and common types of corruption across the EU-15. This book has focused first on understanding why corruption persists despite the introduction and implantation of forces presumed to reduce it, such as competition. Additional research is needed to investigate why, given that these forces can foster corruption in a variety of contexts, there is variation in the prevalence of corruption across countries and across time.

Anticorruption Mechanisms

A legalistic approach suggests that corruption can be curbed through more and better oversight and stronger sanctions, with the latter raising the costs of corruption and the former the likelihood that those costs will have to be paid. Institutions must monitor programs, enforce rules, and sanction those who commit infractions. The key is to avoid giving any office a monopoly (or even overwhelming discretion) in the distribution of a resource.[21] The answer is not more international organizations. Because they are inherently lacking in real oversight and enforcement institutions and offices, and because their tenuous legitimacy compels their leadership to sweep all instances of corruption under the rug, these organizations often become part of the problem. Consider the UN oil-for-food program, the scandal of UN head Kofi Anan's son obtaining UN contracts, the European Commission's history of mismanagement and nepotism, and the Coalition Provisional Authority turning a blind eye to corruption in contracting in Iraq. In addition, international organizations sometimes become the repositories for leaders with dubious domestic records. The European Commission, the Organization of American States, the World Economic Forum, the North Atlantic Treaty Organization—all have had leaders and officials whose corrupt or dubious activities in their country of origin surfaced during their tenure in the international organization.

Reducing corruption in the EU and in other wealthy democracies is less a matter of creating more laws and more a matter of creating contexts in which existing laws are enforced, whether by more staffing of existing investigative and enforcement institutions, by less political intervention in judicial actions, by the creation of institutions that can then enforce laws on the books, or by a change in political culture, which is admittedly hard to effect. The political will to pursue corruption is decidedly lacking. International anticorruption agreements, when codified into national law, have enabled prosecutors to bring charges for transnational corruption. The discovery of these cases is sometimes the result of personal vendetta or unhappiness with remuneration or specific individuals. Thus, one of the important things might be to promote and encourage whistle-blowers and disaffected participants in corrupt practices to come forward and provide information to public authorities. Perhaps anticorruption statutes could be written in such a way that the public, whether as private citizens, interest groups, or NGOs, can sue to obtain enforcement of the law (for example, as provided in the U.S. National Environmental Protection Act and a number of other acts).

It is likely that when penalties wipe out the net gain from corruption—whether access to elected office or a firm's profit—some of those tempted to engage in corruption may be dissuaded. This notion is conjectural in that the data to test the supposition are lacking. One can surmise that the punishment of Serge Dassault, who was given a two-year suspended sentence and fined BEF 60,000 ($1,650) for bribery to land a BEF 6.5 billion ($165 million) contract, had little deterrent effect, whereas the fines levied against ABB by the United States for bribery related to a Nigerian contract, which wiped out the estimated profit obtained from the contract, gave some pause.[22] It is also likely that barring Alain Juppé from public office, if only for a year, sent a stronger signal to other French politicians than did the amnesty granted Jacques Barrot, who later became EU transport commissioner.

Because incumbency tends to make corrupt practices easier and more wide-spread, changing systems of representation and voting to promote easier and more frequent alternation of political parties to national offices might help. It is easy to make these suggestions, but unfortunately, one of the logics of corruption is that politicians have strong incentives to avoid creating the contexts that would reduce corruption. Yet it is politicians who are needed to vote the laws and agencies into existence, or to leave off interfering with the judiciary. The French judges' union complained of political intervention surrounding the prosecution of Alain Juppé, stating that "this affair shows France is a developing country as regards its democracy, where the deputies [members of parliament] have yet to get it into their heads that judges are independent."[23] Certainly, institutions themselves are "sticky" and difficult to change.[24] The failure to increase enforcement and alter political systems partly stems from the vested interests of those who profit from corruption, who are thus not inclined to assign adequate resources to enforcement or to change a status quo from which they have benefited.

It is also easy to observe that a free, vigorous, aggressive press, with an interest in discovering and publicizing corrupt behavior on the part of public officials, may help reduce corruption. Yet trends in media ownership are not promising. In France, Serge Dassault's industrial conglomerate purchased an 80 percent stake in the media group that owns the major French daily paper *Le Figaro* and also publishes *L'Express,* a popular weekly magazine, and about half the regional papers in France.[25] Another weapons manufacturer, Lagardère, owns another major French media group. Bouygues, the French construction and engineering giant, owns a 41.6 percent stake in the leading French television station, TF1.[26] In Italy, former prime minister Berlusconi owns three of the six major television channels (the other three are state owned and thus indirectly were under his control when he was prime minister), a number of the major weekly news magazines, the major publishing house Mondadori (not to mention AC Milan, a popular soccer team). The conflict of interest when he was prime minister was obvious. With media costs, particularly for print, increasing, the dependence of European media on major corporation ownership may also be increasing. This has potential repercussions for the investigative journalism of the mainstream media.

Libertarians and economists would suggest that the solution is to introduce market competition into previously regulated and subsidized areas.[27] As Paolo Mauro argues, "Since the ultimate source of rent-seeking behavior is the *availability* of rents, corruption is likely to occur where restrictions and government intervention lead to the presence of such excessive profits."[28] The conundrum is that, beyond rent-seeking interests, governments and international organizations often have strong policy reasons for *not* allowing the so-called free market to operate in specific sectors. Many of the EU's most important and expensive programs (e.g., Common Agricultural Program, Structural Funds) were deliberately created to *counter* free market forces. Infrastructure projects can create public goods that the private sector might not undertake or would only find feasible to undertake in small disjointed units. There are other areas in which government decisions are still necessary if a country is to retain any semblance of being a governed democracy and its citizenry, values, and beliefs not entirely subject to private market exchanges. Even though corruption subverts the promise of democratic governance, relegating everything to the private sector would do so even more. Furthermore, depending on how they are implemented, market reforms toward a "free" market "can be used as new means to pursue corrupt ends,"[29] as this book and others have shown. The EU, in making market integration and competition the priority, is accidentally pushing firms and politicians to collude to find ways around this competition.

The emphasis in policy circles since 2000 has been to get rid of corruption in order to promote free trade, and the solution to getting rid of corruption is to have more competition and less state regulation.[30] Yet what the EU shows is that competition impels some toward corruption, while leaving intact some opportunities for corruption, and that creating competition within and between states brings with it a heavy overlay of regulation. And neither of the anticorruption solutions addresses the arms race that characterizes campaign and party financing in the Western democracies.

The solution is not to run government like a business, as even the *Financial Times* editorial board recognizes. As it observed of Blair's efforts to make civil servants "more entrepreneurial" and ministries more customer service oriented, "running a government is not directly comparable to running a company." Along with governments being a repository of the public sphere, they are a locus of human interactions, many of which are not based strictly on reducing every object or policy to a discreet value that can be exchanged for a price.[31] In democracies, such an exchange is something that anticorruption and campaign finance laws try to prohibit. Although it was not addressing corruption, the following statement is apt: "A really effective overhaul of central government administration must include the role of the politicians who lead it: *Hamlet* without the Prince is not much of a story."[32] As much as politicians are key players in corruption, the solution is not to get rid of them by transforming government into a firm (which, as Enron, Parmalat, Ahold, WorldCom, and others have shown, may have its own problems with corruption) or by stripping it of all public features and powers. Exploring new ways of limiting what Mark Warren terms "duplicitous exclusion" in public decision making may help.[33]

Reducing corruption requires a concerted effort by activists, judiciaries, industries, and politicians. Yet the efforts of the former two are often stymied by the interests of the latter two. Noting the often convergent interests of those with political and economic power, a political theorist has argued that "democratic accountability may require even more formal, direct, and vigorous control of political *and* socioeconomic elites than even, for instance, contemporary campaign finance reformers propose."[34] Industries will refuse to use bribery only when the risks of being caught and the penalties applied are high relative to the potential profit of bribery. In light of the enormous number of transnational transactions that occur on a daily basis, versus the number of investigations and prosecutions of bribery, the risks are still low. Penalties applied are, in most cases, trivial. Politicians will only eschew or crack down on bribery when doing so does not affect their ability to raise campaign funds, does not hamper their national champions in the global market, and has some value at the polls. The EU's Single Market has not enabled politicians to raise more campaign and party financing legally; it has only increased the extent to which firms might see corruption as a necessary, if unpalatable, business tool in the international market. Nor has the European Union altered the fact that corruption is seldom the key concern of voters when they go to the polls. Finally, the EU has not altered a fundamental aspect of economic and political activity in domestic and international contexts: firms competing for business and politicians competing for power, can, through corruption, give each other what they want—an advantage over and shelter from competition.

KEY DEAD MEN

Carl Algernon, head of the Swedish War Material Inspection Board, in 1987, when Bofors bribery and illegal arms sales in Sweden were being investigated, "fell in front of a subway train, in what police ruled was an apparent suicide."[1]

David Austin, of the Lowry-O'Brien scandal in Ireland, died November 1, 1998, after a long illness. He was the conduit for funds that were illegally diverted to various politicians' and parties' financing schemes.[2]

Jacques Brats was director of the Paris municipal publications office. In 1986, when Jacques Chirac was mayor, Brats was charged with privatizing the publications production. Brats outsourced its work to political friends, who paid two to three times the market price for the deals. During 1986–95 the excess went into the RPR's coffers. Estimates are that the system generated FRF 100 million ($20 million). This scandal, known as Sempap, was one of several associated with Jacques Chirac's tenure as mayor of Paris. Brats's death in 2001 made prosecution of the Sempap affair difficult.[3]

Guido Brunner, German ambassador to Spain during 1981–92, died February 2, 1997. He was allegedly instrumental in the Siemens-PSOE illegal funding scandal.

Gabriele Cagliari, ex-president of ENI, the Italian state-owned energy firm, committed suicide on July 20, 1993, after almost five months in jail. He was accused of corruption in the merger of ENI with Montedison (see Raul Gardini).

André Cools, a leader of the Belgian Socialist Party, was assassinated in 1991. His demise has been directly connected to the Agusta-Dassault affair, from which he was expecting some kickbacks to come to his party's coffers. When he found that rivals in the party had sequestered the funds, he threatened to take the case to the judiciary.

Camillo Crociani, Italy's Finmeccanica president from 1976 to 1989, died mysteriously in exile in Mexico. He had been tried in absentia, convicted, and sentenced to twenty-eight months in jail for having taken bribes from Lockheed in the 1970s.[4]

Robert Feliciaggi was assassinated in Corsica on March 10, 2006. He was allegedly involved in illegal campaign financing of Charles Pasqua, former French interior minister. The police determined that the assassination was the result of a local Corsican vendetta.

Raul Gardini, head of Montedison, was known outside Italy for owning the yacht that took second, sailed by the Italian team, in the 1991 America's Cup. He was involved in the Enimont scandal, in which enormous bribes were paid to Italian political parties to approve the merger of his firm with a state-owned firm; later bribes were again paid to approve the separation. He committed suicide on July 23, 1993, the morning he was to have been interrogated by the Italian judiciary. The Christian Democrats and the Socialists were the primary beneficiaries of the bribes.

Charles Haughey, former Irish prime minister (Taoiseach), died in June 2006 of natural causes. The legal battle of the Dunn supermarket chain over efforts to oust Ben Dunn from the chain's board revealed that Haughey had received substantial illegal financing from Ben Dunn, and that that was the tip of the iceberg. Two tribunals were established to investigate. He had taken over the leadership of Fianna Fail in 1979.

Jörg Hillinger, the primary investigating judge on some major German cases, died in an auto accident April 26, 1999, the day he was to have filed papers with the state's attorney regarding Holger Pfahls, Karlheinz Schreiber, and others involved in the Thyssen tank affair, party funding scandals, and tax evasion.

Wolfgang Huellen, CFO of the CDU parliamentary delegation, committed suicide by hanging on January 20, 2000. He was under investigation for involvement in illegal party financing for Germany's CDU-CSU.[5]

Thierry Imbot, on October 10, 2000, fell from his apartment window or was defenestrated for knowing too much about France's role in the bribery and kickbacks involved in the sale of destroyers to Taiwan. His father, René Imbot, said that the location of the body's landing ruled out accidental death. The senior Imbot was head of France's DGSE from 1985 to 1988.

Étienne Léandri, who died in 1996, was a close associate of Charles Pasqua and was alleged to have been pivotal in several major French corruption cases, including the sale of destroyers to Taiwan, the alleged illegal financing of at least one of Charles Pasqua's electoral campaigns, and the Elf purchase of Ertoil. His death caused one case against Charles Pasqua's son Pierre Philippe to fizzle.[6]

Jacques Lefebvre, of the Agusta-Dassault affair, committed suicide on March 7, 1995. He was formerly commander of the Belgian air force and adviser to Dassault.

Jean-Claude Méry was head of the public housing office of Paris for a number of years when Chirac was mayor. Méry died of cancer in 1999. Before his death, he videotaped a confession in which he exposed and described in detail the system of illegal party financing run out of his office on behalf of the Gaullist RPR, then headed by Jacques Chirac. Although the businessmen involved in the affair faced criminal penalties, politicians were spared because the courts ruled that the videotape could not be considered admissible testimony. Chirac was also spared by the immunity conferred by his presidential office.

Jürgen Mollemann, of Germany's Free Democratic Party (FDP), was under investigation for tax evasion and fraud on behalf of the FDP when he committed suicide on June 5, 2003, by skydiving and unhooking himself from his parachute. His parliamentary immunity had just been lifted prior to his suicide.

Antonio Quatraro, an official in the European Commission, committed suicide on March 30, 1993, by jumping from his office at the commission. He was head of the EU's tobacco subsidy division and was under investigation for accepting a bribe as payment for a vote on subsidies that would affect Italian producers. Although Quatraro was not the only person involved in the network, the EU dropped the inquiry upon his death.

Alfred Sirven, the number-two man at Elf Acquitaine when it was a state-owned firm, died of a heart attack on February 12, 2005. He is infamous for his roles in the Elf and Taiwan destroyer affairs. In May 2001 he was sentenced for his role in the latter to four years in prison, which was reduced to three on appeal. In 2003 he was sentenced to five years in prison and fined EUR 1 million for misuse and embezzlement of Elf funds (EUR 305 million); he was released on bail in 2004 pending the appeal of his convictions. He claimed to have enough information about corruption to "bring down the Republic twenty times over."[7]

Raffaello Teti, CEO of Agusta, died on August 22, 1998, of a heart attack, two weeks before the Agusta-Dassault affair trial was to start.

Alain Van der Biest, one of two protégés of André Cools, was suspected of having ordered Cools's assassination. Van der Biest committed suicide on March 18, 2002, a few months before he was due to go on trial.

Bernard Wilhelm, a businessman who was a facilitator of bribes to French officials to set up a cartel for the construction of the TGV Nord line, died in 1999.

Yin Ching-feng, the Taiwan chief of naval procurement, was assassinated in 1993 after pressing on with his investigation of possible bribery in Taiwan's purchase of French destroyers. He was found dead in a Taiwan harbor. The destroyer affair forced Roland Dumas to resign as head of France's Constitutional Court and to stand trial. He was later cleared by an appeals court.

BRIEF SURVEY OF THE EUROPEAN UNION

The EU's roots lie in the European wars of the first half of the twentieth century.[1] Inspired to keep history from repeating itself, six countries—Belgium, Luxembourg, the Netherlands, France, Italy, and Germany—first formed the European Coal and Steel Community (1952) and then the European Economic Community (EEC) and the European Atomic Energy Community (Euratom). The latter two were brought into existence with the signing of the Treaties of Rome in 1957.[2] The EEC's practical goal was to create a common, integrated market that would allow the free movement of goods, services, labor, and capital. The EEC's first measures included creating a Common Agricultural Policy (CAP) that set prices, quotas, and subsidies for agricultural products of the member states. The CAP still takes up the lion's share of the EU's budget and for a time took up to 70 percent of it. The EEC also began eliminating tariff barriers and other nontariff obstacles to trade. Progress on these fronts was aided by the European Court of Justice's interpretations of the treaty pertaining to the EEC. By the 1970s, the EEC had created a Customs Union, which ensured that a standard duty was paid on all items entering the EEC from "third" countries, no matter the point of entry. Also at that time, the EEC officially became the European Community. Early in the 1970s, the EC began trying to coordinate currency exchange rates to facilitate interstate commerce, which was the beginnings of the European Monetary System. In 1986, after protracted negotiation, the EC members signed the Single European Act (SEA), which eliminated remaining trade barriers and, in 1992, facilitated launch of the Single Market. The Single European Act created the structural funds, giving the EU a budget with which to subsidize development in unindustrialized, rural areas and deindustrializing areas. The Maastricht Treaty (officially known as the Treaty of the European Union), signed in 1991 and implemented in 1993, was meant to further that effort. Formally, it established the European Union, of which the EC was one pillar. The other two—Justice and Home Affairs, and Common Foreign and Security Policy—operated only on a multilateral, state-to-state (intergovernmental) basis. The Maastricht Treaty contained the blueprint for creating the common currency, what came to be called the euro. The common currency was launched electronically in 2000, by fixing participating countries' exchange rates and then converting them to euros, and as a physical currency in 2002.

The EU has added new members a number of times. The first expansion, in 1973, brought in Denmark, Ireland, and the United Kingdom. The second wave of expansion included Greece (1981) and Spain and Portugal (1986). The third brought in Austria, Finland, and Sweden in 1995, and the fourth, and largest, in 2004, Cyprus, Malta, Latvia, Estonia, Lithuania, Poland, Hungary, the Czech Republic, Slovakia, and Slovenia. The fifth expansion saw Romania and Bulgaria become members in 2007.

THE MAJOR INSTITUTIONS OF THE EUROPEAN UNION

European Commission. Headquartered in Brussels, the Commission proposes regulations and directives, and oversees the day-to-day operation of the EU. It is charged with overseeing states' compliance with the treaties and with the subsequent regulations and directives. Each Commission, with a president and a set of commissioners, has a five-year tenure. The number of commissioners and commission portfolios of course expanded along with the EU. Its portfolios range from agriculture to competition to environmental policy and beyond. Commissioners are nominated by member-state governments, and the college must be approved in its entirety by the member states. The Commission may fine firms for violations of competition policy, and it may begin "infringement proceedings" against member states it finds in violation of treaties, directives, or regulations. The proceedings are protracted and may result in a case going before the European Court of Justice.[1]

Council of the European Union. Often known as the Council of Ministers, this institution had its name changed to the Council of the European Union after Maastricht. It is composed of member-state government ministers, who meet to discuss particular policy areas and amend and vote on the detailed policy proposals (sometimes called legislation) from the Commission. When the issue pertains to agriculture, it is the agriculture ministers who meet. A Commission member is also present. Voting in most issue areas occurs under rules of "qualified majority," rather than just simple majority, with states having different voting weights. Some issues, such as expansion, require unanimity. The Council has had a rotating six-month presidency. It is supported by a Council of Permanent Representatives (from each member-state) in Brussels.

European Parliament. Split between its secretariat in Luxembourg, its plenary sessions in Strasbourg, and its committee meetings in Brussels, the European Parliament has always been something of a hybrid institution. Begun as the government-appointed European Assembly, the Parliament's primary institutional thrust has been to try to become more like an actual legislature. Direct elections to it only began in 1979. Elections are not pan-European; each state conducts its own elections every five years, and each has a number of seats somewhat proportional to its population. Those elected sit with their nearest European party family. In 1986 with the SEA, the Parliament gained the right to have a second reading on legislation. Further powers were granted with subsequent treaties.

European Court of Justice. Based in Luxembourg, the ECJ adjudicates the interpretation and application of the EU treaties and legislation, and has decided a number of cases that have been significant in moving European economic integration forward and, more informally, constructing Europe. The number of judges on the ECJ, until 2004, reflected the number of member states. When its case load mushroomed in the late 1970s and 1980s, the EU created a Court of First Instance (1989) to redirect and hear some of the cases. The ECJ has no real powers of enforcement and can only impose fines should a member state fail to comply with an earlier ruling. One way the ECJ's authority or influence has expanded is that national courts began asking the ECJ for a preliminary ruling or interpretation of some aspect of EU law. Whether and when national courts then apply the ECJ's rulings are other questions.[2]

European Council. Composed of the heads of government (prime ministers) plus the French head of state (because the French president has sole authority over French foreign policy), this body meets at least twice a year to determine the broad directions of the European Union and to deal with particularly intractable subjects. The European Commission often takes its cue from the European Council when it initiates proposals for directives and regulations. Along with being photo ops for European politicians, European Council meetings are noted for initiating turning points in the EU's development, such as launching the European monetary system, authorizing negotiations for the Single European Act, resolving budget crises, and expanding the EU's range of governance.

Notes

PREFACE

1. Committee of Independent Experts, *First Report on Allegations regarding Fraud, Mismanagement and Nepotism in the European Commission 15 March 1999*, http://www.euro parl.eu.int/experts/pdf/reporten.pdf; Ann Sherlock and Christopher Harding, "Controlling Fraud in the European Community," *European Law Review* 16/1 (Feb. 1991): 20–36, here at 21.

INTRODUCTION

1. Mark A. Pollack, "Theorizing the European Union: International Organization, Domestic Polity, or Experiment in New Governance?" *Annual Review of Political Science* 8 (2005): 357–98.

2. Mark E. Warren, "Political Corruption as Duplicitous Exclusion," *PS: Political Science and Politics* 39/4 (Oct. 2006): 803–7, here at 804.

3. "Why capitalism, not America, is the real issue," *Financial Times*, 2 Dec. 2002.

4. Günther Verheugen, in Adriano Milovan, "EU commissioner points to possible Croatian admission to the EU by 2008," *Global News Wire*, 3 Dec. 2002.

5. Robert Zoelleck, U.S. Trade Representative, "From Crisis to Commonwealth: CAFTA and Democracy in Our Neighborhood," speech given to the Heritage Foundation, 16 May 2005, http://usembassy.state.gov/panama/cafta.html.

6. Strom C. Thacker, *Big Business, the State, and Free Trade: Constructing Coalitions in Mexico* (New York: Cambridge University Press, 2000).

7. John Gerring and Strom C. Thacker, "Do Neoliberal Policies Deter Political Corruption?" *International Organization* 59 (Winter 2005): 233–54, here at 236.

8. Wayne Sandholtz and William Koetzle, "Accounting for Corruption: Economic Structure, Democracy, and Trade," *International Studies Quarterly* 44 (2000): 31–50.

9. Miriam A. Golden, "Does Globalization Reduce Corruption? Some Political Consequences of Economic Integration," paper presented at the Workshop in Comparative and Historical Analysis, Stanford University, Oct. 28, 2002, 37.

10. Andrew Moravcsik, "Europe without Illusions," *Prospect*, 23 June 2005.

11. Gerring and Thacker, "Do Neoliberal Policies Deter Political Corruption?" 238.

12. Unless otherwise noted, all translations are my own. Renaud Van Ruymbeke, *Ordonnance de renvoi devant le Tribunal correctionnel de non-lieu partiel et de requalification*, no. du Parquet 9418769211, no. instruction 2039/94/29, procédure correctionnelle, Cour d'appel de Paris, Tribunal de grand instance de Paris, 13 Dec. 2002, 514–16.

13. Here I do not mean just the EU as of 1992/Maastricht; I use the term EU even when European Economic Community or European Community would be technically appropriate.

14. Cf. Michael Johnston, *Syndromes of Corruption* (Cambridge: Cambridge University Press, 2005).

15. Thomas Catan and Michael Peel, "Export credit agency 'did little to probe bribery claims over gas scheme,'" *Financial Times*, 22 June 2005.

16. Quoted in Gianni Barbacetto, Peter Gomez, and Marco Travaglio, *Mani Pulite: La vera storia* (Rome: Riuniti, 2002), 677.

17. Open Society Institute, "Monitoring the EU Accession Process: Corruption and Anti-Corruption Policy," http://www.eumap.org/topics/corruption/reports/international/sections/overview/223.

18. A good survey is Mark A. Pollack, "International Relations Theory and European Integration," *Journal of Common Market Studies* 39/2 (June 2001), 221–44."

19. Lawrence H. Officer, "Exchange Rate between the United States Dollar and Forty Other Countries, 1913–1999," Economic History Services, EH.Net, 2002, http://eh.net/hmit/exchangerates/.

20. "Probe into German party official's suicide amid funding scandal," *Agence France Presse*, 21 Jan. 2000.

21. Thierry Jean-Pierre, *Taïwan Connection* (Paris: Laffont, 2003), 184–91.

CHAPTER 1. CORRUPTION DYNAMICS IN THE EUROPEAN UNION

1. Alberto Statera, "Per fortuna per che c'è la tangente unica industria senza recessione," *La Stampa*, 26 Mar. 1992; author interview with UCLAF (Unité coordinatif de la lutte anti-fraude) officials, 4 June 1998; Ulrich Ulrich, "Euro-fraud: Organised Fraud against the Financial Interests of the European Union," *Crime, Law and Social Change* 30 (1998): 1–42; Carolyn M. Warner, "Institutionen der Korruption oder Korruption der Institutionen? Betrug in der Europäischen Union," in *Politische Korruption: Jahrbuch für Europa und Nordamerika Studien,* ed. Jens Borchert, Sigrid Leitner, and Klaus Stolz (Opladen: Leske & Budrich, 2000), 3:225–50; Donatella Della Porta and Yves Mény, eds., *Democracy and Corruption in Europe* (London: Pinter, 1997); Yves Mény, *La corruption de la République* (Paris: Fayard, 1992); Martin Rhodes, "Financing Party Politics in Italy: A Case of Systemic Corruption," *West European Politics* 20/1 (1997): 54–80; Martin J. Bull and James L. Newell, eds., *Corruption in Contemporary Politics* (Basingstoke: Palgrave Macmillan, 2003).

2. In a case of apparent kickbacks granted the local Social Democratic Party (SPD) in Cologne between 1994 and 1998 by construction firms on one project, about $15 million (in deutsche marks) were funneled into and then disappeared from Swiss bank accounts. "Spendenskandal nimmt dramatische Ausmasse an-Streit in Berlin," *DPA-AFX*, 7 Mar. 2002; Celine Le Prioux, "Le SPD de Schroeder aux prises avec un scandale de financement occulte," *Agence France Presse*, 12 Mar. 2002.

3. Gérard Davet and Fabrice Lhomme, "Le parquet de Paris ouvre deux informations judiciaires visant Thales pour 'corruption,'" *Le Monde*, 8 Dec. 2005; Grat Van Den Heuvel, "The Parliamentary Enquiry on Fraud in the Dutch Construction Industry: Collusion as a Concept between Corruption and State-Corporate Crime," *Crime, Law and Social Change* 44 (2005): 133–51; "Siemens Bribery Scandal Escalates," *Financial Times* 16 Dec. 2006; Richard Milne, "Siemens Bribery Scandal Raises Further Questions," *Financial Times*, 22 Dec. 2006; United States Securities and Exchange Commission Form 20-F, Siemens Aktiengesellschaft, *Annual and transition report on foreign private issuers,* SEC Accession no. 0001326932-06-000377; 11 Dec. 2006, 74-75.

4. Wayne Sandholtz and Mark M. Gray, "International Integration and National Corruption," *International Organization* 57/4 (2003): 761–800, here at 787; John Gerring and Strom Thacker; "Do Neoliberal Policies Deter Political Corruption?" *International Organization* 59 (Winter 2005): 233–54, here at 237.

5. Donatella Della Porta and Alberto Vannucci, *Corrupt Exchanges: Actors, Resources, and Mechanisms of Political Corruption* (New York: Aldine de Gruyter 1999), 10; Mark Philp, "Defining Political Corruption," in *Political Corruption,* ed. Paul Heywood (Oxford: Blackwell 1997), 20–46, here at 25; Yves Mény, "Fin de Siècle Corruption: Change, Crisis and Shifting Values," *International Social Science Journal* 48/3 (Sept. 1996): 309–20, here at 311.

6. Tribunal de grande instance de Nanterre, as quoted in "Voici les principaux attendus du tribunal de grande instance," *Le Monde*, 1 Feb. 2004. See also Mark Philip, "Corruption

Definition and Measurement," in *Measuring Corruption*, ed. Charles Sampford, Arthur Shacklock, Carmel Connors, and Fredrik Galtung (Aldershot: Ashgate, 2006), 45–56. Juppé's sentence was reduced on appeal, but the findings of guilt remained. République Française, Cour d'appel de Versailles, no. 2004-00824, 1 Dec. 2004.

7. See Mark E. Warren, "What Does Corruption Mean in a Democracy," *American Journal of Political Science* 48/2 (Apr. 2004): 328–43; Philip, "Corruption Definition and Measurement"; Yves Mény, "France: The End of the Republican Ethic?" in Della Porta and Mény, *Democracy and Corruption in Europe*, 7–21; Susan Rose-Ackerman, *Corruption: A Study in Political Economy* (New York: Academic Press, 1978).

8. Eva Joly and Caroline Joly-Baumgartner, *L'abus de biens sociaux* (Paris: Economica, 2002), 1.

9. They include influence peddling, bribery, corruption, breach of (public) trust, fraud, deceit, dishonesty, collusion (to avoid taxes, the law, etc.), conspiracy (to contravene the law, etc., by a group), obstruction of justice, forgery, tax evasion, breach of duty, malfeasance in office, contravention of public laws, subornation, nepotism (in awarding of public offices), and solicitation (of illegal payments, commissions).

10. Rose-Ackerman, *Corruption*, 2.

11. Good surveys can be found in Susan Rose-Ackerman, *Corruption and Government* (New York: Cambridge University Press, 1999); Alberto Ades and Rafael Di Tella, "National Champions and Corruption: Some Unpleasant Interventionist Arithmetic," *Economic Journal* 107 (July 1997): 1023–42; Arnold J. Heidenheimer, Michael Johnston, and Victor T. Levine, eds., *Political Corruption: A Handbook* (New Brunswick, NJ: Transaction Books, 1989).

12. Gerring and Thacker, "Do Neoliberal Policies Deter Political Corruption?" 235.

13. In reaction to September 11, the EU approved a European arrest warrant, with entry into force (going into effect) by 31 December 2003. At the time of writing, seven of the EU-15 had yet to implement the law. http://europa.eu.int/scadplus/leg/en/lvb/l33167.htm.

14. Interview with Karl Laske, journalist for *Libération*, 25 Nov. 2003; Karl Laske, *Des coffres si bien garnis* (Paris: Denoël, 2004); Fabrizio Calvi and Leo Sisti, *Les nouveaux reseaux de la corruption* (Paris: Albin Michel, 1995).

15. George Parker, "Power begins to shift but nations still dominate," *Financial Times*, 20 June 2006.

16. Pippa Norris, *Democratic Phoenix: Reinventing Political Activism* (New York: Cambridge University Press, 2002), 36.

17. Raymond Fisman and Roberta Gatti, "Decentralization and Corruption: Evidence from U.S. Federal Transfer Programs," *Public Choice* 113 (2002): 25–35.

18. Rose-Ackerman, *Corruption and Government*, 35. Rose-Ackerman goes on to note variations in ways the process can be corrupted.

19. Mény, "France," 18. As Mény states, "Corruption is thus more likely to spread in cases where the 'immune defence systems' of the group tend to weaken and the 'moral cost' drops; as will occur when public behavior is less prized than private, when producing results comes to matter more than observing standards, monetary values more than ethical or symbolic values."

20. See, for instance, the relative absence of voter retribution in Germany to the numerous party financing scandals. Susan E. Scarrow, "Party Finance Scandals and their Consequences in the 2002 Elections: Paying for Mistakes?" *German Politics and Society* 21/1 (Spring 2003), 119–37; Peter Pulzer, "Votes and Resources: Political Finance in Germany," *German Politics and Society* 19/1 (Spring 2001), 1–35.

21. Christophe Deloire, "Secret défense; interdit d'enquêter," *Le Point*, 21 Feb. 2003; see also Thierry Jean-Pierre, *Taïwan connection* (Paris: Laffont, 2003).

22. The Berlusconi government's rapporteur was Giorgio La Malfa, who earlier had

been found guilty of taking a $300,000 payment in a huge corruption case, called Enimont, which involved a state-owned industrial conglomerate and a private firm. Berlusconi had been charged on two counts of false accounting (one involving $6 million, another $1.5 billion), found guilty of the first one, and sentenced to more than two years in prison. The new law, however, forced the courts to drop the charges. To aid the law's passage, some twenty-six members of Berlusconi's coalition in the Italian Senate voted for their absent colleagues by pressing their "yes" buttons during the electronic voting as well as voting yes themselves. Oddly, the vote was considered legitimate. An earlier version of the law, which Berlusconi tried to pass when he was prime minister in 1994, was nicknamed "save the thieves" law by its opponents. On Enimont, see chapter 4. On Berlusconi and La Malfa, see Gianni Barbacetto, Peter Gomez, and Marco Travaglio, *Mani pulite: La vera storia* (Rome: Riuniti, 2002), 655–56; and Peter Gomez and Marco Travaglio, *La repubblica delle banane* (Rome: Riuniti, 2003), 84–132, 362–64, 534. Richard Owen, "European Court asked to review law," *Times*, 28 Oct. 2002; M.D.Fo., "Stop al processo Berlusconi," *Il Sole 24 Ore*, 27 Oct. 2002. On the "banana republic" quote, see "The Fruits of Office," *Economist*, 11 Aug. 2001. Information and sources on the Leuna affair are in chapter 4.

23. Http://europa.eu.int/scadplus/leg/en/lvb/l33099.htm.

24. Andrew Macintyre, *The Power of Institutions: Political Architecture and Governance* (Ithaca: Cornell University Press, 2003), 7.

25. "European Commission criticizes Slovakia over agriculture, aid to iron works," *Financial Times*, 15 Mar. 2004.

26. "EC gives four fail marks to Slovakia," *Financial Times*, 5 Nov. 2003.

27. As a result of the immunity conferred on an officeholder and the strictures on trying a politician for crimes allegedly committed while a minister in the French cabinet, Pasqua's cases are, at the time of writing, being heard by the Cour de justice de la République.

28. Fabrice Lhomme, "Un nouveau proche de Charles Pasqua a été mis en examen pour 'blanchiment,'" *Le Monde*, 15 Sept. 2004; Fabrice Tassel, "Soupçon de blanchiment dans le giron de Pasqua," *Libération*, 15 Sept. 2004.

29. Lhomme, "Un nouveau proche"; Tassel, "Soupçon de blanchiment"; http://www.devinci.fr/home/nous/index-nous.htm; Committee of Independent Experts, *First Report on Allegations regarding Fraud, Mismanagement and Nepotism in the European Commission 15 March 1999* (1999), 71–90; http://www.europarl.eu.int/experts/pdf/reporten.pdf.

30. Firzli's name, transcribed as Elias El-Ferzeli ou Ghazarli, also was on the oil-for-food list. Pasqua was put under official investigation regarding this case in April 2006. Gérard Davet and Fabrice Lhomme, "Ex-cadre de Total au juge: 'Si nous n'avions pas payé, nous n'aurions pas eu de pétrole,'" *Le Monde*, 2 Oct. 2004; Gérard Davet and Fabrice Lhomme, "Deux intermédiaires pour accéder au pétrole irakien," *Le Monde*, 16 Oct. 2004; "Le fils de Charles Pasqua relaxé dans une affaire de corruption," *Le Monde*, 2 Mar. 2006; "Huit proches de Charles Pasqua et son fils renvoyé en correctionnelle dans l'affaire Sofremi," *Le Monde*, 7 Aug. 2006; Gérard Davet, "Affaire 'pétrole contre nourriture': Charles Pasqua est mis en examen," *Le Monde*, 8 Apr. 2006; U.S. Senate Permanent Subcommittee on Investigations, *Report on Oil Allocations Granted to Charles Pasqua and George Galloway*, 109th Cong., 1st sess., 17 May 2005.

31. At the time of writing, Marchiani's convictions are on appeal. Fabrice Lhomme, "Jean-Charles Marchiani mis en cause dans deux nouvelles affaires," *Le Monde*, 21 Nov. 2002; Fabrice Lhomme, "Pourquoi le juge Courroye veut incarcérer Jean-Charles Marchiani," *Le Monde*, 13 May 2003; Pascale Robert-Diard, "Devant le tribunal, Jean-Charles Marchiani règle ses comptes avec MM. Juppé et Léotard," *Le Monde*, 6 Oct. 2005; Pascale Robert-Diard, "Prison ferme pour Jean-Charles Marchiani," *Le Monde*, 16 Dec. 2005.

32. Fabrice Lhomme, "L'ancien conseiller de Charles Pasqua est mis en cause dans plusiers affaires financières," *Le Monde*, 4 Dec. 2003; Fabrice Lhomme, "Le sulfureux," *Le Monde*, 3 Aug. 2004; Pascale Robert-Diard, "Prison ferme pour Jean-Charles Marchiani," *Le Monde*, 16 Dec. 2005. Marchiani and eight others who are close to Charles Pasqua, including Pasqua's son Pierre-Philippe, are due to be tried in 2007 for the SOFREMI/Angolagate affair. "Huit proches de Charles Pasque et son fils renvoyés en correctionnelle dans l'affaire Sofremi," *Le Monde*, 7 Aug. 2006.

33. In 1996, Gaydamak (also sometimes spelled Gaidamak) received France's "order of merit" for his assistance in liberating two French pilots held hostage in Bosnia. Because he had donated $1 million to the 9/11 victims fund, Gaydamak was invited to attend a dinner in Israel held in honor of New York City mayor Rudolph Giuliani; former Israeli prime minister Ariel Sharon was also in attendance. Gaydamak has other notable connections, including a former head of Israel's Mossad, Danny Yatom, and Alimzhan Tokhtakhounov, a Russian of Uzbeki origins who allegedly conspired to fix the results of the pairs skating and ice dancing competitions at the Salt Lake City Olympics in 2002. Holder of Russian and Israeli passports, Tokhtakhounov has faced more serious allegations: that he is "a leading member of the Russian Mafia . . . involved in kidnappings of Russian exiles in Germany and racketeering." U.S. efforts to extradite Tokhtakhounov from Italy, where he had taken up residence after being encouraged to leave France, failed. Jean Chichizola, "Elf, financement des partis, Pasqua, Marchiani, Mitterrand et Attali; Les ramifications de l'affaire Falcone," *Le Figaro*, 11 Dec. 2000; Karl Laske, "Falcone et Cie, armes en tous genres," *Libération*, 13 Dec. 2000; Karl Laske, "L'Etat rattrapé par ses offices d'armement," *Libération*, 23 Dec. 2000; Fabrice Lhomme, "L'autre affaire d'otages qui inquiète l'entourage de Charles Pasqua," *Le Monde*, 26 Jan. 2002; Robert Graham, "French counter-intelligence under surveillance," *Financial Times*, 6 Aug. 2004; Yossi Melman and Julio Godoy, *Making a Killing. The Influence Peddlers* (Washington D.C.: The Center for Public Integrity, 2002), 1; John Tagliabue, "Figure Skating: Details Begin to Emerge of Man Arrested in Plot," *New York Times*, 2 Aug. 2002. Kidnapping and racketeering quote from a Diréction Générale de la Sécurité Extérieure (DGSE) report, France's equivalent of the U.S. CIA, 28 July 1998, reproduced in Melman and Godoy, *Making a Killing*, 3. Gaydamak said he severed ties with Tokhtakhounov in 1994. Global Witness, *All the President's Men* (London: Global Witness, 2002), http://www.globalwitness.org/media_library_detail.php/85/en/all_the_presidents _m11–22.

34. Thomas Lebegue, "Pasqua cherche le salut par le Sénat," *Libération*, 7 Sept. 2004; Hervé Gattegno and Fabrice Lhomme, "Pierre Falcone: 'En France, on peut crucifier un innocent,'" *Le Monde*, 16 Apr. 2002.

35. "L'affaire du trafic d'armes vers l'Afrique," *Agence France Presse*, 11 Jan. 2001; "Renvoi du procès de Jean-Christophe Mitterrand," *Le Figaro*, 18 May 2004; "Les mauvaises fréquentations de Mitterrand l'africain," *Le Point*, 5 Jan. 2001; Stephen Smith and Antoine Glaser, "Les hommes de l'Angolagate," *Le Monde*, 13 Jan. 2001; République Française, Cour de Cassation, Chambre criminelle, no. 01-86063, 14 Nov. 2001.

36. At the time of writing, the case is still in various phases of investigation and prosecution. The international branch of Compagnie générale des eaux later became Vivendi Environnement, which in 2002 posted bankrupting losses of $30 billion. This led to the ouster of its CEO, Philippe Jaffré. Vivendi is now Veolia Environnement.

37. "Policy and Practice," *Financial Times*, 16 Dec. 2004; "Traders de brut et de cash," *La Lettre du Continent*, 1 Mar. 2001; "Glencore, le trader devenu industriel," *Les Echos*, 18 Feb. 2003; Ken Silverstein, "The arms dealer next door," *In These Times*, 21 Dec. 2001.

38. On the illegal financing scheme, see chapter 6. Guilloux was cleared of violating professional secrecy requirements. Fabrice Lhomme, "Cassette Méry," *Le Monde*, 28 Mar. 2002.

39. Karl Laske, "Un axe Hauts-de-Seine-Afrique qui passe par la Corse," *Libération,* 11 Jan. 2001.

40. It is suspected that approximately half their profit went back to officials in Angola, and some to officials in France, including Pasqua and Marchiani. At Elf, the French oil company that did extensive business with Angola, Angolan officials were referred to not by name but by how much of a bribe they charged. Thus, the Angolan itinerant ambassador Elisio de Figueiredo was called Monsieur 20%, and the secretary of the president's cabinet, José Leitao de Costa, Monsieur 30%. Fabrice Lhomme, "Le député européen Jean-Charles Marchiani à nouveau mis en examen dans l'affaire Falcone," *Le Monde,* 21 Sept. 2002; Fabrice Lhomme, "Un témoignage éclaire les dessous des ventes d'armes à l'Angola," *Le Monde,* 23 Apr. 2003.

41. Renaud Lecadre, "L'ombre d'un truand sur le procès Alstom," *Libération,* 11 Jan. 2006; Julien Caumer, *Les requins: Un réseau au coeur des affaires* (Paris: Flammarion, 1999).

42. Guelfi had been a fish industry magnate in Morocco and Norway, a business associate of the founder of Adidas, and had won the publicity contract for the 1980 Moscow Olympics. Denis Demonpion, "Pierre Pasqua; L'éminence de son père," *Le Point,* 13 June 2003; Renaud van Ruymbeke, *Ordonnance de renvoi devant le Tribunal correctionnel de non-lieu partiel et de requalification,* no. du Parquet 9418769211, no. instruction 2039/94/29, procédure correctionnelle, Cour d'appel de Paris, Tribunal de grand instance de Paris, 13 Dec. 2002, 417–49; Markus Dettmer, Jürgen Kremb, Romain Leick, Georg Mascolo, Conny Neumann, Heiner Schimmöller, Holger Stark, and Markus Verbeet, "Finale am Eiffelturm," *Der Spiegel,* 19 July 2004, 42–47; Fabrice Lhomme, "André Guelfi: Homme de réseaux," *Le Monde,* 12 Sept. 2001; Eric Decouty, "Guelfi visé par une affaire de blanchiment de capitaux," *Le Figaro,* 11 May 2004; République Française, Cour de Cassation, Chambre criminelle, no. 02-85089, 31 Jan. 2007; "Les différents volets de l'affaire," *Le Monde,* 18 March 2003; Gilles Gaetner, "Elf. Procès d'une affaire d'Etat," *L'Express,* 13 March 2003; Jochen Hehn, "Gericht verhängt hohe Strafen im Elf-Prozess," *Die Welt,* 13 Nov. 2003.

43. David Pallister and Jon Henley, "British warrant issued in French arms row," *Guardian,* 26 Mar. 2001; Laske, *Des coffres si bien garnis,* 134–38.

44. The police concluded it was an accident; others dispute that interpretation. Pascal Ceaux and Fabrice Lhomme, "Les enquêteurs s'interrogent sur le rôle de Thierry Imbot auprès de M. Falcone," *Le Monde,* 11 Jan. 2001; Jean-Pierre, *Taïwan connection,* 185–90. Imbot was married to an American journalist from CNN who had taken a job in Paris with the *International Herald Tribune* just before Imbot's death on 10 October 2000. Imbot had worked for the DGSE until 1991. See chapter 3.

45. Sonia Falcone's brief biography and statements are at http://www.essante.com/about/founder.html. Catherine Reagor, "Falcones hold record for the priciest estate," *Arizona Republic,* 12 Jan. 2001; Catherine Reagor, "Hopping on the trail of a real estate maze," *Arizona Republic,* 12 Jan. 2001; Anna Kuchment and Malcolm Beith, "Please Return to Sender," *Newsweek,* 29 Jan. 2001.

46. Paul Giblin, "P.V. socialite digs in for a battle over immigration," *East Valley Tribune,* 21 Feb. 2006.

47. Committee on Legal Affairs and the Internal Market, European Parliament, "Report on the Request for Waiver of the Immunity of Charles Pasqua," A5–0032/2002, 20 Feb. 2002.

48. Gaydamak and Falcone are also suspected of having rigged the repayment of Angola's debt to Russia, reserving a healthy commission for themselves and a number of others. Falcone is also being pursued by the French judiciary for tax evasion on profits from arms sales. There is a legal debate in various countries about exactly what kind of diplomatic immunity a UNESCO appointment confers. The 9th chamber of the Court of appeal in Paris ruled that such an appointment does not grant any diplomatic immunity. On

Gaydamak's and Falcone's financial interests, see Nicholas Shaxson, "Murky saga takes the shine off one of Africa's unpolished jewels," *Financial Times,* 9 Dec. 2003; Melman and Godoy, *Making a Killing. The Influence Peddlers;* Global Witness, *A Crude Awakening* (London: Global Witness, n.d.), 11; Global Witness, *All the President's Men.* On Angola's finances, see Human Rights Watch, "Some Transparency, No Accountability: The Use of Oil Revenue in Angola and Its Impact on Human Rights," 16/A, January 2004. Sonia Falcone as quoted in Emily Bittner, "Home fires still burning," *Arizona Republic,* 10 Nov. 2003; Martine Silber, "Abus diplomatique," *Le Monde,* 15 Feb. 2006; "Le procés Falcone pour fraude fiscale a été reporté au mois d'octobre," *Le Monde,* 26 Apr. 2006; "Pas d'immunité diplomatique pour Pierre Falcone," *La Nouvelle République du Centre Ouest,* 14 Sept. 2006.

49. "Affaire Falcone: L'actrice Catherine Deneuve démissionne de l'UNESCO," *Agence France Presse,* 12 Nov. 2003.

50. Karl Laske, "L'Elysée pompier de l'affaire Falcone," *Libération,* 8 July 2004; Hervé Gattegno and Fabrice Lhomme, "L'Angola tente d'obtenir le retraite des plaintes dans l'affaire Falcone," *Le Monde,* 29 June 2005; "Angola declines to renew license for Total," *Agence France Presse,* 5 Nov. 2004; Carola Hoyos, "Angola aims to redistribute its oil wealth," *Financial Times,* 1 Dec. 2005. There are concerns that Angola is showing preference to smaller and non-Western oil firms to evade the transparency pledges that some Western oil firms have recently signed on to.

51. "Is Europe Corrupt?" *Economist,* 29 Jan. 2000, 59.

CHAPTER 2. DOES COMPETITION IN THE EUROPEAN UNION CORRUPT?

1. Dunne's escapade was too much for Dunne's sister Margaret Heffernan. She launched an effort to oust her brother from the board of directors of their company, Dunne, a major Irish corporation. For a number of years, Dunne had been financing Haughey with company money. Haughey, meanwhile, had not been reporting the occasional donations, one of which was IR £1.3 million, to the tax authorities. Haughey thought he bought silence when he paid Dunne IR £85,000. But as the cocaine escapade showed, Haughey was dealing with a loose cannon. In 1997, Dunne was discovered to have financed an IR £300,000–500,000 remodeling job on the home of Irish minister of transport, energy, and communications Michael Lowry, a member of Haughey's rival party, Fine Gael. Haughey died in 2006 at the age of eighty. Kevin Toolis, *Observer,* 3 Sept. 2000. Details also from the *Independent,* 8 and 29 Mar. 1992. Irish GDP growth at http://www.esri.ie/content.cfm?t=Irish%20Economy&mid=4.

2. Peter Gomez and Marco Travaglio, *Bravi Ragazzi* (Rome: Riuniti, 2003).

3. Arve Johansen, memorandum, 4 May 1996, disclosed as evidence at Moriarty Tribunal, morning session, 12 Dec. 2002, 22. Johansen was an executive at Telenor, the state-owned Norwegian telecommunications company that was one of the members of the bid-winning consortium. T. Kiessling and Y. Blondeel, "The EU Regulatory Framework in Telecommunications," *Telecommunications Policy* 22/7 (1998): 571–92.

4. A. G. Dorée, "Collusion in the Dutch Construction Industry: An Industrial Organization Perspective," *Building Research and Information* 32/2 (Mar.–Apr. 2004): 146–56; Grat Van Den Heuvel, "The Parliamentary Enquiry on Fraud in the Dutch Construction Industry: Collusion as a Concept between Corruption and State-Corporate Crime," *Crime, Law and Social Change* 44 (2005): 133–51.

5. Gérard Davet and Fabrice Lhomme, "Un ex-diregeant dénonce un système de corruption chez Thales," *Le Monde,* 27 Sept. 2005.

6. Alberto Ades and Rafael Di Tella, "Rents, Competition and Corruption," *American Economic Review* 89/4 (Sept. 1999): 982–93, here at 988. See also Anne O. Krueger, "The Political Economy of the Rent-Seeking Society," *American Economic Review* 64/3 (June 1974): 291–303.

7. A standard technique in public procurement corruption is to compensate firms for the costs of the kickbacks they are asked to pay by inflating the contract by at least that amount, if not more (to compensate for risk of discovery). Another is to create more public works projects, and thereby grant more business, than the state would have in the absence of corruption.

8. Edward Banfield, "Corruption as a Feature of Governmental Organization," *Journal of Law and Economics* 18 (1975): 587–605, here at 593.

9. Competitiveness in the EU is a complex subject. While the chapter focuses on the microanalysis of the impact of competition in particular cases, the macroeconomic trends show varying levels and types of competition across sectors and years. Patrick Ziltener, "The Economic Effects of the European Single Market Project: Projections, Simulations— and the Reality," *Review of International Political Economy* 11/5 (Dec. 2004): 953–79, here at 962–63; Dominick Salvatore, "Europe's Structural and Competitiveness Problems and the Euro," *World Economy* 21/2 (March 1998): 189–205.

10. Cf. European Commission, *Impact on Competition and Scale Effects: Competition Issues,* Single Market Review Subseries 5: vol. 3 (Luxembourg: Office for Official Publications of the European Communities, 1997), 38–41.

11. The classic statement is George Stigler, "A Theory of Economic Regulation," *Bell Journal of Economics* 2 (Spring 1971): 3–21. See also Gary Becker, "A Theory of Competition amongst Pressure Groups for Political Influence," *Quarterly Journal of Economics* 98 (Aug. 1983): 371–400.

12. On Pasqua, see chapter 4. In Ireland, a lengthy investigation by a tribunal set up by the Irish Parliament has been assessing illegal party contributions connected to changes in zoning regulations for development around Dublin in the 1980s and 1990s. One property developer has stated that he paid Padraig Flynn IR £50,000; Flynn has denied the allegation. Flynn has held various positions in Irish government cabinets: minister of Gaeltacht, minister for trade, commerce, and tourism, minister for environment, and, ironically, considering future charges, minister for justice. Neil Collins and Mary O'Shea, "Political Corruption in Ireland," in *Corruption in Contemporary Politics,* ed. Martin J. Bull and James L. Newell (Hampshire: Palgrave Macmillan, 2003), 164–77, here at 165; http://www.fact-index.com/p/pa/padraig_flynn.html.

13. Case C-237/99, *Commission of the European Communities v. French Republic,* 19 Oct. 2000; case 31/87, *Beentjes v. Netherlands State* [1988]; case C-44/96, *Mannesmann Anlagenbau Austria and Others v. Strohal Rotationsdruck GesmbH Company Law,* 15 Jan. 1998.

14. European Commission, *Single Market: Business Survey Reveals Cautious Optimism* (1997), http://europa.eu.int/comm/internal_market/en/update/score/99.htm, 217, table 12.3; European Commission, *Ninth Survey on State Aid in the European Union* (403 final) (Brussels: CEC, 2001), 23, table 3; European Commission, *State Aid Scoreboard. Autumn 2006 update* (761 final) (Brussels: CEC, 2006).

15. Figures for Italy are lower than those for France, Germany, and Belgium but not the UK. Commission of the European Communities, *Aggregate and Regional Impact: Employment, Trade and Labour Costs in Manufacturing,* Single Market Review Subseries 6, vol. 4 (Luxembourg: Office for Official Publications of the European Communities, 1998), 55–56. The study's authors conclude that the Single Market program of 1986–92 had minimal effect on increased trade, and they credit the effects to mechanisms put in place by the preexisting common market.

16. OECD, *Regulatory Reform in Italy: Enhancing Market Openness through Regulatory Reform* (Paris: OECD, 2001), http://www.oecd.org/dataoecd/20/30/2717506.pdf, 6.

17. Arnaud Leparmentier and Laurent Zecchini, interview with Romano Prodi, "La France sera en minorité si elle n'est pas le levain de l'Europe," *Le Monde,* 18 Oct. 2002. Prodi stated, "I know very well that the stability pact is stupid, like all decisions which are rigid."

18. For the theoretical development of this perspective, see Avner Greif, *Institutions and the Path to the Modern Economy* (Cambridge: Cambridge University Press, 2006), 29–54.

19. Mark Duggan and Steven D. Levitt, "Winning Isn't Everything: Corruption in Sumo Wrestling," *American Economic Review* 92/5 (Dec. 2002): 1594–1605.

20. Giles Tremlett, "German sleaze scandal spreads to Spain," *Sunday Business,* 13 Feb. 2000.

21. The Bonn government had written to the Spanish prime minister saying that relations between the two countries would be damaged should Germany not be awarded a large part of the 1988 train construction contract. Alsthom repeatedly reduced its bid price, undercutting the final German bid but not that of the Japanese. Commentators noted that as a result of Spain's recent entry into the European Community (1986), Spain had to exclude the Japanese and instead figure out how to award the contract to its two most powerful EC "partners," France and Germany. In 2003, Alsthom (renamed Alstom) neared bankruptcy and received a controversial bailout from the French state. Its chief financial officer from 2002–2004 was Philippe Jaffré, brought in from the corrupt French oil firm Elf (now part of Total). Peter Bruce, "Mitsubishi warns Madrid over rail contract award," *Financial Times,* 18 Nov. 1988; Peter Bruce, "French win rail project in Spain," *Financial Times,* 24 Dec. 1988; Peter Bruce, "Europeans shunt Japanese off the tracks," *Financial Times,* 28 Dec. 1988; Martin Arnold, "Alstom in new loans warning," *Financial Times,* 11 Mar. 2004.

22. Manuel Sanchez, "Un dirigente del PSOE cobró cientos de milliones del AVE," *El Mundo* 17 Sept. 1999; Tremlett, "German sleaze scandal."

23. Peter Bruce, "Spain's trains cause EC strains," *Financial Times,* 18 Oct. 1988.

24. Ron Smith, Anthony Humm, and Jacques Fontanel, "The Economics of Exporting Arms," *Journal of Peace Research* 22/3 (Sept. 1985): 239–47, here at 242.

25. Cour de cassation, JC98CN4_2, Brussels, 23 Dec. 1998, title V, chap. 3.3b.

26. Jean-Pierre De Staercke, *Agusta-Dassault: La cassation du siècle* (Brussels: Éditions Luc Pire et le Matin, 1999), 45; Cour de cassation, JC98CN4_B, Brussels, 23 Dec. 1998, sections A1, A2. It appears that Agusta agreed to purchase a significant amount of equipment from a firm with close ties to Cools and Mathot, Trident (as well as from one other, Sabca), in the process bringing revenue (about 70 percent of the contract's value) and patronage to their base in Liège. Agusta officials later admitted they had no intention of honoring the commitment.

27. Cost overruns, kickbacks, and embezzlement eventually caught up with Agusta: by 1995, it was bankrupt.

28. As quoted in De Staercke, *Agusta-Dassault,* 37–38. Interestingly, Agusta was one of the Italian Socialist Party's fiefs. "Tangenti sulla vendita di elicotteri Agusta," *Il Sole 24 Ore,* 11 Apr. 1993.

29. Cour de cassation, JC98CN4_2, Brussels, 23 Dec. 1998, 31.

30. Ibid., 35, 29, 31, 30, 32, 34.

31. Corporate donations to political parties were legal in Belgium until 1989. The problem was that Agusta's and Dassault's "donations" were closely linked to the awarding of contracts to them, which was illegal. Cools's assassination occurred in Liège, birthplace of Georges Simenon, animator of the fictional detective character Maigret. The funds were transferred through screen societies. As Belgian politician Alfons Puelinckx noted, when someone said they preferred a "discreet structure" for the deal, "that automatically meant an off-shore society." Cour de cassation, JC98CN4_2, Brussels, 23 Dec. 1998, title V, chap. 1.2. On links between the cases, see ibid., title III, chap. 3.

32. That statement remained in the Flemish version of the transcribed testimony but was deleted from the French. Some speculate that was to please the French state, which was closely watching the affair. Pierre Bocev, "Son procès s'ouvre aujourd'hui à Bruxelles," *Le*

Figaro, 2 Sept. 1998. In 2002, Serge Dassault, recipient of a two-year suspended sentence in Belgium in 1998, bought a 30 percent share in the group that owns 60 percent of the Belgian paper *Le Soir,* which ran a number of articles exposing the Dassault case; in 2004, his firm bought a large stake in the widely circulated French (conservative) newspaper *Le Figaro.*

33. Cour de cassation, JC98CN4_2, Brussels, 23 Dec. 1998, 39.

34. Hans Rudolf Claussen, Gottfried Herbig, Udo Müller, and Wolfgang J. Schaupensteiner, *Korruption im öffentlichen Dienst* (Berlin: Heymann, 1995); J. Ludwig, *Wirtschaftskriminalität: Schleichewege zum grossen geld* (Frankfurt: Fischer, 1992); M. Möhrenschlager, "Strafrechtliche Vorhaben zur Bekampfung der Korruption auf nationaler und internationaler," *Ebene Juristen Zeitung* (1996): 822–31; K. P. Sommermann, "Brauchen wir eine Ethik des öffentlichren Dienstes?" *Verwaltungs Archiv* (1998): 290–305.

35. Amounts are given in EUR due to time of discovery. "Das Netz der schmutzigen Geschaefte," *Kölner Stadt-Anzeiger,* 10 July 2003; "Der Abfall der Genossen," *Die Zeit,* Dec. 2002; Celine Le Prioux, "Le SPD de Schroeder aux prises avec un scandale de financement occulte," *Agence France-Presse,* 12 Mar. 2002; Georges Marion, "En Allemagne, pots-de-vin autour du traitement des déchets," *Le Monde,* 22 Mar. 2002; "Affaire de corruption à Cologne," *Agence France-Presse,* 13 May 2004.

36. Marion Georges, "En Allemagne, pots-de-vin autour du traitement des dechets," *Le Monde,* 22 Mar. 2002; *Agence France Presse,* 24 Mar. 2002.

37. The EU's approval came on 29 April 1991. Commission des communauté européennes, case no. IV/M.063-ELF/Ertoil, Celex 391M0063.

38. Loïk Le Floch-Prigent, *Affaire Elf: Affaire d'état* (Paris: Le cherche midi, 2001), 183–84.

39. As quoted in Pascale Robert-Diard, "La lutte de plus en plus âpre," *Le Monde,* 8 May 2003. Quotation in the text is from Andrew Spurrier, "Elf tipped to acquire Ertoil from GMH," *Lloyd's List,* 16 Jan. 1991; William Dawkins, "Elf seeks Spanish acquisition," *Financial Times,* 15 Jan. 1991; Stéphane Durand-Souffland, "Procès Nadhmi Auchi," *Le Figaro,* 6 May 2003; Paul Webster and Martin Bright, "Oil scandal billionaire tells French court of bribes," *Guardian,* 7 May 2003.

40. At the time, an Elf spokesman said that they "knew GMH"; another report said that Elf was "confident of its chances of acquiring Ertoil" and that Total was no longer interested. Spanish prosecutors suspected that the sale to GMH, a company based in Luxembourg, was a method of dodging tax liability. They also suspected Ertoil's director (who later became Spain's foreign minister) of having embezzled funds. As quoted in Spurrier, "Elf tipped to acquire Ertoil from GMH"; Dawkins, "Elf seeks Spanish acquisition."

41. As quoted in Reynaud van Ruymbeke, *Ordonnance de renvoi devant le Tribunal correctionnel de non-lieu partiel et de requalification,* no. du Parquet 9418769211, no. instruction 2039/94/29, procédure correctionnelle, Cour d'appel de Paris, Tribunal de grand instance de Paris, 13 Dec. 2002, and cited in "Leuna et Ertoil," *Agence France Presse,* 14 Mar. 2003; Renaud Le Cadre, "Mille facons d'empocher la monnaie," *Libération,* 13 Jan. 2003; Dossiers du Canard, *Elf: L'empire d'essence* (Paris: Roto France, 1998), 70–72.

42. Le Floch-Prigent, *Affaire Elf,* 185.

43. *L'Unità,* 30 Apr. 2003; Gianni Barbacetto, Peter Gomez, and Marco Travaglio, *Mani pulite: La vera storia* (Rome: Riuniti, 2002), 475–76.

44. The sequence of judicial decisions affected by bribery are detailed in Camera dei Deputati, XIII legislatura, "Domanda di Autorizzazione a procedere in giudizio nei confronti del deputato Previti," *Documenti-Relazioni,* vol. II, doc. IV. no. 11, 12 Dec. 1997 (Rome, 1998); ibid no. 11-A-bis, 2–4, 12 Dec. 1997. See also "Sme, Previti condannato a 5 anni," *La Repubblica* 5 Dec. 2005; Barbacetto, Gomez, and Travaglio, *Mani pulite.*

45. As quoted from the court's ruling, in Barbacetto, Gomez, and Travaglio, *Mani pulite,* 479. The ruling did not declare Berlusconi innocent; he remained a suspected "pri-

vate corruptor" but one who did not have to stand trial (and one who refused to testify even while declaring his innocence).

46. Ibid., 480.

47. Moriarty tribunal, 12 Oct. 2001, 1; Ted Harding, "Lowry set for Moriarty Grilling," *Sunday Business Post,* 28 Oct. 2001.

48. O'Brien used much of the proceeds of the BT sale to start a mobile phone business in the Caribbean.

49. Matt Cooper, *Sunday Tribune,* 9 Mar. 2003.

50. Rupert Cornwell, *Financial Times,* 30 Jan. 1985; Anna Tomforde, "Barzel quits," *Guardian,* 26 Oct. 1984. Details of donations from the accountant's records are in Hans Leyendecker, *Das Lambsdorff-Urteil* (Göttingen: Steidl, 1988), 51–59.

51. "West Germany: Flickering On," *Economist,* 21 Feb. 1987; Peter Lösche, *Wovon leben die Partein? Ueber das Geld in der Politik* (Frankfurt: Fischer Taschenbuch Verlag, 1984), 58–60.

52. Rupert Cornwell, "The Flick affair becomes the Kohl affair," *Financial Times,* 27 Feb. 1986. The investigations into Kohl's activities were later dropped because of "insufficient evidence." John Tagliabue, "Insufficient evidence ends Kohl's perjury inquiry," *New York Times,* 22 May 1986.

53. Jean-Pierre Thomas, former treasurer of the Republican Party, quoted in *Le Monde,* 25 July 2001.

54. Jean-Claude Méry, full text in *Le Monde,* 23 Sept. 2000.

55. Ibid., 22 and 23 Sept. 2000.

56. In the Île-de-France case, these firms included Sicra, Baudin Chateauneuf, GTM, Bouygues, Nord-France, Dumez, Chagnaud, CBC, Fougerolles; in Urbatechnic, les Travaux du Midi, la Société lyonnaise (its Groupe de recherches et de construction), and the Société auxiliaire d'entreprise Rhone-Alpes-Mediterranée (SORMAE).

57. Jean-Claude Méry, full text in *Le Monde,* 22 and 23 Sept. 2000.

58. Ibid.

59. BIPE, *The "Cost of Non-Europe" in Public Sector Procurement: Research on the "Cost of Non-Europe" Basic Findings/ Le "Coût de la Non-Europe" des produits de construction: Note de synthèse* (Luxembourg: Commission of the European Communities, 1988), 13:21.

60. Commission of the European Communities, *Aggregate and Regional Impact,* 114, 122, 152, 167, 212, 272.

61. Van Den Heuvel, "Parliamentary Enquiry on Fraud in the Dutch Construction Industry"; W. Bremer and K. Kok, "The Dutch Construction Industry: A Combination of Competition and Corporatism," *Building Research and Information* 28/2 (2002): 98–108; John Groenewegen, "About Double Organized Markets: Issues of Competition and Cooperation. The Dutch Construction Cartel: An Illustration," *Journal of Economic Issues* 28/3 (Sept. 1940): 901–8; Parlementaire Enquête Commissie Bouwnijverheid, *De Bouw uit de Schaduw,* vols. 1 and 2 (The Hague: SDU, 2003).

62. Peter A. Hall and David Soskice, "An Introduction to Varieties of Capitalism," in *Varieties of Capitalism: The Institutional Foundations of Comparative Advantage,* ed. Peter A. Hall and David Soskice (New York: Oxford University Press, 2001), 1–68, here at 8.

63. Alan Doig, "Political Corruption in the United Kingdom," in Bull and Newell, *Corruption in Contemporary Politics,* 179–90, here at 190.

64. Ibid.; author interview with Yves Mény, European University Institute, May 2001.

65. One "cash for questions" led to a parliamentary inquiry, which concluded that a Conservative MP and minister, Neil Hamilton, had accepted £25,000 ($41,000) from Mohamed Al-Fayed. David Hencke, "A liar and a cheat: Official," *Guardian,* 4 July 1997.

66. Tony Blair, as quoted in James Lyons, "Blair embroiled in Labour funding row," *Press Association,* 10 Feb. 2002.

67. Blair's letter, praising the Romanians for choosing a British firm (no mention of the real status of Mittal's firm), was dated 23 July 2001—the same date that Jospin, after much urging from the French firm Usinor, arrived in Bucharest to campaign on its behalf. David Pallister, Vikram Dodd, and Patrick Wintour, "Blair letter 'crucial' to steel firm bid," *Guardian,* 13 Feb. 2002.

68. As Tory MP and overseas development spokeswoman Caroline Spelman asked, "Why is British taxpayer's money being spent on a foreign billionaire who is trying to wreck our steel industry?" This was not the first instance of Mittal getting British and European Bank for Reconstruction and Development (EBRD) aid. In 2005, Mr. Mittal donated £2 million to Labour. Rob Evans and David Hencke, "More Labour help for Mittal revealed," *Guardian,* 8 Mar. 2002; United Kingdom Electoral Commission, Register of Donations to Political Parties, http://www.electoralcommission.org.uk/regulatory-issues/regdpoliticalparties.cfm

69. Some observers have suggested that Blair is only following the path blazed by Margaret Thatcher, who welcomed business's financial contributions to her party and its personnel to her government. The main difference is that as of 2001, British parties are required to disclose the names of all those who donate more than £5,000 (although not the amount). The British media have been quick to jump on the names in order to find out the sums. Others claim that this sort of activity has been going on "even when party politics was a lot cheaper to run." Hugo Young, "That Blair letter," *Guardian,* 12 Feb. 2002.

70. Camera dei deputati, XI Legislatura, "Domanda di autorizzazione a procedere in giudizio nei confronti del deputato Salvatore Grillo," *Documenti-Relazioni,* vol. 2, doc. 4, no. 145, 22 Dec. 1992 (Rome, 1996) 4, 21.

71. Camera dei deputati, XI Legislatura, "Domanda di autorizzazione a procedere in giudizio," *Documenti-Relazioni,* vol. 5, doc. 4, no. 370 (Rome, 1996), 4.

72. The kickback from each firm was to be 5 percent of the value of the contract. Ibid., 3.

73. Eberhard Von Koerber, quoted in Haig Simonia, "Italy's corruption scandal," *Financial Times,* 16 Mar. 1993. See also Camera dei deputati, XI Legislatura, "Domanda di autorizzazione a procedere in giudizio contro i deputati Tognoli, Pillitteri, Del Pennino, Cervetti, Massari," *Documenti-Relazioni,* vol. 1, doc. 4, no. 6, 2 June 1992 (Rome, 1996), 8, in which ABB di Milano is listed as having granted kickbacks in exchange for supplier contracts for the Milan metro system.

74. Camera dei deputati, XI Legislatura, "Domanda di autorizzazione a procedere in giudizio nei confronti del deputato Craxi," *Documenti-Relazioni,* vol. 6, doc. 4, no. 484 (Rome, 1996), 8.

75. Camera dei deputati, XI Legislatura, "Domanda di autorizzazione a procedere in giudizio nei confronti del deputato Cariglia," *Documenti-Relazioni,* vol. 6, doc. 4, no. 509, 22 July 1993 (Rome, 1996), 2.

76. Camera dei deputati, XI Legislatura, "Domanda di autorizzazione a procedere in giudizio nei confronti del deputato La Malfa," *Documenti-Relazioni,* vol. 3, doc. 4, no. 255, 6 Apr. 1993 (Rome, 1996), 5.

77. Camera dei deputati, "Domanda di autorizzazione a procedere in giudizio nei confronti del deputato Salvatore Grillo," 3, 19–20.

78. Examples include Christine Deviers-Joncours in the Dumas affair, Stefania Ariosto in the Berlusconi/Previti judge-bribing cases, the Cools case, and Urbatechnic.

79. Piotr Smolar and Fabrice Lhomme, "Affaires et politique," *Le Monde,* 7 Apr. 2002; "The Count against the Court," *Economist,* 3 Dec. 1983.

80. Michael Cooper, "Major probe into building fraud launched," *Het Financieele Dagblad,* 15 Nov. 2001.

81. John Hooper, "European politics plagued by funding scandals," *Guardian,* 4 Dec. 1999.

82. "Scusa, Palermo! Wie Deutschland zur kaeuflichen Republik und Sizilien zur schmiergeldfreien Zone wurde," *Süddeutsche Zeitung,* 23 Mar. 2002.

83. Richard S. Katz and Peter Mair, "Changing Models of Party Organization and Party Democracy," *Party Politics* 1/1 (1995): 5–28; Jonathan Hopkin, "Political Parties, Political Corruption and the Economic Theory of Democracy," *Crime, Law and Social Change* 27/3–4 (1997): 255–74.

84. Michael Johnston, *Syndromes of Corruption* (Cambridge: Cambridge University Press, 2005); Hall and Soskice, "Varieties of Capitalism"; Peter A. Gourevitch and James Shinn, *Political Power and Corporate Control* (Princeton: Princeton University Press, 2005); Wayne Sandholtz and William Koetzle, "Accounting for Corruption: Economic Structure, Democracy, and Trade" *International Studies Quarterly* 44 (2000): 31–50.

CHAPTER 3. "CORRUPTION IS OUR FRIEND"

The title of this chapter comes from a line of dialogue in the movie *Syriana* (2005).

1. Fabrice Lhomme, "Jean-Charles Marchiani mis en cause," *Le Monde,* 21 Nov. 2002.

2. Nicolas Beau, *La maison Pasqua* (Paris: Plon, 2002), 95; Renaud Van Ruymbeke, *Ordonnance de renvoi devant le Tribunal correctionnel de non-lieu partiel et de requalification,* no. du Parquet 9418769211, no. instruction 2039/94/29, procédure correctionnelle, Cour d'appel de Paris, Tribunal de grand instance de Paris, 13 Dec. 2002, 97–100.

3. Wayne Sandholtz and Mark M. Gray, "International Integration and National Corruption," *International Organization* 57/4 (Fall 2003): 761–800.

4. Stephan Haggard, *Pathways from the Periphery: The Politics of Growth in the Newly Industrialized Countries* (Ithaca: Cornell University Press, 1990).

5. House of Commons, Select Committee on International Development, Minutes of Evidence, Appendix 4, memorandum submitted by the Corner House, "Underwriting Corruption: Britain's Role in Promoting Corruption, Cronyism and Graft," 22 Mar. 2001.

6. Susan Hawley, "Enforcing the Law on Overseas Corruption: A Model for Excellence," Corner House, Dorset, June 2004; OECD, Directorate for Financial and Enterprise Affairs, *United Kingdom: Phase 2. Report on the Application of the Convention on Combating Bribery of Foreign Public Officials in International Business Transactions and the 1997 Recommendations on Combating Bribery in International Business Transactions* (Paris: OECD, 2005), 64–65.

7. Christopher Adams, James Boxell, and Daniel Dombey, "Blair defends ending BAE bribe probe," *Financial Times,* 16–17 Dec. 2006.

8. OECD, *OECD Convention on Combating Bribery of Foreign Public Officials in International Business Transactions* (Paris: OECD, 1997), article 5, http://www.oecd.org/document/21/0,2340,en_2649_34859_2017813_1_1_1_1,00.html.

9. Ernesto Dal Bó, Pedro Dal Bó, and Rafael Di Tella, "'Plata o Plomo?' Bribe and Punishment in a Theory of Political Influence," *American Political Science Review* 100/1 (Feb. 2006): 41–53, here at 42.

10. OECD, Directorate for Financial and Enterprise Affairs, *United Kingdom: Phase 2,* 48–49. The OECD report most likely is referring to a government negotiated deal between BAE, a large British defense firm, and Saudi Arabia. David Leigh and Rob Evans, "BAE accused of arms deal slush funds," *Guardian,* 11 Sept. 2003; David Leigh and Rob Evans, "BAE accused of hiding cash paid to win deals," *Guardian,* 5 Dec. 2003; Christopher Adams and James Boxell, "UK faces storm over abandoning BAE probe," *Financial Times,* 15 Dec. 2006.

11. John Hakes, of Thorn EMI, as quoted in David Pallister, "Thorn admits fees on Saudi arms deal," *Guardian,* 14 Nov. 1994.

12. The chairman of Thorn EMI, Sir Colin Southgate, said he paid a commission of £10 million on a £40 million weapons contract. Pallister, "Thorn admits."

13. Unnamed source, as quoted in Eric Plouvier, "Corruption à la française III," *Le Monde*, 15 Oct. 1992.

14. Jacques Isnard, "Fournisseur et client sont complices," *Le Monde*, 14 Mar. 1998.

15. I thank Andrew Barnes for clarification of this point.

16. As quoted in Neil Cooper, *The Business of Death: Britain's Arms Trade at Home and Abroad* (London: Tauris Academic, 1997), 143.

17. Andrew Wang, quoted in Lukas Hässig, "Frigate King Dethroned," *Weltwoche*, 23 June 2004.

18. High Court of Lesotho, *The Crown v. Acres International Limited*, Accused's written argument, CRI/T/02/02, 22 June 2002, 23.

19. Van Ruymbeke, *Ordonnance*, 372–87.

20. Susan Rose-Ackerman, *Corruption: A Study in Political Economy* (New York: Academic Press, 1978), 193.

21. Unnamed source, as quoted in Plouvier "Corruption à la française III."

22. D. Gibbs, "Secrecy and International Relations," *Journal of Peace Research* 32/2 (1995): 213–28; Ian Davis, *Regulation of Arms and Dual-Use Exports: Germany, Sweden and the UK* (New York: Oxford University Press, 2002), 234.

23. Right Honourable Sir Richard Scott, *Report of the Inquiry into the Export of Defence Equipment and Dual-Use Goods to Iraq and Related Prosecutions: Return to an Address of the Honourable of the House of Commons Dated 15th February*, House of Commons, HC 1995/96, 115 (HMSO: London, 1996), paragraph K8.13. The full text reveals that Sir Richard is challenging the need for secrecy.

24. In describing Elf's convoluted, obfuscating, and anticompetitive legal status, the French parliamentary committee investigating Elf said it was "hardly compatible with [European] community law (to say the least)." Assemblée nationale, Commission des affaires étrangères, "Rapport d'information sur le rôle des compagnies pétrolières dans la politique internationale et son impact social et environnemental," no. 1859, vol. 1, 13 Oct. 1999 (Paris), 61.

25. Total merged with Elf and Fina. International Consortium of Investigative Journalists, *Greasing the Skids of Corruption* (Washington, D.C.: Center for Public Integrity, 2002), 10.

26. OECD, Directorate for Financial and Enterprise Affairs, *United Kingdom: Phase 2*, 8.

27. Public Accounts Committee chair Robert Sheldon, as quoted in *Independent*, 23 June 1997.

28. Hervé Gattegno, "Fregates de Taiwan: L'enquête sur les commissions se heurte au secret-défense," *Le Monde*, 22 June 2002; Gérard Davet, "Frégates de Taiwam: les juges ont clôturé leur enquête," *Le Monde*, 13 Oct. 2006.

29. Terry Macalister, "'Ethical' BP linked to Angola claims," *Guardian*, 27 Feb. 2002; "Making Oil Transparent," *New York Times*, 6 July 2003; Serge Michel and Serge Enderlin, "Les rois du brut," *Le Figaro*, 16 July 2003.

30. Ronen Palan, *The Offshore World: Sovereign Markets, Virtual Places, and Nomad Millionaires* (Ithaca: Cornell University Press, 2003); Leigh and Evans, "BAE accused of hiding cash"; Serious Fraud Office, United Kingdom, "Investigation into Service Contracts with BAE," press statement, 3 Nov. 2004, http://www.sfo.gov.uk/news/prout/pr_337.asp?seltxt=; David Leppard, "Bid to end Saudi probe to safeguard arms deal," *Sunday Times*, 26 Mar. 2006.

31. "London's dirty secret: Crooks can launder money through trusts and companies," *Financial Times*, 29 Oct. 2004; Eric Decouty, "La justice traque le trésor d'Abacha," *Le Figaro*, 11 Oct. 2004; David Leigh and Rob Evans, "'National interest' halts arms corruption inquiry," *Guardian*, 15 Dec. 2006.

32. Palan, *Offshore World*.

33. There has been pressure in recent years to reach agreements limiting export subsidies, but, as usual in international accords, the rules and enforcement provisions are weak. Tied aid has been exempt from the rules. Andrew M. Moravcsik, "Disciplining Trade Finance: The OECD Export Credit Arrangement," *International Organization* 43/1 (Winter 1989): 173–205, here at 181.

34. Christopher Elliott, David Fairhall, and Michael White, "Fresh pressure on arms deals," *Manchester Guardian Weekly,* 20 Nov. 1994.

35. In 1984, India used its British foreign aid to purchase twenty-one British military helicopters. In 1993, two months after Foreign Secretary Douglas Herd promised Indonesia £335 million ($500 million) in aid, Indonesia agreed to a £65 million ($97 million) "soft loan" for a power station. Christopher Bellamy, "Campaign condemns arms sales subsidies," *Independent,* 15 Nov. 1994; Davis, *Regulation of Arms,* 125.

36. In addition, the cost effectiveness of such programs is dubious at best, and besides, because buyers can obtain weapons with ease, they can engage in such risky behavior as civil wars and currency crises—risks the sellers had hoped to offset with export credits. Cooper, *Business of Death,* 143; World Development Movement, *Gunrunners Gold: How the Public's Money Finances Arms Sales* (London: WDM, 1995), 22.

37. R. T. Naylor, *Wages of Crime* (Ithaca: Cornell University Press, 2002).

38. Global Witness, *Time for Transparency* (Washington, D.C.: Global Witness Publishing, 2004), 27–35, http://www.globalwitness.org/reports/show.php/en.00049.html.

39. Van Ruymbeke, *Ordonnance,* 70–74, Houdray at 71. In 2000, the French began an investigation into FIBA's money-laundering activities. Two days after a police raid to collect documents, FIBA was broken into, presumably by someone who hoped to recover and destroy other incriminating evidence. FIBA was liquidated on June 1, 2000. Ibid., 70.

40. A similar argument appears to hold for the United States and other OECD countries. Because this book is about patterns of corruption within the EU and the EU's possible effect on those patterns, this chapter focuses on the EU-15.

41. Randy R. Kessler, sales manager of KTI Corp, as quoted in Gary J. Tulacz, "Finding ways to make it happen abroad," *Engineering News-Record,* 20 May 1996.

42. "Lesotho over the financing hump," *International Trade Finance,* 28 Nov. 1991.

43. The Highlands Water Venture consortium included Impregilo (Italy), Hochtief (Germany), Bouygues (France), Keir International and Stirling (United Kingdom), and Concor and Group Five (South Africa). That consortium was just one of at least thirteen firms and consortia awarded contracts in the Lesotho Highlands Water project. The Lesotho official was ultimately sentenced to fifteen years in prison on eleven counts of bribery and two of fraud. He said he had not demanded the payments but was offered them. As contracts for various parts of the project were signed, payments were made to his Swiss bank accounts via intermediaries (a Mr. and Mrs. Z. M. Bam), whose commissions were approximately 40 percent. Mr. Bam died in 1999. Acres International of Canada, Lahmeyer International of Germany, Schneider Electric of France (which purchased Spie Batignolles), and Impregilo of Italy have been convicted of bribery. Court of Appeal of Lesotho, *Ephraim Masupha Sole and The Crown,* CRI/T/111/91, 14 Apr. 2003; High Court of Lesotho, *Rex v. Masupha Ephraim Sole,* CRI/T/111/99, 20 May 2002, 8 and passim; High Court of Lesotho, *Rex v. Acres International Limited,* Crown's Heads of Arguments on the Merits, 4 June 2002, 50; Court of Appeal of Lesotho, *Lahmeyer International GmbH and The Crown, CRI/6/2002. n.d.;* Court of Appeal of Lesotho, *Acres International Limited and The Crown,* CRI/T/144/02, 6–15 Aug. 2003; Richard High, "Impregilo fined for LHWP bribes," *International Construction,* 13 Sept. 2006; Antonio Tricarico, *Dams on Trial: The World Bank and the "Cancer of Corruption"* (Rome: Reform the World Bank Campaign, 2000), 3; House of Commons, Select Committee on International Development, "Underwriting Corruption," 27 Feb. 2001, 13.

44. High Court of Lesotho, *Rex v. Masupha Ephraim Sole,* 221–23 and passim; Tricarico, *Dams on Trial,* 3; David Pallister, "Blacklisting threat to UK firm," *Guardian,* 6 July 2002.

45. High Court of Lesotho, *The Crown v. Acres International Limited,* Accused's written argument, 12.

46. David Pallister, "Canadian company fined pounds 1.6 m," *Guardian,* 29 Oct. 2002; Court of Appeal of Lesotho, *Acres International Limited v. The Crown,* Maseru, CRI/T/144/02, 6–15 Aug. 2003.

47. House of Commons, Select Committee on International Development, Minutes of Evidence, Examination of Witnesses, Mike Welton, CEO Balfour Beatty, Question 387, 9 January 2001.

48. On financing, see "Lesotho over the financing hump," *International Trade Finance,* 28 Nov. 1991.

49. Tricarico, *Dams on Trial,* 1; Chris Lang, Nick Hildyard, Kate Geary, and Matthew Grainger, *Dams Incorporated: The Record of Twelve European Dam Building Companies* (London: Swedish Society for Nature Conservation, 2000; also published by the Corner House), "Lesotho Highlands Water Development Project" section, n.p.

50. Tricarico, *Dams on Trial,* 9.

51. House of Commons, Select Committee on International Development, Appendices to the Minutes of Evidence, "Recent Cases of Corruption Involving UK Companies and UK-backed International Financial Institutions," 22 Mar. 2001, 1.

52. As of December 2006, his case continues. Rodríguez had been president of Costa Rica in 1998–2002; the executive director of the Costa Rican firm was also implicated. Fabrice Lehoucq, "Costa Rica: Paradise in Doubt," *Journal of Democracy* 16/3 (July 2005): 140–54; "Immigration reform to tackle corruption," *Latin News Daily,* 15 Dec. 2006.

53. OECD, Directorate for Financial and Enterprise Affairs, *Sweden: Phase 2. Report on the Application of the Convention on Combating Bribery of Foreign Public Officials in International Business Transactions and the 1997 Recommendation on Combating Bribery in International Business Transactions* (Paris: OECD, 2005), 65.

54. "Affaire Thales: Le parquet de Paris va ouvrir deux informations judiciares," *Les Echos,* 9 Dec. 2005.

55. As the spokeswoman for ExxonMobil said of odd transactions involving a U.S.-based bank, Riggs, and oil revenue from Equatorial Guinea, "I don't know where our payments are made . . . we have very high business standards and ethical standards." "ExxonMobil says has no knowledge of Equatorial Guinea oil probe," *Platts Oilgram Price Report,* 12 May 2003.

56. House of Commons, Select Committee on International Development, Minutes of Evidence, Balfour Beatty, "Attachment 2: Inaccuracies in Evidence Submitted to the Committee," 24 Jan. 2001.

57. Acres International claimed it had paid the intermediary in the Lesotho case to act as a consultant. The courts rejected the claim that Acres could not and did not know that a large portion of the funds would be transferred to the public official who rigged the contract awards on Acres' behalf. Spie Batignolles's contortions in the court room have been similar. The firm merged with Schneider (a major French electronics firm), which claimed that because all of Spie's assets and obligations were transferred to a subsidiary in Lesotho, Schneider was not responsible for the corruption. The Lesotho judge disagreed, noting that the requisite legal changes were not carried out in Lesotho: "Whatever happened in France, nothing happened in this country." Schneider pled guilty to bribery in order to avoid a trial. The Lesotho court fined the company ZAR 10 million (about $1.5 million). "Electrical company must stand trail in Lesotho bribery case," *Financial Times,* 12 Dec. 2003; "Global company fined R10–M for Lesotho bribery," *Financial Times,* 25 Feb. 2004;

High Court of Lesotho, *Rex v. Acres International Limited,* Crown's heads of arguments on the merits, 4 June 2002; Court of Appeal of Lesotho, *Acres International Limited v. The Crown,* Maseru, CRI/T/144/02, 6–15 Aug. 2003.

58. House of Commons, Foreign Affairs Committee, *Third Report. Public Expenditure: Pergau Hydro-Electric Project, Malaysia, and Related Matters,* vol. 2, *Minutes of Evidence and Appendices* (London: HMSO, 1994), 54.

59. OECD, Directorate for Financial and Enterprise Affairs, *Sweden: Phase 2,* 11, quote in n. 26.

60. Antonio Tricarico, "Oil in the Caspian: The Blue Stream-Black Sea Gas Pipeline Project" (Sept. 2001), 2, 8, 11, http://www.eca-watch.org/problems/oil_gas_miningcaspoil /bluestream.html.

61. Peter Bosshard, "Publicly Guaranteed Corruption: Corrupt Power Projects and the Responsibility of Export Credit Agencies in Indonesia" (2000), http://www.eca-watch.org/ problems/corruption/bosshard_intro.html. Evidence suggests that the European firms Suez and Thames bribed Indonesian president Suharto to privatize Jakarta's water system. Andreas Harsono, "Water Politics and the Fall of Suharto," Center for Public Integrity/ International Consortium for Investigative Journalism, 10 Feb. 2003, http://www.icij.org/ water/printer-friendly.aspx?aid=52.

62. United Kingdom, High Court, Queen's Bench Division, *R v. Secretary of State for Foreign Affairs,* ex parte World Development Movement Ltd., I All ER 611, 1995 1 WLR 386, 10 Nov. 1994, 5.

63. House of Commons, Committee of Public Accounts, Seventeenth Report, *Pergau Hydro-Electric Project* (London: HMSO, 1994).

64. House of Commons, Select Committee on International Development, "Recent Cases of Corruption," 8.

65. House of Commons, Foreign Affairs Committee, *Third Report,* 2: 57–58; House of Commons, Foreign Affairs Committee, *Third Report. Public Expenditure: Pergau Hydro-Electric Project, Malaysia, and Related Matters,* vol. 1, *Report, Together with the Proceedings of the Committee* (London: HMSO, 1994), liv–lv.

66. Unnamed source, as quoted in Plouvier, "Corruption à la française III."

67. Plouvier, "Corruption à la française III."

68. Coverage is not automatic; sometimes other foreign policy considerations prevail. France's electronics group Thomson could not conclude a contract with the Algerian government in 1993 for the sale of communications facilities for about $35 million because the export credit agency thought the commissions, of 10 percent, were too high. Jacques Isnard, "Les commissions sur les ventes françaises à l'étranger ont atteint 10 milliards de francs en 1994," *Le Monde,* 17 Mar. 1995.

69. Saar Golde and Asher Tishler, "Security Needs, Arms Exports, and the Structure of the Defense Industry," *Journal of Conflict Resolution* 48/5 (Oct. 2004): 672–98, here at 676–77; J. Paul Dunn and Eamon Surry, "Arms Production," in Stockholm International Peace Research Institute (SIPRI), *SIPRI Yearbook 2006: Armaments, Disarmament and International Security,* http://yearbook2006.sipri.org/chap9, 1; Congressional Research Service, "CRS Report to Congress: Conventional Arms Transfers to Developing Nations, 1996–2003," RL32547, Aug. 26, 2004, Washington, D.C.; Stockholm International Peace Research Institute (SIPRI), *World Armaments and Disarmament: SIPRI Yearbook* (London: Taylor and Francis for SIPRI, 1984); Ron Smith, Anthony Humm, and Jacques Fontanel, "The Economics of Exporting Arms," *Journal of Peace Research* 22/3 (Sept. 1985): 239–47; U.S. General Accounting Office, *Military Exports: A Comparison of Government Support in the United States and Three Major Competitors,* report to Congressional Committees, May 1995, GAO/NSIAD-95-86.

70. "The transfer takes place as part of a package involving the equipment itself, spares,

training, access to technology, export credits, insurance for payment, offset agreements, and now increasingly counter-trade (barter) arrangements." Smith, Humm, and Fontanel, "Economics of Exporting Arms," 241. Also Leslie Wayne, "Offsets replace bribes to clinch arms deals," *New York Times,* 17 Feb. 2003.

71. Lewis W. Snider, "Arms Exports for Oil Imports? The Test of a Non-Linear Model," *Journal of Conflict Resolution* 28/4 (Dec. 1984): 665–700; Steve Chan, "The Consequences of Expensive Oil on Arms Transfers," *Journal of Peace Research* 17/3 (1980): 235–46; Gregory S. Sanjian, "Great Power Arms Transfers: Modeling the Decision-Making Processes of Hegemonic, Industrial, and Restrictive Exporters," *International Studies Quarterly* 35/2 (June 1991): 173–93.

72. Edward A. Kolodziej, *Making and Marketing Arms: The French Experience and Its Implications for the International System* (Princeton: Princeton University Press, 1987), 240.

73. Davis, *Regulation of Arms,* quotes at 22, 234, 132.

74. Ibid., 53.

75. International Consortium of Investigative Journalists, "The Field Marshal," Center for Public Integrity, 2002, 2.

76. The real economic costs and benefits are seldom examined by exporting governments and their industries. The benefits tend to accrue to the specific industries and to the government officials linked to them, whereas the costs are borne by taxpayers at large (including, of course, those in other countries against whom the weapons are used). This situation is not unlike the economics and politics of cities and major league ballparks. See Campaign against the Arms Trade, "Subsidies Factsheet," February 2002, http://www.caat.org.uk/information/publications/economics/subsidies-factsheet-02 (accessed 28 Mar. 2004). Although this chapter is concerned with practices within the EU, the United States takes the lead in promoting and even fully financing the foreign purchase of its defense equipment. U.S. General Accounting Office, *Military Exports.*

77. The agency was called the Délégation ministérielle pour l'armement (DMA), which soon became the Délégation générale à l'armement (DGA). Pierre Marion, *Le pouvoir sans visage: Le complexe militaro-industriel* (Paris: Calmann-Lévy, 1990), 37–38.

78. U.S. General Accounting Office, *Military Exports,* 23.

79. World Bank, *Anticorruption in Transition: A Contribution to the Policy Debate* (Washington, D.C.: World Bank, 2000), 1–2.

80. Peter A. Hall and David Soskice, "An Introduction to Varieties of Capitalism," in *Varieties of Capitalism: The Institutional Foundations of Comparative Advantage,* ed. Peter A. Hall and David Soskice (New York: Oxford University Press, 2001), 1–68.

81. Davis, *Regulation of Arms,* 147; Scott, *Report of Inquiry into the Export of Defence Equipment and Dual-Use Goods to Iraq and Related Prosecutions,* D1.103-44, 187–292.

82. Mick Lambert, Judith Rattenbury, and Ian Prichard, *The Political Influence of Arms Companies* (London: Campaign against Arms Trade, 2003), 3.

83. Campaign against Arms Trade, "Shut DESO: Time's Up for the Government's Gunrunners," (London: Campaign against Arms Trade, 2006), 2–3, http://www.caat.org.uk/publications/government/DESO-0106-high.pdf.

84. Susan Hawley, "Turning a Blind Eye: Corruption and the UK Export Credits Guarantee Department," Corner House, Dorset, 2003, 32–33, http://www.thecornerhouse.org.uk/document/correcgd.html. Chrissie Hirst, *The Arabian Connection: The UK Arms Trade to Saudi Arabia* (London: Campaign against Arms Trade, 2000), 9. Report available at http://www.caat.org.uk/information/publications/countries/saudi-arabia.php.

85. Andrew Gowers, "UK seeks 2bn pounds loan to help Saudi military deal," *Financial Times,* 27 Nov. 1989.

86. Stevie Cameron and Harvey Cashore, *The Last Amigo* (Toronto: Macfarlane Walter and Ross, 2001), 179.

87. Ojjeh owned Techniques d'Avant-Garde, which is more widely known for TAG

Heuer, an expensive Swiss watch brand. TAG is a conglomerate of aviation firms, hotels, construction firms, and electronics companies worldwide. Cameron and Cashore, *Last Amigo,* 180.

88. Court of Appeal for Ontario, *Federal Republic of Germany, the Minister of Justice, and the Attorney General of Canada v. Karlheinz Schreiber,* docket nos. C41853 and C42701, case heard 5, 6 Dec. 2005, Certified Translation. Augsburg Local Court, warrant of arrest against defendant Karlheinz Schreiber, ref. no. 1 Gs997/97, file no. 501 Js 127135/95, Augsburg Public Prosecutor's Office, 7 May 1997; Hans Leyendecker, "Abgeschmiert ins Nirgendwo," *Süddeutsche Zeitung,* 28 June 2005.

89. Cameron and Cashore, *Last Amigo,* 183.

90. Hans Lyendecker, "Germany: Corruption Notebook," (Washington, D.C.: Global Integrity, 2004); Bertrand Benoit, "Fugitive's arrest reopens old wounds for Germany's CDU," *Financial Times,* 15 July 2004; on CSU payment, see "German challenger's party received illegal funds," *Agence France Presse,* 14 May 2002.

91. Schreiber gave Kiep a total of DM 1 million, DM 420,000 of which Kiep gave to the CDU's tax adviser Horst Weyrauch and DM 370,000 to Uwe Lüthje, "a party insider and friend." Kiep and Schreiber later denied that there was any connection between these sums and the Saudi tank deal. Cameron and Cashore, *Last Amigo,* 206–7.

92. Ibid., 183–87.

93. In Germany, decisions to grant export licenses officially lie with the Ministry of Economics but in practice require assent from Defense and sometimes full government cabinet approval. Davis, *Regulation of Arms,* 169, 195. Kohl testified at Pfahls' trial that bribes were not necessary for the deal. Hans Leyendecker, "Pulverdampf und grosse Gesten," *Süddeutsche Zeitung,* 4 Aug. 2005.

94. Thomson-CSF became Thales in 2001. The weapons export board in question was the Commission interministeriel pour l'étude des exportations de matériels de guerre (CIEEMG). Hervé Gattegno, "Fregates de Taiwan," *Le Monde,* 20 July 2000.

95. "Après de longues négotiations," *Le Monde,* 14 Sept. 1991.

96. One news source states that after fighting in the French resistance, and in the Korean war, Sirven was jailed and served time in Japan for bank robbery. Christine Deviers-Joncour, *La putain de la république* (Paris: Calmann-Lévy, 1998); "Top Elf convict Alfred Sirven dead at 78," *Agence France Presse,* 13 Feb. 2005.

97. Procureur de la République Jean-Pierre Dintilhac, "Requisitoire contre Roland Dumas," extract in *Le Monde,* 11 Feb. 2000.

98. Gattegno, "Fregates de Taiwan," 20 July 2000.

99. "Le pôle financier cherche des bénéficiares," *Intelligence Online,* 23 Jan. 2003; Deviers-Joncour, *Putain de la république;* Karl Laske, "Sirven parle," *Libération,* 7 Nov. 2002.

100. Thomson's then CEO Alain Gomez allegedly did not know about the illicit arrangements until after Thomson had committed to them. Thomson claimed fraud and embezzlement, a claim that France's Cour de cassation upheld. Gattegno, "Fregates de Taiwan" (20 July 2000); Hervé Gattegno, "Deux proches de François Mitterrand soupçonnés d'être intervenus dans l'affaire des fregates," *Le Monde,* 20 Oct. 2000; Cour de cassation, Chambre criminelle, no. 01-88608, audience publique, 12 Mar. 2002.

101. Hervé Gattegno, "Fregates: L'enquête sur les commissions menace tout l'armement français," *Le Monde,* 30 Oct. 2001; "Taiwanese premier backs foreign minister over French frigate scandal," *BBC Monitoring Asia Pacific,* 8 Mar. 2003.

102. The planes were the Mirage 2000-5. Isnard, "M. Joxe veut vendre des Mirage à Taiwan après l'echec finlandais"; William Dawkins, "France and Taiwan cement dollars 2.6bn jet fighter contract," *Financial Times,* 19 Nov. 1992.

103. Wang allegedly was paid $400 million for this set of deals. Gattegno, "Fregates: L'enquête"; Laurent Maudit, "Pots-de-vin et contrats d'exportation," *Le Monde,* 16 Dec. 1999.

104. According to the official version, he fell out the window while trying to "repair the shutter very late on a windy night." Gattegno, "Fregates de Taiwan" (22 June 2002); *Intelligence Online,* 11 Oct. 2002.

105. He was also a friend of French interior minister Charles Pasqua's friends, the arms dealers and Angolagate perpetrators Pierre Falcone and Arcady Gaydamak. "Le pole financier a entendu Lee sur les fregates," *Intelligence Online,* 9 Jan. 2003.

106. As of November 2006, the case is again being investigated, with the aid of the Swiss judiciary. "La justice suisse relance l'enquête sur le sulfureux dossier des fregates de Taiwan" *Le Temps,* 9 Dec. 2003; Fabrice Lhomme, "Quatre morts suspectés dans l'ombre du dossier," *Le Monde,* 19 Nov. 2003.

107. Hirst, *Arabian Connection.*

108. John Hooper, "'Bribes of 600 million pounds' in jets deal," *Guardian,* 21 Oct. 1985.

109. For a variety of political reasons having to do with the United States' and other states' activities and policies in the Middle East, the sale was highly controversial. In addition, phase 1 of the deal included sizeable "offsets"—British commitments of direct investments, subcontracting, and technology transfer to Saudi Arabia. The value of the offsets was also hard to estimate. Al Yamamah phase two was to include a huge offset deal, but as of 1999, one still hadn't been concluded. Hirst, *Arabian Connection,* 10, quoting a *Financial Times* report; on offsets, ibid., 20–21; David White and Robert Mauthner, "Britain's Arms Sale of the Century," *Financial Times,* 9 July 1988.

110. White and Mauthner, "Britain's Arms Sale of the Century." The deal struck many as morally corrupt: it was not just a deal "to supply simply weaponry but an entire military infrastructure to one of the most repressive and corrupt regimes in the Middle East." Will Self, "Addicted to Arms," *Independent,* 26 April 2002.

111. It was also due to the fact that the U.S. Congress was refusing to allow weapons sales to the Saudis.

112. Self, "Addicted to Arms."

113. John Hakes, as quoted in Hirst, *Arabian Connection,* 31. Also David Pallister, "Thorn admits fees on Saudi Arms deal," *Guardian,* 14 Nov. 1994. Related and very complicated cases involving a Conservative minister of defense procurement, Jonathan Aitken, as well as bribes and kickbacks on Westland/Sikorski helicopters and on illegal arms sales to Iraq and Iran also emerged and have been confirmed in varying degrees. Aitken was a glaring case of conflict of interest, and then perjury.

114. Thatcher's defense procurement minister told the House of Commons that "the transaction between Her Majesty's Government and Saudi Arabia was on a government-to-government basis in which no commissions were paid and no agents or any middlemen were involved." Thanks to a law suit filed against one of the firms benefiting from the Al Yamamah deal, it came to light in 1997 that "Thorn Electrical paid 25 per cent on a contract for electrical fuses worth £40 million . . . [and] Rolls Royce paid 15 per cent on a contract for jet engines worth several hundred millions, rising to 100 per cent on money above a target price." Pallister, "Thorn admits fees on Saudi arms deal"; Joe Roeber, "Parallel Markets: Corruption in the International Arms Trade," CAAT 2005 lecture, http://www.caat .org.uk/publications/corruption/parallel-markets-0205.php#4.

115. House of Commons, Select Committee on International Development, Appendix 3, memorandum submitted by the Campaign against Arms Trade, 4.

116. In a plea bargain with the South African prosecutor, Thatcher admitted to contravening South Africa's law on mercenary activity, and was given a four year suspended sentence and a fine of ZAR 3 million ($500,000). "S. Africa gives Thatcher suspended sentence for coup plot," *Deutsche Presse Agentur,* 13 Jan. 2005.

117. The SFO was investigating a "worldwide system of offshore secret payments by BAE Systems," of possibly as much as £1 billion. Evidence indicated BAE had set up a £60

million slush fund to bribe the Saudis. "FAQ: the investigation," *Guardian,* 29 Nov. 2006; James Boxell, Roula Khalaf, Michael Peel, and Peggy Hollinger, "Saudis halt Eurofighter talks in bid to end graft inquiry," *Financial Times,* 28 Nov. 2006; Christopher Adams and James Boxell, "UK faces storm over abandoning BAE probe," *Financial Times,* 15 Dec. 2006.

118. Quoted in Paul Betts, "Hat Trick for British Aerospace," *Financial Times,* 30 Jan. 1993.

119. In the Thomson Taiwan destroyer case, it was the Socialist French minister of finance Laurent Fabius and later the Gaullist Francis Mer who refused to lift the defense secrets block. So far, for any one judiciary to investigate the case, it has required cooperation from authorities in France, Taiwan, Switzerland, and Liechtenstein. Gerard Davet and Fabrice Lhomme, "Deux juges demandent la levée du secret-défense sur les fregates de Taiwan," *Le Monde,* 12 Feb. 2004.

120. Snider, "Arms Exports for Oil Imports?"

121. "Commissions," also referred to as "bonuses," on contracts with foreign governments, such as the regime in Angola, were automatically tax deductible in France until the loi Sapin (1993), which requires that each commission's tax status be decided individually. As of 1999, commissions are not tax deductible if they are given to foreign officials. Assemblée nationale, Commission des affaires étrangères, "Rapport d'information, 67–68. On royalties, see House of Commons, Select Committee on International Development, Minutes of Evidence, supplementary memorandum submitted by BP, 9 Jan. 2001, paragraph 12.

122. House of Commons, Select Committee on International Development, supplementary memorandum submitted by BP, paragraph 12; cf. Van Ruymbeke, *Ordonnance,* 57.

123. House of Commons, Select Committee on International Development, Minutes of Evidence, examination of witnesses (response to question 408), 9 Jan. 2001, Dr. Reg Hinkley.

124. Assemblée nationale, Commission des affaires étrangères, "Rapport d'information," 68. On 5–10 percent, see 69.

125. "Les reséaux africains," *Lettre du Continent,* 1 Apr. 1999.

126. Jens Christian Andvig, *Levels of Corruption in the North Sea Oil Industry: Issues and Assessment* (Oslo: Norwegian Institute of International Affairs, 1995), 14–22; Said K. Aburish, *Pay-Off: Wheeling and Dealing in the Arab World* (London: André Deutsch, 1985).

127. Tarallo handled Africa; Guelfi was the intermediary for most of Elf's dealings elsewhere. Guelfi was recommended to Elf's CEO by managers at another of France's major exporters of corruption, the water systems company, Générale des eaux. Van Ruymbeke, *Ordonnance,* 372.

128. Noël Pantalacci, as quoted in Stephane Marchand and Jean-Alphonse Richard, "Le groupe petrolière français déstabilisé en Afrique," *Le Monde,* 7 May 1997.

129. Assemblée nationale, Commission des affaires étrangères, "Rapport d'information," 61.

130. E.g., House of Commons, Select Committee on International Development, examination of witnesses (response to question 416), Dr. Reg Hinkley; and House of Commons, Select Committee on International Development, supplementary memorandum submitted by BP, paragraph 13.

131. BP noted the condition that might provide an exception: "unless, which is sometimes the case, the technological and scientific expertise provided by the company was clearly superior to its rivals and was judged more essential to the country concerned than immediate revenue." House of Commons, Select Committee on International Development, supplementary memorandum submitted by BP, paragraph 13.

132. Assemblée nationale, Commission des affaires étrangères, "Rapport d'information," 113.

133. In Gabon, Elf paid $40 million into Bongo's personal accounts between 1990 and 1993 for a very valuable license; Elf paid $35 million to private accounts of officials in the Congo between 1992 and 1997 for offshore deepwater permits. To effect the payments, Elf used middlemen, or agents. Once the agent's "efficacy" was verified, Elf used him for other jobs, such as transferring $4 million to the Congo's minister of oil (Mr. Koukebene). Elf's point man in Africa, André Tarallo, claimed that, "given the personal relations between Heads of State in these countries," these sorts of transactions were particularly worthwhile. He cited Omar Bongo for his introductions to successive Nigerian presidents, and Mr. Sassou for Elf's contacts in Angola, and again President Bongo for facilitating Elf's entrance into Chad and the pipeline deal there. Van Ruymbeke, *Ordonnance*, 48.

134. Ibid.

135. Jaffré, in contrast, told a parliamentary committee that Elf's "bad habits" were peculiar to the years 1989–93, when his predecessor, Le Floch-Prigent, was CEO. Assemblée nationale, Commission des affaires étrangères, "Rapport d'information," 70. Other witnesses to the committee contradicted Jaffré's statement. Van Ruymbeke, *Ordonnance*, 88.

136. According to an Angolan newspaper, *Angolense*, these are among Angola's ten richest citizens. Economist Intelligence Unit, *Angola Country Report*, 10 Feb. 2003; cf. *Human Rights Watch*, "Some Transparency, No Accountability: The Use of Oil Revenue in Angola and Its Impact on Human Rights," *Human Rights Watch Report* 16/1A (Jan. 2004): 1–2; Ian Gary and Terry Lynn Karl, *Bottom of the Barrel* (n.p.: Catholic Relief Services, 2003), 32–33.

137. Assemblée nationale, Commission des affaires étrangères, "Rapport d'information," testimony by Jean-François Bayart, 78.

138. Assemblée nationale, Commission des affaires étrangères, "Rapport d'information," testimony by Pierre Péan, 58. Testifying in front of the same commission, Elf's CEO at the time, Philippe Jaffré, contested that view and argued that Elf's history was "extremely banal, identical to those companies which were created by the State, such as ENI, an Italian company or BP, created by the British navy." Ibid., 59.

139. Cour des comptes, "Les relations de l'État avec Elf Aquitaine et les missions de l'E.R.A.P. [Entreprise de recherches et d'activités pétrolières]," 157–73, *Rapport public* 1990, B4141, Bibliothèque de la documentation française, here at 158.

140. In 1992, the company gave the Angola opposition party about $23 million. Van Ruymbeke, *Ordonnance*, 97.

141. "Anyone for ENI now?" *FT Energy Newsletters*, 19 Mar. 1993.

142. Van Ruymbeke, *Ordonnance*, 94–100; Global Witness, *A Crude Awakening* (London: Global Witness Publishing, 1999), 11.

143. Global Witness, *Time for Transparency* (Washington, D.C.: Global Witness Publishing, 2004), 38.

144. UK Trade Minister Richard Caborn, letter to Ilisu Dam Campaign, 6 July 2000, in House of Commons, Select Committee on International Development, "Underwriting Corruption," paragraph 79, 22 Mar. 2001.

145. This is not the first time the bank has tried to prevent investigations into corruption. In the Lesotho dam project, the Lesotho government decided to conduct a management audit because they had detected account irregularities in the Highlands Development Authority. They wanted to suspend the director of the authority and one other individual, but the bank "vigorously opposed the suspension . . . , even threatening legal action." Hawley, "Turning a Blind Eye," 26. Stephen Fidler, "U.S. steps up pressure over power project," *Financial Times*, 8 Mar. 2000.

146. This is another of those extravagant infrastructure projects that seem to be gigantic precisely so they can include a large number of firms from a variety of wealthy countries, thus reducing the risk that any one of them will squeal on the others about

corruption. It reduces risk by being all inclusive. Members of the managing consortium comprised firms from Saudi Arabia, the United States, the UK, Japan, Italy, and France. The "private" financing, underwritten by the publicly financed World Bank, came from a syndicate of banks from Japan, the United States, France (the then state-owned Crédit lyonnais, infamous for bankruptcy and famous for sponsoring the *maillot jaune* of the Tour de France), and Switzerland (UBS). The IMF, for its part, made a $1.2 billion structural adjustment loan to Pakistan contingent on settlement of the dispute. The loan was "the only thing standing between the country and outright default on its debts." "Why Pakistan opted for BOO rather than BOT at Hab River," *FT Energy Newsletters,* 17 June 1991; "World Bank gives Hab River a resounding ECO," *FT Energy Newsletters,* 2 Dec. 1991; "Losing Control," *FT Energy Newsletters,* 23 Oct. 1998; Hawley, "Turning a Blind Eye," 9.

147. Hawley, "Turning a Blind Eye," 9. This time it was the export credit agencies of Germany, Japan, Switzerland, and the United States that applied pressure.

148. Armelle Thoraval, "Ces morts qui hantent les frégates," *Libération,* 20 June 2002.

149. Renaud Lecadre, "Les frégates de Taiwan cherchent preneurs," *Libération,* 29 Oct. 2004.

150. Astri Ghosh, "India: new Swedish government's help sought in gun scandal probe," *Inter Press Service,* 17 Sept. 1991.

151. Johann Rapp, "Weapons maker struggles to regain image against corruption charges," *BC Cycle,* 30 Nov. 1989.

152. "Supreme Court strikes down order quashing Bofors gun deal probe," *Agence France Presse,* 17 Dec. 1992. Olaf Palme may have known some of the terms of the deal; he was assassinated two weeks before Bofors was awarded the contract. Jan Bondeson, *Blood on the Snow* (Ithaca: Cornell University Press, 2005), 198–207.

153. The case's prosecution in India was complicated by the fact that those alleged to have been the intermediaries—Srichand, Gopichand, and Prakash Hinduja—had citizenship in the UK (Srichand and Gopichand) and Switzerland (Prakash). Gopichand obtained UK citizenship in 1997, and Srichand Hinduja appears to have obtained British citizenship after his family made a £1 million donation to the Labour government's Millennium Dome project. The donation led to the resignation of Minister Peter Mandelson, who had contacted the immigration minister about Srichand's application. An Italian businessman, Ottavio Quattrochi, was also involved, but he avoided extradition from Malaysia. "Supreme Court strikes down order quashing Bofors gun deal probe," *Agence France Presse,* 17 Dec. 1992. Bofors went bankrupt in 1991. Ghosh, "India." Beth Lewallen, research notes on the Hinduja brothers, MSS. Arizona State University, 2004. The Hinduja brothers and a major Indian politician, the late Rajiv Gandhi, were cleared of bribery charges in 2004. In 2005, the charges against the Hinduja brothers of conspiring to defraud the Indian government were dropped. Khozem Merchant, "Charges against Hinduja brothers dismissed," *Financial Times,* 5 Feb. 2004; Jo Johnson, "Delhi court throws out case against Hindujas," *Financial Times,* 1 June 2005.

154. Hawley, "Turning a Blind Eye," 9.

155. Self, "Addicted to Arms."

156. Transparency International, "Transparency International Bribe Payers Index 2002" (Berlin), http://www.transparency.org/cpi/2002/bpi2002.en.html (PDF version), 7.

157. Belgium tied with the Netherlands (ibid.). The 1999 version (which was TI's first such survey) shows similar scores. Transparency International, "Transparency International's Bribe Payers Survey 1999" (Berlin), http://www.transparency.org/cpi/1999/bps.html.

158. Marion, *Pouvoir sans visage,* 117–18.

159. This chapter has focused on large-scale business and government projects, not on "petty" corruption such as bribing customs officials. Clearly, as competition gets keener,

access to markets becomes more significant, so customs officials can charge more for access to that market. Firms will be willing to pay, until the cost (including the negligible risks of prosecution) equals the profits.

160. On effects on French businesses, see OECD, Directorate for Financial and Enterprise Affairs, *France: Phase 2. Report on the Application of the Convention on Combating Bribery of Foreign Public Officials in International Business Transactions and the 1997 Recommendation on Combating Bribery in International Business Transactions* (Paris: OECD, 2004), 9–11.

161. Details are accessible in Tweede Kamer der Staten-Generaal, *Rapport van de Commissie van Drie: Onderzoek naar de juistheid van verklaringen over betalingen door een Amerikaanse vliegtuigfabriek*, 13787 nr. 3–5 (Amsterdam: Staatsuitgeverij, 's-Gravenhage, 1976); Guido Campopiano, *Memoria di accusa contro l'onorevole Giovanni Leone* (Milan: SugarCo, 1978); Maurizio De Luca, Paolo Gambescia, and Fabio Isman, *Tutti gli uomini dell' Antilope* (Milan: Mondadori, 1977); David Boulton, *The Grease Machine* (New York: Harper and Row, 1978).

162. Larry Martz, "Payoffs: The Growing Scandal," *Newsweek,* 23 Feb. 1976, 26.

163. Stewart Toy, "Dollar Diplomacy: The Moral Dilemma," *Business Week,* 4 June 1979, 10.

164. Martz, "Payoffs," 26.

165. Umberto Agnelli, as quoted in Richard Steele with Loren Jenkins, "Winner Take Nothing," *Newsweek,* 4 July 1976, 86.

166. Raymond Carroll with Loren Jenkins, "Italy's Fateful Election," *Newsweek,* 10 May 1976, 49; Richard Steele with Loren Jenkins, "Italy: Running Scared," *Newsweek,* 17 May 1976, 53; "Dateline: Rome," *Associated Press,* 1 Mar. 1979.

167. In the Netherlands, Lockheed appears to have bribed Prince Bernhard (husband of then Queen Juliana), in 1959 or 1960, first with the offer of an airplane, then with an offer of cash. Although Bernhard claims he never received the money, Lockheed did pay $1 million into the Swiss account of a friend of his mother. The U.S. Senate report stated: "It . . . had to be assumed by Lockheed that the money had indeed got to [the Prince]." Bernhard evidently took other payments, or at least was open to being offered them, in exchange for facilitating Lockheed sales to the Dutch military. Mark Stevens with Anthony Collings and Friso Endt, "The Prince Pays the Piper," *Newsweek,* 6 Sept. 1976, 21.

168. Davis, *Regulation of Arms,* 234.

169. It scores 8.4 out of 10 on least likely to bribe. Transparency International, "Bribe Payers Index 2002," 1.

170. The classic statement on strategic goods remains David A. Baldwin, *Economic Statecraft* (Princeton: Princeton University Press, 1985), 214–24.

171. Germany, Japan, Belgium, and the Czech Republic have balked at the latest OECD efforts to tackle export credit agency–subsidized corruption. Hugh Williamson, "Export credit agencies' graft crackdown stalls," *Financial Times,* 15 Feb. 2006.

172. Human Rights Watch, "Ripe for Reform: Stemming Slovakia's Arms Trade with Human Rights Abusers," February 2004, 16/2D, http://hrw.org/reports/2004/slovakia0204/slovakia0204.pdf.

173. Davis, *Regulation of Arms,* 164; "Investigate Mbeki's role in arms deal: De Lille," *Financial Times Information,* 3 Sept. 2003.

174. David Leigh and Rob Evans, "British businessman arrested in fresh BAE corruption inquiry," *Guardian,* 8 June 2006; Transparency International, "Bribe Payers Index 2002," 1.

175. Hervé Gattegno, "Philippe Jaffré assume la responsabilité des commissions versées," *Le Monde,* 29 Oct. 2002.

CHAPTER 4. THE MYTH OF THE MARKET

1. Testimony of Loïk Le Floch-Prigent, in Pascale Robert-Diard, "Loïk Le Floch-Prigent reconnait avoir fait payer par Elf le prix du silence de son ex-femme," *Le Monde,* 17 Apr. 2003. Renaud Van Ruymbeke, *Ordonnance de renvoi devant le Tribunal correctionnel de non-lieu partiel et de requalification,* no. du Parquet 9418769211, no. instruction 2039/94/29, procédure correctionnelle, Cour d'appel de Paris, Tribunal de grand instance de Paris, 13 Dec. 2002, 484–504. The divorce of its CEO seems to have cost Elf $5–10 million, in addition to the enormous sums Fatima Belaïd spent annually, using her husband's business credit card, before he divorced her. Canard Enchaîné, *Elf: L'empire d'essence, dossiers du canard* (Paris: Roto France, 1988), 56. Van Ruymbeke, *Ordonnance,* 550. According to Maurice Bidermann, "Fatima [Belaïd] threatened blackmail, and said to Mr. Richard [the other friend] that if we didn't do something for her, the newspapers would call her and she would talk." Van Ruymbeke, *Ordonnance,* 489.

2. As one commentator stated after Elf was privatized, "the problems of Elf Aquitaine's CEO today are more to be found on Wall Street, because of the attitude of American pension funds, than in the African capitals." Jean-François Bayart, director of CERI, testifying before the Assemblée nationale's Commission des affaires étrangères, "Rapport d'information sur le rôle des compagnies pétrolières dans la politique internationale et son impact social et environnemental," no. 1859, 13 Oct. 1999, 128.

3. The figure includes Austria, Finland, and Sweden, states that did not join until 1995. To put this in perspective, the amount is only a third of the total amount of the EU budget for those same years, a budget that annually totals about 1.2 percent of the combined GDP of the member states. On privatization figures, see Judith Clifton, Francisco Comín, and Daniel Díaz Fuentes, *Privatisation in the European Union: Public Enterprises and Integration* (Dordrecht: Kluwer Academic Publishers, 2003), 94–95; on the UK, Steven K. Vogel, *Freer Markets, More Rules: Regulatory Reform in Advanced Industrial Countries* (Ithaca: Cornell University Press, 1996).

4. Colin Talbot, professor of public policy and management, Manchester Business School, as quoted in Nicholas Timmins and Salamander Davoudi, "Sector as opaque as ever on value for money," *Financial Times,* 8 Feb. 2006.

5. John Goetz, Conny Neumann, and Oliver Schröm, *Allein gegen Kohl, Kiep & Co.* (Berlin: Ch. Links Verlag, 2000), 138–39.

6. Elf's consortium was Thyssen Handelsunion, Elf Aquitaine, and DSBK, the latter a firm wanting to sell its products to the Minol network. Untersuchungsausschuss "Parteispenden" Bundestag, *Parteispenden: Bericht des Untersuchungsausschusses* (Berlin: Deutscher Bundestag Referat Öffentlichkeitsarbeit, 2002), 614–15. Hereafter, *Parteispenden.*

7. Ibid., 617.

8. Hans Leyendecker, Michael Stiller, and Heribert Prantl, *Helmut Kohl, die Macht und das Geld* (Göttingen: Steidl, 2000), 179.

9. As with most corrupt deals, the financial figures quoted in the press vary considerably. David Gow, "BP loses in Treuhand deal," *Guardian,* 17 Jan. 1992; Hervé Gattegno "Les déboires d'Elf dans l'ex-RDA," *Le Monde,* 28 May 1997; "Franco-German group clinches deal to buy East German network," *FT Energy Newsletters,* 24 Jan. 1992.

10. *Parteispenden,* 616.

11. Having been French prime minister during the critical time when the Elf-Leuna deal was being negotiated, Cresson later exhibited incredible naiveté when she stated that "it was people from Elf who asked us to send our invoices to Switzerland so they could be paid by Elf International. How was I to know that there might be something fishy about it?" as quoted in Susan Bell, "Cresson named as Elf sleaze scandal deepens," *Scotsman,* 24 Feb. 2000; "Leuna: 'Hypotheses' de financement occulte mais beaucoup de flou," *Agence France Presse,* 28 Apr. 2003; JC, "Procès d'Elf en France," *Service de base français,* 28 Apr.

2003. Cresson is the same person who, as a commissioner of the European Union suspected of fraud and mismanagement (she wasn't alone), triggered the entire commission's collapse in 1999. She was on trial in Brussels for fraud, for having used EU funds to pay her lover (who was her dentist) to do "studies" for the EU, which he never did. The Belgian court later dropped charges that Cresson had violated Belgian law. The European Commission took her to the European Court of Justice, which ruled she had "acted in breach of the obligations" of her office, but it did not impose a penalty. The dentist has, since that time, died. Roland Binder, "Prosecutor drops EU corruption charges," *Financial Times,* 30 June 2004; "Commission européenne: La Cour de justice européenne sasié du cas d'Edith Cresson," *Europolitique,* 21 July 2004; *Commission v. Cresson,* C-432/04, 11 July 2006.

12. Pfahls had been head of Germany's secret service and at one time on the board of Daimler-Benz. Before he was tried, Lethier recorded his own version in Pierre Lethier, *Argent secret* (Paris: Albin Michel, 2001). "Leuna," *Agence France Presse,* 28 Apr. 2003; Pascale Robert-Diard, "Les services secrets invités du volet allemenad du procès Elf," *Le Monde,* 30 Apr. 2003; Stephane Durand-Souffland, "Procès Elf," *Le Figaro,* 29 Apr. 2003; on Lethier's and Holzer's payments, see Van Ruymbeke, *Ordonnance,* 419–37.

13. *Parteispenden,* 640–41; Paul Perraudin, "An die zuständige deutsche Behörde Augsburg," P/1338/99, Judiciary, Canton de Genève, 14 Sept. 2000, reprinted in Thomas Kleine-Brockhoff and Bruno Schirra, *Das System Leuna: Wie Politiker gekauft werden; Warum die Justiz wegschaut* (Hamburg: Rowohlt Taschenbuch Verlag, 2001), 175–200.

14. Commission of the European Communities, case no. IV/M.235, Elf Aquitaine-Thyssen/Minol, article 6(1)(b) non-opposition, 4 Sept. 1992, Office for Official Publications of the European Communities, Luxembourg.

15. Thomas Vanicek, member of the board of directors, Elf Oil AG, 11 May 1995, as quoted in Jutta E. Howard, *The Treuhandanstalt and Privatisation in the Former East Germany* (Aldershot, UK: Ashgate, 2001), 66–67. Le Floch-Prigent to Kohl, letter, reprinted in Kleine-Brockhoff and Schirra, *Das System Leuna,* 202–3.

16. Stevie Cameron and Harvey Cashore, *The Last Amigo* (Toronto: Macfarlane Walter and Ross, 2001), 241; cf. Van Ruymbeke, *Ordonnance,* 430–33. One of the accounts Holzer used was that named Delta, which appears to have also been used by Karlheinz Schreiber to process bribes and commissions. Van Ruymbeke, *Ordonnance,* 441.

17. Leyendecker, Stiller, and Prantl, *Helmut Kohl,* 190

18. She was paid on 27 Apr. 2000, *Parteispenden,* 631, see also 172.

19. Valérie Lescasble and Airy Routier, *Forages en eau profonde* (Paris: Grasset, 1998), 345.

20. The report, by Dr. Burkhard Hirsch, "Bericht über Ermittlungen zum Aktenbestand des Bundeskanzleramtes zu ausgewählten Sachbereichen," 21 June 2000, is reprinted in Kleine-Brockhoff and Schirra, *Das System Leuna,* 232–94; quotes in *Parteispenden,* 996.

21. Peter A. Hall and David Soskice, "An Introduction to the Varieties of Capitalism," in *The Varieties of Capitalism,* ed. P. A. Hall and D. Soskice (New York: Oxford University Press, 2001), 1–68, here at 8. See also Hans Tson Söderström, ed., *Corporate Governance and Structural Change: European Challenges,* trans. Timothy Chamberlain (Kristianstad: Kristianstads Boktryckeri AB, 2003).

22. *Parteispenden,* 630–31. In April 1994, Friderichs stepped down from his position at Airbus. Ironically, he was praised by the German component of Airbus for having moved Airbus away from a "politically motivated model of European integration towards a self-supporting industrial dimension." Deutsche Aerospace, quoted in "Airbus appoints Reuter chairman," *Flight International,* 6 Apr. 1994.

23. Cameron and Cashore, *Last Amigo,* 241.

24. Goetz, Neumann, and Schröm, *Allein gegen Kohl,* 137–45; Cameron and Cashore, *Last Amigo,* 238–40.

25. The judge, Diego Curtò, did a favor to the Socialist Party leaders by freezing Enimont's stocks and putting them into a trust managed by one of Socialist Party leader Bettino Craxi's right-hand men, Vincenzo Palladino. Palladino then paid Curtò CHF 400,000 ($245,000). Curtò, after retrieving the funds from a bank in Lugano, panicked and threw the money into a public trash can, making one Swiss garbageman very happy. Tribunale di Milano, V Sezione penale, *La maxitangente Enimont* (Milan: Kaos, 1997), 70, 148–51; Giani Barbacetto, Peter Gomez, and Marco Travaglio, *Mani Pulite: La vera storia* (Rome: Riuniti, 2002), 153–59.

26. Silvia Colazingari and Susan Rose-Ackerman, "Corruption in a Paternalistic Democracy: Lessons from Italy for Latin America," *Political Science Quarterly* 113/3 (1998): 447–70; Tribunale di Milano, *La maxitangete.*

27. Tribunale di Milano, *La maxitangente,* 69.

28. Ibid., 72, 78, 142–44.

29. Other networks were used for funds going to factions and their leaders in the other parties; one point of transit for some was a Vatican investment house (Istituto per le opere di religione). Ibid., 151–52, 172–94.

30. As quoted ibid., 126.

31. See Camera dei deputati, XI Legislatura, "Domanda di autorizzazione a procedere in giudizio nei confronti del deputato Grippo," *Documenti-Relazioni,* vol. 4, doc. 4, no. 297, 20 Apr. 1993 (Rome, 1996), 2.

32. Justice Feargus M. Flood, *The Second Interim Report of the Tribunal of Inquiry into Certain Planning Matters and Payments* (Dublin: Stationery Office, 2002), 35, 40, 45, 46, 47. Burke asserts that he did not solicit the payment; the facts and the tribunal contradict him. He was also justice minister at the time and, in that capacity, sold eleven passports to an Arab businessman for £20 million. Ibid., 47–48; Neil Collins and Mary O'Shea, *Understanding Corruption in Irish Politics,*(Cork: Cork University Press, 2000) 28, 37. The case is described in Paul Cullen, *With a Little Help from My Friends: Planning Corruption in Ireland* (Dublin: Gill and Macmillan, 2002), 169–205.

33. Flood, *Report,* 36, 40; Burke's quote on 40.

34. Roland-Pierre Paringaux, "Des méthodes et des personalités identiques dans le dossiers parisiens et régionaux," *Le Monde,* 10 May 1996; "Conflit entre élus RPR sur les marchés publics d'Ile-de-France," *Le Monde,* 10 May 1996; Françoise Chirot and Roland-Pierre Paringaux, "Une élue RPR critique publiquement les contrats de BTP en Ile-de-France," *Le Monde,* 10 May 1996.

35. Polaris Institute, "Global Water Grab: How Corporations Are Planning to Take Control of Local Water Services," January 2003, 6; www.polarisinstitute.org/pubs/pubs_pdf/gwg_english.pdf.

36. "Storm over Sofia," *FT Energy Newsletters,* 21 May 1999.

37. Compagnie générale des eaux is the firm Jean-Marie Messier took over in 1996, renamed Vivendi in 1998, and was ousted from in 2002 after Vivendi posted almost $30 billion in annual losses.

38. "Nor any drop to drink," *Economist,* 25 March 2000.

39. William Birnbauer, "The Big Pong Down Under," Center for Public Integrity/International Consortium of Investigative Journalists, Washington, D.C., 14 Feb. 2003, www.icij.org/water/printer-friendly.aspx?aid=59. A case in Bolivia is documented in María Teresa Rondelos, "A Tale of Two Cities," Center for Public Integrity/International Consortium of Investigative Journalists, Washington, D.C., 11 Feb. 2003, http://www.public integrity.org/water/report.aspx?aid=53&sid=100; on Indonesia, Andreas Harsono, "Water and Politics in the Fall of Suharto," Center for Public Integrity/International Consortium of Investigative Journalists, Washington, D.C., 10 Feb. 2003, http://www.public integrity.org/water/report.aspx?aid=52&sid=100.

40. Colin Talbot, as quoted in Timmins and Davoudi, "Sector as opaque as ever on value for money."

41. David Hall and Emanuele Lobina, "Private to Public: International lessons of Water Remunicipalisation in Grenoble, France," Public Services International Research·Unit, August 2001, http://www.psiru.org/reports/2001-08-W-Grenoble.doc.

42. The then CEO of Lyonnaise des eaux, Jérôme Monod, set up a subsidiary with which Grenoble contracted (Cogese); in 2000 he left Lyonnaise des eaux to become a senior adviser to President Jacques Chirac, precisely at the time when Chirac was being named as a participant in illegal party-financing schemes, which collected money from major French public works firms, including Lyonnaise des eaux. Monod had been the general secretary of the RPR (Chirac's party) from 1976 to 1978. The water services firm was bought by Suez and became Suez Environment. Julio Godoy, "Water and Power: The French Connection," Center for Public Integrity/International Consortium of Investigative Journalists, Washington, D.C., 1–4, 4 Feb. 2003; www.icij.org/water/printer-friendly/aspx?aid=47; Cour de cassation, Chambre criminelle, no. 96-83698, 27 Oct. 1997.

43. Hall and Lobina, "Private to Public," 7–9.

44. Ibid., 15.

45. As quoted in R.I., "Milano, scoppia un'altra Tangentopoli. Si dimette l'azzurro De Carolis? Decide Berlusconi," La Stampa, 19 Mar. 2000.

46. Daniel Politi, "Privatizing Water: What the European Commission Doesn't Want You to Know," Center for Public Integrity/International Consortium of Investigative Journalists, Washington, D.C., 2003, 5–6; www.icij.org/dtaweb/report.asp?.

47. The case involves at least the land deputy and head of the SPD group in Cologne's city council, Norbert Rüther, as well as the former SPD-Cologne treasurer and a former local party leader. "Das Netz der schmutzigen Geschaefte," Kölner Stadt-Anzeiger, 10 July 2003; "Der Abfall der Genossen," Die Zeit, Dec. 2002; Céline Le Prioux, "Le SPD de Schroeder aux prises avec un scandale de financement occulte," Agence France Presse, 12 Mar. 2002; Georges Marion, "En Allemagne, pots-de-vin autour du traitement des déchets," Le Monde 22 March 2002; "Affaire de corruption à Cologne: 2 ex-patrons condamnés, un politique relaxé," Agence France Press, 13 May 2004.

48. Author interview with Joachim Stünker, SPD Bundestag member, Berlin, 19 May 2003; author interview with Volker Neumann, SPD Bundestag member and head of Parteispenden commission, Berlin, 21 May 2003.

49. Georges Marion, "En Allemagne, pots-de-vin du traitment des déchets," Le Monde, 22 Mar. 2002; Anon., "Das Netz der schmutzigen Geschaefte," Koelner Stadt-Anzeiger, 10 July 2003.

50. Werner Rügemer, Colonia Corrupta: Globalisierung, Privatisierung und Korruption im Schatten des Kölner Klüngels (Münster: Westfälisches Dampfboot, 2003).

51. Roussin had worked for Compagnie générale des eaux (later Suez) when Monod was CEO. As quoted in Jean-Claude Méry, "On vous en supplie, Jean-Claude, l'élection de Chirac dépend de votre silence," Le Monde, 23 Sept. 2000. The Ordonnance de renvoi, which formed the basis of prosecution, later stated that witnesses and evidence corroborated Méry's statements. His mission was to "assure the financing of the political activities—of the RPR—by collecting funds, notably, from supplier firms." Ordonnance de renvoi, as quoted in Pascal Robert-Diard, "Feu l'affaire des HLM de Paris," Le Monde, 15 Mar. 2006.

52. Jean-Claude Méry, taped testimony, as quoted in "Je tiens à le dire pour que, si cette bande, un jour est utilisée, les choses soient claires, une fois pour toutes," Le Monde, 22 Sept. 2000.

53. Paul Heywood and Vincent Wright, "Executives, Bureaucracies and Decision-Making," in Developments in West European Politics, ed. Martin Rhodes, Paul Heywood, and

Vincent Wright (London: Macmillan, 1997); Fanfani quote in Percy A. Allum, *Politics and Society in Post-War Naples* (Cambridge: Cambridge University Press, 1973), 140; "forest" quote in Vittorio Emiliani, *L'Italia Mangiata* (Torino: Einaudi, 1975), 5.

54. UNISON, "What is wrong with PFI in schools?" September 2003, http://www .unison.org.uk/acrobat/13672.pdf. UNISON is a public services trade union.

55. "The Influence Peddlers," Center for Public Integrity/International Consortium of Investigative Journalists, Washington, D.C., 2002, 5; http://www.publicintegrity.org/bow/ report.aspx?aid=154.

56. Henri Hurand, CEO of SOFREMI in 1997–2001, as quoted in an interview with Eric Decouty and Marie-Amélie Lombard, "Vente d'armes," *Le Figaro,* 9 Jan. 2001; Pascal Ceaux, "De 1989 à 1997, M. Falcone s'est imposé en partenaire priviligié de la Sofremi," *Le Monde,* 17 Jan. 2001.

57. Ceaux, "De 1989 à 1997"; Hurand, as quoted in an interview with Decouty and Lombard, "Vente d'armes."

58. Note from DGSE (one of France's secret services), 7 July 1997, extract reprinted in Karl Laske, *Des coffres si bien garnis* (Paris: Denoël, 2004), 49; Global Witness, *A Crude Awakening* (London: Global Witness, 1999), 11.

59. A later report suggests the amount was $200,000. Ceaux, "De 1989 à 1997"; Fabrice Lhomme, "L'homme d'affaires Pierre Falcone," *Le Monde,* 7 Jan. 2003.

60. Lhomme, "L'homme d'affaires Pierre Falcone."

61. Jean-Pierre Gohon, interview in "Lycées d'Ile-de-France," *Le Figaro,* 18 Dec. 2000.

62. The SEM operated from 1986 to 1998 or 2000. The kickback scheme was interrupted when the new (as of 1998) president of the regional council asked for an audit and denounced audit findings to the judiciary. Luc Leroux and Michel Samson, "La justice enquête," *Le Monde,* 13 Apr. 2000. The regional Court of Auditors had already, in 1997, written and published "severe criticisms" of the operation of the SEM (here, called Semader). Those weren't taken up by the judiciary because the Court of Auditors didn't formally request it to do so. The person most suspected of corruption is the former president of the regional council (from 1986 to 1998), who named himself president of Semader in 1987–93: Jean-Claude Gaudin. He also holds the additional office of mayor of Marseille (1995–present) and, at various times, senator. Semader was created in 1986 for the Lycées réussite program and for construction of a "home" for the regional council. It invested over FRF 7 billion (about $1.4 billion) in various programs.

63. Méry, taped testimony, as quoted in "Je tiens à le dire."

64. Roland-Pierre Paringaux, "Des irrégularités sont dénoncées dans les marchés publics d'Ile-de-France," *Le Monde,* 2 May 1996.

65. Roland Pierre Paringaux, "Des irrégularités sont dénoncées dans les marchés publics," *Le Monde,* 2 May 1996.

66. "Andrew Smith announces sale of 51 per cent of Partnerships UK to private sector," *Hermes Database,* 27 Feb. 2001.

67. Partnerships UK, http://www.partnershipsuk.org.uk/aboutPUK/about-puk.asp.

68. Partnerships UK, http://www.partnershipsuk.org.uk/aboutpuk/about-advisory-members.asp.

69. "The Britain Audit," *Economist,* 14 Aug. 1993, 56.

70. Chris Blackhurst, "The Nolan report," *Independent,* 12 May 1995.

71. Andy Beckett, "How clean was my valley?" *Independent,* 28 Aug. 1994.

72. Anthony Barker, "Governmental Bodies and the Networks of Mutual Accountability," in *Quangos in Britain: Government and the Networks of Public Policy-Making,* ed. Anthony Barker (London: Macmillan, 1982), 3–33, here at 7.

73. "Low marks for private financing," *Labour Research,* 1 Sept. 2004.

74. Martin Wainwright, "Analysis: Municipal corruption," *Guardian,* 24 Mar. 1999.

75. Nick Cohen, "Behind Closed Doors," *New Statesman,* 12 June 2000.

76. Méry, taped testimony, as quoted in "Je tiens a le dire."

77. Karl Laske, "Un axe Hauts-de-Seine-Afrique qui passe par la Corse," *Libération,* 11 Jan. 2001; David Owen, "Europe: Générale des eaux chairman bows out," *Financial Times,* 28 June 1996; now under the leadership of Nicolas Sarkozy (at the time of writing, president of the Hauts-de-Seine Conseil Général, French Interior Minister and Minister of State), these expenditures appear to be continuing (e.g., see Direction générale des services: Culture, Relations Internationales et Economiques. Direction: SEM Coopération 92 *Rapport N.° 04.246 CP. Dossier de Cooperation avec le Gabon. Commune de Lekoni. Intervention avec Cooperation 92,* Département des Hauts-de-Seine, Nanterre, France, 7 May 2004).

78. Fabrice Tassel, "À Issy-les-Moulineaux, la gabegie de Pasqua et Santini," *Libération,* 7 Apr. 2004; Van Ruymbeke, *Ordonnance,* 329–43; Pascale Robert-Diard, "La vente par Elf de terrains à Issy-les-Moulineaux," *Le Monde,* 21 May 2003.

79. Assemblée nationale, Commission des affaires étrangères, "Rapport d'information," 70.

80. Alstom used to be Alsthom. In July 2004, despite protests of shareholders who wanted him out of Alstom entirely, Jaffré was demoted from CFO to the position of general adviser to the firm.

81. David Pallister and Richard Norton-Taylor, "Concern grows over 'revolving door,'" *Guardian,* 9 Sept. 1992.

82. Mark Warren, "What Does Corruption Mean in a Democracy?" *American Journal of Political Science* 48 (2004): 328–43.

83. Alexander Stille, "Emperor of the Air: Berlusconi owns Italian Politics, but He Wants More," *Nation,* 29 Nov. 1999, 16–20; "Your Other Trials," *Economist,* 31 July 2003.

84. "Berlusconi and a web of intrigue," *Financial Times,* 30 July 2003.

85. Amy Kazmin, "Thai premier's corruption pledge meets with skepticism," *Financial Times,* 1 Oct. 2004.

CHAPTER 5. DECENTRALIZATION, DEMOCRACY, AND GRAFT

1. Michel Noir's daughter Anne-Valérie Botton later divorced Alain Botton, who was evidently having an affair with her younger sister (and Noir's youngest daughter). Anne-Valerie allegedly sometimes served as "gopher" in illegal financial transfers from Geneva. Sophie Landrin, "Les comptes suisses," *Le Monde,* 15 Oct. 2003.

2. Yingyi Qian and Barry R. Weingast, "Federalism as a Commitment to Preserving Market Incentives" *Journal of Economic Perspectives* 11/4 (Autumn 1997): 83–92; Joseph E. Stiglitz, "On the Economic Role of the State," in *The Economic Role of the State,* ed. Arnold Heertje (Oxford: Basil Blackwell, 1989), 9–85, here at 58–60; Pranab Bardhan and Dilip Mookherjee, "Decentralization, Corruption and Government Accountability," in International *Handbook on the Economics of Corruption,* ed. Susan Rose-Ackerman (London: Edward Elgar, 2006), 161–88.

3. Paul Heywood, "Analysing Political Corruption in Western Europe: Spain and the UK in Comparative Perspective," in *Corrupt Exchanges: Empirical Themes in the Politics and Political Economy of Corruption,* ed. Donatella Della Porta and Susan Rose-Ackerman (Baden-Baden: Nomos, 2002), 45.

4. EuroStrategy Consultants, *Dismantling of Barriers: Public Procurement,* Single Market Review subseries 3, vol. 2 (Luxembourg: Office for Official Publications of the European Communities, 1997), 20–21.

5. Agatino Licandro with Aldo Varano, *La città dolente: Confessione di un sindaco corrotto* (Turin: Einaudi, 1993), 21.

6. Camera dei deputati, XI Legislatura, "Domanda di autorizzazione a procedere in giudizio nei confronti del deputato Cirino Pomicino," *Documenti-Relazioni,* vol. 4, doc. 4, no. 344, 6 May 1993 (Rome, 1996); Camera dei deputati, XI Legislatura, "Domanda di autorizzazione a procedere in giudizio nei confronti del deputato Craxi," *Documenti-Relazioni,* vol. 4, doc. 4, no. 265, 13 Apr. 1993 (Rome, 1996).

7. République Française, Cour de cassation, Chambre criminelle, no. 01-84922, 10 Oct. 2001; Gérard Davet and Fabrice Lhomme, "Plusiers enquêtes convergent vers Jacques Chirac sans l'atteindre," *Le Monde,* 14 Mar. 2004.

8. Cour des comptes, *Rapport au Président de la République suivi des réponses des administrations* (Paris: Journel Officiel, 1982).

9. Claude Popis, *L'argent, le bâtiment, la politique sous la Vème République* (Paris: Albin Michel, 1992), 90.

10. Vivien A. Schmidt, *Democratizing France: The Political and Administrative History of Decentralization* (Cambridge: Cambridge University Press, 1990), 115, 31, 35.

11. Ibid., 135.

12. Ibid., 120, 121, 129, 302.

13. Raymond Avrillier and Philippe Descamps, *Le système Carignon* (Paris: Éditions la Découverte, 1995), 332. On corruption in Grenoble, see also chapter 4.

14. Ibid., 333, 18.

15. Claude Francillon, "L'affaire Névache éclabousse la classe politique grenobloise," *Le Monde,* 10 Jan. 1995; "L'homme des postes stratégique," *Le Monde,* 10 Jan. 1995.

16. As quoted in Avrillier and Descamps, *Système Carignon,* 333.

17. Water distribution systems, utilities, and transport were excluded from EU procurement rules until the 1990 Utilities Directive, which still gave contracting authorities wide discretion. Utilities Directive 90/531/EEC, adopted 17 Sept. 1990. Peter Rees, "Public Procurement in the Construction Industry," in *1993: The European Market Myth or Reality?* ed. Dennis Campbell and Charles Flint (Deventer: Kluwer Law and Taxation Publishers, 1994), 169–88, here at 183.

18. Luc Leroux and Michel Samson, "La justice enquête sur des marchés publics de la région Provence-Alpes-Côte d'Azur," *Le Monde,* 13 Apr. 2000.

19. Thomas Drysch, "The New French System of Political Finance," in *Campaign and Party Finance in North America and Western Europe,* ed. Arthur B. Gunlicks (Boulder, CO: Westview, 1993), 155–77.

20. Quoted in Anne Chemin, "La validité de la procédure ouverte au Mans Affaire Urba," *Le Monde,* 29 June 1991.

21. Diary, as quoted in Edwy Plenel, "Urbatechnic à livre ouvert. II. Le financement occulte du PS," *Le Monde,* 18 Apr. 1991.

22. Pierre Avril, "Regulation of Political Finance in France," in *Comparative Political Finance among the Democracies,* ed. Herbert Alexander and Rei Shiratori (Boulder, CO: Westview, 1994), 85–95, here at 88.

23. Dossiers du Canard, *L'argent secret des élections* (Paris: Canard Enchaîné, 1988), 53, 14.

24. Ibid., 67, 66.

25. Jean Claude Pierrette and Pascale Sauvage, "Des marchés passés par le conseil général des Yvelines auraient donné lieu à corruption," *Le Monde,* 14 Oct. 1995.

26. Jean Pierre Dubois, "Au procès du conseil général des Yvelies, M. Borotra dénonce le manque de contrôle des marchés publics," *Le Monde,* 7 Nov. 2001.

27. Dossiers du Canard, *Argent secret,* 34–35.

28. Ibid., quotes at 36, 55.

29. Jean-Pierre Dubois, "La corruption ordinaire au conseil général des Yvelines devant le tribunal de Versailles," *Le Monde,* 23 Oct 2001.

30. Robert Belleret, "Les logiques souterraines d'un projet faraminuex," *Le Monde,* 11 Feb. 1998; Claude Francillon, "Pierre Botton est condamné," *Le Monde,* 4 Oct. 1997. The opponents of the road project were able to appeal to France's Conseil d'État on the basis of an EU directive in order to have the contract and concession annulled. Rafaele Rivais, "Le Conseil d'État annule la délibération," *Le Monde,* 9 Feb. 1998.

31. In three years, Bouygues's Nigerian subsidiary transferred $400,000 into a Swiss account from which Noir's activities were financed; another construction firm did likewise, for a total of about $1 million. République française, Cour de cassation, Chambre criminelle, no. 01-83250,13 Feb. 2002; Cour de cassation, Chambre criminelle, no. 94-81398, 31 May 1994; Cour de cassation, Chambre criminelle, no. 99-81788, 8 June 1999; Landrin, "'Comptes suisses,' dernier volet de l'affrontement."

32. Robert D. Putnam, *Making Democracy Work: Civic Traditions in Modern Italy* (Princeton: Princeton University Press, 1993), 85, 98.

33. Camera dei deputati, XI Legislatura, "Domanda di autorizzazione a procedere in giudizio contro i deputati Tognoli, Pillitteri, Del Pennino, Cervetti, Massari," *Documenti-Relazioni,* vol. 1, doc. 4, no. 6, 2 June 1992 (Rome, 1996), 4.

34. See Camera dei deputati, XI Legislatura, "Domanda di autorizzazione a procedere in giudizio nei confronti del deputato Martelli," *Documenti-Relazioni,* vol. 4, doc. 4, no. 284, 15 Apr. 1993 (Rome, 1996); Camera dei deputati, XI Legislatura, "Domanda di autorizzazione a procedere in giudizio nei confronti del deputato Pollastrini," *Documenti-Relazioni,* vol. 7, Doc. 4, no. 614, 8 Nov. 1993 (Rome, 1996).

35. Percy A. Allum, *Politics and Society in Post-War Naples* (Cambridge: Cambridge University Press, 1973); Carolyn M. Warner, "Mass Parties and Clientelism in France and Italy," in *Clientelism and Interests in Transition: The European Experience in Comparative and Historical Perspective,* ed. Simona Piattoni (New York: Cambridge University Press, 2001), 154–89.

36. Miriam A. Golden and Eric C. C. Chang, "Competitive Corruption: Factional Conflict and Political Malfeasance in Postwar Italian Christian Democracy," *World Politics* 53 (July 2001): 588–622; Gary W. Cox and M. F. Thies, "How Much Does Money Matter? 'Buying' Votes in Japan, 1967–1990," *Comparative Political Studies* 33 (2000): 37–57.

37. Martin Clark, *Modern Italy, 1871–1982* (New York: Longman, 1984), 392.

38. Licandro and Varano, *Città dolente,* 28, 59, 38, 44, 47.

39. Ibid., 50, 124.

40. As quoted in Marcella Andreoli, *Andavamo in Piazza Duomo nella testamonianza di Mario Chiesa* (Milan: Sperling and Kupfer, 1993), 36. See also Camera dei deputati, XI Legislatura, "Domanda di autorizzazione a procedere in giudizio nei confronti del deputato Altissimo," *Documenti-Relazioni,* vol. 4, doc. 4, no. 343, 4 May 1993 (Rome, 1993); ibid., no. 345, 6 May 1993.

41. Camera dei deputati, XI Legislatura, "Domanda di autorizzazione a procedere in giudizio nel confronti del deputato Pollastrini," 7.

42. Carol Mershon, "The Costs of Coalition: Coalition Theories and Italian Governments," *American Political Science Review* 90/3 (1996): 534–54.

43. As quoted in Andreoli, *Andavamo,* 51.

44. Ibid., 33.

45. As quoted in Stefano Scotti, ed., *Mani Pulite* (Milan: Panorama-Mondadori, 1992), 23–24.

46. As quoted ibid., 24.

47. Maurizio Prada, as quoted ibid., 24, 23.

48. Testimony of Mario Chiesa, as quoted in Andreoli, *Andavamo,* 33.

49. Ibid., 35.

50. Golden and Chang, "Competitive Corruption."

51. As quoted in Andreoli, *Andavamo,* 35–36.

52. Maurizio Prada, as quoted in Scotti, *Mani Pulite,* 25.

53. As quoted in Andreoli, *Andavamo,* 27.

54. Ibid., 26–27; Licandro and Varano, *Città dolente,* 125–27.

55. As quoted in Andreoli, *Andavamo,* 31.

56. Ibid., 32.

57. Camera dei deputati, XI Legislatura, "Domanda di autorizzazione a procedere in giudizio nei confronti del deputato Craxi," 69–71.

58. Andreoli, *Andavamo,* 32, 34–35, 34, respectively.

59. Ibid., 36.

60. Court of Auditors 1991 report, as quoted in Donatella Della Porta and Alberto Vannucci, *Corruzione politica e amministrazione pubblica* (Bologna: Il Mulino, 1994), 42.

61. Citing a professional from the southern province of Catania, in Della Porta and Vannucci, *Corruzione politica,* 296, cf. 58–59.

62. These transfers represented about 10 percent of state revenue. E. Buglione, F. Merloni, V. Santantonio, and L. Torchia, "L'Italie," in *La réforme des collectivités locales en Europe,* ed. Yves Mény (Paris: Documentation française, 1984), 68.

63. Beginning in 1978, local governments were barred from borrowing to cover running expenses. Carlo Desideri, "Italian Regions in the European Community," in *The European Union and the Regions,* ed. Barry Jones and Michael Keating (Oxford: Oxford University Press, 1995), 65–87, here at 68.

64. Council of Europe, Steering Committee on Local and Regional Democracy, *Structure and Operation of Local and Regional Democracy: Italy. Situation in 1999,* 29.

65. Licandro and Varano, *Città dolente,* 63, 67, 62.

66. Ibid., 63–64, 65; see also Camera dei deputati, XI Legislatura, "Domanda di autorizzazione a procedere in giudizio contro il deputato Manti e contro il deputato Nucara," *Documenti-Relazioni,* vol. 2, doc. 4, no. 106A, 9 Oct. 1992 (Rome, 1996).

67. Licandro and Varano *Città dolente,* 69.

68. Ibid., 71.

69. On self-reinforcing, see Avner Greif, *Institutions and the Path to the Modern Economy* (Cambridge: Cambridge University Press, 2006).

70. Quotes from Martin Wainwright, "Municipal corruption," *Guardian,* 24 Mar. 1999.

71. In 1974, architect John Poulson was found guilty of distributing bribes to facilitate his business interests, which primarily involved the planning, design, and building of public housing. Poulson was sentenced to seven years in prison and was called by his trial judge an "incalculably evil man." The affair prompted outcries for local government reform, namely, for higher ethical standards. It did not prompt, in contrast to what so often happens in Italy and France, accusations that the judiciary was on a politically motivated witch hunt. On Poulson, see Michael Gillard and Martin Tomkinson, *Nothing to Declare: The Political Corruptions of John Poulson* (London: J. Calder, 1980).

72. Chris Hastings, David Leppard, Jonathan Carr-Brown, and Patrick Masters, "Land scandal hits Labour council," *Sunday Times,* 12 Apr. 1998.

73. Ibid.

74. Russ Newton, "Jail is price of corruption," *Doncaster Star,* 31 July 2002; Rob Waugh and Brendan Carlin, "Tory jailed in Donnygate case," *Yorkshire Post,* 31 July 2002; Sean Cronin, "Bribes and punishment," *Estates Gazette,* 23 Mar. 2002.

75. R. J. Johnston and C. J. Pattie, "Great Britain: Twentieth Century Parties Operating under Nineteenth Century Regulations," in Gunlicks, *Campaign and Party Finance in North America and Western Europe,* 123–54, here at 130.

76. David Walker, "The true cost of corruption," *Independent,* 22 June 1995.

77. Allan Massie, "Fit to rule the land of Braveheart?" *New Statesman,* 26 Nov. 2001.

78. Ibid.; Ian Bell, "Tommy and tone," *Independent,* 20 Sept. 1998.

79. Bill Aitken, "The corrosive culture of the Labour party's rotten little fiefdoms," *Daily Mail,* 8 Mar. 2002.

80. Rob Waugh, "Council web of corruption scandal ends in jailings," *Yorkshire Post,* 13 Mar. 2002; Andrew Norfolk, "Expenses paid for a day at the races—in Hong Kong," *Times,* 13 Mar. 2002.

81. Iain Macwhirter, "Ending the crony culture," *Scotsman,* 4 June 1998.

82. Ibid.

83. John Maccalman, "No independent review of local government finances upsets MSPs," *Herald,* 29 Feb. 2000.

84. Bell, "Tommy and tone."

85. Peter John, "The Restructuring of Local Government in England and Wales," in *Local Government in Europe,* ed. Richard Batley and Gerry Stoker (New York: St. Martin's, 1991), 58–72, here at 60, 64.

86. "The Britain Audit," *Economist,* 14 Aug. 1993.

87. "[For instance,] a basic allowance of GBP 431 in Tamworth Borough Council, with an attendance allowance of GBP23.22 per meeting, is not untypical. Some leaders of councils receive little more than GBP1000 a year in allowances. . . . The principle is that councillors should not suffer financial hardship as a result of being elected. In the case of some of the smaller sums involved, it is difficult to believe that this is being achieved." Nolan Committee, *Standards of Conduct in Local Government in England, Scotland, and Wales: Third Report of the Committee on Standards in Public Life* (London: HMSO, 1997), 1:14–15.

88. Ibid., 1:53.

89. Granted, much of the UK's party financing looks, as it does in the United States, "sleazy" and morally corrupt, if not technically (legally) corrupt.

90. I haven't done a systematic study, but it appears that countries with extensive, generous public financing of political parties have less corruption (such as Sweden and Austria), although Spain is a significant exception to that "rule." It also appears that the structure of party competition matters considerably. For example, Italy even more than France has had parties as competitive internally as they are externally, which creates more demand for individual financing.

91. Raymond Fisman and Roberta Gatti, "Decentralization and Corruption: Evidence from U.S. Federal Transfer Programs," *Public Choice* 113 (2002): 25–35.

CHAPTER 6. THE CORRUPTION OF CAMPAIGN AND PARTY FINANCING

1. The names of cases associated with these deaths are in Appendix 1; one could add the suicides of Raul Gardini and Gabriele Caciagli.

2. An example would be the illegal funding by the French Center Party (CDS) of its 1989 European Parliament campaign. Cecile Prieur, "Trois anciens ministres centristes mis en examen dans l'affaire du CDS," *Le Monde,* 6 June 1997.

3. Lord Razzall, in his testimony to Chairman Lord Neill, Committee on Standards in Public Life. *The Funding of Political Parties in the United Kingdom, Fifth Report,* vol. 2: *Evidence.* (London: HMSO, 1998), 100 1:100.

4. For entry to a vast literature, see Ben Clift and Justin Fisher, "Comparative Party Finance Reform" *Party Politics* 10/6 (2004), 677–99; Robert E. Mutch, "Three Centuries of Campaign Finance Reform" in *A User's Guide to Campaign Finance Reform,* ed. Gerald C. Lubenow (Berkeley: University of California Press, 2001), 1–24; Karl-Heinz Nassmacher, ed. *Foundations of Democracy: Approaches to Comparative Political Finance* (Baden Baden: Nomos, 2001); Jonathan Hopkin, "The Problem with Party Finance" *Party Politics* 10/6 (2004), 627–51; Alan Gerber, "Estimating the Effect of Campaign Spending on Election

Outcomes Using Instrumental Variables," *American Political Science Review* 92 (1998), 401–11.

5. On the United States, see Sanjay Gupta and Charles W. Swenson, "Rent Seeking by Agents of the Firm," *Journal of Law and Economics* 56 (Apr. 2003): 253–68.

6. Pascale Robert-Diard, "Les chefs d'entreprise décrivent le chantage du RPR," *Le Monde*, 2 Oct. 2003.

7. Alberto Statera, "Per fortuna che c'è la tangente, unica industria senza recessione," *La Stampa*, 26 Mar. 1992.

8. Quotes from Camera dei deputati, XI Legislatura, "Domanda di autorizzazione a procedere in giudizio contro il deputato Craxi," *Documenti-Relazioni*, vol. 3, doc. 4, no. 166-quater, 13 Jan. 1993 (Rome, 1996), 6, 7.

9. Author interview with Volker Neumann, chair, Parteispenden investigative committee, Berlin, 25 May 2003; Joanna McKay, "Political Corruption in Germany," in *Corruption in Contemporary Politics*, ed. Martin J. Bull and James L. Newell (Basingsoke: Palgrave, 2003), 53–65, here at 60.

10. Rt. Hon. Alan Beith, uncorrected comments, House of Commons, Constitutional Affairs Committee, "Party Funding," *Uncorrected Transcript of Oral Evidence*, to be published as HC 1060-iii, 4 July 2006, 4; http://www.publications.parliament.uk/pa/cm200506/cmselect/cmconst/uc1060{endash002.htm.

11. Karl-Heinz Nassmacher, "Political Finance in West Central Europe," in *Foundations for Democracy: Approaches to Comparative Political Finance*, ed. Karl-Heinz Nassmacher (Baden-Baden: Nomos Verlagsgesellschaft, 2001), 93.

12. Chairman Lord Neill, Committee on Standards in Public Life, *Fifth Report*, 1:43; Treasurer, Committee on Standards in Public Life, *Fifth Report*, vol. 2, *Transcripts of Oral Evidence* (London: HMSO, 1998), 75, paragraph 854. See also Michael Pinto-Duschinsky, "British Party Funding, 1983–1988," in *Comparative Political Finance among the Democracies*, ed. Herbert E. Alexander and Rei Shiratori (Boulder, CO: Westview, 1994), 13–28, here at 14, 17.

13. Cour de cassation, Brussels, no. JC98CN4_2, 23 Dec. 1998, title V, chap. 3.1; Jean-Pierre De Staercke, *Agusta-Dassault: La cassation du siècle* (Brussels: Éditions Luc Pire et le Matin, 1999), 111. The Dassault case is discussed in chapter 2.

14. Terry Moe, "Political Institutions: The Neglected Side of the Story," special issue of *Journal of Law, Economics, and Organization* 6 (1990): 213–53, here at 232.

15. Andreas Schedler, "Restraining the State: Conflicts and Agents of Accountability," in *The Self-Restraining State*, ed. Andreas Schedler, Larry Diamond, and Marc F. Plattner (Boulder, CO: Lynne Rienner, 1999), 333–50, here at 334.

16. Gianstefano Frigerio, former (Lombardy) regional secretary for the DC, interrogation of 5 July 1992, in Camera dei deputati, XI Legislatura, "Domanda di autorizzazione a procedere in giudizio contro il deputato Craxi, 7."

17. Martin Rhodes, "Financing Party Politics in Italy: A Case of Systemic Corruption," *West European Politics* 20/1 (1997): 54–80, quote at 58, data at 61.

18. Luís De Sousa, "Political Parties and Corruption in Portugal," *West European Politics* 24/1 (Jan. 2001): 157–80.

19. John Goetz, Conny Neumann, and Oliver Schröm, *Allein gegen Kohl, Kiep & Co.* (Berlin: Ch. Links, 2000), 211, 210.

20. Ingrid van Biezen and Karl-Heinz Nassmacher, "Political Finance in Southern Europe (Italy, Portugal and Spain)," in Nassmacher, *Foundations for Democracy*, 131–54, here at 151–52; Sesto Mariolina, "Referto della corte dei conti sui bilanci elettorali," *Il Sole 24 Ore*, 21 Sept. 2000.

21. Goetz, Neumann, and Schröm, *Allein gegen*, 210.

22. For instance, the cases against Dr. Riedl ended on 9 March 2000; the ones against Pfahls, Schreiber, and Max Strauss ended on 26 January 2001; there were two cases against Kiep, which were terminated (no date given), as were the cases against Uwe Luethje and Horst Weyrauch.

23. Fabrice Tassel, "Des députés européens très protégés," *Libération*, 27 Nov. 2003.

24. Pascale Robert-Diard, "Le tribunal examine le scandale de corruption des HLM de Paris, naguère affaire d'Etat," *Le Monde*, 25 Jan. 2006; Pascale Robert-Diard, "Dernier jour du procès des HLM de Paris, en l'absence des politiques," *Le Monde*, 5 Apr. 2006; Pascale Robert-Diard, "Attendus sévères et peines légères au procès des HLM de Paris," *Le Monde*, 7 July 2006; "Affaire de corruption à Cologne: 2 ex-patrons condamnés, un politique relaxé," *Agence France Presse*, 13 May 2004; "Staatsanwaelte und Eisermann legen Revision eine," *General Anzeiger*, 18 May 2004.

25. Committee on Standards in Public Life, *Fifth Report*, vol. 1; Herbert E. Alexander, "Money and Politics: A Conceptual Framework," in *Comparative Political Finance in the 1980s*, ed. Herbert E. Alexander with the assistance of Joel Federman (Cambridge: Cambridge University Press, 1989), 9–23, here at 16.

26. For a view that denies there has been too much money in politics in the United States, see Steven Ansolabehere, John de Figueiredo, and James Snyder, "Why Is There So Little Money in U.S. Politics?" *Journal of Economic Perspectives* 17/1 (Winter 2003): 105–30.

27. Committee on Standards in Public Life, *Fifth Report*, 1:194–207. The no-limits countries were Germany, Sweden, Austria, Belgium, Denmark, and the Netherlands. Until 2000 the United Kingdom only limited spending by a candidate's constituents, not by the national party.

28. Committee on Standards in Public Life, *Fifth Report*, 1:24.

29. Rt. Hon. Jack Straw, uncorrected comments, House of Commons, Constitutional Affairs Committee, "Party Funding," *Uncorrected Transcript of Oral Evidence*, to be published as HC 1060-iii, 4 July 2006, 9; http://www.publications.parliament.uk/pa/cm200506/cmselect/cmconst/uc1060{endash

30. Pinto-Duschinsky, "British Party Funding," 21.

31. BBC reporter Michael Crick, to the Committee on Standards in Public Life, *Fifth Report*, 1:112.

32. In Spain, it is the reverse. Ingrid van Beizen, "Party Financing in New Democracies: Spain and Portugal," *Party Politics* 6/3 (2000): 329–42.

33. Jean-François Médard, "Finanziamento della politica e corruzione: Il caso Francese," in *Finanziamento della politica e corruzione*, ed. Fulco Lanchester (Milan: Giuffrè, 2000), 165–97, here at 192; Thomas Drysch, "The New French System of Political Finance," in *Campaign and Party Finance in North America and Western Europe*, ed. Arthur B. Gunlicks (Boulder, CO: Westview, 1993), 155–77, here at 158–59.

34. Drysch, "New French System," 158.

35. By law, presidential candidates were allowed FRF 250,000 ($42,500). Candidates also could be reimbursed for the costs of printing and mailing programs and other election materials (including 154,000 election posters). Candidates in National Assembly elections received minor financing, provided they won 5 percent or more of the vote in the first round. The extreme limits of the laws are evident in that candidates were allowed to display only four types of election posters (two for the campaign program and two for campaign events) and were reimbursed only up to about FRF 10,000 ($1,700) for them. Candidates were required to put up a deposit of FRF 1,000 ($170), which was refunded if they won 5 percent or more of the vote in the first round. Parties with seats in the National Assembly were allotted approximately twenty minutes per month of television time (the channels were all state owned). During campaigns, this amount was increased to about three hours before the first ballot. Parties without seats in the parliament could only get

air time if they put up seventy-five candidates for the first ballot, in which case each candidate received seven minutes for the first-ballot campaign and five minutes for the second. Clearly, the governing parties were protecting their oligopoly.

36. Presidential candidates could receive up to FRF 40 million ($8 million) in 1995, and parliamentary candidates up to FRF 50,000 ($10,000). Parties also began to receive subsidies on the basis of their presence in the National Assembly and Senate. After 1992, parties without seats in that national legislature became eligible for subsidies. The 1988 law made it legal for parties to receive corporate and private-person donations, with limits of FRF 500,000 ($84,000) and FRF 50,000 ($8,400), respectively, per year. Drysch, "New French System," 164, 169, 170.

37. Elf's CEO Le Floch-Prigent claimed he had no knowledge of payments (or at least of their details), having told his staff, "I don't want to hear of it." Renaud Van Ruymbeke, *Ordonnance de renvoi devant le Tribunal correctionnel de non-lieu partiel et de requalification,* no. du Parquet 9418769211, no. instruction 2039/94/29, procédure correctionnelle, Cour d'appel de Paris, Tribunal de grand instance de Paris, 13 Dec. 2002, 552.

38. The late Gérard Monate (former director of the PS consultancy Urba) said that the kickbacks ("commissions") were set at FRF 3,500 ($600) per square meter (of the proposed project). Emmanuelli claimed the charge was only FRF 600 ($100) per square meter. Renaud Lecadre, "Les hypermarchés qui hantent Emmanuelli," *Libération,* 24 Apr. 2001; Jean-Marc Leclerc, "Financement occulte," *Le Figaro,* 9 Dec. 2003; Hervé Gattegno, "L'enquête sur l'affaire Destrade," *Le Monde,* 15 May 2001.

39. Hervé Gattegno, "Les politiques et les circuits de la corruption," *Le Monde,* 4 June 1999.

40. As quoted from letter of Destrade to investigating judge Jean-Louis Lecue, 29 Aug. 1995, "J'ai permis d'apporter au PS 33 millions de financement occulte," *Le Monde,* 4 Oct. 1995.

41. Gattegno, "Les politiques et les circuits de la corruption."

42. Cases are described in chapters 2 and 5.

43. Ruud A. Koole, "Political Finance in Western Europe (Britain and France)," in Nassmacher, *Foundations for Democracy,* 73–91, here at 87. The law passed in 1995.

44. Robert-Diard, "Les chefs d'entreprise decrivent le chantage du RPR." This view was also expressed by Jacques Bonnet, president of the Commission nationale des comptes de campagne et des financements politiques (CNCCFP), in an interview with the author, 26 Nov. 2003, Paris. Cour d'appel de Versailles, 1 Dec. 2004, 2004-00824.

45. Robert-Diard, "Les chefs d'entreprise decrivent le chantage du RPR."

46. This is the crime for which Alain Juppé, among others, was prosecuted and of which he was found guilty. He appealed the original sentence. On 1 December 2004 he was barred from public office for one year and given a fourteen-month suspended sentence. République Française, Cour d'appel de Versailles, no. 2004-00824, 1 Dec. 2004.

47. In a five-year period, the head of the Milan metro system collected kickbacks totaling about 5 percent of the more than ITL 200 billion ($200 million) paid to contractors, which he then redistributed to the major parties according to a precise plan. The parties skimmed from every economic sector, so the sums gained were enormous. Camera dei deputati, XI Legislatura, "Domanda di autorizzazione a procedere in giudizio contro i deputati Tognoli, Pillitteri, Del Pennino, Cervetti, Massari," *Documenti-Relazioni,* vol. 1, doc. 4, no. 6, 2 June 1992 (Rome, 1996), 9–13. Of these kickbacks, 25 percent went to the main Socialist Party (PSI), 25 percent to the DC, 25 percent to the Communist then Democratic Left Party, 12.5 percent to the Republicans (PRI), and 12.5 percent to the minor Socialist Party (PSDI). Ibid., 7–8.

48. Luigi Carnevale Miyno, interrogation, as quoted in Camera dei deputati, XI Legislatura, "Domanda di autorizzazione a procedere in giudizio contro il deputato Craxi," 9.

49. Berlusconi's political successes are the result of a variety of factors, not merely campaign finance laws that starved the regular parties and politicians and gave a competitive advantage to a wealthy media magnate. Jonathan Hopkin and Caterina Paolucci, "The Business Firm Model of Party Organization: Cases from Spain and Italy," *European Journal of Political Research* 35/3 (May 1999): 307–39; Alexander Stille, *The Sack of Rome* (New York: Penguin, 2006).

50. Tony Barber, "Italian vote of confidence used to protect Berlusconi TV," *Financial Times,* 18 Feb. 2004; Stille, *Sack of Rome.*

51. Guy Goodwin-Gill, Rubin Director of Research, Institute of European Studies, University of Oxford, in Committee on Standards in Public Life, *Fifth Report,* 2:270–71, paragraph 3286.

52. When a 1958 Constitutional Court ruling eliminated tax breaks for making contributions to political parties, a massive decline in contributions occurred, and the parties ran into serious financial difficulties. So, in 1959, the Bundestag (under CDU-CSU majority) decided to establish direct state contributions to partially fund the parties represented in the Bundestag. An SPD-governed state, Hessen, filed suit against this method of funding the parties (i.e., state support). The Constitutional Court ruled, in a July 1966 decision, that the method was indeed unconstitutional because it interfered with the "free and open" process of the creation of public opinion concerning political issues. The court said, however, that it would be constitutional for the state to fund the *costs* of running election campaigns. *Parteispenden,* 231. Untersuchungsausschuss "Parteispenden" Bundestag, *Parteispenden: Bericht des Untersuchungsausschusses* (Berlin: Deutscher Bundestag Referat Öffentlichkeitsarbeit, 2002).

53. Thomas Saalfeld, "Court and Parties: Evolution and Problems of Political Funding in Germany," in *Party Finance and Political Corruption,* ed. Robert Williams (Basingstoke: Macmillan, 2000), 89–122, here at 101.

54. *Parteispenden,* 232.

55. Press conference, 14 Jan. 2000 in Goetz, Neumann, and Schröm, *Allein gegen,* 195. The persons who created the story about the origin of the undocumented and ultimately illegal contributions to the CDU of Hessen were Casimir Prinz zu Sayn-Wittgenstein, who was the treasurer of the CDU-Hessen from 1976 to 1998, and Roland Koch, ministerpraesident of the CDU in Hessen. Hans Leyendecker, Michael Stiller, and Heribert Prantl, *Helmut Kohl, die Macht und das Geld* (Göttingen: Steidl, 2000), 214–15.

56. Pierre-Angel Gay, "Les dons des entreprise fournissent 13% des recettes des partis" *Le Monde,* 20–21 Nov. 1993.

57. As quoted in Committee on Standards in Public Life, *Fifth Report,* 2:123, paragraph 1459.

58. As self-interested individuals, members of the general public would rather use their money as they see fit, donating if they have a particular interest in a particular party. This tendency varies according to a national culture's view of public expenditure. It is perhaps not surprising that the British have no public funding, whereas the Austrians and Spanish have extensive public funding.

59. A rigorous study of the effect of public subsidies on party and candidate spending awaits an author. Anecdotal evidence is suggestive, although the correlations may be spurious: in Sweden, for instance, expenditures rose dramatically and in step with increases in public funding. Gullan Gidlund and Ruud A. Koole, "Political Finance in the North of Europe (The Netherlands and Sweden)," in Nassmacher, *Foundations for Democracy,* 112–30, here at 114. Claire M. Smith, "Money to Burn: Party Finance and Party Organization in Germany and Austria," paper presented to the Midwest Political Science Association, Chicago, 15–18 Apr. 2004.

60. Van Beizen, "Party Financing in New Democracies."

61. Details of Spanish party financing can be found in Pilar del Castillo, "Problems in

Spanish Party Financing," in Alexander and Shiratori, *Comparative Political Finance among the Democracies,* 97–104, here at 100.

62. Ibid., 98, 102.

63. Fernando Jiménez, "Political Scandals and Political Responsibility in Democratic Spain," *West European Politics* 21/4 (1998): 80–99; Paul Heywood, "Sleaze in Spain," *Parliamentary Affairs* 48/4 (1995): 726–37.

64. Gilles Paris, "Le CDS reconnait avoir été financé grace à une caisse noire en Suisse," *Le Monde,* 23 Mar. 1995.

65. Prieur, "Trois anciens ministres centristes."

66. The shell society in which some funds were sent was cynically named SOS Christians of Libya. The CDS's vice secretary, François Froment-Meurice (and then European Parliament deputy), was, by the time of the trial in 2000, a member of the Conseil d'état, France's highest administrative justice tribunal. Also directly involved in the illegal financing scheme were a former minister of transportation, and a minister of labor and social affairs: Bernard Bosson, in the Edouard Balladur government, and Jacques Barrot, in the Alain Juppé government. Pierre Méhaignerie, Barrot, and Bosson were convicted of illegal party financing, and on appeal the former two were given eight-month suspended sentences and the latter a four-month suspended sentence. They immediately benefited from an amnesty law passed just after Chirac's 1995 presidential election victory. Barrot became France's EU commissioner in 2004, assigned to Transport after he turned down the Justice portfolio. Bosson, a parliamentary deputy since 1986, switched parties and became mayor of a resort town in the Alps, Annecy. Méhaignerie also switched parties and became general secretary of Chirac's party (UMP, which replaced the RPR in 2003) in 2004. He had been a deputy in the parliament since 1973 and has held other major ministerial portfolios, such as agriculture, since 1976.

67. The cases are discussed in chapters 2, 4, and 5.

68. Author interview with Jacques Bonnet, 26 Nov. 2003.

69. Three former Alstom directors were convicted of corruption in this affair. The bribes they paid went into the account of Étienne Léandri, a Pasqua confident who died in 1995. Jacques Foloorou, "Trois anciens dirigeants d'Alstom condamnés pour corruption," *Le Monde,* 4 Mar. 2006; "Le fils de Charles Pasqua relaxé dans une affaire de corruption," *Le Monde,* 2 Mar. 2006.

70. Robert Feliciaggi, who had also been under investigation, was assassinated in Corsica in March 2006. The police ruled it a local vendetta. Ariane Chemin, "Le dernier nabob corse," *Le Monde,* 16 Mar. 2006; "Pour la première fois, Charles Pasqua est renvoyé en correctionnelle," *Le Monde,* 23 June 2006. On the use of the casino for Pasqua's campaign financing, see République Française, Cour d'appel de Bastia, 18 Sept. 2002, no. 2002/00324.

71. At its initial public offering in 1998, GEC-Alsthom became Alstom. Fabrice Lhomme, "Trois dossiers devant la Cour de justice de la République," *Le Monde,* 23 Feb. 2004; "Charles Pasqua, d'Annemasse à la Haute Cour," *Le Temps,* 6 Feb. 2004; Karl Laske, "Au bout des comptes, Pasqua père et fils," *Libération,* 28 Sept. 2004; Karl Laske, "Triple mise en examen pour Pasqua," *Libération,* 9 Oct. 2004; quote on financing by Pierre-Henri Paillet, former director of France's office of the planning and management of territory (DATAR), in Fabrice Lhomme, "Entendu lundi par la police, l'ancien ministre reste cerné par les 'affaires,'" *Le Monde,* 5 Oct. 2004; on the international arrest warrant, "Le fils de Charles Pasqua relaxé dans une affaire de corruption," *Le Monde,* 2 March 2006.

72. Hervé Gattegno, "Comment Pasqua a fait peur à l'Elysée pur se réfugier au Sénat," *Le Monde,* 5 Oct. 2004.

73. Elie Barth and Nicolas Weill, "Le project de fondation de l'UMP reveille le débat," *Le Monde,* 17 Oct. 2003; Denis Demonpion, "Des fondations a doublés fonds," *Le Point,* 24 Oct. 2003.

74. Gidlund and Koole, "Political Finance in the North of Europe," 127.

75. Justin Fisher, "Party Finance and Corruption: Britain," in Williams, *Party Finance and Political Corruption,* 15–36, here at 26–27.

76. By about 1995, Labour received "40 per cent [of its income] from members and small donations, 30 per cent unions, 20 per cent wealthy entrepreneurs and 10 per cent commercial activities." Brian Groom, "Paying for the party," *Financial Times,* 9 Jan. 2001.

77. Once out of office after the 1997 election (won by Labour), the Conservatives were soon down to corporate donations of only £359,059, in contrast to £2.5 million their last year in office. Ibid.

78. Committee on Standards in Public Life, *Fifth Report,* 1:32.

79. Ironically, Méhaignerie was minister of justice when the case later broke (in March 1995, discovered by the investigative paper *Canard Enchaîné*) in a government that advertised its propriety and distance from illicit party financing. He was convicted and amnestied. Renaud Lecadre, "La justice absout les pecheurs du CDS," *Le Monde,* 24 Feb. 2000.

80. Author interview with Volker Neumann, 21 May 2003. Clay Clemens, "A Legacy Reassessed," *German Politics* 9/2 (Aug. 2000): 25–50.

81. *Parteispenden,* 229.

82. The court reasoned that, as a result of the progressive income tax, the wealthy were able to deduct their contributions to an extent not possible for the economically less privileged, which violated the principle of equality before the law. The court also expressly stated in its decision that it was legal to finance the parties through public funds.

83. *Parteispenden,* 230.

84. The SPD established an organization similar to the SV and developed other mechanisms to hide money, the most common being to charge exorbitant annual fees to receive its publications; the excess over the real costs went into party coffers.

85. *Parteispenden,* 233.

86. "Tony Blair has been accused of selling peerages after four businessmen who gave Labour £4.5m in unpublicised loans were subsequently nominated for peerages. Labour went on to reveal it had been secretly loaned nearly £14m ahead of the last election. The Conservatives borrowed £16m from 13 wealthy backers. The Liberal Democrats have said they owe £850,000 to three backers." "Q&A: Cash for Peerages," BBC News, 14 July 2006.

87. Bundeskriminalamt, "Bundeslagebild Korruption 2001," annual report, http://www .bka.de/lageberichte/ko/bl2001korruption.pdf.

88. Sir Stanley Kalms, chairman of Dixons Group plc, in Committee on Standards in Public Life, *Fifth Report,* 2:32. See also Thomas Jefferson, "A Bill for Establishing Religious Freedom," in *The Papers of Thomas Jefferson,* ed. Julian P. Boyd (1950), 2:545.

89. Jason Beattie, "Labour ranks call for state funding of parties amid sleaze allegations," *Scotsman,* 17 Apr. 2002.

90. A study of disclosure in the United States finds some increase in the public's sense of efficacy when there are stricter disclosure rules. David M. Primo and Jeffrey D. Milyo, "Campaign Finance, Political Efficacy, and Citizen Trust: Evidence from the States," Harris School Working Paper series 03.15, University of Chicago, 2003.

91. E. Auci, "Verità e problemi dei bilanci dei partiti," *Il Mulino* 253 (1978): 65–73.

92. On party factions, see Alan S. Zuckerman, *The Politics of Faction: Christian Democratic Rule in Italy* (New Haven: Yale University Press, 1979).

93. Rhodes, "Financing Party Politics in Italy," 64. Ciaurro writes of the accounting by factions of the Christian Democrats that "there is no trace in the official balance sheets of the huge sums used to finance this phenomenon, and so it is impossible to ascertain the source of the funds used by the 'currents' for their operations, how much they cost and who subsidized them." Gian Franco Ciaurro, "Public Financing of Parties in Italy," in Alexander with Federman, *Comparative Political Finance in the 1980s,* 163.

94. Dave Barry, *Dave Barry Hits below the Beltway* (New York: Ballantine Books, 2001), 109.

95. Van Biezen and Nassmacher, "Political Finance in Southern Europe," 135; Saalfeld, "Court and Parties," 97.

96. James Newell, "Party Finance and Corruption: Italy," in Williams, *Party Finance and Political Corruption*, 61–88, here at 79.

97. Rafael Rivais, "Le Parlement européen lève assez peu l'immunité," *Le Monde*, 13 May 2003.

98. Committee on Standards in Public Life, *Fifth Report*, 2:122.

99. Newell, "Party Finance," 71–72.

100. National party expenditures during general elections are limited to about £20 million per party and require the reporting, to a new electoral commission, all donations over £5,000 per year along with the donors' names. At the time of writing, data were available at http://www.electoralcommission.gov.uk/regulatory-issues/regdpoliticalparties.cfm Jill Sherman, "Parties to have pounds 20m election spending limit," *Times*, 18 Nov. 1999.

101. Croce was quoted by Marco Pannella of the reform-minded Partito Radicale, in Sergio Turone, *Agonia di un regime: Il caso Abruzzo* (Bari: Laterza, 1993), 39.

CHAPTER 7. THE PATHOLOGIES OF AN INTERNATIONAL ORGANIZATION

1. House of Lords Select Committee on the European Union *Fiftieth Report, HL Paper 270-I* (London: HMSO, 2006).

2. Lothar Kuhl, "Protecting the Finances of the European Union: Investigating Corruption in Public Procurement," in *Corruption in Public Procurement: Proceedings. Programme of Action against Corruption. Reports of the 2nd European Conference of Specialised Services in the Fight against Corruption,* Council of Europe, Tallinn, Estonia, 27–29 Oct. 1997 (Strasbourg: Council of Europe, 1998), 59–72, here at 59.

3. Quote from Marta Andreasen, Letter and Memorandum, 11 July 2006, in House of Lords, *Fiftieth Report,* vol. 2, HL 270-II (London: HMSO, 2006); Commission of the European Communities, *Green Paper on Criminal-Law Protection of the Financial Interests of the Community and the Establishment of a European Prosecutor,* COM (2001) 715 final (Brussels, 2001).

4. Wayne Sandholtz and Mark M. Gray, "International Integration and National Corruption," *International Organization* 57/4 (2003): 761–800.

5. Committee of Independent Experts, *First Report on Allegations regarding Fraud, Mismanagement and Nepotism in the European Commission 15 March 1999,* 79; http://www .europarl.eu.int/experts/pdf/reporten.pdf. François d'Aubert, *Main basse sur l'Europe* (Paris: Plon, 1994); François d'Aubert, *Coup de torchon sur Bruxelles* (Paris: Plon, 1999); House of Lords, *Fiftieth Report.*

6. Commission of the European Communities, *Report on the Functioning of Public Procurement Markets in the EU: Benefits from the Application of EU Directives and Challenges for the Future,* 3 Feb. 2004, http://europa.eu.int/comm/internal_market/publicprocurement/docs/public-proc-mar, 2.

7. Ibid., calculated from data at 6–8.

8. *Commission v. France,* C-225/98 (2000), pr. 89.

9. EuroStrategy Consultants, *Public Procurement. Single Market Review Subseries III: Dismantling of Barriers, vol. 2* (Luxembourg: Office for Official Publications of the European Communities, 1997), 146.

10. Council of Europe, *Steering Committee on Local and Regional Democracy: Structure and Operation of Local and Regional Democracy. Italy. Situation in 1999* (Strasbourg: Council of Europe, 2000), 9.

11. *Commission v. Italy,* 194/88R (rec. 1988), 4559. See also Becket Bedford, "Powers of the EC Commission," in *Public Procurement in Europe: Enforcement and Remedies,* ed. Alan Tyrrell and Becket Bedford (London: Butterworths, 1997), 11–24, here at 14; Sue Arrowsmith, *A Guide to the Procurement Cases of the Court of Justice: Procurement in the European Community* (Winteringham: Earlsgate, 1992), 2:220–25.

12. Stephen Martin, Keith Hartley, and Andrew L. Cox, "Public Procurement Directives in the European Union: A Study of Local Authority Purchasing," *Public Administration* 77/2 (1999): 387—406, here at 390.

13. Commission of the European Communities, *Special Sectoral Report No. 1: Public Procurement* (1997), sec. 3.2; http://europa.eu.int/comm/internal_market/en/publproc/sector/publrep.htm.

14. Ibid., sec. 2.2.

15. The ratios vary significantly in the large states: Germany is the "worst" at .29; Spain, .39; Italy, .42; United Kingdom, .55; and France, .67. The changes between 1987 and 1994 in public-sector import penetration are as follows: United Kingdom from 4 to 12 percent; Italy from 1 to 6 percent; France from 5 to 12 percent; Belgium from 12 to 20 percent; Germany from 4 to 5 percent. EuroStrategy Consultants, *Dismantling of Barriers,* 249–50, quote at 24.

16. BIPE, *The "Cost of Non-Europe" in Public Sector Procurement: Research on the "Cost of Non-Europe" Basic Findings,* vol. 13, *Le "Coût de la Non-Europe" des produits de construction. Note de synthèse* (Luxembourg: Commission of the European Communities, 1988), 12.

17. *Independent,* 26 Apr. 1995.

18. Nino Ciravenga, "Truffa alla CEE," *Il Sole 24 Ore,* 7 Oct. 1992; Mario Tortello, "Un ingegnere: Hanno bocciato i miei progetti senza spiegazioni," *La Stampa,* 1 Oct. 1992; Commission of the European Communities, *Annual Report from the Commission on the Fight against Fraud: 1992 Report and Action Programme for 1993,* COM (93) 141 final (Brussels, 1993).

19. Press release, Commission of the European Communities, COM IP/03/601, "Public Procurement: Commission Gives Green Light to Thessalonika Metro Contract," Brussels, 30 Apr. 2003, http://europa.eu/rapid/pressReleasesAction.do?reference=IP/03/601&format=HTM

20. Complaints reported to the Commission averaged 1,346 between 1999 and 2002, up from the average of 536 between 1983 and 1989. The EU's membership and scope had, of course, considerably expanded between 1983 and 2002. Commission of the European Communities, *20th Annual Report on Monitoring the Application of Community Law 2002,* COM (2003) 669 final (Brussels, 2003), 6.

21. Commission of the European Communities, *Green Paper. Public Procurement in the European Union: Exploring the Way Forward* (Brussels, 1996).

22. Lisa Conant, *Justice Contained: Law, Politics, and Policy-Making in the European Union* (Ithaca: Cornell University Press, 2002).

23. See Peter Rees, "Public Procurement in the Construction Industry," in *1993: The European Market Myth or Reality?* ed. Dennis Campbell and Charles Flint (Deventer: Kluwer Law and Taxation Publishers, 1994), 169–88.

24. House of Lords, Select Committee on the European Communities, Session 1987–88, *Twelfth Report: Compliance with Public Procurement Directives with evidence,* HL 72 (London: HMSO, 1988), paragraph 53.

25. Denis Waelbroeck and Mark Griffiths, "Case Law. National Courts. *French Cour de Cassation: T.G.V. Nord et Pont de Normandie,* Judgment of 5 October 1999," *Common Market Law Review* 37 (2000): 1465–76.

26. Rees, "Public Procurement," 187.

27. European Court of Auditors, *Annual Report concerning the Financial Year 1996, Together with the Institutions' Replies,* official journal C348, vol. 40 (Brussels: European Commission, November 1997), 79; Carolyn M. Warner, "Creating a Common Market for Fraud in the European Union," *Independent Review* 8/2 (Fall 2003): 249–57.

28. David Conradt, *The German Polity* (New York: Longman, 1993); Rolf G. Heinze, *Verbandspolitik zwischen Partikularinteressen und Gemeinwohl: Der Deutsche Bauernverband* (Gütersloh: Verlag Bertelsmann Stiftung, 1992); John T. S. Keeler, *The Politics of Neo-Corporatism in France: Farmers, the State and Agricultural Policy-Making in the Fifth Republic* (New York: Oxford University Press, 1987); S. Von Carmon-Taubadel, "The Reform of the CAP from a German Perspective," *Journal of Agricultural Economics* 44 (Sept. 1993): 394–409; quote in Francesco Paolo Giordano, "Major Problems Arising from the Preparation of Criminal Proceedings against Community Fraud," in *The Legal Protection of the Financial Interests of the Community: Proceedings of the Seminar Organised by the Directorate-General for Financial Control and the Legal Service of the Commission of the European Communities on the 27, 28 and 29 Nov. 1989 in Brussels* (Brussels-Luxembourg: ECSC-EEC-EAEC, 1990), 53–66, here at 56.

29. K. A. Fikkert, "The Policy of the Ministry of Agriculture on EC Fraud," in *The Dutch Approach in Tackling EC Fraud,* ed. M. S. Groenhuijsen and M. I. Veldt (The Hague: Kluwer Law International, 1995), 119–26, here at 123.

30. *La Stampa,* 14 Aug. 1994.

31. In 1995, the member states agreed to a "convention" that included a common definition of fraud. By 2002, it had been ratified by the EU-15 but not implemented.

32. Technically, these funds are part of the European Economic Community. The EEC became one pillar of the European Union, when the EU was officially created with the Maastricht Treaty. I use "EU," rather than EEC, here, for simplification. Mireille Delmas-Marty, "Incompatibilities between Legal Systems and Harmonisation Measures: Final Report of the Working Party on a Comparative Study on the Protection of the Financial Interests of the Community," in Directorate-General for Financial Control, Commission of the European Communities, *The Legal Protection of the Financial Interests of the Community: Progress and Prospects since the Brussels Seminar of 1989* (Dublin: Oak Tree Press, 1994), 59–93, here at 61.

33. Giovanni Grasso, "The Harmonization and Coordination of National Dispositions Relating to Penalties," in *Legal Protection of the Financial Interests of the Community: Proceedings,* 245–70, here at 254–55.

34. House of Lords, Select Committee on the European Communities, *Fraud against the Community with Evidence, Sessional Papers,* 1988–89, *Fifth Report,* HL Paper 27, vol. 9, 13.

35. Marta Andreasen, Letter and Memorandum.

36. Marc Landré, "Grosse pagaille à la Insee européen," *L'Expansion,* 1 Nov. 2004.

37. George Parker, Ralph Atkins, and Kerin Hope, "Greece stays in the Euro despite giving false data," *Financial Times,* 15 Nov. 2004. The Commission could decide to withhold EUR 500 million in aid to Greece and could decide to impose fines.

38. Aldo Angioi, "The Court of Auditors and the Protection of Community Finances," in *Legal Protection of the Financial Interests of the Community: Proceedings,* 311–20, here at 318.

39. European Court of Auditors, *Annual Reports concerning the Financial Year 2004,* official journal of the European Union, C301, vol. 48 (Luxembourg: European Commission, November 2005), 14.

40. As the House of Lords noted in 1988, "Traditionally revenue offences have not been extraditable. This reflects the international law principle that states do not assist one another to enforce their revenue law, and this principle has not been adapted to take account

of Community law, under which Community money belongs in effect to all Member States." House of Lords, *Fraud against the Community,* 30; Ronen Palan, *The Offshore World* (Ithaca: Cornell University Press, 2003).

41. John Spencer, uncorrected transcript of "File on 4-EU Fraud," British Broadcasting Corporation, Radio 4, Current Affairs Group, transmission of 26 July 2005, no. 05VY3022LHO, http://news.bbc.co.uk/nol/shared/bsp/hi/pdfs/26_07_05_eu_fraud.pdf.

42. Some officials in the EU's Competition and Internal Market divisions have said that the states generally act in good faith, although on occasion states may be "economic" with the facts they report to the Commission and that most cases of noncompliance are not "political" or related to fraud or corruption but to misunderstandings or different interpretations of directives. Author interviews, DG Competition, DG Internal Market, Brussels, 7 Feb. 2001.

43. Mark A. Pollack, "Delegation, Agency and Agenda Setting in the European Community," *International Organization* 51/1 (Winter 1997): 99–134.

44. Ian Harden, Fidelma White, and Katy Donnelly, "The Court of Auditors and Financial Control and Accountability in the European Community," *European Public Law* 1 (Winter 1995): 599–632.

45. George Parker, "Suspended EU chief accountant fears dismissal for her public allegations," *Financial Times,* 30 Sept. 2004.

46. "European Commission: Andreasen Sacked for Whistleblowing," *European Report,* 16 Oct. 2004; Frank Fitzgibbon, "Shoot the messenger," *Sunday Times,* 3 Oct. 2004.

47. Murray Ritchie, "Whistleblower returns to face his former Euro chiefs," *Herald* (Glasgow), 28 Apr. 2003; Doreen Carvajal, "The value of blowing the whistle," *International Herald Tribune,* 23 June 2004.

48. "Budget: Anti-fraud unit backs court action against former EU auditor," *European Report,* 13 Nov. 2002; Murray Ritchie, "I was right," *Herald* (Glasgow), 25 Oct. 2002.

49. Committee of Independent Experts, *First Report on Allegations regarding Fraud;* Gail Edmondson, "The Fighting Dutchman," *Business Week,* 26 July 2004.

50. Romano Prodi, "Eurostat and the OLAF Action Plan," 5; "Communication to the Commission from Vice President Kinnock in agreement with the President, Mr. Solbes and Ms. Schreyer. Subject: Eurostat enquiries," Commission: 18.11.2003 SPEECH/03/551, 1–2; "Questions and Answers by Mr. Solbes," COCOBU (Commission du Contrôle Budgétaire), 17 June 2003; "Questions and Answers by Mrs. Schreyer," COCOBU, 17 June 2003, 3. All are from Press Releases on Eurostat, http://ec.europa.eu/archives/commission_1999_2004/schreyer/en/ms_estat_en.htm#Pr

51. Tobias Buck, "Eurostat faces Paris corruption probe," *Financial Times,* 16 May 2003; Tobias Buck, "'To safeguard the interests of the institution'—but was action taken quickly enough?" *Financial Times,* 17 June 2003.

52. Lattanzio was arrested in 1995 for having accepted kickbacks from a major contractor not related to this case and was named by another who had major illegal dealings in Sicily. Lattanzio was, however, acquitted. The relevant 1994 European Commission antifraud unit report by UCLAF only describes a fraudulent export of tobacco to Romania; it does not address this case, nor the broader issue of a tobacco cartel. The EU did stop heavily subsidizing tobacco exports. "Prese tangenti per 2 miliardi destinate alla dc di Bruxelles? Suicida funzionario Cee," *La Stampa,* 31 Mar. 1993; Commission of the European Communities, *Protecting the Community's Financial Interests: The Fight against Fraud Annual Report 1994,* COM illegible final (Brussels, 1995), 50–51; Gianni Barbacetto, Peter Gomez, and Marco Travaglio, *Mani Pulite: La vera storia* (Rome: Riuniti, 2002), 346–47; Lirio Abbate, "Nella città dove bisona pagare 150 euro per essere riforniti dalle autobotti," *La Stampa,* 19 May 2002; "Ho pagato tutti i partiti," *La Stampa,* 4 Dec. 1997.

53. Kelvin Mackenzie, "A truly nonsensical law for television," *Financial Times,* 6 Sept. 2006.

54. Buck, " 'To safeguard the interests of the institution'—but was action taken quickly enough?"

CHAPTER 8. THE EUROPEAN UNION, THE INTERNATIONAL POLITICAL ECONOMY, AND CORRUPTION

1. W. Michael Reisman, *Folded Lies: Bribery, Crusades and Reforms* (New York: Free Press, 1979), 18.

2. République Française, Cour d'appel de Versailles, no. 2004-00824, 1 Dec. 2004; "Deux décisions, deux visions," *Le Monde,* 3 Dec. 2004.

3. Patrick Ziltener, "The Economic Effects of the European Single Market Project: Projections, Simulations—and the Reality," *Review of International Political Economy* 11/5 (Dec. 2004): 953–79; M. Haller, "European Integration and Sociology: The Difficult Balance between the Theoretical, Empirical and Critical Approach," *European Societies* 2/4 (2000): 533–48.

4. Cf. Michael Johnston, *Syndromes of Corruption* (Cambridge: Cambridge University Press, 2006); Jonathan Hopkin, "The Emergence and Convergence of the Cartel Party: Parties, State and Economy in Western Europe," paper presented at the London School of Economics, 30 Jan. 2003.

5. Andrei Shleifer and Robert W. Vishny, *The Grabbing Hand: Government Pathologies and Their Cures* (Cambridge: Harvard University Press, 1998).

6. Andrew Moravcsik, *The Choice for Europe: Social Purpose and State Power from Messina to Maastricht* (Ithaca: Cornell University Press, 1998), 76–77.

7. Avner Greif, *Institutions and the Path to the Modern Economy* (Cambridge: Cambridge University Press, 2006).

8. Another way of looking at the situation is to note that it is remarkable that there is as much compliance with EU and member-state law as there is. See Karen J. Alter, *Establishing the Supremacy of European Law: The Making of an International Rule of Law in Europe* (Oxford: Oxford University Press, 2001); Lisa Conant, *Justice Contained: Law and Politics in the European Union* (Ithaca: Cornell University Press, 2002); Tanya A. Börzel, "Non-Compliance in the European Union: Pathology or Statistical Artifact?" *Journal of European Public Policy* 8/5 (2001): 803–24. Conant shows that it takes considerable support of the Commission and member states before an European Court of Justice ruling has an impact beyond the particular case it concerns.

9. *United States v. ABB Vetco Gray, Inc. and ABB Vetco Gray UK, Ltd.,* case no. 04-CR-279-01 (S.D. Texas); *United States Securities and Exchange Commission v. ABB Ltd.,* case no. 1-04-CV-01141, 7 June 2004.

10. K. Griffiths, "Oh what a lovely war on terror it's been for Halliburton," *Independent,* 27 Mar. 2005; S. Bodzin, "Pentagon aided Halliburton, official charges," *Los Angeles Times,* 28 June 2005; Henry A. Waxman and B. L. Dorgan, *Halliburton's Questioned and Unsupported Costs in Iraq Exceed $1.4 Billion,* joint report of the U.S. House of Representatives, Committee on Government Reform, Minority Staff Special Investigations Division, and the U.S. Senate, Democratic Policy Committee (Washington, D.C., 2005), http://www.democrats.reform.house.gov/Documents/20050627140010–82879.pdf.

11. "China supplies funds with fewer conditions," *Financial Times,* 14 Nov. 2005; John Reed, "A peace dividend is elusive as Angola embraces 'petro-diamond capitalism,' " *Financial Times,* 14 Nov. 2005.

12. See Ch. 3 for details. David Leppard, "Bid to end Saudi probe to safeguard arms deal," *Sunday Times,* 26 Mar. 2006.

13. Hugh Williamson, "Export credit agencies' graft crackdown stalls," *Financial Times*, 15 Feb. 2006.

14. Michael Peel, "Big money, high politics and Nigerian oil interests make a murky mix," *Financial Times*, 8 Aug. 2006.

15. Independent Inquiry Committee into the United Nations Oil-for-food Programme. *Manipulation of the oil-for-food programme by the Iraqi regime*. 27 Oct. 2005, 608–22, and tables 1–8, http://www.iic-offp.org/story27oct05.htm; Mark Turner, Michael Peel, and Haig Simonian, "Most Iraq oil-for-food scandal perpetrators go unpunished," *Financial Times*, 9/10 Dec. 2006.

16. George Parker, Daniel Dombey, and Kerin Hope, "Bulgaria, Romania to face 'tough' EU entry," *Financial Times*, 5 Sept. 2006.

17. John Gerring, "What Is a Case Study and What Is It Good For?" *American Political Science Review* 98/2 (May 2004): 341–54.

18. There have been considerable advances in the causal logic of necessary condition counterfactuals. See Gary Goertz and Jack S. Levy, eds., *Causal Explanations, Necessary Conditions, and Case Studies: World War I and the End of the Cold War* (London: Routledge, forthcoming).

19. Miriam A. Golden and Lucio Picci, "Proposal for a New Measure of Corruption, Illustrated with Italian Data," *Economics and Politics* 17/1 (Mar. 2005): 37–75; see also Charles Sampford, Arthur Shacklock, Carmel Connors, and Fredrik Galtung, eds. *Measuring Corruption* (Aldershot: Ashgate, 2006).

20. Cf. Johann Graf Lambsdorff and Sitki Utku Teksoz, "Corrupt Relational Contracting," in *The New Institutional Economics of Corruption*, ed. Johann Graf Lambsdorff, Johann Markus Taube, and Matthias Schramm (London: Routledge, 2005), 138–51.

21. Josephine Andrews and Gabriella R. Montinola, "Corrupt Democratization: The Importance of Institutional Design in the Multi-Dimensional Political Environments of Transition," paper presented at the Annual Meeting of the American Political Science Association, Boston, 3–6 Sept. 1998; cf. Edward Banfield, "Corruption as a Feature of Governmental Organization," *Journal of Law and Economics* 18 (1975): 587–605; Ann Sherlock and Christopher Harding, "Controlling Fraud in the European Community," *European Law Review* 16/1 (Feb. 1991): 20–36, here at 25.

22. Jean-Pierre De Staercke, *Agusta-Dassault: La cassation du siècle* (Brussels: Éditions Luc Pire, 1999), 17. On ABB, see note 9.

23. As quoted in Robert Graham, "The 'Juppé effect,'" *Financial Times*, 5 Feb. 2004.

24. Political science and sociology have much to say about that. Paul Pierson, *Politics in Time* (Princeton: Princeton University Press, 2004); James Mahoney, ed., *Comparative Historical Analysis* (Cambridge: Cambridge University Press, 2003).

25. Laurence Frost, "French defense tycoon takes helm of media empire," *Associated Press*, 30 Sept. 2004.

26. "La justice Belge condamne des socialistes pour corruption," *Le Temps*, 24 Dec. 1998; Cour de cassation, Brussels, no. JC98CN4_2, 23 Dec. 1998; Jo Johnson, "A well-armed custodian of press freedom," *Financial Times*, 18 Mar. 2004.

27. Christopher Bliss and Rafael Di Tella, "Does Competition Kill Corruption?" *Journal of Political Economy* 105/5 (1997): 1001–23, here at 1005.

28. Paolo Mauro, "Corruption: Causes, Consequences, and Agenda for Further Research," *Finance and Development* 35/1 (Mar. 1998): 11–14, here at 11 (emphasis in original).

29. Luigi Manzetti and Charles H. Blake, "Market Reforms and Corruption in Latin America: New Means for Old Ways," *Review of International Political Economy* 3/4 (Winter 1996): 662–97, here at 662; Simon Johnson, Daniel Kaufmann, and Pablo Zoido-

Lobatón, "Regulatory Discretion and the Unofficial Economy," *American Economic Review* 88/2 (May 1998): 387–92; Daniel Kaufmann and Paul Siegelbaum, "Privatization and Corruption in Transition Economies," *Journal of International Affairs* 50/2 (Winter 1996): 419–58; Yan Sun, *Corruption and Market in Contemporary China* (Ithaca: Cornell University Press, 2004).

30. World Bank Institute, *Anti-Corruption in Transition: A Contribution to the Policy Debate* (Washington, D.C.: World Bank, 2000), 23; G8 Chair's Summary, St. Petersburg, 17 July 2006, http://en.g8russia.ru/docs/25.html.

31. Alan Fiske, "The Four Elementary Forms of Sociality," *Psychological Review* 99 (Oct. 1992): 689–723; Ruth Grant, "Ethics and Incentives: A Political Approach," *American Political Science Review* 100/1 (Feb. 2006): 29–39.

32. "Yes, minister . . . but," *Financial Times*, 20 July 2006.

33. Political theorist John McCormick goes so far as to suggest "institutional affirmative action for common citizens," including "the participation of the entire citizenry in accusation/appellate processes dealing with political offenses." John P. McCormick, "Contain the Wealthy and Patrol the Magistrates: Restoring Elite Accountability to Popular Government," *American Political Science Review* 100/2 (May 2006): 147–63, here at 161; Mark E. Warren, "Political Corruption as Duplicitous Exclusion," *PS: Political Science and Politics* 39/4 (Oct. 2006): 803–807.

34. McCormick, "Contain the Wealthy and Patrol the Magistrates," 147.

APPENDIX 1. KEY DEAD MEN

1. Johann Rapp, "Weapons maker struggles to regain image against corruption charges," *BC Cycle*, 30 Nov. 1989.

2. Colm Keena, "Lowry 'can say why Smurfit man gave (pounds) 150,000'" *Irish Times*, 5 May 2001.

3. Chirac was mayor of Paris from 1977 to 1995 and president of the RPR from 1976 to 1994. Charles Vial, "Paris, banc d'essai des privatisations," *Le Monde*, 19 Feb. 1989; Gérard Davet and Fabrice Lhomme, "Plusiers enquêtes convergent vers Jacques Chirac sans l'atteindre," *Le Monde*, 15 Mar. 2004; Fabrice Lhomme, "Le six dossiers qui convergent vers M. Chirac," *Le Monde*, 30 Mar. 2001.

4. "Rome," *Associated Press*, 1 Mar. 1979.

5. "Probe into German party official's suicide amid funding scandal," *Agence France Presse*, 21 Jan. 2000.

6. Renaud Lecadre, "L'ombre d'un truand sur le procès Alstom," *Libération*, 11 Jan. 2006; Julien Caumer, *Les requins: Un réseau au coeur des affaires* (Paris: Flammarion, 1999).

7. "Top Elf convict Alfred Sirven dead at 78," *Agence France Presse*, 13 Feb. 2005.

APPENDIX 2. BRIEF SURVEY OF THE EUROPEAN UNION

1. Studies of the EU are almost beyond number. For a basic survey, see Desmond Dinan, *Ever Closer Union? An Introduction to European Integration*, 3rd ed. (Boulder, CO: Lynne Rienner, 2005); for a complex analysis of the dynamics of the EU's development, which also covers extensive historical ground, see Andrew Moravcsik, *The Choice for Europe: Social Purpose and State Power from Messina to Maastricht* (Ithaca: Cornell University Press, 1998). The EU itself gives a brief history and explains its institutions at http://www.europa.eu.int.

2. The Treaties of Rome are what the Treaty establishing the European Economic Community and the Treaty establishing the European Atomic Energy Community quickly came to be called. Both were signed on 25 March 1957 in Rome.

APPENDIX 3. THE MAJOR INSTITUTIONS OF THE EUROPEAN UNION

1. For fuller descriptions and analyses of the institutions, see John McCormick, *Understanding the European Union: A Concise Introduction,* 3rd ed. (New York: Palgrave, 2005); Andreas Follesdal and Simon Hix, "Why There Is a Democratic Deficit in the EU: A Response to Majone and Moravcsik," *Journal of Common Market Studies* 44/3 (2006), 533–62.

2. See Lisa Conant, *Justice Contained: Law, Politics, and Policy-Making in the European Union* (Ithaca: Cornell University Press, 2002). For a rival view, see Karen Alter, *Establishing the Supremacy of European Law* (New York: Oxford University Press, 2001).

Index